# Of Spies and Spokesmen

Nicholas Daniloff

# Of Spies and Spokesmen

*My Life as a Cold War Correspondent*

University of Missouri Press
Columbia and London

Library of Congress Cataloging-in-Publication Data

Daniloff, Nicholas, 1934–
    Of spies and spokesmen : my life as a Cold War correspondent / Nicholas Daniloff.
        p.   cm.
    Includes bibliographical references and index.
    Summary: "A riveting look at Cold War journalism behind the Iron Curtain by a
Russian-American reporter who was later falsely accused of spying and thrown into a
Russian prison. Daniloff sheds light on such prominent figures as Nikita Khrushchev,
Henry Kissinger, and suspected spies Frederick Barghoorn, John Downey, and Sam
Jaffe"—Provided by publisher.
    ISBN 978-0-8262-1793-6 (hard cover : alk. paper)
    ISBN 978-0-8262-1804-9 (pbk. : alk. paper)
    1. Daniloff, Nicholas, 1934–   2. Journalists—United States—Biography.   3. Foreign
correspondents—United States—Biography.   I. Title.
    PN4874.D353A3 2008
    070.4'332092—dc22
    [B]

                                                                                                2007044526

Designer: Jennifer Cropp
Typesetter: BookComp, Inc.
Printer and Binder: Thomson-Shore, Inc.
Typefaces: Palatino, Garamond, and RageJoi

The University of Missouri Press offers its grateful acknowledgment to James Stellar,
Dean of the College of Arts and Sciences, Northeastern University, and to Stephen
Burgard, Director of the School of Journalism, Northeastern University, for a generous
contribution in support of the publication of this volume.

In memory of Anna Politkovskaya and the other Russian and Soviet journalists who died under mysterious circumstances after the collapse of the Soviet Union.

And for Baboota—Anna Nikolaevna Danilova—who, after all, put me on the train for Russia . . .

# Contents

# Preface

Some fifteen years have elapsed since the Soviet Union collapsed and the Cold War gave way to the age of terrorism. People interested in recent history often ask what it was like to live in Moscow and Washington as an American correspondent during that earlier period. As a journalist since 1956, I reported the twists and turns of the superpower relationship. Those were exciting and frightening years. On one occasion—the Cuban missile crisis of 1962—peace hung by a thread, and for a few days the apocalypse seemed upon us.

I began writing these recollections long after I was expelled from Moscow in 1986 on false allegations of espionage. Taking up the pen so many years afterward, of course, raises questions. As a professor of journalism today, I wanted to document how we journalists covered a lengthy conflict that the current generation often knows little about. I wanted, also, to show some of the journalistic tricks of the trade that characterize media operations.

Writing long after the events has both advantages and disadvantages. On the minus side, the memory dulls and sometimes misleads. On the other hand, official documents are declassified, and some mysteries are cleared up. You can often say, "Now we know!" From the beginning of my career in 1956, I suspected I might write a memoir, so I kept copious notes. I was lucky, too, because my UPI boss, Henry Shapiro, donated the entire files of the UPI Moscow office from 1934–1974 to the Manuscript Division of the Library of Congress. There I was able to review what I had written during my first assignment in Moscow, 1961–1965. I preserved my own files from my second assignment in Moscow, 1981–1986, for *U.S. News and World Report*. And, naturally, I made Freedom of Information requests to U.S. government agencies and benefited from memoirs of both Soviet and American officials.

In 1983, President Reagan denounced the Soviet Union as "an evil empire." The Soviet Russia I came to know was much more complex than a simple generator of evil. Americans and Russians had a love-hate relationship during the Cold War. It was us against them. The Soviets envied what we Americans had built up over the years. But they distrusted us, fearing we wanted to undermine their socialist system. We resisted Soviet attempts to spread communism around the world and feared their espionage against us was aimed at destroying our way of life.

As an American of Russian heritage, I used to joke that on Mondays, Wednesdays, and Fridays the Soviet authorities abhorred what I stood for, but on Tuesdays, Thursdays, and Saturdays I somehow passed through the looking glass into the Russian universe. I found a world of spontaneous hospitality, warm friendships, and ancestral ties. I also discovered a wilderness of propagandists, manipulators, and intelligence agents. To get information during the Cold War, you often had to dance with spooks.

The Russian Federation is today the successor state to the Union of Soviet Socialist Republics (USSR). It is still finding its way toward a new social and political order. What seems undeniable is that the seventy years of Communist rule have left a deep impression on the nation's psyche and its bureaucracy. Russia is struggling with its Communist and czarist past—sometimes successfully and sometimes not—as it wrestles with the present. The Cold War is over, and Russia and the United States are nominally friends, certainly partners in the war against terror. Whether Russia will move toward a political system that we in the West will recognize as a democracy remains to be seen. More likely, Russia will re-create some kind of authoritarian order enveloped in a benevolent overcoat.

I hope that these pages throw some light on that heritage as well as the ways of journalism in times of crisis.

# Acknowledgments

In writing about journalism in Moscow and Washington, I wanted to probe as much as possible beneath the surface of what Ruth and I observed in both cities. I am very grateful to the families of Henry Shapiro, Sam Jaffe, and Stewart Hensley for reading the chapters where their kin are named, correcting mistakes, questioning assumptions, and sharing additional information.

I am especially grateful to my son, Caleb, a skilled writer in his own right, who went over the entire manuscript and helped me make countless improvements. Thanks also to his wife, Chris, who was extremely helpful in processing the photographs included in this book. I want to thank my daughter, Miranda, who contributed recollections, and Ruth, who read chapters and evaluated particularly sensitive passages.

I am obliged to Mark Kramer of Harvard University, editor of *Journal of Cold War Studies,* for pointing me toward many relevant declassified Soviet documents, and to Professor Stuart Loory who introduced me to the University of Missouri Press. I owe a debt, too, to my Northeastern University colleagues—Jim Chiavelli, Juli Jerzyk, Laurel Leff, Gladys McKie, and Phyllis Strauss—who read and commented on parts of the manuscript.

I would like to thank my journalist colleagues who answered questions, read sections of the manuscript, and commented to good purpose. Among them are Robert Estabrook, Joe Fromm, Bernard Gwertzman, Greg Jensen, Ozzie Johnston, Murrey Marder, Norman Runnion, and Dottie Wood.

Similarly, I am indebted to several Northeastern students—Nik Coates, Sean Maher, Charlotte Nazareth, Tinkerbelle Ready, and Ye Zhao—who served as research assistants and went scurrying hither and yon to find ordinary and exotic facts that have enhanced the narrative.

Obviously, I am solely responsible for all interpretations and errors, which creep into manuscripts like gremlins no matter how hard I fight against them.

# Of Spies and Spokesmen

Chapter 1

A Peck of Trouble

It's harder to live a life than to cross a field *(prozhit' zhizn' ne polye pereidti),* according to an old Russian saying. Unexpected events, near and far, intersect the lives of individuals and nations, throwing routines wildly off course. The Japanese attack on Pearl Harbor in 1941 brought the United States into the Second World War. The launching of Sputnik in 1957 raised the worry that Soviet communism was overtaking the United States. The assassination of John F. Kennedy in 1963 threw America into turmoil and sadness. These events affected our family too.

August 30, 1986, brought another totally unexpected challenge to the top leaders of the United States and Soviet Union, and to my family. On that Saturday, I was winding up a five-and-a-half-year assignment in Moscow as chief of the *U.S. News and World Report* bureau when the Soviet secret police arrested me. My wife, Ruth, and I were about to turn over the bureau to my successor, Jeff Trimble, and his wife, Gretchen. President Ronald Reagan and Communist leader Mikhail Gorbachev were making plans to hold a summit meeting in the fall. None of us—neither family nor superpower leaders—had any inkling that events in New York and Moscow were about to slip out of control.

Throughout 1986, the Reagan administration had been seriously concerned about the growth of Soviet espionage in Washington, New York, and San Francisco. The Federal Bureau of Investigation was especially worried about one Russian, a thirty-nine-year-old physicist employed by the U.N.

Secretariat in New York, who seemed to be breaking the rules of the spy game. He had arrived in 1982 from Moscow, and his aggressive behavior had come to the attention of FBI counterintelligence. Although his work was for the Science and Technology Committee of the United Nations, he frequently visited university campuses and masqueraded as a "Russian professor" named Genrick, befriending graduate students, especially those concentrating on physics and computer science. With the lure of easy money, he persuaded four of them to serve as "research assistants," digging up open information, then moving stealthily to more furtive assignments.

The bureau got a break in 1983 when Leakh Bhoge, a student from Guyana at Queens College in New York, contacted the FBI about Genrick, whose real name was Gennadii Zakharov. Bhoge agreed to cooperate with the FBI to see where Zakharov's requests would lead. The task involved keeping the FBI informed of the Russian's activities, occasionally wearing a hidden tape recorder. By August 1986 the FBI had collected sufficient information to incriminate Zakharov. The bureau could document that the Russian had paid Bhoge six thousand dollars for information and had also urged him to get a job with a defense subcontractor. In a meeting before leaving for Moscow on vacation in the summer of 1986, Zakharov made Bhoge an unusual request: he asked him to sign a contract formalizing their relationship over the long term. Zakharov dictated the text to Bhoge, unaware that the student was wearing a wire. Bhoge wrote the agreement in pencil, signed it, and handed it back to Zakharov. It stated:

I hereby agree to continue this cooperation with the USSR mostly in obtaining the information required. This agreement is for a term of ten years initially and after that period the agreement is to be reconsidered for renegotiation. I understand that my assignments would include materials which could not be obtained by a citizen of the USSR and which are of a classified nature. I also agree to follow the instructions as to the fulfillment of my assignment. My understanding is that the level of my reimbursement is to be decided by the institution on the basis of quality and quantity of information (quantity meaning importance in nature and character of the material).

Toward the end of the summer, the FBI requested permission of the Department of Justice to arrest Zakharov and charge him with espionage under Article 794 of the U.S. Criminal Code. Before acting, the FBI asked for and received approval for the arrest from the Defense Department, State Department, National Security Council, U.S. Mission to the United Nations, as well as the Senate and House Intelligence Committees. John Evans, whom I had known in Moscow and who now was with the Soviet desk of the State Department, replied to the FBI request: "There is no foreign policy objection to the arrest of Zakharov."

Then on August 22, 1986, FBI Special Agent Daniel K. Sayner applied to U.S. magistrates for warrants to arrest and search Zakharov's apartment and car. FBI agents planned an elaborate arrest scenario during which Bhoge would pass Zakharov three authentic, secret air force documents relating to jet engines and, they hoped, receive payment for his good work. The exchange was to take place the next day, August 23, in the parking lot of the Finast Supermarket at Glendale in Queens, New York. When they met, Bhoge immediately asked for his money, but Zakharov put him off, saying he would pay him later when the documents were handed over, but for now he could sign a receipt. Bhoge signed the paper, and Zakharov stuffed it in his pocket. Possibly sensing something amiss, Zakharov switched the handover to a Queens subway station some distance away.

Bhoge pleaded that his leg hurt and said it would take him about twenty minutes to get to the site. As Zakharov left, Bhoge radioed the change of plans to the arrest team. They rushed to the subway stop and got into position as Bhoge arrived. The team consisted of a male-female couple, dressed as joggers, and a third agent who took a position nearby on the platform. Bhoge approached Zakharov and handed him an envelope. Zakharov opened it, and glanced hurriedly at the contents. At this moment, the joggers, who had been embracing, split apart and glided toward Zakharov. The FBI man seized Zakharov's arm, but the Russian broke away and ran until he tripped, sending the envelope sliding along the platform. The agents jumped on him; Zakharov resisted, punching the woman agent in the face. Nonetheless, they managed to handcuff Zakharov and read him his Miranda rights, in Russian and English. He had the right to remain silent and have the assistance of a lawyer.

Zakharov was next transported to the FBI field office where a counterintelligence supervisor, Joseph Hangenmuller, a thirty-five-year veteran of the bureau, "chatted" with him for more than an hour before Zakharov asked for counsel. During that time, Zakharov identified several KGB agents in the Soviet Mission and tried various ploys to persuade the FBI to release him. "He said he was expecting his wife Tatiana and daughter Irina to arrive the next day and did not want them to be arrested," Hangenmuller said later. When Zakharov insisted a "misunderstanding" had occurred, Hangenmuller and his associates dismissed his pleadings. Zakharov then offered to become a double agent for the FBI in Moscow. The FBI might have been prepared to consider him as a double agent in New York, where they could keep a close eye, but they rejected his Moscow offer, assuming that he would quickly turn into a "triple" agent, feeding disinformation to the United States. When all ploys failed, Zakharov broke down in tears and was carted off to the Manhattan Correctional Center to await Soviet consular officers and an American lawyer experienced in defending Soviet spies. Before leaving the field office, Zakharov expressed regret that he had socked the woman agent and inquired if she would be all right. Then he embraced Hangenmuller, thanking him for treating him in an unexpectedly courteous manner.

News of Zakharov's arrest in New York was picked up almost immediately by the news media. Ruth and I heard the BBC news program in Moscow on Sunday morning, August 24, but we took little notice because our Jack Russell terrier, Zeus, was barking. We learned later that the U.S. Embassy had discreetly warned several prominent U.S. businessmen in Moscow to be careful in the days after Zakharov's detention because a retaliatory arrest was a distinct possibility, given the history of tense U.S.-Soviet relations during the Cold War. No such warning came to me or any other American journalist, however. That evening, a Soviet contact of mine, Mikhail Luzin, called to say he would be in Moscow the next week and would like to get together. I had met Misha on a trip to the Soviet republic of Kirghizia (now Kyrgyzstan) and had wanted to see him again to say good-bye. He had been a good source on Soviet attitudes toward the war in Afghanistan, and supplied me with information from time to time. I had recently bought him a set of Stephen King novels in the United States that he hungered for, and I was anxious to get them to him. So I was pleased with his call and looked forward to the meeting, which we set for Saturday, August 30.

We met at the Leninskii Prospekt subway station at about eleven in the morning. I decided not to take Zeus with me because we had already had our morning walk. Misha was a few minutes late, and I ribbed him about that. "Today you're late. Last time you didn't show up at all!" He seemed embarrassed. "Excuse me. I know I should've been there last time. But, you know, I got involved with friends, we drank a little, and everything got away from me."

We walked slowly down a path to the Moscow River bank, which curves through the center of the capital. It was a clear autumn day with a slight chill in the air. The banks of the river form a park that is frequently used by strollers in the summer and skiers in the winter. After walking for about a half hour, we sat down in a little A-frame shelter. From a white plastic bag I had been carrying, I pulled out the Stephen King novels. "I'm leaving Moscow soon," I said, "but I hope to come back, and I want to keep in touch with you. Perhaps I'll send you a postcard to let you know."

Misha then produced from under his jacket a black envelope, measuring about six by eight inches, the kind used to hold photographic paper, and handed it to me. The envelope, he explained, contained candid shots by soldiers in Afghanistan and clippings about how Gorbachev's policies of glasnost and perestroika were being introduced in the faraway provinces. I did not open the envelope; he had given me such envelopes before, and I felt no need to check its contents. No money passed hands. In the fourth year of our friendship, I had no reason to suspect Misha.

Finally, Misha announced that he had to leave—a little precipitously, I thought, but I did not reflect on it for long. I offered to walk with him to the nearby Sportivnaya metro station, but he insisted he was in such a hurry it would be inconvenient. So we said good-bye, and he left in one direction while I began walking home for lunch with Jeff and Ruth. The road leading out of the riverside park divides into two branches. As I began walking up the right branch, I spotted a white unmarked minibus coming my way. That was odd because there was usually very little traffic on this road. Suddenly, as the van drew abreast of me, six individuals jumped out and sailed toward me. Several were photographing the scene, and a videographer was shooting tape. I had that strange feeling that I was observing the action from a point outside myself. Suddenly, two of the husky men threw me against the van, pulled my arms behind my back, and handcuffed me. I made a split-second decision not to resist and said not a word.

I was bundled into the van, and we took off at high speed for Lefortovo Prison. In some respects my arrest was the mirror image of Zakharov's arrest in New York, except that it all took place in utter silence. No Miranda rights here. No one told me that under the Soviet criminal code I could remain silent. I remember saying to myself, as we drove at high speed over Moscow roads, "Boy, am I in a peck of trouble now." One of the arresting officers fished my wallet out of a pocket and flipped through it. "A foreigner!" he exclaimed, as if he had no idea what this arrest was about.

As it turned out, there was little doubt that I had been arrested in retaliation for Zakharov in New York, although I did not immediately realize that as we bumped along. The Soviet secret police had purposely taken a hostage with which they hoped to bargain for the release of their man. This was one of the last big incidents of the Cold War, a major crisis for President Reagan and Soviet leader Gorbachev, a family crisis for me, an American of Russian heritage.

# Chapter 2

## Serge

One of my English friends likes to joke that I am not really a "paid-up and practicing American." What he means, I am sure, is that I have only passing interest in those things that characterize so many Americans: love of football, or Halloween, or Charlie Brown. I suffer these failings because I grew up in an extended family consisting of a Russian father, an American mother, a Russian grandmother, an American grandmother, and an older sister. Our common language was neither English nor Russian but French, because the American side of the family never mastered Russian and the Russian side of the family, with the exception of my father and uncle, never mastered English. This unusual family arrangement would never have happened except for the Russian Revolution in 1917.

My father, we all called him Serge, was more stunned than angry when word reached him in Italy in 1917 that the provisional Russian government had been overthrown by Lenin and his cohorts on November 7. He had left St. Petersburg in mid-October of that year to take up a position as secretary to a Russian delegation charged with buying Italian armaments for Russia's efforts in the First World War. At nineteen, his concerns were more about parents and future than about the destiny of Russia or the world. On one point he was not confused: he and his colleagues at the Russian Mission in Padua were not going to join the Communists. They divided up the funds of the mission, and my father suddenly found himself nine hundred dollars richer, the equivalent of nine thousand dollars today.

Serge (Sergei Yuryevich Danilov) considered himself a man without a country. His first move was to try to join the army of Serbia, a traditional Russian ally, but his application was refused. So he accepted the invitation of the czarist ambassador and went off to await further events in Rome. Months later, he learned from his older brother in Paris that a group of American educators was organizing a program to bring Russian refugees from the revolution to the United States. He succeeded in joining that group and sailed from Bordeaux on the French liner *Le Chicago* for New York, where he arrived on October 28, 1918. A prospective student, with money in his pocket, he did not go through Ellis Island. His very first outlay was twenty dollars for a horse-drawn cab, which he imagined to be the New York equivalent of a Parisian *fiacre* or a Roman *carrozzo,* to a hotel on Twenty-eighth Street.

Upon my father entering this establishment, a black porter sidled up to him and lifted off his hat. Irritated at what he took to be unwarranted familiarity, my father looked around with contempt. "But, sir," the porter explained, "the band is playing 'The Star Spangled Banner'!" Serge did recognize this was the national anthem and retired to his room in shame. My father's entry into the United States may have been humiliating, but compared to the experiences of so many immigrants it was smooth. The next day he visited the Carnegie Endowment for International Peace, where Dr. Fred Thompson and Dr. Schofield urged him to enter Harvard. A few days later he was riding the train to Boston.

Serge was always concerned with appearances. He had bought a pipe to smoke on shipboard because he thought it made him look more American. Now he was in for a surprise. He considered gray spats and a cane a mark of European chic and frequently donned these accessories while parading around Rome. In Harvard Yard, he was laughed at by his classmates training to become military and naval officers toward the very end of the world war.

Despite his best efforts, minor annoyances kept popping up in his life. When he opened a bank account in Cambridge, the clerk asked him for his birthday. In those years, Russia still lived by the Julian calendar, which had fallen thirteen days behind the Western Gregorian calendar. Standing before the bank clerk, Serge had difficulty adjusting his birth date of August 25, 1898, to the equivalent date of September 7, 1898. "Wait a minute," he confessed to the bank clerk. "I can't remember. Let me go look at my driver's license."

These embarrassments probably reinforced a feeling that in some ways he must be different, that is, superior, to boorish Americans. Harvard, he occasionally told me when I myself was a Harvard student, was a snap, so easy he thought he might have mistakenly entered a high school.

Serge was punctilious to a fault. He loved leather-bound books, and tailor-made suits. I remember that his suits always had to be hung according to color and shade—dark suits at one end of the closet, light ones at the other. Wines were another point of sophistication. Having grown up in Europe, he had a penchant for good French wines, which he found in short supply in the New World. Serge was always well dressed, good-looking, and sociable, with a mischievous habit of encouraging ice-cold shots of vodka, downed in a single swallow.

He was certainly more than a party animal. Technology intrigued him, especially cameras, racing cars, and airplanes. He started a photo collection in St. Petersburg in 1914 that he continued until his death in 1984. As a teenager, he would be allowed to drive his father's Bugatti, under parental supervision, and in the First World War he drove an ambulance of the Moscow Stock Exchange and Merchants Association. He saw his Harvard training in engineering as an extension of his studies at the Petrograd Polytechnical Institute and approached life in the early 1920s with the optimism of a young man who knew that professional life could be fulfilling. His work ethic was almost puritanical. "Remember," he would drum into me, "in this life, no one owes you a living."

Serge and his brother, Mikhail—or Mish (pronounced "Meesh")—graduated in the class of 1921 with honors. Leaving Cambridge, Serge went to work for the Saco Lowell Shops, the largest builder of textile machinery in the United States at that time. As an apprentice and later a patent engineer in Lowell, he made his way into the middle class. His gregariousness helped, but he had trouble being completely accepted. His Russian-accented English set him apart, and his Slavic surname—meaning son of Daniel—was so unfamiliar to New Englanders that he contemplated changing it to McDaniels. He and Mish made quite a splash in Lowell; they were friendly and exotic characters from another world.

At a charity dance, Serge made the acquaintance of Ellen Crosby Burke. Her family roots traced back to Richard Burke, born in England in 1640 and died in Sudbury, Massachusetts, in 1693. Some of her relatives fought in the Revolutionary War, and she was tempted, but only slightly, to petition for membership in the Daughters of the American Revolution. For her to marry a Russian immigrant was nearly inconceivable, but her father eventually agreed on the condition that Serge become an American citizen first. Serge complied in spirit if not in letter. He married my mother on May 23, 1925, and was naturalized in Boston a few weeks later, on July 7.

Mother was the glue that held our family together. I remember her as a warm, industrious woman much admired by our neighbors, who marveled at the way she balanced her responsibilities. She had an artistic flair and loved painting floral decorations on trays and tin boxes. Mother maintained harmony between the two grandmothers who moved in with us during the World War II years. This unusual combination of Baboota (Russian) and Mimi (American) produced in our family a heavy European influence. Furthermore, my father's love of *la douce France,* his continual drive to reside in Paris on an American salary, drove an un-American spike into our family. I believe Serge wanted me to be what he could not, a 100 percent American, but he also created obstacles to my Americanization. He never took me to a baseball game and forbade me to read the comics.

We spent the World War II years at Grosse Pointe, Michigan, outside of Detroit. I entered the second grade at Kirby Elementary School, where the only thing I remember is practicing air raid drills by crawling under our desks, drawing up our legs, hugging our knees. The fear was that Germany would dispatch long-range bombers on suicide missions over the North Pole to bomb our major industrial center. After school, I would sneak off to play war games with my friends in the backyard, pretending to be a bomber pilot perched on a high branch of an old apple tree. The reality of war in America's heartland was brought home by the appearance of "gold star" mothers, women whose sons had paid the ultimate price, as announced by pennants in the windows. We were in this conflict until unconditional surrender in Europe and Asia. Unlike subsequent wars in Korea, Vietnam, and Iraq, every corner of the United States was involved and sacrificing. Meat and gasoline were rationed, copper and steel scarce. I contributed by hauling scrap iron to a recycling center in my red Express wagon.

In the summers we moved to the family house at Little Boar's Head, New Hampshire. This had been a summering spot for the Boston wealthy after the Civil War, and its sandy beaches and salt air continued to attract celebrities well into the 1930s and 1940s. Former Massachusetts governor Alvin Fuller, who upheld the death sentences in the Sacco-Vanzetti case, had a mansion facing the sea, as did former New Hampshire governor Rolland Spaulding and former secretary of the navy John L. Sullivan. Sculptor Malvina Hoffman, who had studied in Paris with Auguste Rodin, made regular appearances. Ogden Nash, the whimsical poet, kept a summer house overlooking the Atlantic, whose bathing beaches inspired his ditty "Seaside Serenade."

Those were lazy days when I memorized poems before getting up in the morning and penned some of my own. On one occasion Mother persuaded me to recite before Ogden Nash. He listened politely as I voiced these lines reflecting a love of the sea and my adolescent pessimism (I include only the opening lines):

> Lo, 'tis my boat that has capsized,
> And 'tis I that am floating away.
> I am the prize of the ocean

On this lonely gray-blue day.
I must try to swim to an island,
An island but one mile away.
Off in the distance I see a wave
A wave of tremendous height.
It is headed my way with a shark in its spray
A shark of both teeth and of fight.

In 1942, we all knew there could be greater trouble than sharks from the sea. By day, I chatted with the coastguardsmen in white uniforms who patrolled the Atlantic coast from Maine to Florida or scanned the waves through binoculars from ugly watchtowers. At night we pulled down blackout curtains made of oilcloth to prevent any errant light from giving German U-boats a bearing on our shores.

My relations with Serge evolved through stages. The early years were a period of obedience. Formality characterized our relationship. When given a task, it was always, "Yes, sir!" or "No, sir!" I was often decked out in short pants, jacket, and necktie. When we moved to Grosse Pointe, I graduated to knickerbockers. Serge was an intimidating presence—not someone you could confide in.

The Second World War was the period when I became aware of his political views. In the Detroit years, he considered himself a conservative. He criticized the Roosevelt administration for forging an anti-Nazi partnership with the Soviet Union. I remember him lashing out at the Communists. "Those bandits stole my country, and the Nazis would do us a favor by marching to Moscow. The world would be better served if the Nazis gobbled up those bloody bastards in the Kremlin."

After the war, Serge was often absent, as he traveled for months at a time to Latin America and war-torn Europe on behalf of his employer, the Packard automobile company. So Mother ran the household, bringing us up and handling the grannies. "Waste not, want not" was her rule, undoubtedly bolstered by the memories of the Depression years. We were always to clean our plates for "Lord John Manners" or feel guilty for not shipping leftovers to the starving children of China. On leaving a room, Mother instructed us to turn out the lights to save electricity. She forbade dirty language on pain of washing our mouths out with soap and water. Mother confided to me, "There will be a dangerous period when this horrible war ends. Then there is a chance that Russia and America will find themselves fighting against each other." I found this hard to fathom. My Russian father was living peacefully in the United States with my American mother, and at thirteen I could not figure out why we might find ourselves at war with his native country.

In the fall of 1949, my father was assigned to Paris to manage Packard's exports to Europe and the Middle East. We sailed from New York on the French ocean liner *De Grasse* in September. Serge, Mother, the two grand-mothers, and my sister all settled in a large apartment in the suburb of Ver-sailles facing Louis XIV's chateau, and I began going to the American Community School in Paris, where I sharpened my French. I also took Rus-sian lessons with Baboota, who fed my interest in Russia. If anything, Serge's reserve increased. He brushed aside my desire to learn Russian and tried to quash any thought of my going to Russia, an adventure his own mother was promoting behind his back. "Never go to Russia, my son," he would declare in what amounted to a tacit admission he was losing influence over me to his mother. "If you do go, you will be arrested and be sent to the salt mines. You can be sure your American passport will do you no good."

My father had a point, but it turned out he was only partly right.

Chapter 3

Russia in My Life

Bad luck, or what I thought was bad luck at the time, pushed me accidentally into journalism and turned me into a correspondent of the Cold
War. Journalism was never on my mind as a high school student; rather, it
was diplomacy that attracted me. This idea began when we moved to
France. Always encouraging my interest in Russia, Baboota one day introduced me to a fellow unfortunate, Colonel Dmitrii Chikachov, who had fled
the Russian Revolution for Paris, where he ran a nightclub called Din-
erzade. I remember as a teenager sitting with this stocky officer and his even
more corpulent wife, Valya, in their apartment, examining czarist china sold
abroad by the Communists to make money. The blue-and-gold-bordered
plates, with the imperial crest, inspired my imagination. "You should become a diplomat who can bring Russia and America together," the colonel
prodded. That thought took root, particularly since the military dangers of
the Cold War were palpable in Paris in the early 1950s.

Truth to tell, I had no conception of what diplomats really did and, even
more important, no idea how to prepare for the U.S. Foreign Service exam.
After the school day in Paris, I would conjugate Russian verbs and decline
nouns with Baboota. She had the fanciful idea that I might improve my Russian by going to classes at the Russian high school just down the street from
the American school in Paris. When he found out, Serge put a stop to that. Interestingly, I found out later that one of my future American classmates,
whose father was a U.S. diplomat, did go to that Russian school for a year.

During those Paris years, I became close friends with a French lad, Yannic Mercier, who had spent the Second World War with his parents in New York and was now also attending the American school. Sometimes students learn more from their peers than they do from their teachers, and this was the case with Yannic. He was no bookish intellectual. He was a doer. His specialty was thinking "outside the box." One of the best examples of his flair occurred during a summer vacation in Brittany. His mother had a house in the Côtes du Nord district and encouraged her son to invite American friends to the seaside town of Trégastel. On one occasion, Yannic and I set off for the railroad station at Lannion to meet Don Harper, a high school pal. On the way, we came across a small circus that was setting up.

"Why don't we rent a camel," Yannic mischievously proposed, "and take it to the station to surprise Don?"

"Great idea!" I agreed. "Let's see you do it."

And Yannic, seventeen, blond, and six feet tall, immediately sought out the circus manager. After a short chat, Yannic convinced him to rent us a mangy camel for a modest price. A circus attendant led the camel, and we walked the remaining distance to the station. On the way, Yannic rushed into a photo shop and got the manager to rent us a camera to record the scene. When we got to the station, Yannic wanted to take the camel onto the platform to greet Don who, we pretended, was the camel's owner. To do so, Yannic insisted we would need a *billet de quai*—a platform ticket for the camel. With no hesitation, Yannic approached the stationmaster and said with a straight face, "Je voudrais un billet de quai pour un chameau" (I would like a platform ticket for a camel). The stupefied chief replied, "Pour un chameau? Vous plaisanter! C'est pour votre belle-mere?" (For a camel? You must be kidding! For your mother-in-law?). In the end, the stationmaster refused to allow the camel on the platform, and our adventure ended with the camel craning its neck over a fence outside the station to glimpse its supposed owner.

Another of Yannic's capers involved falsifying the final exams in our senior year at the American Community School. By bribing the janitor, Yannic got into the files of the headmaster's office, where the exams were kept. He called on me to fashion answers for his closest friends. I was not troubled in those days by the theft, rather impressed by Yannic's incredible savoir faire. As a university professor of journalism today, I would have a harsher view of our misdeed. For this illicit exercise, I realized the need to create answers appropriate to the abilities of Yannic's friends. So I went to work as a consultant and sketched out plausible answers for each student. Assured of passing grades, they goofed off during the final weeks of the school year and came away with the Bs and Cs they deserved.

Looking back at those years, I would say I became an adult on April 16, 1950, in an episode that is painful to remember yet impossible to forget. It was just after six o'clock in the morning at our Versailles apartment. I could hear the telephone ringing and ringing; it went on with unconscionable persistence. I was too drowsy to shake off the covers and answer the call, especially since now I could hear Baboota padding down the hall of our six-room apartment in the direction of my parents' room. My father and mother were away on an Easter vacation at St.-Jean-le-Thomas in Normandy. I reflected hazily on the troubled night. I had woken up about two with a strange feeling that I was very close to Mother. I imagined that she was looking down at me; I could sense warmth coming from her. This was odd because in recent months we had been quarreling, as I acted out my teenage rebellion. And in any event, she was nowhere near at all. She had fallen ill during the holiday with a stomach ailment and was hospitalized at Avranches, at least three hundred miles from Versailles.

As I began to come to, I could hear Baboota struggling to comprehend what my father was saying from Normandy. She kept asking him to repeat the message, and still she couldn't understand. Finally, she called me to the phone and thrust the receiver at me. My father said to me in utterly clear, perfectly controlled English, "Your mother died this morning at two of an intestinal embolism. Tell the rest of the family." That was it. I was so stunned, I did not know what to say. So I hung up. Turning to Baboota, I said cryptically in French, "Maman est morte." Baboota gasped and started to cry. For years afterward, I recalled that I made sure to emphasize the final *te* in *morte* as I explained the message to Baboota. (In French the past participle must accord in gender and number with the noun it modifies.) Some might say this insistence on the *te* was incipient pedantry; I prefer to think that it showed a determination under difficult circumstances to report accurately.

In the ensuing weeks and months, our family grieved. The rest of that evil day, I walked alone around the Parc de Versailles, trying to comprehend the incomprehensible. Why did Mother die? How could she die before her own mother? And now what? I felt vulnerable, wondering how life could continue without her. I wrote in my schoolboy diary that night that Mother was such a good person, she must certainly have migrated to heaven . . . if heaven really existed.

Her body was cremated and buried in the Père LaChaise cemetery in Paris at a ceremony I did not attend. I was frightened of seeing her body. We had no strong religious sense in our family and no rituals to assuage our grief. Mother and Mimi were Episcopalians and frequent churchgoers, but failed to transmit their faith to me. Serge and Baboota were nominally Russian Orthodox, but Serge declared himself an atheist, and Baboota, I guess, was the same, for she claimed that religion was the opiate of the people. I did not know what was involved in a cremation and was afraid to ask.

Three decades later memories of Mother flooded back to me. Rooting around in the possessions of my father, who died in 1984, I found a picture of Mother in a silver-painted wooden frame taken when my parents were first living in Paris in the early 1930s. My father had stretched a pink ribbon across the lower left corner of the picture. Turning it over, I found a paper square, about four inches on a side, pasted to the back of the frame. I scraped it free with a knife and found that my father had recorded Mother's last words, spoken between five in the afternoon on April 15 and two o'clock the next morning: "Turn on the light," she had said. "It is time to get up, isn't it?" And then, "Those awful horses." No further explanation. I can only guess that this had to do with my father's obsession with horseback riding. Then something that must have connected her to family and children in a foreign land: "I want to build a house." Nearing two o'clock, these pathetic words: "It is practically the end." My sister, Aya, later confirmed the peaceful way that Mother slipped away, recalling that Serge reported she also said, "Everything is so beautifully sparkling, like a diamond."

Now, more than a half century later, it seems to me that Mother's death opened the way for Baboota—a corruption of the Russian word for "grandmother," *babushka*—to compete actively with Mimi for our affections. Grandparents are special. When parents are absent or distracted by earning a living, grandparents often exert more influence on children than parents. Baboota used to say, "How I wish you were my child. How I would spoil you!" On that April day in 1950, her chance arrived.

Baboota, more properly Anna Nikolaevna Danilova (née Frolova), came from a Russian military family. She was the granddaughter of a revolutionary, Alexander Frolov, who joined a conspiracy that tried unsuccessfully to overthrow Nicholas I on the day he was to receive oaths of loyalty from his troops, December 14, 1825. Baboota's father, son of the mutineer, was Colonel Nikolai Aleksandrovich Frolov, who commanded the artillery garrison of the Moscow Kremlin. In those years, Moscow was merely a great provincial town, the capital of the empire being in St. Petersburg. Baboota was born in a Kremlin apartment on December 31, 1874, during the reign of Alexander II, "the Czar Liberator," so named because he freed the serfs in 1861, two years before Abraham Lincoln's Emancipation Proclamation. As a young woman, she had been introduced to Captain Yuri Nikiforovich Danilov, a rising star, whom she married in 1895.

These connections, along with her family heritage, gave her an unusual sense of place in Russia's history. She was undoubtedly a Russian patriot, a lover of the Russian language, and a devotee of its literature. When Lenin and his cohorts overthrew the Provisional Government of Aleksandr Kerensky in November 1917, she and her husband, now a general in retirement, broke with the Bolsheviks and made their way to Paris. "Le Général," as we used to call him, died there in 1937, and when World War II engulfed Europe, Baboota fled by ship to Buenos Aires, Argentina, where my father was the Packard export manager for Latin America. Baboota found herself a refugee for a second time. In one sense she was lucky because both her sons were out of Russia and working for American corporations. My mother took her in, and she became part of our family.

One day in Buenos Aires in December 1941, I remember my father announcing, "The Japanese have attacked the American naval base in Hawaii. The United States is going to war! Our days in Argentina are coming to an end!" His prediction proved correct. In January 1942, he was recalled by Packard, and we embarked on a five-day trip in the lumbering two-engine DC-3s of Pan American Grace Airways over the Andes, north along the west coast of South America, and on to Panama, Cuba, and Miami. One of our pilots joked with me, now seven years old, that I might buy the plane one day and gave me a certificate after we crossed the equator made out to "Condor Nicholas Daniloff."

During the Second World War, I began growing closer to Baboota. We were now living near Detroit, where my father was employed as an inspector of Rolls-Royce marine engines that Packard was producing under license for U.S. PT boats. What brought us together at first was my curiosity about language. We spoke French at home, and occasionally I heard Baboota conversing in Russian, a language that seemed totally meaningless to me. In the evenings, like so many families across America, we gathered around the radio to hear Edward R. Murrow report the war from London and to listen to such children's programs as *Captain Midnight* and *The Shadow*. Occasionally, when excerpts of Adolf Hitler's rantings were broadcast, my father would interpret into English.

In the summers we traveled by train to Boston, and on to New Hampshire, where Mimi owned a three-story cottage called "Little Grey House." It was during those wartime summers that I began to appreciate Baboota's spirit. She could be both frivolous and serious. When she surveyed the beach, noting that the young men were all at war, she would sometimes say within hearing of the conservative matrons, "But where are all the luvairs?" She was full of risqué sayings like, "La banane est peu couteux, je lui en donne autant qu'elle veut" (The banana is cheap, and I give her as much of it as she desires). My grandmother even encouraged my sister to have an affair whenever possible. Around 1942, Baboota began taking me for walks along the seacoast. On a bluff overlooking the Isles of Shoals, she would sit on a rock and regale me with stories of her previous life. Russia, she emphasized, was a special place on earth; it was not a geographical entity, but a state of mind.

Some of her recollections I had trouble understanding. The turmoil of the general strike of 1905 and the proclamation of a constitution by Nicholas II seemed distant and irrelevant. Her descriptions of the revolution, the repressions launched by the Bolsheviks, the confiscation of jewelry and apartments from the wealthy, hit closer to home. "People who owned dogs were protected by them," she would recount. "They would bark in the night, warning of the approach of Red guards. That allowed families to hide their valuables under the floorboards. Often they kept no record of the hiding places, and later many were unable to find what they had hidden."

Her stories ranged over all the members of her family. One of the most curious was a cousin named Sasha Manganari, grandson of the conspirator. He was the son of Nadezhda (Hope), daughter of Alexander Frolov, who had married a Russian naval officer of Greek heritage. In Greek the name was pronounced Manganaris, but to make it slide more easily into Russian it got shortened to Manganari. Sasha, she told me, was convinced he could fly and set about making himself a pair of wings as a young boy. Then he climbed to the top of a tall clothes closet and jumped. Instead of taking off, he crashed like a rock, seriously injuring one of his legs. "He limped for the rest of his life," Baboota said. "We sometimes called him 'le diable boiteux'" (French for "the limping devil").

Looking out over the Atlantic, she confided to me, "The waves remind me of the Black Sea off the Crimea and of Uncle Peter's dacha." Uncle Peter, Frolov's younger son, served in the Russian army for forty-nine years, becoming a general and a member of the State Council, the upper house of the Russian parliament before the First World War. Turning maudlin, she would sometimes add, "I've often wondered what would have happened if Lenin had not succumbed so young. He was only fifty-four when he died in 1924. He was a more reasonable man than Stalin and the others who came after him."

Unconsciously—or maybe consciously—she was transmitting to me a longing for her lost world. She encouraged thoughts of improbable return through tales of her husband's achievements. "He was an important general, you know, very close to the czar," she would say. "He was decorated by many governments for his service during the First World War. Medals from Russia, England, France, and the emir of Bokhara. In Moscow there is a coffer of medals, and you will go there one day and find that coffer." I believed everything she said, and was ready to leave the next day.

I have no clear recollection of her husband, "Le Général." He died in Paris when I was two years old. Yet for some reason I carry about a recollection that goes back to those Paris days. Actually, this is a memory of a memory, an image called up intermittently in childhood that has since faded from my mind. I am crawling on the floor when an august presence enters the room. I sense an intruder; I am scared and scramble into the darkness under a table. This might have been an encounter with "Le Général."

Baboota's accounts of General Danilov's service would cause me to begin hunting out his story in later years. I learned that he had been born in Kiev in 1866. As a young man, he had wanted to become a mining engineer in the Urals, but his plans were brushed aside by his father, Colonel Nikifor Akimovich Danilov, a distinguished veteran of the Russo-Turkish war of 1877, and forced to join the army. His career moved forward swiftly; he was selected as a young officer for the Nicholas General Staff Academy, where he developed a handbook on mobilization of manpower for war. Its publication brought him early recognition, and in 1898 he was assigned to the General Staff headquarters in St. Petersburg.

After a tour as colonel in charge of a regiment in the Kiev Military District, he was brought back to the Russian capital in 1908 as first assistant to the deputy chief of staff and, at forty-two, promoted to major general. The family lived in a spacious apartment at No. 4 Nevskii Prospekt, provided by the General Staff, near the archway that links that central avenue to Palace Square. My father and uncle received their early education at home, provided by a series of German, French, and English tutors.

Although they lived in military housing, any thoughts of entering the military were discouraged. My father wrote in a 1924 account that his father insisted his sons avoid the military, his own sweet revenge for having been denied a civilian career. "His sons were going to be free to select their own professions," my father wrote, "all except one—the military. And so from the tenderest age, everything which could give rise to military inclinations was banished from the nursery; no drums, no wooden soldiers, no swords. His sons were going to serve their country to the best of their ability but not in the way he served her himself."

In 1909 my father was sent to the private school of Prince Tenishev, a progressive institution without schoolboy uniforms that banished the study of Greek and Latin in favor of modern languages. Among his classmates was the precocious Vladimir Nabokov, future author of *Lolita*, a book that my father later denounced in a letter to his former classmate as neither pornography nor art but "a waste of time and effort." On graduation from Tenishev, both my father and my uncle entered the Petrograd Polytechnical Institute on their way to becoming engineers. But World War I intervened, and my father took advantage of the family's position to transfer to the Kadetskii Korpus (also known as the Corps des Pages), an elite institution created in 1802 by Czar Alexander I to turn generals' sons into junior officers. During the riots of the "July Days" of 1917, my father and classmates were sent to protect Sir George Buchanan's British Embassy, where they were invited to lunch for a job well done.

Shortly before the war, General Danilov was promoted to deputy chief of staff and served in that capacity until 1915, when Nicholas II assumed the position of commander in chief and shook up the General Staff. General Danilov was dispatched to field commands during the next two years, first with the Twenty-fifth Army Corps and later the Fifth Army. In March 1917 he was serving as chief of staff to General N. V. Ruzskii, commander of the northern front, when new riots broke out in the capital, precipitating the first stage of the Russian Revolution.

Nicholas II, who had been visiting the front, found his return to St. Petersburg blocked by Communist railroad workers. The Russian Duma sent several representatives to Pskov to urge abdication as a way to resolve the crisis. The czar summoned his field commanders, among them General Danilov, for emergency consultations. Danilov, who backed the notion of a constitutional monarchy on the English model, urged the czar to hand over the reins of power to his son Alexei and a regent. In a recollection published in 1929 in Paris, Danilov described the abdication scene in the czar's railroad carriage:

> The Sovereign approached the table and, apparently oblivious of others, looked several times at the carriage window whose blind had been pulled down. His face, which was usually impassive, flinched in a way I had never seen before, his lips grimacing to the side.
>
> The ensuing silence was unbroken. The door and windows were tightly closed. If only . . . if only this terrible silence would come to an end!
>
> With a brusque motion, the Emperor suddenly turned around to face us and in a strong voice announced:
>
> "I have decided. I have decided to abdicate the throne in favor of my son Alexei." At this point he crossed himself, and we did the same.
>
> "I thank you for your excellent and loyal service. I trust it will continue under my son."
>
> It was a deeply solemn moment.

Shortly afterward, Nicholas II changed his mind and abdicated in favor of his brother Michael who, in turn, abdicated immediately. This brought to an end three hundred years of the Romanov dynasty and prompted the creation of Kerensky's Provisional Government.

General Danilov's active career came to an end in 1917. As a field commander, he had been constantly concerned about deteriorating army discipline. Danilov backed the efforts of General Lavr G. Kornilov, Russian chief
of staff in 1917, to restore the death penalty at the front. Kornilov's further
actions soon took on the appearance of political maneuverings against
Prime Minister Aleksandr Kerensky. For his support of Kornilov, Danilov
narrowly escaped being arrested by his own soldiers. After the Kornilov incident, he resigned his command and returned to St. Petersburg (now renamed Petrograd to avoid the German-sounding name) to await the
hoped-for disintegration of the Communist regime.

Seeing the storm clouds gather over the summer and fall of 1917, Danilov
(like South Vietnamese generals in Saigon decades later) got his two sons
out of the country. Meanwhile, in the capital, General Danilov was thrown
into a new episode that I found mysterious. The War Ministry suddenly
called him out of retirement on the night of February 24, 1918, to serve on
the Soviet delegation that would sign a separate peace with Germany at
Brest Litovsk, taking Russia out of the war. After some hesitation, "Le
Général" agreed to accompany the Soviet plenipotentiaries. Why would a
czarist general who believed in constitutional monarchy agree to serve the
Communists? Why was he betraying the British and French allies with
whom he had worked tirelessly? And what caused him later to join the anti-
Bolshevik movement of the "White" generals? These questions intrigued
me, especially after I became a journalist. They beckoned me to Moscow,
even more than my grandmother's tale about a coffer of medals.

# Chapter 4

## Cards I Was Dealt

I easily won admission to Harvard College before graduation from the American Community School in June 1952. That fall, Serge and I boarded a Pan American Strato-Cruiser and flew from Paris to Boston to begin my freshman year. In PanAm's first-class cabin we slept in full-length bunks, traveling in the sort of luxury during a twelve-hour flight that I have rarely experienced since. But I was not happy. I remember looking out the window at Orly airfield as the pilot revved the four engines before takeoff and feeling I was being ripped away from a life in France that I did not want to give up.

At Harvard, I began breaking away from Serge's thrall. This was when our first serious arguments began. He said I was a fool to take calculus to fulfill a science distribution requirement. He scorned my growing interest in government and philosophy. On the other hand, he was delighted when I was elected in my sophomore year to the Spee Club, a secret society that he thought would give me the contacts to rise in the Eastern Establishment. He pressured me subtly to become a banker or a businessman and was pleased when I showed a fleeting interest in Morgan and Company. I would occasionally put on a Brooks Brothers tweed suit with waistcoat when he visited. He clearly hoped I would find a well-connected debutante for a wife.

The necessity of finding a job, much less a spouse, struck with full force during my senior year. Although the college maintained a career placement center, the deans did relatively little to encourage students to prepare for "the real world." Harvard was not about entering the labor force; it was about the life of the mind. To be a "success" at Harvard meant graduating with an honors degree. The higher the honors—cum laude, magna cum laude, summa cum laude—the more you would be a success, or at least that was what I thought.

In this elitist world, I pictured two roads into the future: more education or two years of obligatory military service. Hopes for more education centered around Oxford University or the University of Paris. One of the revelations of my Harvard years was an enthusiasm for political philosophy. This was inspired by a single professor, Carl J. Friedrich, a transplant from pre-Nazi Germany. Known for his work on ancient Greece, Friedrich would lecture in an amphitheater to one hundred or more students in Government 101. He would begin his lectures in a barely audible voice, speaking louder and louder, in an ever more pronounced German accent, as he emphasized important points, until he reached a crescendo at the forty-fifth minute. Friedrich's lectures opened my eyes to the Greeks and the Romans who two thousand years before had thought through many aspects of man's relationship to authority and the state.

In my senior year, I read the French existentialists such as Jean-Paul Sartre and Albert Camus and decided to write a senior thesis on their views of the social contract between man and state. I was still nostalgic for France, and these thinkers appealed to me because of their determination to rebuild from the ashes. Man had to take control of his destiny. The notion that God was not going to be of help had been gaining ground since the writings of Friedrich Nietzsche. It seemed completely plausible to me that there was no Creator, no guiding force, no self-evident morality provided by God. Could it be that the American Declaration of Independence, with its stress on inalienable rights bestowed by man's Creator, was founded on a false premise? According to the existentialists, it was up to man to make the best of a disorderly, Godless world. Impressed, I wrote directly to Camus for further explanations and, to my surprise, received a kindly answer with minor elucidations.

As graduation in June 1956 approached, I began applying for fellowships to study abroad. I applied for a Rhodes Scholarship to Oxford University because it was known as a great center of philosophy. The Rhodes stipends were conceived in the early twentieth century by British magnate Cecil Rhodes, who wanted to encourage young men (and later young women) who possessed intellect, athletic ability, and leadership abilities. Rhodes designated the United States, Germany, and a number of British colonies as sources of future imperialists. They would receive support to study for several years in one of the twenty colleges that make up Oxford University.

My father was skeptical. The academy, he asserted, was for idlers. He often cited Oscar Wilde's epigram that "those who can, do; those who can't, teach." Still, he said, if I insisted on applying, I should take his advice—advice that I thought then, and think now, was totally absurd and out of touch with the real American world: bribe the judges! How a twenty-one year old could go about doing that, I had no idea then and have not learned since.

The Rhodes selection process was conducted at different levels of scrutiny that began in the individual states and progressed to a half-dozen regions in the United States. First, universities would approve a list of candidates who could apply to state selection boards. These panels would then create short lists of two candidates per state and send them to the regional boards that made the final selection. The examiners were distinguished citizens who twenty, or thirty, or forty years earlier had won Rhodes Scholarships themselves. Knowing I could not fulfill my father's instructions, I boarded a train at Boston with trepidation for the state examination in Concord, New Hampshire. From the start, my interview went badly. One of the examiners asked what I thought of states' rights. Harvard had not required me to take any course in American history, nor had I ever given any thought to the relationship of the federal government to the states. My ignorance shone through, and I was rejected.

My interview for the Sorbonne in Paris was similarly dismal. I was questioned by Dr. Martin Malia, then an assistant professor who would become a distinguished scholar of Russian history at the University of California. We spoke in French, and on that score my performance was creditable. But Malia and others sensed I had no clear program in mind. Weeks later, I received my next rejection. These two failures confirmed to me that I did not have the right stuff for academic life.

My next step, therefore, was to grapple with the military draft that bore down on all able-bodied males. In 1955, we were only a few years from the messy end of the Korean War, and conscription awaited those who did not volunteer. Here my father's advice proved more reasonable. "Avoid the military at all costs," he warned. "Wars are made by old men who send young men out to die." I think my father knew next to nothing about the Selective Service system. But he did have one further suggestion: "If you have to go into the military, get into intelligence. That way you can sit behind a desk and cheat the bombs."

My preference was the navy. I loved the sea and learned to sail in small boats from Rye Harbor, New Hampshire. One summer my cousin Dickie Burke and I designed and built a primitive diving mask out of a truck inner tube. At Harvard, I was active on the lightweight crew and earned a letter as bowman of the junior varsity boat during my last two years. My naval leanings were encouraged, too, by my friend Stephen Hopkins, a direct descendant of the colonial governor of Rhode Island who signed the Declaration of

Independence in 1776. His relatives had many connections to the navy. His grandfather was Admiral William Sims, who had supported General Billy Mitchell's notion that seaborne aircraft could sink ships with bombs. In the fall of 1955, my naval hopes were rising. I pictured myself in a naval officer's uniform, fantasized that I would have it custom-tailored, wear sparkling white shirts with starched collars.

So, on a cold December day, I reported with Stephen to the Federal Building in downtown Boston to take the preinduction physical required for officer candidate school. Once accepted, I expected to train at Newport, Rhode Island, in June and in July be commissioned an ensign with one gold stripe. It didn't work out that way. Being examined for service with two dozen other naked men was a shock after the gentility of college life. We were ordered to line up against a wall. The examining physician was a Dr. Green, assisted by a medical corpsman, who by my reckoning measured six feet five and weighed no less than three hundred pounds. I came to know "Teenie" quite well in the months ahead, but on this occasion Teenie succeeded in humiliating all of us when he commanded, "OK, mates! Bend over and spread your stern sheets!" Thus were splayed open twenty-four bottoms for Dr. Green's official inspection.

I knew I was in trouble when I was unable to fulfill the next order, for a urine specimen. Try as I might, I could not open my bladder that by this time was uncomfortably full. My "bashful bladder" was at it again. This problem—psychological at root—has been with me a lifetime, and I remember exactly how it began. One summer when I was ten, a childhood chum named Zab Warren and I were jousting in a pissing match against a stone wall. He glanced over at my uncircumcised member and exclaimed, "That's the queerest dick I've ever seen! What the hell is the matter with it?" I was speechless. But beginning that afternoon, I developed difficulty opening a stream under scrutiny. It crossed my mind that this drawback might be a handicap on a storm-tossed destroyer in the North Atlantic. Still, I was willing to play out the line to the end.

There was more bad news. Since my teenage years in France, I suffered from unstable blood pressure. In times of stress, my BP rises above normal levels and then gradually falls back. Talking with your boss about your future or having your blood pressure taken are stressful situations. On this December occasion, my blood pressure checked in at 180/100, compared to normal at 125/70. Dr. Green looked on disapprovingly. The navy's limit for recruits, he explained, was 130/80. The fact that I rowed bow on the Harvard lightweight crew suggested I should have another chance. So for the next six months, I trudged to the Federal Building periodically to have "Teenie" take my blood pressure, but it never complied with navy standards. At one point, Dr. Green referred me to a cardiac specialist at the Chelsea Naval Hospital. This experience came out badly too. The young cardiologist informed me that one of my heart valves was not closing properly. This report wounded me even more deeply than the stern-sheets humiliation. I kept asking myself: Why was I born defective? Why was this happening to me?

The injustice of the situation was reemphasized by unsuccessful efforts to enter the coast guard. Finally, I decided to challenge the military directly. I would volunteer for the army and hope they, too, would reject me. Before taking the bus with some fifty other candidates to the examination station, I drank cup upon cup of coffee, hoping to boost my pressure. That worked. My pressure came in at 200 / 100. My draft board in Exeter, New Hampshire, listed me as 4-F (unfit for service), with the provision I might be reexamined on demand every year until age thirty-five.

In the fall of 1956, I moved to Washington, D.C., where relatives of mine by marriage were living. My step-brother-in-law, Jere Dykema, was employed in the general counsel's office at the Pentagon, and I found a temporary place to live with him and his wife, Annette. I had never been to Washington before, and it immediately seemed a logical place for someone with international interests. I applied for work everywhere I could think of without success. I even visited an employment agency, where a counselor looked at me curiously and asked, "What did you study in college?" "Government," I replied. I didn't bother to explain that at Harvard the Political Science Department is called Government. The man grimaced but asked no further questions. "Then you should seek a job in government," he concluded solemnly. He gave me a list of possibilities, including a clerk's job at the Securities and Exchange Commission. I went away disgusted and started to understand I would probably be my best employment counselor.

About this time, a New Hampshire family came to my rescue. Cord Meyer Sr. had been a pilot in the "Escadrille Lafayette," an American squadron that fought with the French during the First World War. The wooden propeller of his biplane fighter and the gray canvas of one of its wings hung in his New Hampshire barn. Cord Meyer's son, Cord Jr., was a key person in this rescue plan. He had served in the Second World War, led the World Federalists after the war, and later joined the Central Intelligence Agency. At the CIA, he became notorious in the 1960s when his activities became public: infiltrating and influencing journalistic organizations and literary groups. The Meyers thought my Russian background might make a good fit for the CIA. By this time, I was willing to become a spy. Like so many young men, I sought adventure; the morality of Cold War espionage was no concern.

I met Cord Meyer Jr. in the temporary CIA buildings in Washington, which were arrayed between Constitution Avenue and the Potomac, in the fall of 1956. From him, I learned that the CIA ran a junior officers training program. He arranged for me to take the entrance exam and swore me to secrecy. I did not, however, fully comply and let slip a few details at a Georgetown cocktail party. Months later, I received the famous white envelope with no return address: again, rejected. No reason given. I succeeded in renewing my application one more time, but the result was the same.

The obstacles of life are not always what they seem. One morning after the navy refused to give me a waiver for blood pressure, I saw a sign hanging from a building at Sixteenth and L Streets, Northwest, that proclaimed the *Washington Post and Times Herald.* On the spot, I decided to walk in and ask for a job. I imagined they would be delighted to see a Harvard graduate and would soon send me abroad as a foreign correspondent. The head of the human resources department, Elsie Carper, sat me down at a typewriter for an initial test. At dictation speed, she read me an article from that morning's *Washington Post.* It reported that President Eisenhower had approved a bill sent to him by Congress. It began, "President Eisenhower today signed . . ." My typing was not perfect, but I did not stumble too badly. She checked my work and looked at me approvingly. "You'll do," she said. "You spelled 'Eisenhower' right!"

She sent me next to the newsroom for an interview with the crusty city editor, Ben Gilbert. He didn't care about my education, my interests, or my health. I was a warm body willing to take any order, run any errand, convey any copy, confront any burden, attack any foe for the success of journalism. We kept in touch for weeks by phone until the final roadblock to the real world fell away as the team of editorial assistants turned over yet again. On October 29, 1956, I went to work at the *Washington Post* as the lowliest of all copyboys. My life in journalism was about to begin.

Chapter 5

The Magic Dateline

Washington was still a provincial southern town in the late Eisenhower years. There were few haute cuisine restaurants, marginal cultural life, and the old segregationist habits were still hanging on. To the newcomer, Washington seemed to offer only one product: government. The three newspapers, the *Washington Daily News, Washington Evening Star,* and *Washington Post and Times Herald,* covered the world, to be sure, but devoted much of their news hole to the inner workings of the government bureaucracy.

The *Washington Post* in those days was a far cry from what it would become during Watergate under the leadership of publisher Katharine Graham and editor Ben Bradlee. It had an impressive White House staff, but covered poorly the African American community that made up the majority of the city's population. A white-centric provincialism hung over the newsroom. It had no foreign correspondents and relied heavily on seventeen wire services. Yet its future looked bright. Eugene Meyer had bought the newspaper at auction and entrusted its running to his son-in-law, Philip Leslie Graham.

As a new employee, I had a memorable run-in with Phil Graham. Copyboys were gophers who might be ordered to do anything: run copy to the composing room, deliver messages about town, bring coffee to the editors on the "graveyard shift," take dictation from reporters, answer the telephones. On one occasion, Graham called the newsroom, and I answered in an offhand manner. Before I transferred his call to the person he was seeking, he berated me for my rudeness and emphasized that my voice represented the newspaper, not myself, a lesson I never forgot.

My duties during the fall of 1956 when Eisenhower was running for re-election consisted of inside and outside chores. I was totally lacking street smarts. Thinking on your feet was not what Harvard did for you. On one occasion the chief copyboy, Frank Wilson, ordered me to the Treasury Department to find George Humphrey and get from him some special document. I had no idea who Mr. Humphrey was and didn't bother to ask. Security in those days was lax, and I entered the Treasury Department without challenge. Asking the way, I suddenly found myself in the office of George M. Humphrey, President Eisenhower's secretary of the treasury, before I realized that Wilson had played a practical joke on me.

My hours usually began in the afternoon about four o'clock and ended at midnight or later. Somebody told me that I should be happy with these conditions because I was getting entrée to Washington's top journalists. Maybe so, but I was not impressed. The top reporters were always bent over their typewriters, pounding out copy on deadline, and not inclined to talk. Bud Nossiter, the economics expert, was particularly dramatic. A one-finger typist, he looked more like an excited orchestra conductor approaching a crescendo than a cool brain, crafting copy.

During the Hungarian uprising and the Suez crises of 1956, I kept both the foreign and the national editors instantly informed of the latest developments. I would read the dispatches coming over the wires from Reuters, the Associated Press (AP), and United Press (UP), wishing all the time that I was in the thick of the action. I wanted badly to be abroad, but how to get there was a mystery. There was no clear upward route, and I was as ignorant of journalistic ways as it was possible to be. Harvard did not teach journalism, and believed that all a budding journalist needed was a liberal arts education. I had not worked for the *Harvard Crimson* and did not have the slightest idea how newspaper stories were written. In college I had not read newspapers until the 1954 Supreme Court decision of *Brown v. The Board of Education*. I followed the Army-McCarthy hearings sporadically, mostly on a television set located at the Newell Boat House, after coming in from crew practice. I found it hard to swallow news: you needed a lot of background on a lot of subjects before the reports made any sense.

To be a journalist, as I was finding out, there are qualities you must develop. You have to be curious about everything. Some called it a "garbage-can mind" in which you store the trivial along with the weighty. You have to have a sense of the dramatic so that you can cast your story in a way that piques the reader's interest and draws him into the report. You have to be flexible, willing to drop anything you are working on to shift to more urgent stories. Friendly reporters would occasionally nudge me to think up a story idea and do it. It was months before I tried.

My first enterprise effort focused on International House at 1825 R Street, Northwest, a Quaker residence for foreign students. I visited, talked to students, and produced my first copy. It was thrown back in my face. An editor told me the "lede" was no good. I had no idea what a "lede" was—the opening paragraph of a story whose purpose is to hook the reader. I had no idea what journalists call the "inverted pyramid"—the structure of a story where the most important information comes first, descending to the least-important detail. Disappointed and confused, I went back to International House and rereported the story, rewrote it, and flailed about without asking for help. The story finally passed and was published on August 2, 1957, with photographs.

As time went on, I began to undertake night assignments for the city and suburban desks. After six or seven months, I had risen to head copyboy, directing a staff of some fifteen subordinates. My schedule now began at ten in the morning and finished about six. I would grab a sandwich for dinner and journey by bus out to northern Virginia to cover school board and zoning meetings. No one at the *Post* explained to me the role that the press plays in local issues. I had no sense that what I was witnessing was the bedrock of American democracy. I felt no connection with these communities and possessed no interest in them. Why should I? I lived in the Burleith section of Washington, not northern Virginia. I had no wife, no house, no mortgage, no debts, no children.

On the bus I would often read Joe Alsop's columns on international events and wonder how night assignments were going to bring me closer to my dream. Often I would get home at midnight or one. The exercise was supposed to be good for the soul and might eventually push you to become a reporter on the obit desk. I found the experience hateful. A question constantly hovered in the back of my mind: are journalists born, as some of the *Post*'s editors claimed, or could you develop the skills to become a journalist through training? The answer was not obvious to me, and I mistakenly concluded I was probably not the born kind, did not have the wide-ranging curiosity needed, did not have the flair for the dramatic. Thinking that I could not stand copyboy work much longer, I applied to several Oxford colleges as a way out, never considering journalism schools such as Columbia or Missouri. Rather, I wanted to follow my incipient interest in philosophy. Magdalen College accepted me for the fall of 1957.

One day Ed Gritz, the fastidious night world editor, pulled me aside. He probably acted solely from curiosity, but his comments made a deep impression on me, and I mulled them over literally for years afterward.

"Daniloff," he said, "who are you? Tell me about yourself." Gritz, a Pole by origin, was about forty-five and spoke with a slight Middle European accent. He was a natty dresser, always wearing a neat bow tie and often a pink shirt. He sat ramrod straight at the desk, facing the picture window that enclosed the wire room, concentrating intently. He was one of the few who was easy to talk to; he grinned and quipped, portraying himself as an expert on almost every subject. Awkwardly, I related my education, described my father's flight from Petrograd in October 1917, revealed my interest in Russian and philosophy. "With that kind of background," he said, "you should concentrate on the Soviet Union. The Soviet Union is the greatest threat to American security; in fact, Soviet communism is a serious menace to the whole world. You should become a Soviet expert."

It was an obvious thing to say, but until that conversation I had accepted uncritically my father's prejudices about Russia. Everything about Russian power was bad, and it was better not to get mixed up in it. Now an editor at the *Washington Post* was advising me to do exactly what my father had forbidden. This would probably produce another conflict with my father. Maybe it wasn't a problem at all. After all, I was planning to quit the *Washington Post* in the fall.

Finally, on September 6, 1957, I walked out of the newspaper, armed with letters of recommendation from Alfred Friendly, the managing editor; Ben Gilbert, the city editor; and suburban editor Dick Malloy. I sailed for England from New York aboard the USS *United States* with the successful candidates of that year's Rhodes competition. I had no feelings of jealousy toward them; rather, it seemed like a good idea to get to know the Rhodes scholars before arriving in Oxford. The ship dropped us off at Falmouth. After going through customs, we took the night train to London. This was my first visit to England, and I spent several days walking about Trafalgar Square and the Strand. Although I had a letter of introduction to the UP London bureau chief, Bill Sexton, from Dick Malloy, I did not act on it. That was a mistake, but I was still very much in my antijournalism mood. After a few days, I took the train from Paddington Station to Oxford.

At the beginning of October, Oxford grows damp and cold. The cold seeps into the marrow of your bones, and nothing, except a hot bath, will alleviate it. Magdalen is one of Oxford's older colleges, tracing its origins back to the early part of the fifteenth century before Columbus discovered America. The college authorities provided me with ample rooms in the New Building, which was constructed in the year of the French Revolution of 1789. I was assigned a "scout" who would clean my room and manage the housekeeping chores, such as providing punch, bowls, and glasses if I wanted to organize a small party. Breakfast I took in Hall, where the temperature in the mornings was about forty degrees and the fare was usually kippers or kedgeree on a damp piece of toast. The English students were standoffish, offended that "colonials" and foreigners were appearing in ever increasing numbers. Within days I was hopelessly depressed, and convinced that I had made a terrible mistake in coming to Oxford.

My desire to study philosophy all but disappeared. It seemed clear to me now that what I really needed was a way into a career. I began to question my decision to study philosophy, politics, and economics (PPE), the so-called modern greats, which would lead to a second B.A. degree. It was not unusual for Rhodes scholars to pursue the English B.A., which at that time was rated the equivalent of an American M.A. In fact, the tradition at Oxford, dating back to the Middle Ages, was that if a holder of a bachelor of arts degree survived five years and paid twenty pounds sterling, he was awarded the title master of arts. It was assumed he had increased appropriately in knowledge and wisdom.

The Oxford B.A. was considered the university's major academic degree—more important than a doctorate in those days—and much depended on the brilliance with which you completed your work. A first-class degree was roughly the equivalent of a summa cum laude at Harvard, whereas a second-class degree lay somewhere between cum laude and magna cum laude. Many Oxford dons possessed no more than a B.A. and looked down on the doctorate as some form of German pedantry. Oxford had added a doctoral degree called the D.Phil. to satisfy the needs of American scholars-to-be and offered a variety of other research degrees called the B.Litt. and the B.Phil.

In my confusion, I never really considered shifting from PPE to a research degree, which, in retrospect, is what I should have done. In those days, I made decisions on my own without seeking counsel. Like many young people, I was embarrassed to ask for help. To seek advice, I thought, was to demonstrate weakness, not wisdom. It was a long time before I learned different.

And so I decided to study law. Oxford taught law as an undergraduate subject, and American students sometimes spent two years getting a B.A. in law. Then they would transfer back to an American law school, which would usually credit them with one full year of graduate law work. Since law in the United States was derived from English common law—except in Louisiana, whose legal roots go back to the Napoleonic Code—this was a tested path. The English experience usually endowed American students with an appreciation of the history of law, especially since they were required to take one course in Roman law. Traditionally, examination questions in this subject required students to comment on statutes and expressions in the original Latin. That was always a challenge for the Latinless Americans, but did not stop them. They memorized endless citations. I began my law studies with a blind professor who tutored me one-on-one on torts. I remember one of my first cases involved a man who had discovered a worm in a soft drink he was consuming.

When I informed my father that I had shifted from political science to law, he exploded. His anger was evident. I should drop law immediately, go back to studying whatever it was I was foolish enough to want to study at Oxford, complete the academic year, return home, and get a job. To study English law was ridiculous, he asserted, since it had nothing to do with law in the United States, where presumably I was going to make a living. Feeling desperately alone, I shifted back to philosophy, politics, and economics.

During the first few months in Oxford, I would occasionally go to London. On these trips I visited Murrey Marder of the *Washington Post*, whom I had known slightly as a copyboy. He had been sent by the *Post* to open the newspaper's first foreign bureau and had leased an office on Fleet Street from the *Manchester Guardian*, where Victor Zorza turned out analyses of Soviet affairs. Murrey arranged for me to meet Zorza, a Polish émigré, who frightened me with accounts of what it would take to become a competent Soviet expert. His tales of reading Moscow newspapers fourteen hours a day only added to my insecurities, which were so bad that my heart beat uncontrollably whenever I walked into his or Murrey's office.

By March 1958, my depression began to lift and for one very specific reason. I finally worked up the courage to walk into the London offices of United Press just off Fleet Street and made the acquaintance of Bill Sexton, the bureau manager, and Roger Tatarian, the European general manager. They were pleased to meet an American student with an interest in Russia. They took me out for a steak lunch, washed down with beer in silver flagons, and told me I might be a potential candidate for the three-man Moscow Bureau.

These two wire-service men seemed much more approachable and much more international than the journalists at the *Washington Post*. They made me feel comfortable. Roger, an American Armenian from Fresno, California, had long experience in the wire service. During the Second World War he had worked for the Office of War Information, then joined the Washington Bureau of UP. He had run the overnight desk in Washington until he was called by New York headquarters to head the Rome Bureau. He covered movie stars and the pope and was rewarded by being made the top European editor in the early 1950s.

"Go back to Oxford," Tatarian counseled. "Get your degree, but study as much Russian as you can. Be our stringer in Oxford and come to London during your vacations and work on the desk. It's some of the best training in the world." I was always grateful that Roger recognized my interest in completing the degree; he could easily have persuaded me to go to work full-time right away. In this competitive, fast-moving business, Roger always seemed to understand the other fellow's interest. He had a warm personality, and his colleagues called him a "prince of a man."

Suddenly, the gloom was brushed aside by the realization that I had discovered a path. Did I have the right stuff? I had no way of knowing. If I failed, what would happen? I did not know. Did it matter? Here was something I could grasp: I wanted and I was wanted. My apprenticeship on the London desk was conveniently structured around my availability. I came to London when I could, worked as long as I cared. I would sit on the rim of the desk and bat out three- and four-paragraph stories for the slot man or editor who controlled the flow of copy to New York. Occasionally, I would decipher dispatches written in "cablese," that arcane language of contractions used by foreign correspondents to defeat high cable tolls.

Some of the more exciting work involved taking telephone dictation from the Moscow Bureau. Until 1961, the Soviet authorities censored the work of Moscow-based foreign correspondents. Usually, they sent their dispatches by press telegram to London, where deskmen reworked the copy into readable items that were then forwarded to New York by radio teletypewriter. On major stories, the UP Moscow correspondent, Henry Shapiro, or one of his two colleagues, Aline Mosby and Bud Korengold, would telephone London. Once in a while, I would be thrown into the dictation booth to capture their breathless words. This work was often tedious, and I would emerge from the booth sweating and headachy. In my hypochondriacal way, I attributed my troubles to labile blood pressure and told myself I would probably die of a heart attack by forty, and, therefore, I had to achieve everything I wanted in life by that time.

In the late 1950s, UP, AP, Agence France Presse (AFP), and Reuters were the major purveyors of news around the planet. They had long histories: the AP was conceived in 1848, Reuters in 1870, and the UP in 1907. London was a major hub because of the telegraph lines and favorable tariffs created during the days of the British Empire. UP London serviced cables from as far away as Hong Kong and India, North Africa, the Middle East, and Eastern Europe. Moscow was special because the Iron Curtain had isolated the Soviet Union from the international community. Most readers in the West had only sketchy knowledge of Russia.

Tatarian used to call Moscow the "Magic Dateline" because anything written from the mysterious Soviet capital would get printed. The Moscow Bureau intrigued me, too, because Shapiro had worked there an incredibly long time—since 1934, to be exact—and had an international reputation. He had covered such stories as the murder of Stalin rival Sergei Kirov, the onset of the Great Terror, the purge trials of the late 1930s, the Second World War, the death of Stalin, the rise of Khrushchev, the launching of Yuri Gagarin and other cosmonauts into space. I could see that UP journalism would connect me with the future as well as with my family's past.

My father's disapproval was now irrelevant and could no longer hold me back. Ed Gritz's advice resonated in my mind, and I began to follow Soviet affairs more closely. Oxford was poorly structured to allow students flexibility outside their field, so I cast around and found an elderly Russian widow who was willing to give me Russian lessons. But my most daring plunge was a "secret" trip to Moscow—secret because I hid it from my father.

This journey was organized by John Cochrane of the Oxford Conservative Club to take advantage of the new possibilities of tourism in Russia following the death of Stalin in 1953. Cochrane's plan was to buy an old double-decker London bus, recruit thirty-six students, and drive to Berlin, Warsaw, Minsk, Moscow, Novgorod, Leningrad, Helsinki, Copenhagen, and back to London. The Soviet Embassy in London gave him help, arranging through Intourist to send guides to the Soviet-Polish border to meet us.

At the time of our departure, British Labour Party leader Hugh Gaitskill announced he would be traveling to Russia at the same time. I calculated that Russian authorities would not wish to cause an international scandal by arresting some members of our Oxford group. We sailed from Dover with our bus on August 9, 1959. Our journey proceeded smoothly enough until we reached Brest Litovsk, where the bus proved a few inches too tall to pass under an arch on the Soviet side of the border crossing. No one thought of letting the air out of the tires and loading down the bus to make it squeak under. Instead, the Russians, over the course of several hours, cheerfully unbolted the arch, and we chugged through this hole in the Iron Curtain.

The red bus, bearing advertisements on its sides for Black&White Scotch Whisky, drew crowds wherever we stopped. The intense curiosity about the West was palpable after so many years of isolation. In Minsk, we stood on a street corner for four hours answering questions about daily life. How much are workers paid in England and the United States? How much do they pay for housing? For health care? For education? One of our interlocutors was a French girl whose father had repatriated to Russia in 1946, only to become disillusioned with the Soviet "paradise." At one point, she raised a particularly sensitive question. Nodding toward Wale Olumide, one of our colleagues from Nigeria, she said, "If that nigger stands out in the sun, will he get sunburned?" That question stumped us; none of us knew how to respond.

Throughout our trip such questions popped up again and again, under-lining the thirst for information. The U.S. Embassy in Moscow gave us one hundred copies of the American propaganda magazine *Amerika* that it had been blocked from distributing because the Soviet equivalent, *Soviet Union*, did not sell well in the United States. We came very near to causing a riot in Novgorod as crowds rushed around the bus. I remember seeing quite a few legless war veterans wheeling themselves in our direction on homemade carts fitted with roller-bearing wheels. In a few instants we had passed out all our copies of the magazine.

Sometimes our replies caused irritation, if not outrage, from our new So-viet friends. References to Leon Trotsky, Stalin's major opponent in the late 1920s, were turned back with disdain. "Don't mention that name," one young woman told me. "It's not a good idea to talk about him here." In Moscow, we were invited to do a radio program aimed at spreading good-will among nations. Our comments about one-party rule, orderly transfer of power, and freedom of information were so critical that the radio jour-nalists were deeply disappointed. Our interview was never broadcast.

During our Moscow stay, I finally met Henry Shapiro in his apartment at 3/5 Ulitsa Furmanova, bordering the old Arbat section of the capital. Henry was one of the few Westerners who did not live in a diplomatic ghetto and was not guarded by a Soviet policeman. He had inherited his five-room apartment from Eugene Lyons, a UP correspondent who had gone to Russia in 1928 and returned seven years later disillusioned with Stalin's Russia, dis-appointments that he wrote about in his book *Assignment in Utopia*. I walked in off the dusty street near Gogol Boulevard, mounted the stairs, and rang the bell of apartment 17. Raya, the Tatar maid, opened the door and, skating over the parquet floor in her cloth slippers, led me to Henry's office.

Henry, a stocky, balding man with bushy eyebrows and a broad mus-tache, was seated in a darkened room, lit by a small desk lamp. His office was lined with shelves overflowing with books, reports, papers, encyclo-pedias, reference books going back to the early 1930s. I warmed to this bookish atmosphere, and we chatted amiably for some time.

"So what brings you here?" Henry asked. He spoke deliberately, with something of an accent that I could not identify. I recounted the same sorts of things I had told Ed Gritz but in more detail—my growing interest in Russia, my grandfather's role in advising Czar Nicholas II to abdicate in March 1917, and his unexplained willingness to serve on the Soviet delega-tion at the Brest Litovsk peace treaty of 1918 as senior military adviser.

"Yes, I've heard of General Danilov," Henry replied uncertainly. I was im-pressed by Henry's profession of interest; he was so different from the edi-tors in Washington who knew everything about the District of Columbia but not much more. In Henry I sensed an appreciation of history and a determination to understand developments in Russia, where so many things were shrouded in secrecy. Henry seemed more like a college professor than a newshound, more like a researcher, a thinker, a mentor. How wonderful, I thought, to work with a man who had seen so much history firsthand. Henry was intriguing. Why would a correspondent spend more than a quarter century in the Soviet capital, particularly during the malevolence of the Cold War?

Was it simply because he was a Soviet expert with a Russian wife? Or had he become an agent of Soviet influence, as some of his colleagues claimed? Or was it something else?

In parting, we promised to keep in touch. I walked out of his apartment in a trance. Moscow was beckoning. Even the dust in the streets and the shabby state of the buildings seemed magical. I was twenty-four and starting a desk job in London for United Press in October. I was more determined than ever to join the ranks of Cold War correspondents by sneaking through a hole in the Curtain to take up residence in the Magic Dateline.

# Chapter 6

## London, Paris, Geneva

"If you want to get ahead in this company, don't get married and don't buy furniture." Bill Sexton, London bureau manager, was confiding to me his formula for success in the European operation of United Press. His advice was forbidding, but, as I was to find out, there was more to getting ahead than junking family life. For the moment, I put Sexton's advice aside as I became a full-time employee of UP London. I returned to London from my "secret" trip on September 12 and was enormously grateful that Roger Tatarian had made good on his promise to hire me. However, within days I learned that my position was more precarious than I imagined. In early October 1959, New York headquarters announced that United Press was acquiring Hearst's International News Service (INS) to form a new company called United Press International (UPI). Tatarian was recalled to New York after many years in Europe to become managing editor, and Sexton was leaving to become the New York bureau chief.

Paul Allerup, managing editor of INS, was transferred to London to head the European Division of the new UPI. Thus, my future would depend on making a good impression on Allerup, who had no part in my hiring. Furthermore, Allerup's main preoccupation was entertainment and good writing. He loved feature stories, particularly scandals about the English royals, a far cry from the conflicts of the Cold War that Ed Gritz told me threatened Western civilization. Around the news desk, editors and deskmen made wisecracks about Allerup's obsession with the marital problems of Princess Margaret when the world was blowing up around us.

To work for UPI in those days, you had to be a news junkie. We all worked six days a week, ten hours or more a day. My schedule usually called for me to begin about noon, with a day off in the middle of the week. That eliminated most social life other than an occasional beer with a colleague. Life in England was still austere in 1959; we were only fourteen years after the Second World War. I had been hired at twenty pounds a week (about sixty dollars), which I thought modest. But English university graduates were paid even less by British publications. In fact, I had turned down a tentative offer from Donald Tyreman, editor of the *Economist,* for a full-time job on American politics at seven pounds a week.

Before Roger left for New York, he arranged for me to ease into the bureau's operations by writing a number of timeless features. Here's a story he inspired, which moved some months later:

LONDON, Jan. 7—(UPI)—The ancient British bell foundry which cast America's Liberty Bell 207 years ago said today it would be happy to repair the crack.

Master Founder Albert A. Hughes of Whitechapel Foundry said he would gladly recast the whole bell if Philadelphia's town fathers would send it to him—he did not mind at all that the bell was once rung to proclaim America's independence from Britain.

He expressed doubt that the Philadelphia authorities would part with the bell and send it back to his foundry which has been casting bells— including London's Big Ben—for four centuries . . .

UPI ran a complex operation out of No. 8 Bouverie Street, just off Fleet Street, the British media center in those days. London was a busy hub— not because Britain was brimming with news but because of the favorable press rates of the British imperial telegraph system. Press telegrams were written in "cablese," a kind of pidgin English intended to save on transmission fees. Definite and indefinite articles were usually eliminated; two words were often merged into one. Pronouns fell by the wayside, except for "I," which was usually written "eye" to ensure that a harried telegrapher would not drop that single letter without a trace. Code words were created to designate special clients, competitors, key individuals. A correspondent traveling to Damascus, for example, might wire: "UNIPRESS LONDON—EYE DAMASCUSWARDING SMORNING FOR MAJOR PRESSER PARA ROX AND RAND ALREADY THERE PARA DOWNHOLDING EXPENSES PARA WILL FILE SAPPEST DUGAN." In plain English: "I'm traveling to Damascus this morning for a major press conference. The Associated Press and Reuters are already there. I'm keeping expenses to a minimum. Will file as soon as possible. Dugan."

Special code numbers used by telegraphers in the nineteenth century lived on and cropped up in copy until the 1980s. The AP, for example, preceded their urgent dispatches with a "95" that caused the teletypewriters down the line to ring three bells, thus alerting editors. When we wanted to conclude a cable with warm greetings, we would write "73s." I have no idea where that came from. The term *30* was used to indicate the end of a dispatch. This grew out of a mid-nineteenth-century practice of trying to avoid confusion with the telegraph. Correspondents would type an *x* at the end of each sentence, *xx* at the end of each paragraph, and *xxx* at the end of each story. If some of the story got lost in transmission, the *x*'s would alert the editor that something was missing. The three *x*'s—Roman symbols for thirty—were converted to "30" over time and are still used today to mark the end of a story or a press release.

Many of our staff correspondents or stringers in the Middle East and Asia were local hires whose English left much to be desired. The desk puzzled out what their fractured English meant, filled in the holes with background, and transmitted their stories in finished form to New York by radio teletypewriter at sixty words a minute. It was cheaper to do this corrective work in London where wages were lower than in New York. Simultaneously, the Euro Desk at UPI London rewrote dispatches for Europe, highlighting European angles and sending them back to the Continent. In 1959, UPI was still serving as an internal news service for Germany, where the Deutsche Presse Agentur was only just getting started after de-Nazification. Similarly, UPI made a special effort to supply news for the Japanese market because Japanese newspapers could not yet afford to send their own correspondents abroad. Reporting for Spain and Portugal was as sensitive as the AP's reporting for southern newspapers in American Civil War days. We had to remember that Madrid and Lisbon were the dictatorial outcasts of Europe. News that was acceptable in democratic countries would not always go down well on the Iberian Peninsula.

An overeducated person like myself had difficulty grasping that United Press International was writing for ordinary people who had a high school education but probably not much more. Our clients wanted the top of the news, the headlines. They were not looking for erudite analyses, which is what a university education pushes you toward. Our job was to package information succinctly—no big story was worth more than seven hundred words in those days—and to use clever, intriguing, or entertaining phrases. Time and again, Bill Sexton would pound into me, "You are writing for the

Kansas City milkman, someone with a ninth grade education." This theme was sounded so often, by so many editors, that it became a catchphrase. One correspondent, Reynolds Packard, used it as the title of his humorous novel about UP and its Paris Bureau.

Another slogan was "Get it first, but first get it right." This dictum grew out of a general perception that United Press was less conscientious than the Associated Press in verifying information. The reputation for sensationalism traced back to a dispatch sent from Paris in 1918 by Roy W. Howard, UP's hard-driving president, ending the First World War four days before the Armistice was signed on November 11, 1918. Howard, who got an unauthorized tip from the U.S. admiral commanding U.S. ships in French waters, filed this cable on November 7: "UNIPRESS NEWYORK—URGENT ARMISTICE ALLIES GERMANY SIGNED ELEVEN SMORNING HOSTILITIES CEASED TWO SAFTERNOON SEDAN TAKEN SMORNING BY AMERICANS. HOWARD SIMMS." UP played, up, the, news, only to have it denied within hours by the U.S. State Department in Washington. Howard filed a clarification, but experience shows that corrections never catch up with the original mistake.

Editors constantly pushed correspondents to produce exclusives, not exclusives that stayed unmatched forever but exclusives that would be confirmed within hours. I felt that a few minutes over the AP did not really make much difference in the light of history. I was wrong. This was the sort of elitist attitude that did not endear college graduates to ink-stained editors. From a business point of view, beating the opposition was all-important since UPI had clients all over the world, and deadlines occurred every minute.

Getting a beat on the AP often required ingenuity since "Rox" (the UPI code word for AP) usually outstaffed and outspent its competitors. An example was the way UP covered the sinking of the *Flying Enterprise,* a freighter that foundered off Land's End, England, in a storm on December 31, 1951. Captain Kurt Carlsen managed to transfer crew and passengers to the American troopship USS *General Greeley,* which came to the rescue. But the freighter, listing at 60 degrees, finally sank, carrying to the bottom a Stradivarius violin and other precious cargo. Paddy Thornberry, a veteran "Unipresser" in the London Bureau, was sent to Falmouth to report the drama with little money for expenses. "They gave me ten pounds and wished me good luck," Paddy told me years later. "When I got to Falmouth I found the AP had rented an oceangoing tug with radio-telephone. They had several staffers aboard, and they circled the sinking ship right up to the moment Captain Carlsen stepped off the stern and rowed away in a small boat." Thornberry said he was so depressed he could not match this blanket coverage that he retired to a bar to spend the ten pounds. As luck would have it, he sat down next to a former Royal Navy radioman. Eventually, they got to talking, and the radioman invited Paddy home to his own radio shack. From there, they monitored the frequent transmissions that the thirty-seven-year-old Carlsen, an accomplished radio operator, was sending to Admiralty House in London and to his superiors at the Isbrandtsen Line. Thornberry's stories, based on these inside conversations, gave UP clients an insight that the AP missed entirely and cost Paddy only a few drinks.

Then came the wind-up press conference at Falmouth at which Captain Carlsen described his ordeal. The British newspapers staffed the conference heavily. To maintain order, the organizers decreed that no one would be per-mitted to file copy until the conference was over; policemen were posted at the doors to enforce the edict. Bob Musel, who directed UP's special cover-age, told me that he instructed his four correspondents to disregard the order and leave every fifteen minutes to file to New York. He led the way by going first. "When I got to the door," Musel explained to me in the fall of 1959, "the bobby stopped me. He said, 'You can't leave. Orders.' I replied, 'But I've got a pass!' And I opened my wallet where I had placed a five-pound note in plain view. The bobby replied, 'Aha. You have a pass,' and let me and my col-leagues out with no further argument." That gave UP a series of very con-firmable beats over the AP. The Associated Press in London was deluged with "rockets" from New York headquarters, saying something to the effect of "The *World Telegram and Sun* [a prime UP client in New York in the 1950s] is front-paging Carlsen's press conference. Where are you?"

Musel was a gifted writer with a world reputation who worked out of the London Bureau. He had joined the UP in 1927 when he was eighteen and came to London in 1943 as a war correspondent. He had never been to col-lege, but as he peered at his typewriter his words flowed with magical ease. He began his report on Queen Elizabeth's coronation in 1952 this way: "Golden trumpets stilled the tumult of modern London today, and the world's largest city rolled back the centuries to hear Elizabeth II proclaimed Queen." Musel knew every trick, every twist, and his enthusiasm never flagged. In his many years in London, he specialized in covering the enter-tainment world, movie stars, and any story that needed a special touch. Ob-viously, Paul Allerup was in awe.

There were others notables at No. 8 Bouverie. Joe Grigg Jr. was the flushed-face pro with a clipped mustache who seemed more English than American. His father, Joe Grigg Sr., had been a foreign correspondent in Eu-rope after World War I, and Joe Jr. was raised in England and graduated from Trinity College–Cambridge in 1932. Joe had been assigned to Berlin at the start of the Second World War and contributed some of the earliest re-ports on the Holocaust. When I knew him in the 1950s and 1960s, he seemed to be acquainted with every political leader worth knowing in Europe. He was as comfortable covering British elections as running the Paris Bureau or watching for the telltale plume of white smoke that signaled the selection of a new pope at the Vatican.

K. C. Thaler was my favorite because he covered diplomacy. A refugee from Poland who looked like a diplomat in his gray double-breasted suit, Karol Thaler began as a translator at the BBC radio monitoring service at Caversham in the immediate postwar years. He was in constant competition with the free-swinging Arthur Gavshon of the Associated Press, a fact that made him put more of a spin on his stories than I thought warranted. But he got wide play—we used to say he got "plenty of house"—and was immensely knowledgeable about the international world. I found his skepticism about Russian intentions to be similar to my father's.

Dick Growald, from Fort Worth, Texas, was a rotund rewrite man, with a partially amputated index finger, who could compose stories in his head faster than a teletypewriter could gobble them up. Dick had an uncontrollable temper and was known to have thrown a typewriter in anger out a window onto Bouverie Street. A few minutes later, all was forgotten; he could not recall his outburst or hold a grudge.

By contrast, Greg Jensen, the senior news editor, seemed to have ice water in his veins. No matter how dramatic the story, he never betrayed the slightest emotion, and his fingers flew over the keyboard silently, relentlessly, never missing a stroke.

Daniel F. Gilmore, who replaced Sexton as bureau manager, was an excitable Irish American slave driver who exuded an infectious enthusiasm. Danny, who had been a copyboy in New York when the war started, joined the U.S. Army Air Corps as a belly gunner on a B-17 with the Eighth Air Force. He was shot down but helped by the French Resistance to travel across France to the Pyrenees. As he tried to cross over into Spain he was captured by the Germans and sat out the rest of the war in a prison camp. When liberated by American forces in 1945, a G.I. gave him a rifle that he pointed at one of his German tormentors. "Get ready to die!" he shouted at the guard who was now cowering. Danny confessed he did not have the guts, at the last moment, to pull the trigger.

An intriguing deskman was Don Larrimore, a 1956 graduate of Princeton, a rapid-reaction man with a steel-trap mind and considerable knowledge of Soviet affairs. Larrimore, like me, was fascinated by the Cold War and knew Russian well. He had come to UP London from Radio Liberation, then financed by the CIA to broadcast news into Russia, to improve his newswriting skills over a six-month period. Who sent him I did not know then, and do not know now. Desk colleagues thought he was secretly connected to the

CIA. Larrimore traveled to Moscow after Princeton, hoping to become a student at Moscow State University and the following year went to the Soviet-sponsored Youth Festival in Helsinki in 1957. When his six-month training period in London was up, he had become so enthusiastic about wire-service work that he asked to be hired full-time. Tatarian pegged him for the Moscow Bureau, and assigned him to go there ahead of me.

For editors and deskmen, the daily work on the London desk was a grind. There were not many outside events to cover, since the Press Association and ExTel, two British wire services, covered all major happenings and not a few of the minor ones. Occasionally, I would be detached to cover events that I often found trying—like an exhibition of men's underwear. Even more difficult for me was my first death watch. The ambassador from Colombia was dying. For UPI, this was a major event because our extensive Latin American service was considered better than that of the Associated Press and the Colombian ambassador was an important political figure at home.

Jay Axelbank, one of my rewrite colleagues, and I were assigned to report on the ambassador's waning health no fewer than two times a day—for the A.M. and P.M. news cycles. This involved calling up his widow-to-be morning and evening to ask how far gone the ambassador was. Like so many cub reporters before me, I thought that if this was journalism, I wouldn't be able to stand it. Fortunately, the ambassador's wife was a highly experienced public person herself and fielded the calls with grace. I finally realized that such people have an interest in keeping their constituencies accurately informed. Suddenly, the death watch seemed less forbidding.

Death intruded into my life that winter in a more piercing way. Serge and his second wife, Martha, came to London to see me receive my B.A. degree from Oxford over the weekend of December 11–12. We had dinner together in a little restaurant off King's Road on Thursday night. I still remember that meal—prawns in avocados served with chilled white wine. The next morning, December 9, when I went to work I received an unexpected call from Serge, speaking again in his controlled, tense voice. It was April 16, 1950, all over again: "Martha died of a heart attack this morning."

I rushed to Brown's Hotel, wondering if our meal the night before had anything to do with this tragedy. At the reception desk, I told the attendant that I was going up to see Mr. Daniloff. He replied cryptically, "It is not advisable to visit Mr. Daniloff at this time." A few more words of explanation, and I was upstairs in my father's suite. Martha lay on the bed, her body covered by a white sheet. A few moments later, there was a knock at the door. My father opened it, and a tall man, dressed in striped trousers and black coat, announced, "I am the coroner." Not understanding his British accent, my father snapped, "I can see you are in the corridor. Go away!" The medical examiner finally managed to explain himself, and Serge allowed him to view Martha's body. The rest of the day was spent informing relatives in Detroit by telephone that Martha had suddenly died. For UPI, this was also news. Martha was the widow of Henry Sheldon, an investment banker and Republican Party activist in Grosse Pointe, Michigan. In recent years, she had been elected president of the International Social Service, and the *Detroit Free Press* wanted all the details. The office, not realizing that I was related, never reached me for details, and I was too street-dumb to offer any on my own initiative.

Saturday, the next day, the family participation in the degree ceremony at Oxford went ahead as planned. It was a joyless occasion attended by Serge and Martha's daughter, Annette. She had flown from Washington to London despite her pregnancy to help Serge through this difficult moment and accompany him back to Grosse Pointe for the funeral.

Because of the long hours, life on the general desk was tedious. But in 1958 a chance encounter had brought a glimpse of happiness. It happened one night in February as I was returning to Oxford from a short stint at UPI in London. I was pleasantly exhausted when I arrived at Paddington Station. On a whim, I decided to check out all the women passengers on the train. This London-Oxford train, and its Oxford-London counterpart, was famously dubbed the Flying Fornicator because of the high jinks that sometimes occurred during and after the run.

"I'm going to meet the prettiest girl on the train," I said to myself as I climbed aboard. I ambled down the passageway of all the carriages until I spotted a young woman with chestnut hair. Brashly, I slid the compartment door open and plunked myself down opposite her. From my bag, I pulled out a copy of the *London Times* and began to read. As the train lurched out of Paddington, I leaned over and asked if she would like to glance at it. Soon we were deep in conversation, and by the time we reached Oxford at one in the morning, I realized this had been no ordinary encounter. Soon I was inviting her to my college rooms for what I conceived as exotic liaisons, namely, drinking Lapsang Souchong tea with guavas, and she was inviting me back to her digs for dinners with her roommates. In retelling the Fornicator frolic over the years, Ruth would offer a far more sober version than mine. "I was returning to Oxford when this pompous American came into my compartment and forced his boring newspaper on me," she would say. In the months ahead there would be many ups and downs, but little by little we were slowly binding ourselves to each other.

Slowly, life at UPI returned to normal, but not always for the good. Inevitably, I made some bad mistakes in the early days. One of them occurred at the Anglo-American Press Club, an association formed by American correspondents in London after the war for hosting and interviewing British personalities. Occasionally, I would be invited to go by a senior colleague. This time it was Norm Runnion, one of the top writers in the bureau, who took me along to hear British Foreign Secretary Selwyn Lloyd. Before lunch was served, I spotted a group of journalists surrounding someone who was speaking at length about the Russians. Fascinated, I wriggled into the inner circle. Not knowing who this person was, I took advantage of a lull to ask, "Are you a Soviet expert?" The person turned out to be the foreign secretary. My senior colleagues were horrified, and I slunk away in disgrace.

I suppose it was events like this, plus my inexperience at desk work, that made me appear to Allerup to be a questionable member of his team. In April I took advantage of a short vacation to fly to the States and chat in New York with Tatarian. We talked, as I recall, of the possibility that I might be assigned to the Rome Olympic Games. Roger also thought that I would gain valuable experience if an opening occurred in the one-man bureau in Geneva, the European headquarters of the United Nations. On returning to Europe, I flew to France, not London, to work temporarily in the Paris Bureau during the summit conference in early May between President Eisenhower and Soviet leader Nikita Khrushchev. At the end of the Khrushchev visit, Allerup would decide whether I had passed the six-month probationary period.

My job in Paris was to help the desk in any way that seemed useful over a daily shift of ten to twelve hours. Art Higbee, the bureau manager, had deployed his best troops to cover the Eisenhower-Khrushchev summit along with an infusion of personnel from London and Washington. The meeting, or rather the unmeeting, as it turned out, unfolded in high drama. The Soviets on May 1 had shot down one of the American U-2 spy planes that had been flying over key industrial targets at the very high altitude of sixty thousand feet or more since 1955. The pilot, Francis Gary Powers, had parachuted safely and refused to commit suicide with a poisoned pin.

From the start, the Eisenhower administration prevaricated, claiming the U-2 was a weather plane that had gone astray through navigational failure. Now Khrushchev announced that Powers had been captured alive. To heighten the drama, Khrushchev had the wreckage of the plane displayed in Gorki Park in central Moscow with all the attendant publicity. At a Paris press conference, Khrushchev demanded that President Eisenhower apologize on behalf of the United States for violating the sovereignty of the Soviet Union . . . or else. Eisenhower refused, and Khrushchev and the Soviet delegation walked out in anger and returned to Moscow.

During this same period a drama of another kind exploded one evening while I was on the Paris desk. Prince Ali Khan, the presumed successor to the fabulously wealthy Aga Khan, died in an automobile accident in the Paris suburb of Suresnes on the night of May 13, 1960. As he approached the intersection of Boulevard Henri Senier and the rue du Mont Valerien, his gray Lancia crashed into an oncoming Simca. Agence France Presse sent out an urgent story that I quickly refashioned and sent to London for final processing. Charlie Ridley, one of UPI's most seasoned jack-of-all-trades, bustled into the office, having heard the news on the radio, eased me off the desk, and took over the story. Minutes later, special correspondent Serge Fliegers rushed breathlessly into the newsroom, seized a typewriter, and pounded out a dramatic "eyewitness" account for the Hearst newspapers: "Paris—'Oh my God! My Ali! My man!' cried out Bettina, the girl friend of Prince Ali Khan, just moments after his car crashed in a Paris suburb, killing him instantly."

None of us thought that Fliegers had actually seen the wreck or heard the words. I thought Fliegers's invention was pretty disreputable, certainly unworthy of the journalism I hoped to do. Later, the Paris police announced that Ali Khan died in a hospital, not in his car. But Fliegers's copy was a classic tearjerker, one that did not simply repeat wire-service information. And, as one of the office wits was fond of declaring, "Don't let the facts get in the way of a good story!"

I flew back to London after the remains of the nonsummit were cleaned up to learn that my work in Paris had been appreciated. Allerup approved my becoming a full-time Unipresser. It was back to the six-days-a-week grind again, this time compounded with once-a-week duty as overnight editor. That meant coming into the office at midnight and working until seven. The months merged one into another until midsummer when Allerup summoned me to his office. "Jon Randal in Geneva has quit to join the *Paris Herald Tribune*," he said. "How about you taking over the bureau?"

I should have been delighted. But a new consideration was growing in my life—that chestnut-haired English girl called Ruth. Sexton's words cycled ominously through my mind: "Don't get married and don't buy furniture." Allerup looked as if he expected me to accept immediately and be on my way the next day. His face brooked no argument or conditions. In fact, at this moment UPI looked to me like an ogre, a heartless organization, interested only in getting the news out first with maximum speed and minimum cost. I agonized over Allerup's proposal for several days, consulted like a grown-up with Joe Grigg and other members of the senior staff without revealing the real nature of my concerns. I recalled Charlie Ridley's words when I left Paris after the failed summit conference. "Keep this in mind," Ridley told me. "UPI is the worst company to work for, but it has a policy of hiring only the nicest people."

After days of indecision, I accepted the Geneva assignment. Ruth and I promised each other that we would not let this separation harm our relationship. Before flying to Geneva, I had a final meeting with Allerup and Harry Ferguson, UPI's top roving correspondent. "Fergie," an authority figure so great I hardly dared approach him, turned to me spontaneously and said, "Remember, whatever interests you in Geneva will probably interest me and our clients. So don't hesitate to send in the oddball story from time to time." Good advice, and it stuck.

The UPI operation in Geneva was conducted out of Room 74 on the ground floor of the Palais des Nations, the old League of Nations building that had become the European headquarters of the United Nations. The diplomatic story of the day was the U.S.-British-Soviet negotiations to ban atmospheric nuclear tests. As the U.S. election campaign geared up during that summer of 1960, pitting Senator John F. Kennedy against Eisenhower's vice president, Richard Nixon, the trilateral negotiations slowed to a crawl. Occasionally, Soviet negotiator Semyon K. Tsarapkin would get off a memorable remark, but more often than not, the U.S., British, and Soviet delegations would meet briefly, set a new date, and adjourn. No one was prepared to offer a dramatic proposal until the future leadership of the United States was decided. I had only to file brief reports alerting editors down the line that the talks, though moribund, were not dead.

"The whole trick in covering these negotiations," my predecessor Jonathan Randal explained to me, "is to look for progress. That's what it's all about." Randal's counsel, like Ferguson's, was excellent advice for a cub, especially since I had no mentor hovering over me to correct errors or deflect foolishness. London hardly ever offered guidance. But on one occasion I did get applause from Allerup when I wrote a whimsical article about the possibility—much discussed under Soviet pressure—that U.N. headquarters should be transferred from New York to Geneva. My story focused on the flock of peacocks that roamed the lawns around the U.N. buildings, indifferent to the political upheavals of the world. The feature depended on a clever play on words and began this way: "If U.N. headquarters is transferred to Geneva, nine old peacocks who inhabit the grounds won't ruffle a feather."

If you looked hard, you could find all sorts of unusual stories in Geneva's back streets and watering holes. I particularly liked this one:

GENEVA (UPI)—The man who punched Stalin in the face and lived to tell the tale is rounding out his long life denouncing the brutal terror of the communist system, whose founders he once plotted with.

At 75, white-haired Khariton Chavichvili is a man who has known conspiracy, revolution and terror.

In a Geneva café, just a stone's throw from his present dingy, second-floor lodging, he plotted during 1908 with Lenin for the overthrow of Russia's Romanov dynasty and the end of the reign of Nicholas II, czar of all Russia . . .

When life was active in Geneva, it provided a great introduction to diplomatic reporting. Here were headquartered many organizations that made news, such as the International Labor Organization, International Committee for European Migration, General Agreement on Tariffs and Trade, World Health Organization, International Committee of the Red Cross, and others. You picked up their press releases, scooped up some background, and introduced yourself to their spokesmen in the hopes they would feed you some good stuff sometime in the future. This was where I learned the technique of cultivating sources by forsaking the telephone and taking them out to lunch. It was essential to be gregarious, and it helped to speak French.

One of my more memorable efforts occurred at the Villa Rose with Soviet negotiator Semyon K. Tsarapkin. The interview was arranged at my request by Yuli Vorontsov, the negotiator's spokesman, a promising young diplomat with whom I would meet in happy and unhappy circumstances in decades to come. Tsarapkin owed his rise to the Bolshevik Revolution. He was born in 1906 and went to work in a smelting plant at seventeen. While he was still in his twenties, he was plucked from the factory floor and sent for political training. In the post–World War II years, he served in the Soviet Mission to the United Nations and also in the embassy in Washington, where he held the rank of minister-counselor. He was well liked by Western diplomats who appreciated his ability to distinguish policy from personality. He might deliver a serious blast at the West but usually made clear he was not impugning his interlocutors personally. Behind his back, British and American envoys called him "Scratchy," because his surname was derived from the Russian verb *tsarapat'*, meaning "to scratch."

Tsarapkin had made news during my Harvard years when he received two editors of the *Harvard Crimson* at the Soviet Mission in New York in April 1953. They presented him with a copper ibis, a large storklike bird stolen by pranksters from atop the Harvard Lampoon building in Cambridge.

In my meeting, Tsarapkin chatted amiably about the Russian Revolution that forced my father to flee Petrograd but gave the Soviet official the chance to make a career as a diplomat. We sat on chairs in the garden of the villa and discoursed about the state of the world. If I wished to be well informed on Soviet matters, "Scratchy" insisted, I should read the Soviet press attentively. It was reliable and authoritative, he assured me. I nodded dutifully, pretending to take notes. I came away with no scoop and no news, a fact that Tsarapkin probably considered excellent press management by Vorontsov.

The Palais des Nations, where the nuclear-test-ban negotiators met, brought together journalists from all over the world—AP, Reuters, UPI, Agence France Presse, the *New York Times, Manchester Guardian*, and many European newspapers. Its press room was a hangout for the down-and-out, for the freelancers from France, Switzerland, India, Pakistan, and assorted lost souls who sought warmth and company. Between rounds of major conferences, Geneva lapsed into somnolence. A. M. Rosenthal, future editor of the *New York Times,* spent months in Geneva after being expelled from Poland for reporting too critically. He wrote that the city, where so many international initiatives had failed in the past, had the aura of a cup of warm chocolate at bedtime. A more cynical colleague quipped, "It's really a place where you eat sticky cakes and commit adultery."

On the surface Geneva appeared to be well ordered and proper. The Lac Leman, impressive hotels such as the Beau Rivage, and the view of Mont Blanc projected a picture of serenity. Yet underneath, scandalous and mysterious doings were going on. On one occasion, the head of the Geneva Bar Association was accused of murdering his wife's lover. On another, a prominent lawyer was arrested for indecent exposure in the Vieille Ville, or Old Town. Still later, the newspaper *La Suisse* produced details of the gory murder of Felix Moumié, a political exile from Cameroun.

In the fall of 1960 a Harvard classmate, Jamie Barnes, brought intrigue into my own office without my realizing it. He would suddenly appear, plop down in a chair, address me in the lingo of the Harvard clubbie—"You Big Bomber, you!"—then entertain me with hysterical stories from college years. Later, he confided he was actually using my office as cover. He served, in civilian clothes, as a member of U.S. Army Intelligence exploring some secret situation in Geneva until Swiss counterintelligence identified him and forced him out of the country. I never did learn what his mission was, but I was not pleased.

At the turn of the year, Ruth decided to join me to set up housekeeping in my studio apartment at 14 rue de la Madeleine in the Old City. This was a daring decision because living in sin in those days was not generally considered acceptable, as it is today. Ruth's father could raise no objections. A naval officer, he had died some years before. He had played a role in arresting Leon Trotsky off Halifax, Nova Scotia, in 1917 as he sailed from New York to join the Russian Revolution. Ruth's mother, an eccentric and literary widow, had no complaints. Actually, she was delighted because she guessed the arrangement would lead to marriage.

Ruth's first preoccupation was to find a job while I honed my journalistic skills. Her first employment was as a girl Friday to Dr. Said Ramadan, the Jordanian delegate to the European Office of the United Nations. Dr. Ramadan was a shadowy figure whose main concern was to spread Islam throughout Europe. He was forever traveling, setting up Muslim cultural centers, and handing out copies of the Koran. Word circulated in the corridors that he was closely linked to the fundamentalist Muslim Brotherhood in Egypt and that President Nasser had put a price on his head for his activities. Ruth and a coworker, a Turkish girl named Aishe, edited Ramadan's flowery English prose and ran errands. They also rejected his sexual advances and chortled over his more quotable lines, uttered in a U.N. lilt, "Aishe, Aishe, he stands for you!" Eventually, Ruth left Dr. Ramadan after spotting surreptitious agents tailing her and joined an English-language tabloid, the *Geneva Tribune*, owned and operated by an American woman, Casey Herrick. There Ruth began her own journalistic career.

Our Geneva apartment soon became a stopping-off spot for college friends on the rise. Among the visitors were Alston Chase, later a distinguished environmentalist and author of *Harvard and the Unabomber*, and Barry Bingham Jr., future publisher of the *Louisville Courier-Journal*. One of the most important drop-ins was not an American at all but a Russian. Yuri Korolyov, a well-known war photographer, came to Geneva for a week to cover the Soviet team at an international hockey match. Yuri was employed part-time by the UPI Moscow Bureau, and Henry Shapiro had asked him, when he had time, to assess discreetly my suitability for a Moscow posting. Yuri and I quickly became friends, and he proved to me that *homo sovieticus* could also be a real human being and avid consumer. Yuri also spent a good deal of time with Ruth, who guided him on an even more important quest—loading up on watches, dresses, and a fur coat for his lady friend, Tonya. This encounter was worth the effort: we passed inspection.

Once President Kennedy was inaugurated in January 1961, activity in Geneva began to pick up. The United States presented new proposals to the nuclear-test-ban talks, then turned to the problem of growing Communist inroads in Indochina. Fearing an expanded insurgency, Kennedy backed an effort to ensure the neutrality of neighboring Laos. A major international conference was convened in Geneva to bring together leaders from Cambodia, Vietnam, Laos, China, the Soviet Union, the United States, and Britain.

I was suddenly hyperbusy organizing communications, negotiating arrangements with Swiss officials, booking hotel rooms for the UPI team that would come to take over the coverage. Yet in the midst of these long working days, Ruth and I managed to slip off to the Hotel de Ville on June

24, 1961, and get married. Taking advantage of our chief diplomatic correspondent, Karol Thaler, London Bureau manager Danny Gilmore, rewrite
man Dick Growald, and my father, who flew in especially, we arranged a
wedding luncheon beside Lake Geneva. The next day, I was back at the conference, covering the Communist delegations.

Finally, in September 1961, the instructions I had been waiting for during
the past three years came through from London. Allerup informed me that
Don Larrimore was to go to Moscow to replace Aline Mosby, who was
winding up a three-year assignment. I was to follow a month later to become the third and most junior member of the bureau, as Henry Shapiro
was leaving on a break. Within days, I traveled to the Soviet Embassy in
Berne to apply for a journalistic visa, which came through within weeks.
This was none too soon, because Larrimore's Moscow assignment was canceled by UPI management without explanation as he was driving his VW
Bug across Eastern Europe. Rumors circulated that UPI vice presidents had
learned belatedly that Larrimore had some dubious connections that could
cause trouble for him and the company. I was told to speed up my departure. By the end of November 1961, Ruth and I wound up our affairs in
Geneva and made our way to Paris. At the Gare du Nord, we boarded the
dark-green Russian sleeping car for the two-and-a-half-day journey
through Berlin and Warsaw to the Magic Dateline.

# Chapter 7

## Genri

Henry sent his assistant, Bud Korengold, to meet us when the train pulled into the Byelorussian railroad station on November 28, a day that I remember for the -25 degree cold that bit through our clothes. My first professional encounter with the chief occurred a day or two later after we had settled temporarily into the Ukraine Hotel, across the street from the UPI office. This meeting was quite different from our initial encounter two years before. Henry summoned another newly arrived correspondent, Sam Jaffe of ABC, to the office at 15 Kutuzovsky Prospekt for that first working meeting.

I knew nothing about Sam in those early days. As we waited, I could see by his determined face and body language that Sam was likely to be an energetic, even aggressive, correspondent. He had worked earlier for CBS and had participated in the coverage of U-2 pilot Francis Gary Powers's espionage trial in August 1960. He had covered the United Nations in New York, where he had made friends with many Soviet diplomats. Those friendships, and new ones, would make him a formidable competitor.

At last, Henry bustled into the sparsely decorated front room in his heavy overcoat and settled down behind the desk. Then, looking at both of us in a rather skeptical way, he said, "Well, you've got to Moscow. Welcome." We smiled appreciatively, expecting that Henry would now endow us with some unusual insight, some special word, that would finally make us members of that exclusive, sought-after fraternity of Moscow correspondents. He didn't. The conversation took a surprising turn, as he continued rather sternly, "Forget everything about the Soviet Union you've ever read elsewhere. You'll find out more about this place by being here than by reading what's published by the nincompoops in the West. And, keep in mind, we are on duty twenty-four hours a day. This isn't London, where you've been working six days a week. Here we're on duty every day of the week, including Saturdays and Sundays." Stunned, Sam and I remained silent.

Henry went on to explain how Moscow journalism had developed since Stalin died. Considered the dean of foreign correspondents, he launched into an explanation of the "alliance system" that began to evolve during the Second World War. The purpose of this arrangement was to cope with the cascade of news that could easily overwhelm any single correspondent or bureau. The system divided Western correspondents into two competing groups. UPI, Agence France Presse, and a bevy of newspaper "specials" (special correspondents of large newspapers) formed one camp; the Associated Press, Reuters, and their satellite "specials" formed the other. News collected by one wire service would be shared with alliance partners but never with the opposing cartel. The point was to help each correspondent by widening his ability to get the fullest, most interesting, most timely accounts of the day's events while maintaining competition.

Both groups were free to develop as many allies as they liked among the "specials" and television networks. Henry was always recruiting new members, and that was undoubtedly why Jaffe was included in this first meeting. If a newsman joined Henry's camp, he would be free to read and plagiarize our files. Probably, the correspondent would give us no credit in print—journalistic ethics were not as highly developed in the 1960s as they became in the 1990s. If we were not credited, there was one important benefit to us nevertheless. Stories lifted from our files and printed by the "specials" would appear to be confirming our own stories. We gained credibility through this circuitous process, although we probably should not have.

There was one favor Henry would do for all correspondents whether they belonged to our camp or not: share his notes from Soviet receptions. After decades in Moscow, Henry was fluent in Russian and got on easily with the top Soviet leaders. Nikita Khrushchev would sometimes endearingly call him "Shapirka," a diminutive suggesting easy familiarity. Very often at receptions, Khrushchev would seek out Shapiro and other correspondents who huddled around to banter with him for fifteen or twenty minutes. These were the days before pocket-size tape recorders and everyone scribbled down whatever they could on notepads and envelopes. Immediately afterward, correspondents would go over the quotes and agree on an unofficial "transcript" of what had been said. This avoided wildly differing quotes and reduced misunderstandings that could arise from an imperfect understanding of the Russian language.

Henry brought our first meeting to a close with a word about KGB surveillance of Western residents, a murky subject that evoked images of spying and counterspying. "The authorities will be looking you over, probably for the next six months," Henry declared. "They'll try to find out if you are up to anything suspicious. You're going to be so busy, I wouldn't pay much attention to their efforts if you should notice them. You'll have enough to do around here not to get into trouble with them."

Trouble was something Sam would court soon enough. Predictably, he got off to a racing start, looking up Soviet acquaintances from his New York days and making new contacts. Henry knew a lot about trouble, too; a lengthy career in Moscow had left its mark on him. Although he was a charming host and brilliant raconteur with outsiders, he tended to be secretive, especially when talking on telephones, which were monitored by the KGB. He was extremely possessive of exclusive information, and astonishingly resourceful in transmitting his bombshells to the outside world. He reveled in his scoop of Stalin's death on March 5, 1953, which he recounted to me and his other assistants.

The failing health of the dictator, who had ruled the Soviet Union for a quarter century, did not come entirely out of the blue. On March 2, the Soviet leadership was informed secretly that the dictator had suffered a stroke, and they began planning how to handle his passing. Around midnight on March 3, Henry was working on stories for transmission to London at the Central Telegraph when he received a phone call from an old friend. The caller—Henry never identified him, but I guess it was a Soviet journalist—asked him to come out onto the street. The friend told him of Stalin's illness. Henry returned to the Central Telegraph and prepared an urgent message for New York headquarters, with copies for London and Tokyo. But the receptionist, to whom he handed the copy, took one look and refused to accept it.

March 4 passed quietly with no further information, but Moscow radio played sad music by Bach, Beethoven, and Chopin, alerting the nation that an important person was either dead or dying. On the evening of March 5, Henry sent his chauffeur, Viktor Pavlovich, to Pushkin Square to pick up the government newspaper, *Izvestia,* which ordinarily came out in the evening. When Viktor returned empty-handed to Henry's apartment, he told this astounding story: "The paper is not coming out this evening. It's coming out tomorrow morning simultaneously with *Pravda.* In fact, the place is in turmoil. Employees are leaving the building in tears. When I asked them what was wrong, one of them said, 'Stalin died.'" The official announcement would come only hours later, at three on the morning of March 6.

Henry rushed to the Central Telegraph to telephone UP London with the news that the driver had brought him. The correspondent for the Associated Press and Harrison Salisbury of the *New York Times* had already gathered there, waiting for the official announcement. Henry handed the receptionist urgent copy announcing the death. She tore it up, saying that there had been no announcement. Henry next ordered an expensive telephone connection to London. It was against the rules to hold an open line without talking. So Henry filibustered by reading the Bible over the line. In the booth next to his, Henry could hear the AP correspondent shouting, "Send me another five hundred dollars!" which was prearranged AP code for Stalin's demise. But the man in the AP London Bureau had forgotten what these words were supposed to mean and replied matter-of-factly that five hundred dollars had been sent and no more was available.

At last, UP's ace reporter Bob Musel came on the line in London, and Henry lobbed an innocuous question to him: "Guess what happened here today?" Musel, who had been working on the story from London since the news of Stalin's stroke was announced on March 3, snapped, "Stalin died!" "I had a split second to say yes, and the line was cut off," Henry told me. "But the news was out, and Musel did the rest, filling in the background and summing up Stalin's rule." Sometime later on March 6, the radio monitors of the British and American governments detected the Soviet news agency TASS transmitting the news of Stalin's death by radio to provincial newspapers.

Henry always said this moment announced the happy beginning of a new life for him. The first five years of the Cold War had been worse for Henry and Ludmilla than the Second World War or Stalin's reign of terror. The Cold War was a U.S.-Soviet conflict, pitting Americans against Soviets. On February 9, 1946, Stalin addressed a meeting at the Bolshoi Theater to proclaim that communism would rule the future, whereas on March 5, Winston Churchill declared at Fulton, Missouri, that an "Iron Curtain" was descending across Europe. The Big Chill and its afflictions touched all American citizens then living in Moscow: diplomats, correspondents, hangers-on, and the Russian wives of foreigners.

Official paranoia was growing. Stalin and his cohorts were concerned that the United States, sole possessor of the atomic bomb, might attempt to destroy their regime if not the whole country. They pushed a crash program to develop a similar weapon and succeeded. In recent years, Russian archives have revealed that the Soviets knew the United States was inserting spies and subversives in Soviet territory in an effort to weaken the Kremlin. An atmosphere of hostility engulfed all foreigners in Moscow; sources began to dry up; Western newspapers closed their bureaus. Editors in America were content to surrender the Soviet scene to the news agencies.

By 1948 only five Western reporters remained: Henry Shapiro of UP, Thomas Whitney and Eddy Gilmore of AP, Jean Nau of the French news agency AFP (all of whom were married to Russian women), and Harrison Salisbury, a bachelor, representing the only newspaper that stayed on, the *New York Times*.

In 1947, the Soviet government adopted several new laws that increased the isolation of these journalists. One law prohibited Soviet citizens from marrying foreigners; another made secret any information that had not been published in the official press. Correspondents were constantly monitored. "The Cold War was probably the worst period I experienced in the Soviet Union, even worse than the purges," Henry said in a lengthy interview for an oral history project of the American Jewish Committee. "During the purges, of course, there was a generally oppressive atmosphere, but the Cold War was directed mostly against the United States. . . . I had a policeman outside my building day and night, and I had a car following me day and night."

His wife, Ludmilla Nikolaevna, confirmed this. She recounted that the Russian women who had married foreigners during and immediately after the world war were arrested almost daily. They would be walking down a street when suddenly the door of a car parked on the street would open, and they would be pulled inside. These women would be summarily tried, sentenced for high treason, and sent off to the prison camps for fifteen years. "By the time Stalin died," Ludmilla said, "only six of about one hundred wives of Americans or Britons remained at large. If Stalin had lived a few more days, I am sure my turn would have been next."

Henry added more details. "I didn't feel my life was in danger. But all my Russian contacts were scared of me. I had no Russian friends by this time. There were times when for weeks I couldn't see a single Russian except one or two officials in the Press Department of the Foreign Ministry. My wife's relatives were afraid of her." The U.S. Embassy counseled Henry to leave Moscow for fear that he might be arrested. He refused. He said he was prepared for Siberia, but if he left he was sure his wife and daughter would be nabbed. For five years, he never ventured outside of Moscow. He read the newspapers incessantly, filed whatever was newsworthy, never took a break.

I often wondered how Henry got himself in this fix. He could have become a successful New York lawyer after receiving a law degree from Harvard in 1932 and working briefly for a Manhattan law firm. But life took a different turn. He was born in Romania in 1906 into a family of four sons and four daughters who entered the United States through Ellis Island in 1920. He might well have grown to manhood in Romania were it not for the Balkan wars of 1912–1913. In 1913, Henry's father sent the eldest son to the

United States to escape conscription as well as the eldest daughter. In 1920, the two sent one thousand dollars, and the rest of the family, minus Henry's mother, who died of typhus in 1916, made their way to France and sailed from Le Havre for New York.

At fourteen, Henry's life in the New World began in a tenement at Twelfth Street and Second Avenue. A bookish boy, he perfected his English quickly while attending East Side Evening High School and eventually entered that free institution that has provided a bridge for so many immigrants to mainstream America—the City College of New York. At CCNY he majored in philosophy and minored in history. He read all he could about the Soviet Union, and even published a few minor newspaper pieces. He was admitted to Columbia University Law School as well as Harvard, but chose Harvard to experience a city other than New York. At this time he made contact with a travel organization called the American University in Europe and was asked to lead students to England, France, Germany, Scandinavia, and Russia in the summer of 1929.

After graduating from Harvard Law in 1932, Henry went to work for a New York law firm whose clients included Macy's and the Metropolitan Opera. But his interest in the law dwindled after he was assigned to resolve a problem involving a New York society hostess and her misplaced panties. About this time Professor Manley Hudson of Harvard said to him, "I think we're going to recognize the Soviet Union. One thing you might care to look into is Soviet law. There isn't anybody in this country who knows anything about Soviet law, and when we establish diplomatic relations, business will develop and you'd be in on the ground floor."

Henry took a leave from the New York law firm and led another group of students to Moscow in 1933. At the end of the tour, he decided to stay on. He called on the director of the Moscow Institute of Law and apparently impressed him with his Harvard Law School diploma, which was written in Latin. The director gave him permission to attend any lectures he wished. In the fall of 1933 he met Ludmilla Nikolaevna Nikitina, adopted daughter of a Moscow University professor, through a mutual acquaintance. They immediately took to each other. Ludmilla called him "Genri" (most English words starting with *H* get turned into *G*s in Russian, such as Gitler and Gamlet), and it stuck as an endearing nickname. Within months they married. In November, just as Professor Hudson predicted, President Roosevelt announced U.S. diplomatic recognition of the Soviet Union.

His visa running out, Henry left Moscow in January 1934 for the United States but returned months later as a correspondent for the British news agency Reuters. One of his early assignments was to report on a meeting of physiologists in Leningrad. On the train, he ran into Walter Duranty, the

Moscow correspondent of the *New York Times,* who clearly intimidated him. "How can I compete with you?" he asked the *Times* man. Duranty replied, "Don't worry, I'll help you." But on arriving in Leningrad, Duranty abandoned Shapiro and headed for a bar. Henry shifted for himself, made the acquaintance of the famous Russian academic Ivan Pavlov, and even interviewed the man who embalmed Lenin's body. His enterprising spirit served him well, and in the end it was Henry who helped out Duranty by passing a few tips to the senior man.

Another major story was the Red Square funeral of Sergei Kirov, the Leningrad communist boss who was mysteriously murdered at his offices on December 1, 1934. Kirov's death served as the pretext for Stalin to begin his infamous purges, culminating in the Great Purge of 1937. In that year, Henry was hired full-time by United Press at a salary of one hundred dollars a week, with a weekly expense account of twenty-five dollars. He inherited the five-room apartment of his predecessor, Eugene Lyons, where he lived rent free and income tax free. In his oral memoir, Henry estimated that his total income in 1937 was eighteen thousand dollars, equivalent to about one hundred thousand today.

His career really began to take off with the sensational disclosures of Stalin's efforts to liquidate his opponents in the Communist Party. He was on hand to cover the three major purge trials that ran from August 1936 to March 1938 and eliminated Lenin's Old Bolshevik comrades, using false accusations, forced confessions, and no independently verifiable evidence. Henry and other correspondents attended these public sessions, writing up the major developments speedily and passing them through censorship. "The censors listened to the proceedings on loudspeakers outside the courtroom and passed almost all copy promptly," Henry explained in a seminar paper prepared for the Kennan Institute of Advanced Russian Studies, in Washington, D.C., in 1976. He recalled that Karl Radek, one of the authors of the Stalin constitution, testified at trial that he had conversed with Marshal Mikhail N. Tukhachevsky, chief of the General Staff and first deputy war commissar. Sensing that the highest professional military man was on the verge of arrest, Henry rushed from the chamber and dispatched a bulletin to London reporting that Radek had implicated Tukhachevsky of treason.

The telegram was passed instantly and sent off. But a minute later the presiding justice ordered Tukhachevsky's name stricken from the record. The censor came back to Henry, insisting he withdraw the story. Henry complied, sending off an urgent two-word message in cablese to United Press in London: *Kill Tukhachevsky*—meaning "Do not release the story." The censor threw this cable back in Henry's face, protesting, "Why do you want to kill Marshal Tukhachevsky?" The official was only doing his duty, but Henry's instinct about treason was on target. Marshal Tukhachevsky was arrested on May 23, tried in secret, and convicted of being a German agent intent on seizing political power. He was executed on the night of June 11, 1937.

Henry's job, like that of wire-service correspondents all over the world, was to report the facts accurately and speedily, not to interpret them. Yet anyone with intimate knowledge has opinions even if they do not appear in print. Frequently after the day's court session, Henry and other correspondents would repair to the residence of Ambassador Joseph E. Davies for beer and cheese. The reporters saw the purge trials essentially as a political struggle between Stalin and his opponents. Davies, on the other hand, has gone down in history as an incompetent observer who was convinced that Germany, conniving with treasonous Soviet officials, was plotting Stalin's overthrow. "There will be war," Ambassador Davies predicted, "but they'll have no fifth column." Henry also remembered Davies making a disclosure, extraordinary for its naïveté: "You know, I was a district attorney in Dane County [Wisconsin]. And I prosecuted a lot of criminals. I can tell a criminal when I see one. When I look at those people in the dock, I can see they are guilty."

Henry disagreed. As he recounted in his oral memoir:

> Perhaps, when men of such remarkable intelligence and achievement, as some of the defendants we watched, have spent a year in jail, are in the dock surrounded by armed guards, and are at the mercy of so crafty a prosecutor as Andrei Vishinsky, they do look like criminals. What I did think was that by the rules of the game, some of which the defendants had helped work out, and might have applied if the situation had been reversed, and Stalin stood in the dock—the opponents had never given up the struggle to unseat Stalin.

Henry pressed his critical point on the chief military justice, General Vasilii Ulrich, whom he ran into at a reception at the ambassador's residence. General Ulrich snapped back, "Too bad what the reaction abroad is. It's our problem, and we're handling it the best we see fit."

On one point, of course, Ambassador Davies was correct. War, devastating and draining, did erupt. Despite the Nazi-Soviet friendship pact of 1939, Hitler launched a surprise attack on Russia in the early hours of Sunday, June 22, 1941. This war, like most wars, turned out to be the friend of ambitious journalists. Young reporters in war either jump-start their careers or lose their lives. On June 22, Henry was on the upward escalator—thirty-five, energetic, with a blossoming reputation. Of course, he also had serious concerns for his family's safety. He sent his wife and newborn daughter, Irina, beyond the Ural Mountains, where they would be physically safer than in Moscow. But conditions there were extreme. Food was rationed, intestinal illnesses were rampant, and doctors were few since many had been sent to the front. Henry's wife, Ludmilla, who was nursing Irina, shared some of her milk with those close to her.

Although the Nazi invasion apparently stunned Stalin, it did not surprise Henry. Everybody knew it was coming, he recalled. Intelligence services reported the massing of 170 German divisions along Soviet borders. Stalin's own spy, Richard Sorge, had sent word from sources in Japan of Germany's intentions. Both President Roosevelt and Prime Minister Churchill had warned Stalin. British Ambassador Sir Stafford Cripps had confided to Henry the attack would probably come in June. In midspring, German Ambassador Count Friederich Werner von der Schulenburg sent his family and furniture back to Germany. U.S. Ambassador Lawrence Steinhardt, who replaced Davies, saw his wife off to Stockholm on June 10. "On Saturday, June 21, 1941," Henry would recount during his relaxed moments, "I went to the American Embassy to lunch with some friends to await the beginning of the German-Soviet war." Though war did not break out that day, on Sunday morning at seven o'clock—three hours after the initial German attack—Henry's bedroom telephone rang. It was his German colleague Dr. Hermann Poerzgen of the *Frankfurter Allgemeine Zeitung,* who said in a mournful voice, "What we expected has happened. I am interned at the embassy and want to say auf Wiedersehen under better circumstances."

In the years ahead, Henry had his share of adventures. He was now an American war correspondent in Moscow. He was nearly killed in Kharkov when the jeep traveling ahead of him struck a land mine. He was the first American to fly into besieged Leningrad and to report the story of the nine hundred–day blockade and the city's refusal to surrender. The achievement he was proudest of was his reporting from Stalingrad. He was the first Westerner to report from that battle on the eastern front, predicting the end of the Nazi advance into Russia and the turning point in World War II. These reports were published in the *New York Times,* which gave him the unusual honor of publishing his byline. President Roosevelt was reported to have been impressed, too, by Henry's dispatches because until that point he did not believe the Russians had blunted the German advance.

But the story that made the greatest impression on me led back to the assassination of Nicholas II. As Henry told it, he got permission to travel to the Urals in December 1941 to visit Ludmilla and daughter Irina. He was met at Sverdlovsk by a Mr. Shaumyan, editor of the newspaper *Uralskii Rabochii.* As they were driving into town, Shaumyan pointed out a prerevolutionary mansion and asked, "Do you know what that house there is?"

When Henry said no, Shaumyan replied it was the Ipatiev House, where Czar Nicholas II and the imperial family had been held under house arrest in the early days of the Bolshevik government in 1918. Henry asked to visit it. In 1941, the house was being used as an ammunition dump, and entry required special permission. Several days later they entered the house and went down to the basement where the imperial family had been executed in the early-morning hours of July 17, 1918. "He took me down to the cellar where you could still see the bullet marks in the wall. So I said, 'How did it happen?' Shaumyan replied, 'Do you want to see the man who shot them?' I said, 'Well, of course.'"

The next day, Henry recalled, he went to Shaumyan's office:

> He had a stenographer there. Then this man came in—he must have been seventy or more by that time. Shaumyan said, "There's the executioner: Yakov Yurovsky." He told me the whole story, how they did it. He said he was a member of the czar's guard, how the place was being besieged by the White Army, and it looked like they would arrive any day. The local Soviet did not want the czar to fall into the hands of the White Army for fear they would restore him to power. So they passed a resolution condemning the royal family to death for crimes they had committed against the Russian people. Yurovsky told me that no one survived the execution.

He said that the women were wearing corsets in which they had secreted jewels. After the killing, Yurovsky and his cohorts tallied up the corset buttons and concluded that no one had escaped. Unknown to Henry, Yurovsky made a detailed oral and written report on the execution that came to light only in the mid-1990s.

When Henry returned to Moscow he tried to file the story of his encounter with the executioner of the imperial family. The censors refused to approve it on the grounds that the account would disrupt the U.S.-British-Soviet wartime alliance. "Keep it for your memoirs," the censor counseled. Considering all the impostors who appeared in the West after the slaughter—especially the Anastasia pretenders—Henry certainly should have published that story after the war. But Henry, who was an excellent reporter though not a facile writer, never managed to compose his memoirs in retirement.

Chapter 8

Henry's Bureau

One of the oddities of the Cold War was that living in the enemy's camp could be pleasant, even luxurious, at least from a physical point of view. Correspondents were leased warm, ample housing, near the center of town. They could hire servants, chauffeurs, secretaries, language teachers, which they could hardly have afforded in the West. They could import choice food from abroad and pay nothing in duty during their first twelve months. They could consort with their own kind, attending diplomatic receptions (some in black tie and evening dress) almost every night. The downside of Moscow life, of course, was that we were closely watched, so closely that some of us developed the jitters, if not paranoia.

The center of my professional life was now Kutuzovsky Prospekt, a grand avenue honoring Marshal Kutuzov, who defeated Napoléon in 1812. Our complex was about a mile west of the Kremlin and a half mile east of No. 26, where the Politburo, the highest decision-making body, maintained residences for some of its members. The office was a fifteen-minute walk, over the Moscow River, to the U.S. Embassy and a stone's throw from the Ukraina Hotel, one of seven "wedding cake" high-rises of the Stalin era. Kutuzovsky, or "Kootoo," as the French correspondents called it, was one of several complexes constructed to house and monitor foreign diplomats, correspondents, and their dependents and servants. The other was a squat brown nine-story building continually rattled by a stream of two-ton trucks cruising along the circular Sadovoyoe Koltso, or Garden Ring. The address of this ghetto was Sadovo-Samotechnaya 12/24 and better known to Americans as "Sad Sam."

Our Kutuzovsky residence consisted of a collection of nine-story buildings surrounding a vast parking lot in the rough form of a C. Its entrance was guarded by a police booth, manned twenty-four hours a day by "milimen," our name for the Soviet police. These guardians of the peace would come to know residents and their cars by sight and prevent anyone who did not have official business from entering. Russian acquaintances, and they were very few in those years, would be stopped and turned away unless accompanied by their foreign host. Russian officials explained that these measures were required by security considerations that traced back to the murder of the German ambassador in Petrograd at the start of the First World War. We felt the arrangements were less than hospitable and were intended more to track our habits. "Sure, we live in a ghetto," one of my correspondent friends admonished. "But you know there are some advantages. You bump into all sorts of diplomats in the parking lot, and occasionally they tell you something that makes a story. And they are much more willing to talk out there in the open air than in their offices!"

UPI was located in apartment 67 on the seventh floor at the back of the C. It was a converted two-bedroom apartment whose living room had been turned into the newsroom, the bedroom into Henry's office, the spare bedroom into a storeroom, the bath into a darkroom, and the kitchen into a utility room. A balcony that looked out onto the parking lot frequently served as the locus of confidential conversations.

Adjoining the office on the same floor was apartment 68, a one-bedroom flat occupied by Bud Korengold and his French bride, Christine. From the bedroom, Korengold could hear the tapping of the TASS teletypewriter as well as the muffled rings of the telephones at any time of day or night. These rumblings could be tip-offs that something serious was happening. *Vigilance* was Henry's byword, a tool for beating the Associated Press to the punch.

The apartment that Ruth and I would occupy for the next four years was located across the courtyard in the lower arm of the C, a two-minute walk from the office. It was a "railroad apartment," consisting of a long corridor, with unvarnished parquet flooring, which gave into a living room, a bedroom, a kitchen, and toilet. The walls were covered with atrocious, rough, greenish wallpaper. The double windows gave out onto the inner courtyard. Aline Mosby had occupied this apartment, No. 210, during the past several years and had installed a deep freeze, six feet long and two feet deep, covered with brown stick-on paper. In this huge *morozilnik*, Ruth and I would store six months of edibles that we ordered from Stockmann's Department Store in Helsinki or from Osterman-Petersen in Copenhagen.

Viktor would be dispatched to the central customs house to receive these valuables. If you were in good favor with the authorities, your goods would be handed over quickly on payment of duty. If, however, you had offended someone in the chain of command—and that chain could lead back to the Foreign Ministry or higher—your frozen meats might be held for a day or more on some improbable excuse. Spoiled meat was clearly a signal, but it was usually difficult to decode its meaning. Still, the message made you feel guilty that you had violated some unpublicized rule.

Henry, it was said, had once found himself in trouble with customs when he imported an excessively large amount of toilet paper as gifts for favored sources. When Viktor was called to account by a wary inspector, he replied in his ingenious peasant manner, "You don't understand, comrade inspector, this is copy paper for Mr. Shapiro's news bureau!" Professional supplies theoretically entered the Soviet Union free of duty. The inspector was unforgiving. But Viktor insisted, "It's true, comrade, the UPI correspondents write their dispatches on this type of paper!" That was an evident lie, but the shipment was handed over on payment of a vodka bribe.

Correspondents in the early 1960s were generally treated by officials as if they had the status of a high embassy official. Of course, we had no diplomatic immunity and were subject to the laws of the Soviet Union. Because we were few in number, American correspondents were allowed to buy essential supplies at the embassy PX (post exchange). We could use the embassy snack bar and buy caviar from the majordomo of the ambassador's residence. Our cars could be serviced and washed at the embassy garage. Because a KGB office in the International Post Office read incoming mail from abroad, correspondents were allowed to communicate with their families and stockbrokers through the diplomatic pouch. We were not allowed to send journalistic copy, however, through the embassy.

"The pouch" sounds as if it were a bag handcuffed to the wrist of a diplomatic courier. In fact, it was much more. Often, it consisted of an entire railroad car linked to the Helsinki train and filled with trunks of sensitive equipment, packages, and mail. KGB baggage handlers were said to rifle through the baggage on the overnight run, in violation of diplomatic practice. Correspondents' mail was the least-secure item and could be scrutinized by both sides in the Cold War. To comply with Foreign Ministry rules, a U.S. press officer would check correspondents' mail to make sure it contained no press articles. How intrusive that check was we never knew, but we suspected one embassy official, with initials T. C., read our mail with vicarious enthusiasm.

The Directorate for Service to the Diplomatic Corps, otherwise known as UPDK, made an effort to be helpful to correspondents. One section of this bureaucracy was housed in a mansion on Kropotinskaya Street that had once been used after the revolution by American dancer Isadora Duncan for her ballet school for Soviet kids. If you needed staff, you applied to UPDK, which would send you a choice of personnel. If you wanted to travel, you asked UPDK to make hotel and travel reservations. If you had a particularly troublesome problem—your toilet did not flush, your telephone did not work—UPDK would send someone to fix it.

Of course, the sinister side was that UPDK was in league with the KGB. Everyone expected that your maid, but most particularly your secretary-translator, would be quietly summoned from time to time to the KGB office at UPDK. What were you, the correspondent, like? Did you have anti-Soviet attitudes? Were you Jewish? Whom were you seeing? What was your work routine? With whom did you consort? What stories were you planning? Did you drink excessively? Did you have homosexual tendencies? Were you on good terms with your spouse? We guessed that the KGB was always looking for our vulnerabilities. If you were not targeted for immediate entrapment, the KGB was building up a negative file on you for the day the Foreign Ministry or the Central Committee ordered your expulsion.

UPDK employees put up with these debriefings since being attached to a Western organization had material benefits. The salary of a UPDK worker was higher than usual Soviet salaries, and correspondents would sweeten the pot with gifts from abroad. In December, correspondents were required to pay the UPDK worker a "thirteenth salary," a New Year's bonus. Over time, some employees became reluctant to tattle on their bosses. Too great a loyalty to a foreigner was dangerous, however. Henry's chauffeur Viktor paid the price about a year after our arrival when he announced unexpectedly, "I'm saying good-bye because I am off on an extended vacation." He offered no further explanation, but we understood he had been forced out.

All of us believed our offices and apartments, especially our bedrooms, were bugged. In the 1960s when there were relatively few foreign residents in Moscow, we presumed that our indoor conversations were meticulously scrutinized. In later years when the expat population exploded, conventional wisdom held that tapes of recorded conversations were examined only when particular key words popped up. Henry warned us, "If you find a bug in your apartment, leave it alone. Don't mess with it. If you really have something important to discuss, go outside. Or turn up the radio." We were living in a fishbowl, and, accordingly, we developed protective habits. Henry was a perfect example: say little on the telephone; talk in elliptical terms. Some correspondents went to lengths to disguise a planned meeting with a Soviet source. Whatever time was mentioned in telephone conversations, the real meeting time would be a half hour earlier. This was a questionable practice because if the arrangement became known to Soviet counterintelligence, it would look suspicious and prompt additional surveillance.

One of the enduring facts of the Cold War was "reciprocity." Because of distrust on both sides, the two superpowers limited the number of correspondents in each other's capitals to roughly the same number. In the early 1960s there were some twelve mainstream American news organizations with a total of about twenty journalists accredited to Moscow, and the same number of Soviet correspondents in Washington and New York. If some particularly outrageous incident befell an American correspondent in Moscow, the American authorities would arrange an equivalent difficulty for a Soviet correspondent in the United States. Expulsion of an American correspondent from Moscow would result in expulsion of a Soviet correspondent from the United States.

Reciprocity often came into play when reporters traveled. By the end of the Second World War, the Soviet Union had marked off certain areas as closed military zones. The United States, a far more open society, responded by closing off similar acreage in the United States to Soviet travel. These American closed zones took in U.S. military bases, but because there were far more Russian zones, a fair number of perfectly innocent areas in the United States were prohibited. For a long time, the Russians prevented Americans from sailing down Russia's famous Volga River. In retaliation, the American side regularly prohibited Russians from cruising down the Mississippi. Foreign-affairs groups in the heartland of America would sometimes invite a second secretary of the Soviet Embassy to lecture on U.S.-Soviet relations only to learn with astonishment that the peaceful prairies of Kansas were actually "closed zones."

Travel for me was very limited. As the most junior correspondent in the UPI bureau, I was given little opportunity to leave Moscow. And Henry wasn't joking when he said his correspondents worked seven days a week. We began about eight thirty in the morning when the UPDK secretary-translator arrived and started reading the morning papers, of which there were about twenty, the provincials (another fourteen), and the journals (another dozen).

We had two regular translators, Arthur Krivovyaz (to make it easier for London, Henry called him Arthur Kress) and Lev Shtern. Arthur's family had emigrated from Ukraine to New York City in the 1920s. But when the Great Depression struck, the Krivovyaz family returned to the Soviet Union. Arthur's New York accent, his love of the Big Apple, never left him, and on occasion, recalling his lost youth in Manhattan, he would choke up. He sometimes acknowledged he wished he could return, if only for a visit. But he knew that would never happen. It was clear to me that Arthur, now in his fifties, had been caught in the web of the Cold War, living a life the best he could against his will.

Lev, on the other hand, appeared to be a fine example of *homo sovieticus*. A young man in his early thirties, he had never traveled outside the Soviet Union and respected Soviet regulations scrupulously. He was a hungry gatherer of English colloquialisms, collecting dictionaries of all sorts, constantly noting slang expressions and the latest high-tech twist of modern America. Lyova, as we called him, was superlative as a simultaneous interpreter of Khrushchev's speeches. Coming to a crucial point, his eyes would widen, a smile would spread over his face, his tongue would scramble frantically over the vowels; he would gesticulate with his right index finger, signaling to us what he thought might be "the lead" of the story. Because he did not know the context of American life, his pointers were sometimes misleading, but his staying power was enormous. He could work twenty-four hours without stop, and we dubbed him "Iron Man."

Henry insisted that the bureau be staffed from early morning until Moscow radio signed off at midnight. This meant that his two assistants had to be in the office, or nearby—certainly no farther than the American Embassy—from dawn to dark. We divided the duty into two shifts: the morning from ten to six and the afternoon from five to midnight or one. About noon (four in the morning in the eastern United States), Henry would arrive at the office, and we would go over the day's outlook. After that, we would send a "night sked" to London, informing them of the stories we planned for the morning news cycle in the United States.

The second correspondent would have the morning off and show up during the afternoon, frequently well before the five o'clock shift started. His job was to update the morning report, especially when *Izvestia* arrived in the bureau between six and seven. Reading *Izvestia* and the mainstream Soviet newspapers required a certain knack; usually, the critical information was in the last paragraphs. The next important moment was the nine o'clock national newscast *Vremya*, which was heavy with official announcements. We recorded radio and television newscasts on a large reel-to-reel tape recorder so that we could easily play back any section that was unclear or needed further study.

The afternoon correspondent was charged with updating the top of any developing story, and then refashioning it for the afternoon newspaper cycle in the United States. This made the evening shift onerous because new forward-looking angles had to be teased out of your tired brain. That required breaking news on radio and TV, or advice from Henry, followed by more hours of writing and punching out stories on the telex tape, running that tape through the machine, and getting an acknowledgment from London before closing down at midnight or later.

The end of censorship and the arrival of the telex machine with its instant communications changed the style of Moscow journalistic life enormously. In the late Stalin years, London and New York were reluctant to send the bureau "a rocket" asking for minor clarifications. Telephone calls and telegrams were costly. Editors in London and New York did their best to unscramble any unclear paragraph. But with the installation of the telex, London began sending "callbacks" for the most trivial reasons. Our splendid isolation was ending.

Henry suffered from the demands of the new technology much as my generation suffers from the caprices of digitization and the Internet. The dean of Moscow correspondents was largely a self-taught journalist. For decades he had been scooping up substance and whipping it off to London, where it would be polished into final form. Now the telex required the Moscow correspondent to produce attention-grabbing leads, dramatic releads, inserts, substitute paragraphs, and occasionally corrections, all in a style requiring little or no reworking in New York. You learned these techniques on any UPI desk in the United States or on the foreign desk in New York or the general desk in London. Thirty years in Moscow had not provided Henry with such training, and to some extent he was at the mercy of his assistants. In reaction, it seemed to me, he became a stern taskmaster, insisting that any news story, whether written by him or not, carry his initials at the bottom of copy along with the initials of the writer.

This kind of collegial collaboration had not been the case before. In pretelex days, each reporter signed his name at the end of his cable and let London or New York decide who would get the credit. Now, we duly lumped Henry's initials on copy along with our own. The placement of initials had meaning. If he was the sole author and I punched the story on the telex, the dispatch would be signed "hs-nd." If I was the sole author, I would sign off "nd-hs." Henry never mastered the telex and left it to us, or our hired telegrapher, to punch and transmit copy. The system made us Henry's slaves. It also gave the misleading impression that Henry was involved in writing all the stories the bureau filed. Some of his assistants objected that they were not getting enough credit for their work. I was not particularly offended and was happy enough just to be in Moscow. Leaving such details aside, it was Henry who had the worldwide reputation, and New York signed his byline to all major stories, whether he was the author or not. That made good marketing sense for the company. We junior reporters got bylines mostly on the feature stories we developed by ourselves and occasionally on a follow-up story to Henry's.

Henry was, undoubtedly, one of the jewels in the UPI's crown. His lengthy service in the adversary's capital, however, raised questions for some. Why had he stayed so long? I concluded that, in part, he found the Soviet story compelling and was exceptionally well equipped to cover it. In part, his Russian wife loved Moscow and wanted to be close to her relatives. In part, he had good living conditions and exceptional status in the foreign community. When I worked with him, he was in his midfifties, and transferability to other wire-service duties was diminishing.

Henry did, in fact, contemplate leaving Moscow for other assignments. After the war in 1945, he departed, expecting that his family would follow shortly. But they could not get permission from the Soviet bureaucracy, and he returned in 1947. As the Cold War deepened, the U.S. Embassy urged him to quit for his own safety, but he refused, knowing his wife and daughter would be vulnerable to arrest without him. After Stalin died, he did leave with his family and spent two years at Harvard as a Nieman Fellow. At that time, he began looking for a house in Cambridge, thinking that he would now begin his American life. But United Press urged him to return to Moscow. He agreed on the condition that the company send him an assistant to cope with the ever increasing workload.

As his assistants, we sometimes thought that Henry was excessively secretive about his personal life as well as his sources. I also found him rough on non-UPI colleagues he quarreled with and was reluctant to forgive. When it came to news gathering, I do not doubt that Henry was sometimes used by officials to float information or a trial balloon. But that tends to be true of any correspondent, and I never saw evidence that he had concluded any special deals with the Soviets. In any event, Henry had qualities we came to appreciate. He had lived Soviet history since the 1930s and was a walking encyclopedia. When Francis Gary Powers was shot down on his ill-fated U-2 flight in May 1960, Henry could describe Vladimir Prison where the flyer was imprisoned. Henry's inside details came from his German friend Dr. Poerzgen, who had been interned in Vladimir for eleven years during and after the Second World War.

Henry often railed against "those correspondents who think history began on the day they were born." He was skeptical of American experts who thought they knew the Soviet Union better than he from their academic researches. He was always insistent that we double-check our facts, describe the context in which news was happening, and mention the positive side, if there was one. He urged us not to jump to conclusions but to seek out confirmation. Yet these qualities would sometimes recede when he would ask us—somewhat plaintively, I thought—how best to write his story. Was his new information really a reader-grabbing intro (the new lead of the story, in journalistic terms) or merely a high-up insert?

In later years, our boss would be sometimes criticized by American colleagues who believed he was trying to impose his version of events through the alliance system. Jerrold Schecter asserted in his book *An American Family in Moscow* that Henry used the alliance system to boost his own prestige, a claim that drew an angry rebuttal from our boss. Murray Seeger of the *Los Angeles Times* charged that Henry went easy on news that was unpleasant for the Soviet leadership, and even ordered his subordinates not to cover events such as the grain failure of 1963 or the appearance of dissidents in the 1970s. Such accusations are not correct. Admittedly, Henry had a vested interest in not being thrown out of Moscow, and, indeed, he was threatened with expulsion on several occasions. I believe he may have gone easy on some of the stories he wrote himself, but I know of no case when he suppressed the news or ordered his subordinates not to touch it.

By early December 1961, I was beginning to learn the hard realities of constant work at the Magic Dateline. Ruth and I had arrived in a hurry to replace Aline Mosby. A week later, Aline flew home, and I was summoned to the Foreign Ministry to receive my official accreditation, a two-by-three-inch photo ID in an elegant blue leather holder from a Mr. Simonov. He and his assistant urged me, "Follow the customary rules of journalists, and you'll be all right." But they did not explain what the rules were. They offered no maps of the closed zones, no specifics of what to do, or what not to do. This silence was hardly unusual for a closed society where some rules were unknowable because they were purposely kept secret.

After my half-hour meeting, I walked back to Kutuzovsky from the Foreign Ministry, over the Borodinsky Bridge, down Bolshaya Dorogomilovskaya street. It was a cold day, and a light snow was falling. I remember passing a meat store that displayed in its plate-glass window, without any attempt at artistry, a pathetic piece of beef with yellowing fat. That was the first signal to me that there was something rotten not just in the government store but in the Soviet state.

Later that afternoon, I reported to Henry on my accreditation. "It was pretty routine so far as I could see," I said, "except for one thing."

"What was that?" Henry asked.

"Well," I continued, "they did ask about Larrimore. They clearly wanted to know why his Moscow assignment was canceled at the last moment."

"And what did you tell them?"

"What I was instructed in London: that he developed a heart problem, and it was thought better not to let him proceed."

Henry nodded but made no comment. I could not tell whether Henry knew something none of the rest of us did. I dare say no one guessed on that dreary afternoon that Larrimore would be reassigned, as a consolation prize, to Poland, where in 1963 he would run into the sort of trouble none of us wanted.

Chapter 9

## The Cuban Crisis of 1962

In the year that followed our arrival, the world moved inexorably toward the brink of nuclear conflict. I thought that President Kennedy contributed to this tendency at his inaugural on January 20, 1961. He had offered a stunning address that we mostly remember for that exhilarating phrase, "Ask not what your country can do for you, ask what you can do for your country!" The view from Moscow was much darker. Some of Kennedy's assertions struck me then, and strike me now, as bordering on recklessness if you took them seriously:

> Let the word go out from this time and place to friend and foe alike, that the torch has been passed to a new generation of Americans, born in this century, tempered by war, disciplined by a hard and bitter peace, proud of our ancient heritage, unwilling to witness or permit the slow undoing of those human rights to which this nation has always been committed, and to which we are committed today at home and around the world.
>
> Let every nation know, whether it wishes us well or ill, that we shall pay any price, bear any burden, meet any hardship, support any friend, oppose any foe to assure the survival and success of liberty.

Pay any price? Bear any burden? In 1962, the Kennedy administration would begin sending military advisers to Vietnam to counter what it viewed as the creeping Communist threat. By 1967, the United States was

71

fully engaged in a war that killed five hundred American boys every week. It was becoming clear the nation would *not* pay any price to ensure the success of liberty in South Vietnam. Liberty—that word always troubled me. Living in Moscow, I found it hard to explain to Russians that liberty does not mean that you can do anything you want anytime. Liberty, as nineteenth-century English philosopher John Stuart Mill said, carries the notion of individual responsibility and restraint, but that qualification is often lost in American political rhetoric.

As I recalled Kennedy's address before leaving for Moscow, I must confess I did not focus on such philosophical considerations. My knowledge of philosophy and history in those days was young. Rather, I was struck by Kennedy's Boston accent, his manner of speaking. Here was the first American leader I could feel close to. At Harvard, John Fitzgerald Kennedy (class of 1940) had belonged to the Spee Club, a secret society created in 1882. I, too, had joined that club in 1954 and, through it, felt something of a bond to Kennedy. The oil portrait of Kennedy in the Kennedy School of Government at Harvard shows him wearing a Spee tie, a tie that I occasionally wore too.

In the spring of 1961, the United States suffered the first of a series of shocks. On April 12, the Russians successfully launched the first man into space. Yuri Gagarin became an instant hero whom Khrushchev would boast about. Five days later, another blow. A CIA-backed invasion of Cuba, intended to topple Fidel Castro, met an ignominious defeat on the Cuban coast at the Bay of Pigs. This invasion force of armed Cuban refugees had been organized under the Eisenhower administration and allowed to go forward by Kennedy.

Six weeks later, Kennedy left for Vienna to meet Khrushchev on June 3–4, 1961. The sixty-seven-year-old Khrushchev believed he could bully the forty-three-year-old American president, whom he considered young and inexperienced. The major topic was the future of the Western occupation zones in Berlin, a city whose independent status within East Germany had never been formalized by a peace treaty at the end of the Second World War. High on the agenda, too, was the search for a ban on atmospheric nuclear tests and an easing of Communist pressures on Laos, whose government was split between Communist and neutralist factions.

In the meeting, Khrushchev demanded that the West recognize the post–World War II borders in Europe, including those of East Germany, or the Soviet Union would conclude a separate peace treaty with East Germany by the end of the year, canceling Western rights in Berlin. Kennedy came out of the meeting looking disconsolate. By prearrangement, he met briefly with

James Reston of the *New York Times,* who had disappeared from the crowd of reporters into the U.S. Embassy.

Such an exclusive meeting would not happen today. But in 1961 it was still possible. The media culture of those days was to respect high officials, to believe they were better informed than ordinary citizens, to accept that they would do the right thing, and to overlook personal indiscretions when such peccadillos did not encroach on public policy. Trusted journalists, in effect, became informal spokesmen for the administration. Reston had complained previously to Kennedy that the president's penchant for one-on-one interviews with favorite journalists was unethical. So the Kennedy-Reston meeting was something of a payback. "It's going to be a cold winter," Reston quoted the president as saying as he detailed the Khrushchev ultimatum. "Things are going to get worse before they get better."

The month of June also saw the opening of the Laos conference in Geneva that was intended to shore up that country's neutrality, under threat from Communist North Vietnam. I was thrilled to be a full member of the team, reporting on the comings and goings of the Russian, Chinese, Laotian, and Cambodian delegations. These international efforts at East-West conciliation were buffeted once again on August 13, 1961, when East Germany began erecting a wall that would stand for the next forty years as a symbol of repression. And in October, the Twenty-second Party Congress convened in Moscow, and Khrushchev again shook the world, especially the West. He announced that the Soviet Union had exploded an enormous sixty-megaton bomb. Next he angered the Chinese, admirers of Stalin's anti-Western, anticapitalist stance, by ordering the dictator's body removed from the Lenin mausoleum and buried in semidisgrace at the foot of the Kremlin walls.

In Moscow, Ruth and I realized that we were living in a target zone of American missiles. Young journalists often consider covering a war as a way to boost a career. We never really thought much about that. We were seeking excitement and knowledge, not unusual punishment. Yet much of our daily lives resembled chastisement more than exhilaration. The hours were long, and a good deal of time involved rewriting stories for the next newspaper cycle with little new information. This was drudgery that made you question whether it was worthwhile. The long hours also meant that Ruth was often left to her own devices. In those days before the women's liberation movement moved into high gear, she believed that a wife's duty was to support a struggling husband's career. She did so, and never complained. She used the time to good purpose, developing friends in the Moscow community and writing freelance stories for the Hollywood entertainment sheet *Variety* and the British pacifist publication *Peace News.* UPI management in London frowned on *Peace News* as an inappropriate outlet for the wife of a UPI correspondent. Danny Gilmore, the London manager, asked her to quit. But Ruth, who has a strong will and sense of justice, went right on writing under the pseudonym Allison Palmer.

Bud Korengold ran the bureau when Henry was absent. He was five years older than me, a graduate of the Medill School of Journalism at Northwestern University. In the early 1950s he had bummed around Europe working for the U.S. Army newspaper *Stars and Stripes* before joining United Press in Paris. The way he commanded me and my junior colleague Joe Smith (Smith was sent to Moscow after Larrimore's assignment was canceled) suggested that Bud was somewhat insecure. Not wanting anything to go wrong on his watch, he made sure we all expended more effort than was probably necessary.

One of the first stories he sent me to cover flowed from the deteriorating Russian-Chinese relations. Even before Khrushchev had met President Eisenhower at Camp David in 1959, China's Communist leader, Mao Zedong, had become increasingly critical of Khrushchev for "selling out to the West." Albania, China's tiny Communist satellite on the Adriatic Sea, followed the Beijing line. In the fall of 1961, Moscow suspended relations with Albania as a way of showing displeasure at Beijing's criticisms of Soviet policies.

"Go over to the Albanian Embassy right away," Bud ordered a few days after our arrival, "and find out what is going on. You can flag down a taxi and get him to take you there." This was a daunting assignment. I had no idea how the Moscow subway system worked, had not yet tried to buy anything in a store. My tongue in those early days produced only survival Russian, hardly enough to conduct an interview or even ask directions. Somehow, I managed to get to the gates of the embassy. What I saw was a closed building. Locked gates. No sign of life. I rang the bell, dreading that someone would answer. If they did come out, what would I say? "I am an American correspondent—talk to me!" And then what? I had not prepared any follow-up questions. To my great relief, no one appeared, and I returned to the bureau empty-handed, never an impressive result.

Another one of my first jobs in Moscow was to man the desk from five to midnight. On one night shift, a Sabena airliner accidentally crossed into Soviet territory and was forced by fighters to land in the North Caucasus. Following the U-2 incident of May 1960, this story caused enormous interest abroad because passengers were involved. What would happen? Would Moscow charge espionage? Would the passengers be mistreated? Several days later, the travelers were flown to Moscow on a Soviet jetliner. Bud Korengold drove to Vnukovo Airport to catch them for comment. They had been quite well received. Bud phoned in the passengers' grateful comments late in the evening. I took dictation at the office and struggled to assemble two stories for American morning and afternoon newspapers.

The year ended with a Christmas party at the Shapiros' Furmanova apartment. Though Christmas was not officially celebrated in this country of "scientific atheism," Russians were always ready for an end-of-year bash, or two, or three. The New Year would be marked officially on the night of December 31–January 1, and again on January 12–13, which was the "Old New Year." They were taking advantage of the fact that the Russian Orthodox Church still operated on the Julian calendar, which in the twentieth century had fallen thirteen days behind the modern calendar.

Among the guests was Leonid M. Zamyatin, who had recently replaced Mikhail A. Kharlamov as head of the Press Department of the Foreign Ministry. This was my first encounter with a master of the put-down. I tried to converse with him in Russian, but my sentences tumbled out awkwardly. Zamyatin looked at me scornfully, and said, "Your name is Danilov, and you can hardly speak Russian!" I was humiliated and left the party shortly afterward with Yuri Korolyov, by now a good friend.

Yuri suggested we go to his apartment at Chistiye Prudy in central Moscow to meet Tonya, his girlfriend. Like me, Yuri had had far too much to drink, and as we drove past the Foreign Ministry at Smolensk Square, a drunk ran in front of the car. Yuri slammed on the brakes but knocked the man down as we screeched to a stop. "Get out and get lost," he yelled, not wanting me to become involved in the inevitable police investigation. I slipped out of the car as a crowd began to gather and made my way to the apartment to tell Tonya what had happened. Yuri later visited the hospital, where the victim acknowledged he had been at fault and should have used the pedestrian underpass. Yuri lost his license for six months but not his good humor. He told me that the police grilled him about "a woman who got out of the car and fled the scene" but finally gave up on that line of questioning.

In early March 1962, we got word that the Soviet government was appointing Anatoly F. Dobrynin ambassador to Washington. He would replace "Smiling Mike," the Eisenhower-era ambassador. This nickname stuck because Menshikov grinned a lot but said little. When he did talk at parties, he sometimes embarrassed himself. At one diplomatic dinner, Menshikov pronounced an eloquent toast, then raised his glass of vodka and commanded, "Up your bottoms!"—an awkward rephrasing of "Bottoms up!"

Dobrynin would turn out to be a very different kind of envoy, serving no fewer than twenty-five years in Washington and developing unusually close relations with top American leaders. He would strike most people as a Westernized "reasonable Communist." Originally an aircraft engineer, Dobrynin had been recruited as a diplomat during the Second World War. At the time of his Washington appointment, he had been working as chief of the North American Department of the Foreign Ministry but had never served as ambassador. Acting on a tip, Bud Korengold turned to me one evening in early March and said, "Dobrynin is leaving for the United States in the next few days. Go out to Sheremetyevo early tomorrow morning and see if you can nab him for an interview." This was an excellent idea, but, of course, we had no idea what flight he would be leaving on, and the ministry's Press Department was not about to disclose it. So what was involved was a stakeout with no certain outcome.

By this time I was familiar with Sheremetyevo Airport, the terminal for Western flights. In the early 1960s, the principal Western airliners serving Moscow were Finnair, British European Airways, Air France, Sabena, KLM, and SAS. The terminal consisted of a relatively small building constructed on what once had been the lands of Count Sheremetyev. The main hall led directly to customs and passport control. This was long before the war on terrorism, and airport security was lax. At Sheremetyevo there were no metal detectors, no frisking or lengthy identity checks. Outgoing passengers assembled in the waiting room until their flight was called.

Important passengers were easy to spot by the way they dressed, so it was a good bet that if the ambassador was leaving, he could easily be approached. We often took advantage of lax security to accost total strangers and persuade them in the men's room to carry out news photos or 16-millimeter film, thus skirting the ban on unauthorized pictures. We called such passengers "pigeons." I remember once giving film to a French traveler who, on demand, handed it over to the Soviet customs official when he went through the departure gates. That evening, we received a message from Paris: "Monsieur Jacques says he left the film with the customs officer in Moscow. How do you plan to ship it now?" We laughed. There was no way to recover confiscated film.

On the appointed morning I rose early, and shuffled out to the parking lot in a blinding snowstorm. It was pitch-dark since the sun in March would rise only at about eight. I drove my Renault slowly out the Leningrad Highway, wondering all the time what would happen if the car should suddenly break down. There were few cars on the streets, and it was a lonely, unpleasant drive. Parking the car, I made my way into the terminal to find no ambassador-looking figure among the travelers. After several hours, I gave up and returned, again, empty-handed. Korengold was sympathetic but ordered me out the next morning, with the same result.

Ambassadors were a continuing source of news in a capital where information was highly restricted. One important source was the briefing that the American ambassador would occasionally give on Friday afternoons. Attending the briefing on the seventh floor of the embassy were reporters of the mainstream press: AP, UPI, the *Washington Post*, the *New York Times*, ABC, CBS, NBC. These meetings were useful to both sides. The ambassador and his aides picked up gossip from the reporters, while correspondents had an opportunity to probe for information or solicit interpretations. We figured that the Russian security services monitored these briefings, which were held in an unsecured room, giving them some sense of what was on the minds of adversary diplomats.

At the end of 1961, the ambassador was Llewellyn Thompson, one of the few diplomats trained by the State Department as a Soviet expert in the years after the Russian Revolution. It was exciting to attend these confidential briefings and listen to the views of this experienced public man. Mostly, I remained silent, being the new boy on the block. Unfortunately for me, Thompson was called to Washington to help President Kennedy deal with Soviet-American relations even before Dobrynin departed for the United States.

Arthur Shields, the American correspondent of the communist *Daily Worker*, never appeared at these gatherings. His presence would probably have inhibited the conversation. Shields was one of the "gray men" of Moscow—men of unclear loyalties—who quietly eked out a living with the Soviet government's blessing. Among the others were Wilfred Burchette, an Australian journalist, abhorred in the West because he supported the North Koreans during the Korean War; Ralph Parker, formerly of the *New York Times*, who lived with his common-law Russian wife and worked for the Soviet Ministry of Culture; and Robert Dagleish, who stayed on after the war to run the *Anglo-Soviet Journal*, a leftover of British-Soviet wartime cooperation.

Our coverage in 1962 was extremely active. In July a dozen editors from the American Society of Newspaper Editors (ASNE) arrived on tour. In August, the Soviets launched two manned spacecraft that chased each other in space to see if such ships could eventually link up. Then in August and September, visitors started coming one after another—poet Robert Frost, Representative Morris Udall, and Russian émigré composer Igor Stravinsky, who suffered a mild heart attack while conducting a concert at Tchaikovsky Hall.

One of the most dramatic political developments, however, remained hidden from view. That summer, Khrushchev, while traveling in Bulgaria with Defense Minister Rodion Malinovsky, conceived the idea of deploying medium-range missiles in Cuba. The Soviet leader saw the deployment as a way of defending Cuba against another Bay of Pigs–type invasion. In his memoirs, Khrushchev displayed considerable anger that the United States was maintaining similar missiles in Turkey "right under our noses." He saw the missiles in Cuba as countering that American advantage and "cutting down America's arms." There was another major benefit. Having missiles in Cuba was a way of overcoming the missile gap that favored the United States. Although he would later call these missiles "defensive," they could in fact reach New York and Chicago. If deployment could be achieved secretly, the Soviet Union would win major new bargaining power—possibly enough to make the United States recognize postwar boundaries in Europe, the East German government, and special status for Berlin. Did Khrushchev believe he could get away with installing these missiles secretly? Apparently he did, and that was a mistake. But he was not prepared to accept dissenting views from among his closest advisers.

Until September, the German question dominated superpower relations. Then reports began flowing that the Russians were doing something with rockets in Cuba. Senator Kenneth Keating (R-NY) declared on August 31, 1962, that the Russians were deploying missiles and urged President Kennedy to act. In the following days, the American media began to focus more heavily on this Soviet threat, but we, in Moscow, picked up only snatches of the anti-Soviet rhetoric over shortwave radio.

On September 11, Western correspondents were summoned to the Soviet Foreign Ministry for a briefing on an unannounced topic. Henry sent me to the Stalinesque building on Smolensk Square, where I and about a hundred other correspondents were led into the imposing Blue Room. Aleksei Popov, deputy chief of the Press Department, read a lengthy official statement in Russian that I barely understood. I rushed out to a phone booth near the grocery store opposite the ministry with a copy of the statement in English. I tried to transmit the highlights to Henry, but he waved me off, knowing that the eight-hour time difference with New York gave us time. "Come back to the apartment, and let's go over it here," he said.

Once at Furmanov Street, we pored over the statement, which warned that any U.S. attack on Cuba could lead to nuclear war. In Washington, Ambassador Dobrynin was conveying the same message to Bobby Kennedy. Toward the end of September, Foy D. Kohler, who had headed the Berlin task force in the State Department, was scheduled to arrive in Moscow to replace Ambassador Thompson. On September 19, I wrote the overnight copy:

MOSCOW, Sept. 20 (UPI)—Foy D. Kohler, sixth U.S. post-war ambassador to the Soviet Union, was scheduled to arrive here today and face a new East-West crisis over Berlin in the early months of his assignment.

Naturally, Kohler will be facing the varied unsolved problems of East-West relations.

"I would put Berlin first, then Cuba, then the ban on nuclear testing," one of his future associates said.

The next day I went to Sheremetyevo Airport to record Kohler's arrival. In those days UPI promoted the notion of a "double-threat" or "triple-threat" correspondent—a jack-of-all-trades approach to journalism and an early version of what today is called "convergence." Reporters were expected to handle print, radio, and TV reports with equal skill. In the 1960s, a UPI reporter in Moscow would be asked to file copy, take an arrival photo, shoot a sequence on 16-millimeter film for TV, and do an audio spot. On this occasion, I phoned in a few details updating the overnight story, noted that chargé d'affaires John McSweeney was there to meet Kohler, snapped the new envoy's picture, and jumped into our office car, which Viktor piloted back to the office.

During the trip back to the office, I deployed our secret weapon: a black bag to develop the film in the car. My interest in photography was originally inspired by Serge, an amateur photographer who filled up hundreds of photo albums beginning in 1914. As a teenager, I took photos and outdid my father by learning to develop and print. The black bag I used on this occasion was about eighteen inches square, with sleeves on both sides through which you could thrust your arms to manipulate the film inside the bag without any light getting in. You took the film cassette out of the camera, put it in the bag, and closed the bag tightly. You could then open the cassette safely, feed the 35-millimeter roll onto a spool that then went into a small stainless-steel developing tank. Once that was done, the lightproof tank could come out of the lightproof bag.

Next I poured in developer, waited the requisite number of minutes, poured out the developer, poured in the stopper, out the stopper, in and out the fixer that would make the development permanent. Finally, I ran the film through alcohol and hung it out the car window as we sped into town. The film, trailing in the wind stream, would be dry on arrival. Back in the office, I rushed to our darkroom, made prints, dried them on shiny plates in a low oven, typed up captions, and sped by car to the downtown TASS office for electronic transmission to London. In this fashion, we regularly got a one-hour beat over the Associated Press.

Toward the middle of October, Bud and his wife, Christine, left for a week's vacation. They returned on October 22, 1962, just hours after Henry and Ludmilla departed for a year's sabbatical leave in California and Hawaii. Bud reached the bureau to learn that President Kennedy would be

making an urgent address to the nation that night. At seven in the evening
Washington time—two in the morning Moscow time, October 23—we tuned
the bulky Zenith radio to the Voice of America to hear the president's words:

> This urgent transformation of Cuba into an important strategic base—by
> the presence of these large, long-range, and clearly offensive weapons of
> sudden mass destruction—constitutes an explicit threat to the peace and
> security of all the Americas . . .
>
> I call upon Chairman Khrushchev to halt and eliminate this clandestine,
> reckless, and provocative threat to world peace and to stable relations be-
> tween our two nations. I call upon him further to abandon this course of
> world domination and to join in an historic effort to end the perilous arms
> race and transform the history of man . . .

Bud turned to me and Jay Axelbank (who had replaced Joe Smith in mid-
September) and said, "I guess I got back just in time. We're in for it now."
What we did not know until later was that on that same October 22, 1962,
the KGB arrested Colonel Oleg Penkovsky, who had been spying for the
United States and Britain. Reports circulated later that Penkovsky got off a
secret message to the CIA as he was being detained, but made a serious mistake. Instead of sending a previously prepared message, he mistakenly sent
another message that the Soviet Union was about to attack the United
States. That false information was ignored in Washington.

Our colleagues in the West were seriously frightened by the course of
events because of the much greater availability of information in Washington than in Moscow. Norm Runnion, the chief rewrite man for UPI in Washington, sent his family off to Vermont, fearing that this might be the start of
nuclear war. By contrast, Moscow was calm. The controlled Soviet press
never mentioned the secret installation of Soviet missiles in Cuba until the
crisis was over. Furthermore, this was not a conflict over Berlin, which earlier in the year had caused Moscow housewives to begin hoarding food. Ordinary Russians believed this crisis was between faraway Cuba and the
United States and did not directly affect them.

Meanwhile, on the world stage, diplomacy moved into high gear. The
United States announced it would impose a "quarantine" on Soviet ships
heading for Cuba and would inspect any suspicious cargoes. At the United
Nations, diplomats began casting around for a nonviolent solution with the
cooperation of Secretary-General U Thant.

Marvin Kalb, the correspondent for CBS, remembered that on October 23
he got a message from CBS executive Blair Clark (a Kennedy roommate at
Harvard) in New York, suggesting that it would be a good idea for Kalb's

wife, Madeleine, to go to Copenhagen for a shopping trip. In the conversation, Clark referred only to his college roommate, which Kalb understood by prearrangement meant President Kennedy. The suggestion reflected the growing fear in Washington that armed conflict was imminent. Kalb disregarded the suggestion, however.

In Moscow, the atmosphere turned ugly. The Soviet media repeatedly denounced the United States. Newspapers warned that the Soviet Union would come to Cuba's defense, possibly plunging the whole world into war. On October 24, the *New York World Telegram and Sun* published a dispatch from Bud that the limousine of Ambassador Kohler was stoned as he drove through the capital. No significant injuries or damage occurred.

Inevitably, a "rent-a-crowd"—the term we used to describe a well-prepared demonstration by "angry" citizens—began to gather outside the U.S. Embassy. Many of us were at the Sklifosovkii Institute watching surgeons graft the head and lungs of one dog onto the body of another. This was one of several precursor experiments to an actual heart transplant that Dr. Christian Barnard was first to perform on a human in South Africa in 1967. We correspondents were also to witness a blood transfusion from a cadaver. According to Soviet specialists, such bleeding was a superior method for obtaining donor blood. Religious and family considerations were never mentioned. On this day, we never saw the bleeding because we received a panic call just before the transfusion began. "Get over to the U.S. Embassy right away," Bud shouted down the line. "A demonstration is beginning."

Memoirs by former Soviet officials reveal that Khrushchev never contemplated an attack on the United States despite the hot rhetoric. On Wednesday, October 24, he took time out from meetings to receive William Knox of Westinghouse and Robert Frost, the New England poet. Later in the evening, he went to the Bolshoi Opera to hear Jerome Hines, an American basso, sing in the opera *Boris Godunov*. Marvin Kalb attended the performance, too, because his wife, Madeleine, wanted to hear Hines, who hailed from Scotch Plains, a town near her home in New Jersey. Kalb worried he might miss some official announcement if he went, but in the end he was rewarded with a scoop. Members of the Politburo showed up, and afterward Khrushchev went backstage to congratulate the American singer.

Spotting Kalb, Khrushchev volunteered some positive comments about U.S.-Soviet relations. When Kalb asked if he was thinking of Cuba, Khrushchev replied that the superpowers would find a way out of the crisis. Kalb flashed Khrushchev's comment to the world through CBS, but it did not seem to make any impression on the officials in Washington. Years later I could find no mention of it in the transcripts of White House crisis deliberations.

In Washington on the morning of October 26, one of my future colleagues, John Scali of ABC, became involved in a secret meeting with the Russians. Alexander Feklisov, an intelligence officer at the Soviet Embassy in Washington (who went by the name of Fomin), invited Scali for lunch at the Occidental Restaurant. Fomin proposed a plan to end the crisis: The Soviet Union would dismantle and remove the missiles under U.N. inspection. Moscow would pledge to withdraw the missiles if the United States would pledge not to invade Cuba. Apparently, Khrushchev had personally authorized the Soviet agent, rather than a diplomat, to pass on the message. Fomin asked Scali to get this proposal to the highest U.S. authorities. Scali immediately sought out Roger Hilsman, head of the Bureau of Intelligence and Research at the State Department. The message went next to Secretary of State Dean Rusk, who summoned Scali and authorized him to tell Khrushchev's agent that the United States would, indeed, be interested. In parting, the secretary of state told Scali, "John, you have served your country well. Remember when you report this that we were eyeball to eyeball— they blinked first."

In later years, Fomin would publicly state that it was Scali, not Moscow, who originated the proposal. I saw him on Russian television as late as October 2002 asserting that Scali was a CIA man in touch with the highest authorities in the United States. Fomin's TV account was misleading. The telegram he filed to Moscow on October 26, 1962, has since become public and does not support his later protestations. Furthermore, Scali's own notes and accounts by American officials corroborate Scali's version, not Fomin's. Even Soviet Foreign Minister Andrey Gromyko states in his *Pamyatnoe* (Memoirs) that the Soviet government conceived of the final compromise. So why would Fomin make such an outrageous claim, which offended Scali deeply?

Murrey Marder, diplomatic correspondent of the *Washington Post*, offered me an explanation. In the postcrisis period, Communist China accused the Soviet Union of "adventurism and capitulationism" in deploying the missiles and then withdrawing them. Seeking to counter these charges, the Soviet government tried to shift blame onto the United States. One ploy was to persuade the American media that the proposal was an American initiative, thereby lessening Moscow's responsibility. The Soviet Embassy, which cultivated relations with key correspondents in Washington, invited Marder for an exclusive interview. The number-two Soviet diplomat sought to convince him orally that the CIA had thought up the compromise and gotten Scali to transmit it to Fomin. Skeptical of this version, Marder asked to see the embassy's telegrams to Moscow. "That brought a you-must-be-off-your-rocker reaction," Marder explained to me years later. "That was the end of that maneuver for me."

As the United States began preparations for an invasion or surgical strike against Cuba on October 26, the U.S. Embassy received a personal letter from Khrushchev to President Kennedy. It was divided into four parts, containing marginal notes in Khrushchev's handwriting. Since no dedicated Moscow-Washington communications line existed in those days, the U.S. Embassy was obliged to translate the message, encode it, and send it by commercial cable—a process that took about eight hours. Soviet Ambassador Dobrynin revealed in his memoir, *In Confidence,* that his embassy, too, relied on commercial cable to telegraph dispatches to Moscow. He notes that the embassy would call Western Union, which would send a courier on a bicycle to pick up the text. Dobrynin says he never felt confident that the courier would bicycle straight back to the cable head without stopping at a bar for a drink.

This first Khrushchev message, not published at the time, has since been much discussed because of its discursive and emotional tone:

> Let us therefore show statesmanlike wisdom. I propose: we, for our part, will declare that our ships, bound for Cuba, will not carry any kind of armaments. You would declare that the United States will not invade Cuba with its forces and will not support any sort of forces which might intend to carry out an invasion of Cuba. Then the necessity for the presence of our military specialists in Cuba would disappear.
>
> Mr. President, I appeal to you to weigh well what the aggressive, piratical actions, which you have declared the USA intends to carry out in international waters, would lead to. You yourself know that any sensible man simply cannot agree with this, cannot recognize your right to such actions.
>
> If you did this as the first step towards the unleashing of war, well then, it is evident that nothing else is left to us but to accept this challenge of yours. If, however, you have not lost your self-control and sensibly conceive what this might lead to, then, Mr. President, we and you ought to not now pull on the ends of the rope in which you have tied the knots of war, because the more the two of us pull, the tighter this knot will be tied. And a moment may come when that knot will be tied so tight that even he who tied will not have the strength to untie it, and then it will be necessary to cut that knot . . .

In the afternoon of that same day, a second Khrushchev message was read on Moscow television and radio. It had been drafted during an eight-hour session of the Politburo leaders who believed that the boss had not used his bargaining power to the full in his first personal letter to Kennedy. This second letter upped the ante, demanding the United States dismantle its medium-range Jupiter missiles in Turkey as part of the deal. In the UPI bureau, Korengold, Axelbank, and I skimmed the message off television with the help of our translator, Arthur. Its key passage read:

> You are worried over Cuba. You say that it worries you because it lies at a distance of over 90 miles across the sea from the shores of the United States. However, Turkey lies next to us. Our sentinels are pacing up and down and watching each other. Do you believe you have the right to demand security for your country and the removal of such weapons that you qualify as offensive, while not recognizing this right for us?
>
> You have stationed devastating rocket weapons, which you call offensive in Turkey literally right next to us. How then does recognition of our equal military possibilities tally with such unequal relations between our great states? This does not tally at all.

These two messages—the first soft and secret and the second stern and public—posed a dilemma for the Kennedy administration. The demand to remove U.S. Jupiter missiles from Turkey was difficult because these missiles formed a part of NATO defenses, especially important to Ankara. Kennedy argued they could not be removed immediately. However, he was willing to give secret assurances—transmitted by Attorney General Bobby Kennedy to Ambassador Dobrynin—that they would be removed in the course of four or five months if no public mention was made of these secret assurances.

In Washington, the White House released the text of Kennedy's public reply based on Khrushchev's first, unpublished, letter but ignored the second with its strident demand for removal of the missiles in Turkey. UPI's chief diplomatic correspondent, Stu Hensley, told me he was stumped when he read Kennedy's reply because it did not track with Khrushchev's second, public, message. Something important was missing that probably went to the heart of the matter, Hensley said. "It was the damnedest thing. The reply was apparently also based on the unpublished first Khrushchev letter, and something did not add up. We got no official guidance; we were left in the dark to figure it out for ourselves. I decided all I could do was write it straight. I threw my copy on Harry Franz's [the Saturday-night editor] desk. He looked at it, and without saying a word, marked it up, made no changes, and gave it to the telegrapher to punch out on the wire." In fact, Hensley and his AP counterpart, Hightower, did exactly what the administration wanted, reporting Kennedy's public reply but revealing nothing of the secret side deal on the Jupiter missiles.

Behind the scenes, the Americans were pressing the Kremlin for an immediate acceptance of the Kennedy reply, warning that a surgical attack to take out the Soviet missiles could be imminent. Because of the eight-hour time difference with Moscow and the slowness of telegraphic communications, Khrushchev and his colleagues were under withering pressure. On the morning of Sunday, October 28, Khrushchev agreed to accept Kennedy's formulation with no reference to withdrawal of U.S. missiles from Turkey. Fearing that a U.S. attack on Cuba could come at any time, he rushed an aide to Moscow radio for a 4:00 P.M. broadcast (8:00 A.M. in Washington). The message was read by Yuri Levitan, the famous World War II radio announcer with the stentorian voice.

American journalists in Moscow were now about to play a critical role because they would transmit the key information much faster than commercial cable. We were alerted by a Soviet source that an important announcement would be coming that afternoon. At the UPI office, Korengold hastily called in Arthur on his day off to give a running translation of Khrushchev's message. We switched on the television, started the Grundig tape recorder. When the announcement began, Jay and I feverishly typed out the words as translated by Arthur. Bud grabbed the copy from our typewriters, fashioning Khrushchev's announcement into a lead.

He ran fifteen feet from our newsroom, across a small corridor, to the Siemens teletypewriter located in our makeshift wire room. He punched out a yard of tape through the tape cutter, then began running the yellow five-hole tape through the teletypewriter while continuing to compose, as the machine clacked away at sixty words a minute. We continuously fed him short takes of about two hundred words as the TV droned on.

The Associated Press was less fortunate. In the office were bureau chief Preston Grover and Gus Ensz, neither of whom knew Russian well enough to understand Khrushchev. George Syvertsen, the third AP man, had studied Russian for one year before coming to Moscow. Syvertsen managed to keep up until he came to the key decision on missiles. "I don't know what he's saying," Syvertsen cried to Grover in desperation. "I don't know if he said they would stay in or out!" Grover ran down the hall to *France-Soir*'s Claude Day, a Russian speaker, who explained that Khrushchev had agreed to remove the missiles.

At the Central Telegraph, CBS correspondent Marvin Kalb, a former Harvard doctoral student and the only TV correspondent who was fluent in Russian, ordered up a telephone line to New York for *The World Today*. Interviewed by David Schoenbrun of the CBS Washington Bureau, Kalb declared that Khrushchev had "caved" by agreeing to withdraw the missiles.

In Washington, President Kennedy, anxious for resolution, followed network reports on three television sets. The verb *caved* alarmed Kennedy, and he asked his spokesman, Pierre Salinger, to urge CBS to handle the news with restraint. During a commercial break, Salinger contacted Schoenbrun and urged Kalb not to use the C word. Kalb refused to do as the president wanted. "I told David that's what the Russians had done, and I would stick to the use of the word," Kalb recalled years later.

Unknown to us at the time, ABC's correspondent, Sam Jaffe, secured an unusual scoop on that critical Sunday. One of his confidential sources told him that Khrushchev had argued with hard-liners in penning his first, softer, letter and had imposed his view. Khrushchev, who was growing increasingly authoritarian, brooked little opposition, and the Soviet media were instructed to play up the notion of a "reasonable compromise." I wrote UPI's lead for American morning newspapers of October 29, beginning this way: "MOSCOW (UPI)—The government newspaper Izvestia told the Soviet people tonight the United States had been poised to invade Cuba and that the Soviet decision to dismantle rocket bases there showed 'the wisdom of the Soviet government.'"

Like Washington, Moscow had engaged in its own kind of news management as the crisis headed toward resolution. These tense days demonstrated a serious weak point in Cold War relations. Communications were so antiquated that a conflict could spark a planetary catastrophe unless the two sides could quickly converse with each other. In the days following the crisis, UPI New York asked its bureaus to cooperate in an experiment designed to discover how fast a message could actually travel between Moscow to Washington and return. We were glad to participate. Since news agencies had no direct line from Moscow to Washington, the message would have to travel through several relay points. We sent a brief text—"The quick, brown fox jumped over the lazy dog"—to Finland, where the Helsinki bureau manager sent it on to Frankfurt, which relayed it to London. From there, alert editors forwarded the message to New York by radio link (usually reliable if there were no solar flares), and New York forwarded it to Washington by landline. Washington turned the message around and sent it back to Moscow through the same series of relays, arriving about sixty seconds after leaving.

UPI was pleased to announce the remarkable result. The Cuban missile crisis demonstrated one thing that had not been so obvious before: there were rules of behavior between adversaries during the Cold War, unlike the surprises and confusions of the current war on terrorism. Henceforth, Cold War etiquette would include a "hotline" between the Kremlin and the White House. Enemies had to talk to enemies if planetary war was to be avoided.

Chapter 10

The Paradox of Censorship

In the days following the Cuban crisis, I scanned the morning newspapers for any new details or admissions from the Soviet side. As I leafed through *Komsomolskaya Pravda* with Arthur, we came across a feature article describing the dismantling of Soviet missiles in Cuba. I informed Bud, and he reacted instantly. "That's the first real revelation for the Soviet public of the missile issue!" he shouted. "There's a good story there. Make the most of it!"

As I was learning, the controlled Soviet media often practiced censorship by omission. Throughout the week of the missile crisis, the media heaped blame on the United States for planning to attack Cuba without ever mentioning the secret deployment there of Soviet missiles. That action, which had stirred such deep reactions in the Kennedy administration, was unknown to the Soviet mass public, although a few thousands might have heard about it on the Voice of America. This article was my first encounter with one of the elements of Soviet opinion molding: Don't rush to tell the whole truth; distort the facts if need be, and lie when necessary to avoid embarrassment or guilt. This kind of manipulation made discussion between Soviets and Westerners in the early 1960s very difficult because each side argued from widely differing knowledge.

What puzzled me was why the Russian public found the Soviet version of events credible. Was it because this was their media talking to them in their own language? Was it xenophobic distrust of anything foreign? Was it lack of access to alternative information? In any event, that article in *Komsomolskaya Pravda* started me thinking about censorship. Was it a useful tool for governing and, if so, for how long?

What was undeniable was that the Kremlin's desire to control information over a period of decades hobbled truthful discussion of public issues. Any citizen who was aware of a local tragedy could identify inaccuracies in the media that were always trying to put the best face on a bad situation. Over the long term, that tendency would damage credibility. Thus, the first paradox of censorship: it was a tool intended to boost the Soviet system, but over the long term it encouraged its unraveling. We were always running into examples big and small. Bud recalled how he had once rushed to Sheremetyevo Airport to check out a plane crash. When he arrived, he saw bodies being carried off the field on stretchers. He asked the first responders in accented Russian what had happened and how many had died. The answer he got was: "Plane crash? What plane crash? There was no plane crash here."

Catastrophes and other unpleasant occurrences were supposed to be on the wane under the forward march of communism. Accordingly, the Soviet media rarely published reports about aviation mishaps, poor harvests, crime statistics, or automobile fatalities. There was one exception, however. When foreigners were killed in plane crashes, the press acknowledged the deaths of non-Soviet travelers because these were difficult to keep hidden. Often their deaths would be well reported abroad, and those reports would trickle back into the Soviet Union.

Particular secrecy surrounded space programs that had both military and propaganda uses. The main base for launching cosmonauts into space was called the Baikonur Cosmodrome, after a small settlement in Kazakhstan. The name was located on maps. But when Western scientists traced back the orbits of space flights to their launch site, they arrived at Tyur-Atam, several hundreds miles distant from Baikonur.

Foreign correspondents in Russia operated under censorship after the revolution until the early 1960s. They reported to the Central Telegraph in downtown Moscow, where they would pass their copy to a receptionist behind a counter who, in turn, would pass it through a second door covered by a green baize curtain, to unseen censors. Often, correspondents waited long hours for their dispatches to emerge from the Green Door, stamped with approval and ready for dispatch, or denied without explanation.

We now know that censors sometimes referred particularly sensitive topics to Stalin's administrative apparatus, and that could take many hours. One former censor has described how she would not only translate journalists' dispatches but also write summaries for the secret police and Foreign Ministry. Harrison Salisbury's reports to the *New York Times* in the early

1950s were so perceptive that the secret police actually considered poisoning him. The plan was never enacted, however.

Bud remembered an incident in the early 1960s that typified the frustrations of foreign correspondents with censorship. A French reporter compared Khrushchev in one of his dispatches to Marlon Brando. His copy was delayed for a long time until a censor emerged and asked, "Who is Marlon Brando?"

The Frenchman answered, "A very famous movie actor."

"Does Mr. Brando play serious or comic roles?"

"Serious, *naturellement.*"

There was more delay, until the copy finally emerged, approved for sending—but with all references to Khrushchev and Brando blacked out. From the Soviet point of view, these bureaucratic delays were helpful. They made the foreigners' work exhausting and inefficient and, most of all, kept them from digging too deeply into other subjects.

Henry would sometimes share with us his experience with censorship going back to the mid-1930s. In the wake of the Russian Revolution, the censors were intellectuals who had lived abroad in places such as Paris, London, Geneva, and New York. "They knew languages, they were very well read, often had a sense of humor, and were fun to talk to," he recounted. "You could not only talk to them, but you could actually get some helpful guidance."

Henry remembered that one of the censors tried to influence him to recast a sensitive article. "You know that I can't pass that story. Why don't you rewrite it a little bit?" On another occasion a censor told him, "You are too negative. Why don't you write something positive? There are good things in this country, too." Still a third censor, trying to be helpful, urged, "Why don't you send it out by mail?" Mailers were not subject to scrutiny.

During the purge trials of 1937, the censors started getting tougher and more distant. They would pass what had appeared in the Soviet press but little more. It became increasingly difficult to write fully, or to question why Stalin was putting his former comrades on trial. Henry recalled that you could write whatever you wanted without fear, but critical dispatches would probably go nowhere. "If there had been no censorship, everybody would have been expelled because all correspondents would have written what they felt under the stress of emotion. But as it was, they handed in their copy, and it was killed by the censors." When Stalin concluded the Non-Aggression Pact with Hitler in 1939, the authorities eased censorship for a while on German correspondents. They were allowed to call Berlin at will, and Shapiro, in his shrewd way, occasionally got copy out by calling UP's Berlin Bureau.

By the late 1930s and into the World War II years, the erudite censors had disappeared, replaced by linguists who were more loyal than competent. Not surprisingly, this created humorous situations. Henry remembered that one of his colleagues tried hard to inject some color into a description of a state funeral in the House of Trade Unions. The reporter wrote of the ever present red banners: "There was a symphony of clashing shades of red." When the censor got through, it read, "There was a symphony of clashing shades." In one dispatch, Henry described Ilya Ehrenburg, a famous Soviet writer, as a "Francophile." The adjective *Francophile* was deleted because the censor informed Henry it was libelous "to call Mr. Ehrenburg a friend of [Spanish dictator] Franco's."

One of the more ludicrous deletions that Henry joked about concerned Georgii Dimitrov, general secretary of the Communist International, Moscow's organization for spreading communism around the world. When Dimitrov stepped down as a deputy of the USSR Supreme Soviet but remained general secretary of the Comintern, Shapiro wrote that he had retained his secretaryship. "The censor very indignantly said to me, 'Now Mr. Shapiro, you know that the Comintern has no navy. What do you mean by saying 'secretaryship'?" The censor solved the problem by dropping the ending "ship," and Henry's dispatch went out saying: "Dimitrov retains the secretary of the Comintern."

Western correspondents were never informed what were "censorable" subjects. Thus, they confronted the second paradox of censorship: ignorance of secret regulations is no excuse for violating secret regulations. Correspondents made no effort to develop their own list of sensitive topics. To do so would have been prudent, but it would have encouraged self-censorship. Henry did share with us his assessment of sensitive issues. Avoid insulting Soviet leaders gratuitously, like reporting a grease stain on Prime Minister Kosygin's necktie. Go easy on vandalism against Jews such as bricks being thrown through the windows of the Central Synagogue in Moscow. Sidestep Nikita Khrushchev's growing rift with Mao Zedong or other Soviet-Sino problems. Be careful about reporting disputes within the Soviet leadership, should you learn of them. But he never told us, his subordinates, we had to comply.

The censorship issue increasingly gnawed at foreign correspondents after Stalin's death, and by 1961 American newsmen started pushing for the end of restraints on dispatches going abroad. Correspondents discussed among themselves a variety of arguments that might be made to the Soviet leadership. They reasoned that censorship betrayed an insecurity that was unworthy of a superpower. Furthermore, the work of foreign correspondents was destined to be published abroad, not in the Soviet Union. Finally, censorship could be evaded on less urgent stories by having them carried abroad by travelers, and, in fact, photographs and television film were regularly sent out secretly with tourists leaving for the West.

Edmund Stevens, the chief of *Time* magazine and a longtime Russia hand, took the lead. On February 12, 1961, he sent a letter to Khrushchev calling censorship "a formality alien to the spirit of the times and not capable of improving relations between the USSR and other countries. Knowing your uncompromising attitude towards all kinds of bureaucratic routine and your desire to improve international relations in which the press plays a considerable role, I request consideration of such frankness. I hope you will not take offense at my words or misinterpret them."

Khrushchev's reply came a month later. Correspondents were summoned to the Soviet Foreign Ministry, where press chief Mikhail A. Kharlamov announced obliquely the end of censorship. Because the mere existence of censorship was secret, as was the list of forbidden subjects, he announced circuitously that "measures are being taken to facilitate communications between correspondents and editors at home. From this day forward, correspondents will be able to use facilities at the Central Telegraph in Moscow and in their offices, homes, and hotel rooms to telephone directly." The British news agency Reuters got the first telex machine at the end of 1961, which would provide uncensored communications. United Press International and the Associated Press received their telexes in March 1962.

Despite easing censorship for foreign reporters, censorship continued to function for all Soviet media. Censors and chief editors were responsible for hiding issues described in the List of Forbidden Topics. This list was jocularly called "The Talmud" because of its detailed descriptions. The Communist Party apparatus issued supplementary instructions from time to time to deal with unusual situations, and the criminal code provided sanctions for unauthorized disclosures. Many Soviet journalists began their careers as we did, wanting to tell an accurate story of what happened. Most were ground down by the restrictions and eventually became propagandists for the regime. However, by the 1960s, the younger generation of journalists became increasingly dissatisfied and engaged in give-and-take with the censors. True, reporters would occasionally rewrite to suit political demands or requirements of "The List." But increasingly, they would write in oblique Aesopian ways to permit experienced citizens "to read between the lines."

By the 1970s, emigration of Jewish citizens was eased, and many of them were willing to act as sources for Western correspondents. Freethinkers gave up on the system entirely and would write for *samisdat* (self-publishing), circulating ten carbon copies among friends who would each make another ten carbon copies for their friends. Or writers might pen their observations for *tamizat* (publication abroad). Out of frustration, they would write occasionally only for "the drawer"—material to be published in better times. Once in a while, especially in the laxer years of General Secretary Brezhnev, journalists and writers might succeed in slipping something into print despite the censors. And reports by Moscow-based foreign correspondents could seep back into the Soviet Union through the Voice of America, the BBC, and some Western TV broadcasts receivable from Finland and Poland. I considered this the third paradox of censorship: the system was massive, but it was not perfect; it could develop holes and let the fresh air in.

Media control naturally complicated the ability of Soviet officials to keep up with events around the world, especially when attempting to negotiate arms-control agreements with the West. This required the bureaucracy to allow key officials to read Western publications on a need-to-know basis. (When Aeroflot was granted landing rights in the United States in the 1970s, its airliners were rumored to fly dozens of copies of *Aviation Week and Space Technology*, with its detailed reports on space exploration, regularly to Moscow.) Necessity also forced the Soviet news agency, TASS, to create classified news bulletins for high officials. They were compiled from unedited reports of its correspondents and were known as Red TASS and White TASS. White TASS, the most honest and objective, circulated only among the highest officials.

The authorities, of course, remained concerned about influencing Western correspondents once censorship of foreign reporters was removed. How did they nudge Americans to reflect their views? There were a variety of gambits. Occasionally, they would call a press conference, for example, in connection with space flights. They could be very lengthy affairs, lasting two hours or more, in which the organizers would trot out key scientists. These performances were conceived without much regard to possible headlines. They were basically opportunities for the Soviet side to show off.

Briefing correspondents confidentially was only just getting started in the early 1960s. Sometimes Leonid M. Zamyatin would lunch with a bureau chief and feed him the line. My position as a junior reporter excluded me from such encounters, but I have no doubt that Henry would meet with Zamyatin or his deputies and trade information. What young correspondents discovered was that the KGB was adept at sending them into the embrace of an authorized source, or "nanny." This would be a journalist specifically authorized to be "your friend." His job was to gain your trust through friendly gestures and then feed you exclusive information.

My *nyanka* (nursemaid) was a man about my age, Vadim Biryukov. As a boy he had lived in France and spoke good French. In the early 1960s he was employed by the Novosti Press Agency (APN) as an "observer" and as such had access to briefings on a wide range of subjects. At the time, I suspected he was KGB; decades later, I learned he was associated with the Second Chief Directorate for internal security and counterintelligence. Early on, Vadim helped me buy a pair of cross-country skis, and introduced me to splendid tracks in the birch woods around Moscow. One of the "scoops" he pitched me concerned Valentina Tereshkova, the first woman in space. After her flight in 1964, she married fellow cosmonaut Andrian Nikolayev and became pregnant. Months later, Vadim called me to say that she would deliver by C-section and would not be allowed to fly again. Not a word of this appeared in the Soviet press, and my exclusive boosted my reputation.

An even more important scoop went to the heart of the Cold War. In 1963 a member of the Soviet disarmament delegation in Geneva defected to the United States. He was Yuri Ivanovich Nosenko, a counterintelligence operative. The American authorities flew him to the United States and, at first, prevented Soviet officials from seeing him. This angered his Moscow bosses, who asserted Nosenko had been entrapped by the Americans. When Vadim called me at the UPI office, he said, "You know about the case of Nosenko in Geneva?" I replied that I did. "Well, if your guys don't let our diplomats get to him, we will walk out of the disarmament talks." Excited, I wrote this scoop, attributing it to well-informed sources. I was being used, but I did not object because, once again, this exclusive story would boost my career. In the following days, Soviet diplomats were finally allowed to visit Nosenko. He declined their pleas to return home.

Toward the end of my first tour in Moscow in 1965, my relations with Vadim soured. On one occasion I had spent many hours on the Kremlin grounds watching official limousines drive in and out for an unannounced Central Committee meeting. The Central Committee was composed of some five hundred of the Communist Party's top officials and served as a forum for discussion and ratification of policies proposed by the ruling Politburo. When Vadim asked me how I learned about the meeting, I replied that another source had tipped me off, which was true. "If you want reliable information," he scolded, "I urge you to count on me and not on what some uninformed character tells you."

There were other sanctions aimed at influencing us. Bud told me that he had once angered the Press Department of the Foreign Ministry by revealing some inside information from a closed party meeting. As punishment, the Foreign Ministry refused to authorize his exit visa for a two-week period. In those days, every time you wanted to leave the country, you had to request an exit and reentry visa. This action ruined his planned vacation.

Sometimes dirty tricks would come into play. This happened to my predecessor, Aline Mosby, in March 1961. She rejected a sexual advance from

Alexei Adzhubei, Khrushchev's son-in-law and editor of *Izvestia*. Days later when she was having lunch with a person she believed to be a source, she found her drink was spiked. She was taken out of the restaurant to a sobering-up station and photographed in a disheveled state. This picture was published by *Izvestia* with unflattering commentary about how badly Western correspondents conduct themselves.

The ultimate sanction that officials invoked against Western correspondents in the 1960s was expulsion. This was the fate of Whitman Bassow, bureau chief of *Newsweek*, who had previously worked for Henry as a UP correspondent. He was kicked out in 1962 for an unexplained transgression. Expulsion also ended the Moscow career of Steve Rosenfeld, the *Washington Post*'s first correspondent in Moscow in the mid-1960s, following his newspaper's publication of the papers of Colonel Oleg Penkovsky, a secret U.S. spy. Patrick McGrady, correspondent for *Newsweek* after Bassow, was withdrawn when Soviet press authorities complained about his romancing Russian women. Even Henry Shapiro was once threatened with expulsion for having participated in a television interview in the United States during which another panelist described Khrushchev as a "country bumpkin."

Expulsions and refusals to renew visas have continued as a sanction right up to the present. Andrew Nagorsky of *Newsweek* was expelled in 1982 because the magazine published an unflattering picture of Brezhnev on its cover. ABC Television lost its resident American correspondent early in the twenty-first century because it broadcast an interview with Chechen terrorist Shamil Basayev, presenting the Chechen view of the conflict, which the Kremlin wanted to suppress. Despite the tentative openness of Russian society under President Vladimir Putin, the Kremlin has not forgotten what levers to pull to manipulate, nudge, or control the media, foreign and domestic.

Chapter 11

Life and Death in 1963

In our first year in Moscow, Ruth and I broke every rule for getting ahead in UPI, according to Bill Sexton's guidance. We had married and bought furniture. And now in our first summer, Ruth announced that she was pregnant. I was not overjoyed by this development. Still unresolved for me was the place that professional work should occupy in our lives. Children would be fine sometime, but having a child now was an unwanted complication for someone still very insecure about his work. Ruth, on the other hand, was delighted.

Throughout that summer of 1962, new questions intruded: Should this child be born in Moscow or at Ruth's home in England? If Moscow, what claim might the Soviet state make on the child? If a girl or a boy, what would its nationality really be? A child born abroad of two American parents is American, according to U.S. nationality laws. But a child born abroad of one American and one English parent would be . . . what?

Equally important was the physical setting of childbirth in Moscow. Generally, Russian women gave birth in lying-in hospitals without pain relief, which was usually in short supply. The thought of a husband attending the birth in the delivery room was inconceivable. Conservative rules obliged women to recover in the hospital for nine days. No visitors were permitted for fear of infection, but the new mothers were allowed to look out the windows at their husbands standing on the sidewalks below. We even heard horror stories of Western women who had anesthesia because of complicated births only to find, on recovery, that they had been subjected to a hysterec-tomy without consultation.

We decided to cut short the speculation and have Ruth fly back to England. That way the child would definitely have English nationality and probably American, too. Ruth's mother, Molly, would help in the immediate postnatal period. Still, we opted for the Russian prenatal care rather than relying on the American embassy doctor. Children are born everywhere in the world, and we thought that Russian prenatal care would be adequate, especially if Ruth went to Botkin Hospital, which served the diplomatic corps.

Ruth's Russian obstetrician turned out to be a plump, grandmotherly woman with gray hair named Dr. Litvinova. From the start, she seemed a caring person with plenty of experience. When I delicately asked about abortion, she immediately frowned. "No, no, you mustn't think of that," she responded. "Abortion—not good. You must have first child." And she handed us a little green pamphlet, published by the Russian Ministry of Health, titled *About the Harm of Abortion*. Its message was that aborting a first pregnancy could lead to infertility.

This pamphlet was probably written for the wives of foreign diplomats. We did not know at that point that abortion was the major means of con-traception in the Soviet Union and that most Russian women averaged six to seven abortions during a lifetime. For our part, we were pleased with our Moscow "babushka." We met her regularly, and she reassured us con-stantly. She always seemed concerned for the health of the baby. When Ruth admitted to using a lot of salt, pepper, and salad dressing, Litvinova snapped in Russian, "Everything spicy—no good for baby. No drink either. Walk—full hour—every day. Oxygen—good for baby."

Toward the end of 1962, as Ruth's due day approached, Litvinova intro-duced us to huff-and-puff. "You breathe deeply through nose and out slowly through mouth. If first stage slow, help it with self-massage." She demonstrated to Ruth how to massage the lower regions of the pelvis and back. In the second stage of labor, Litvinova recommended quick pants in-terrupted by deep breaths while bearing down. "Practice exercises and everything—all right," she said comfortingly.

Our biggest problem was informing Litvinova that, in the end, Ruth had decided to fly to England to have the baby because of the nationality issues. Litvinova was clearly disappointed, although she said she understood. We promised to bring the baby back to show her. Ruth later wrote about our consultations with Litvinova for the *Manchester Guardian,* a story that was reprinted in the *San Francisco Chronicle* on November 4, 1963, under a ban-ner headline, "My Experiment Baby." Editors can't resist sensational and misleading headlines: they sell papers.

None of these meetings with Dr. Litvinova would have been possible without Natasha. It was she who helped us improve our Russian to the point that we could converse. Usually, correspondents hired teachers, chauffeurs, and secretaries through the official diplomatic service bureau. This practice was convenient and usually efficient. But such helpers were always being interviewed by the KGB about their employers. We short-circuited UPDK in this case and found Natasha through a friend.

Her father, Vassilii P. Nalimov, had been a professor at Moscow University before the revolution. Natasha (her actual name was Nadezhda Vassilievna Nalimova) had spent eight years in Stalin's Gulag and now looked like a wraith. She was extremely thin, with a moonlike face and white hair. You sometimes thought that a gust of wind might blow her away. As we got to know her, we discovered that she was very well versed in Russian literature. She exuded a real enthusiasm for the language, never failing to point out that the case endings of nouns and adjectives allowed Russian to have a flexible sentence structure, permitting all sorts of twists and turns in poetry that are not possible in English. In the summers of 1962 and 1963 Natasha and I would sometimes drive out to Nikolina Gora (Nicholas Mountain) outside Moscow and sit by the stream in the bright sun and read the Russian classics.

The better I got to know Natasha, the more I learned of her story. She was an "internal émigré" or, more popularly, a "refusenik." Natasha had opted out of Soviet society and desperately wanted to leave the country. The authorities probably threatened her from time to time with expulsion from Moscow, but on the whole they ignored her, possibly because of the British Embassy's interest in her case. During the Second World War, when relations between the USSR and Britain were friendly, she had met and married a British naval attaché, Captain Clifford Henry Whitehead. When his assignment ended, he was ordered back to London. Stalin's government did not look kindly on its citizens marrying foreigners and going abroad. So it was not unusual that Natasha was barred from leaving.

The couple grew more and more disconsolate as departure day approached, and they decided on a desperate scheme. Captain Whitehead dressed Natasha as a British sailor and tried to smuggle her aboard his ship leaving Leningrad for England. As she tried to force her way past Soviet border guards, she was seized from the gangplank. For attempting to depart without permission she was sentenced to a lengthy term in a labor camp. In the camps she was raped and subjected to other brutality. Captain Whitehead, meanwhile, sailed away. After seven years with no news from his wife, Whitehead had Natasha officially declared dead and married an English woman.

When Nikita Khrushchev came to power in 1953, one of his first actions was to review the cases of persons who had been imprisoned during the last years of Stalin. Natasha was released in the mid-1950s, along with thousands of other prisoners. Once in Moscow, she began her efforts to rejoin Captain Whitehead in England. The British Embassy supported her case as much as possible. Many foreigners befriended her, none more so than Nicholas Carroll, the London-based diplomatic correspondent of the *Sunday Times.* Prime Minister Harold Wilson, on a trip to Moscow, received her for a half hour and raised her case with high Soviet officials to no avail. She even instituted a legal suit against Captain Whitehead for abandoning her, but the Law Lords of the House or Lords (Britain's supreme court) found in favor of Whitehead and his current wife. After that, the Soviet authorities warned British diplomats that harping on her case could only endanger British-Soviet relations.

All of those terrible emotions hung over our lessons, but on the whole poor Natasha struggled on. She insisted that we visit the cultural sites of Moscow, including the many art galleries. Because of her I can't forget the painting of Boyarina Morozova, the defiant Old Believer being hauled away on a sledge making the two-fingered sign of devotion. Or, the picture of the haggard Russian prisoner, released from czarist incarceration, titled *Ne Zhdali...* (translated roughly, *They Never Expected Him...*).

I particularly remember a visit to the Tretyakov Gallery during the winter of 1962. As I gave my overcoat to the cloakroom attendant, he picked up my American accent and volunteered, "Privet Kenne'-dee!" (Greetings to Kennedy!). That might seem unusual at the height of the Cold War, but the outburst reflected a deep curiosity among Russians about America and warm feelings for our handsome president. I promised that as a journalist, I would see that his friendly words were transmitted.

Living in Moscow in those days was an education. Henry liked to tell his subordinates that a year's work in the Moscow Bureau was equivalent to a master's degree in journalism, if not more. I remember that summer brought some important lessons to Henry's "graduate course." An old adage has it that "You're only as good as your source." On May 31, 1962, there was no source and therefore no story. But on June 8, the story of May 31 emerged: A U.S. consular officer told Bud that an American defector to Russia, his Soviet wife, Marina, and their Soviet-born daughter, Yulia, had boarded a train for Warsaw on their way to America. We filed 250 words to London about this unknown returnee, normal for such a story. This defector turned out to be Lee Harvey Oswald, who would assassinate President Kennedy more than a year later.

In the postwar years, some two hundred American families had renounced their U.S. citizenship to live in the Soviet Union, which they thought was a more just society than the United States. Oswald was one of three Americans who came to Moscow in 1959 in search of a new life. We tried to keep in touch with these malcontents. Nicholas Petrulli, forty-two, a sheet-metal worker from Long Island, tired of the Soviet experience within weeks and went home. Robert Edward Webster, a plastics technician from Cleveland, succeeded in renouncing his American citizenship, acquired Soviet nationality, shacked up with a woman in Leningrad, but abandoned her in 1962, also to return.

Our bureau knew a fair amount about Oswald before he was sent off to live in the provincial town of Minsk. My predecessor, Aline Mosby, had interviewed him on November 15, 1959, and Priscilla MacMillan, a freelancer for the North American Newspaper Alliance, got to him the following day. Like Webster, Oswald tried to renounce his U.S. citizenship and got as far as writing out a declaration at the embassy on November 2, 1959, stating, "I affirm that my allegiance is to the Soviet socialist republic." But U.S. Consul Richard Snyder advised him to think over the seriousness of what he was doing and delay the renunciation. The two women journalists found Oswald despondent that neither the United States nor the Soviet Union seemed to take him seriously. Shortly after those journalistic interviews, he tried to commit suicide by cutting his wrists, was found in time, and was carted off to Botkin. After that, he was exiled to the provinces.

In July 1962, we all got a lesson on how *not* to conduct public relations at the highest level. The occasion was the visit of a dozen editors from the American Society of Newspaper Editors. Among the visitors was Robert Estabrook, who had been chief of the *Washington Post*'s editorial page when I was a copyboy. The editors had been invited by the Union of Journalists, including Alexei Adzhubei, the abrasive editor of *Izvestia*. This was the first-ever tour of Soviet Russia for American journalists since Stalin's death.

After visiting Leningrad, Kiev, Volgograd, Tashkent, Samarkand, and Tbilisi, the editors sat down in the Kremlin for the high point—an interview with The Boss. In the course of a two-hour *tour d'horizon*, Khrushchev bragged that the Soviet Union had a "global weapon" that could hit any target on earth and was invulnerable. He claimed, too, in his runaway enthusiasm, that the military possessed an antimissile missile that could hit "a fly in the sky." The editors winced, took copious notes, while an official stenographer recorded the session. Rockets in space always made a story, especially if they could be targeted at the United States.

When Khrushchev asked if the Americans had been able to see everything they wanted, Estabrook and his colleague Loren Soth of the *Des*

*Moines Register* shouted, "No!" They explained that they had not been allowed to deviate from the official itinerary (a common refusal in those days) to take a close look at a beautiful cornfield in Ukraine. The disappointment was noted by the stenographer.

In closing, Khrushchev and his aides asked the editors not to file until they received the official transcript, but, of course, they began roughing out their stories in advance. Days later, the transcript was finally handed to Estabrook and Lee Hills, editor of the *Miami Herald,* at a ceremony in the offices of *Pravda,* liberally accompanied by champagne. The editors checked the document against the drafts they had already written and found discrepancies. The transcript had toned down sharp exchanges over availability of consumer goods and distorted elements of the Baruch Plan that the United States had proposed after World War II for controlling nuclear weapons. But the most egregious alteration concerned that uninspected Ukrainian cornfield. Instead of recording that Estabrook and Soth had answered "No!" the transcript boldly stated "Yes!"

Estabrook steamed into the UPI bureau both angry and amused. "Here is a 180-degree falsehood," he declared, "and I'm writing it!" He handed me his copy to transmit to Washington, and I started punching what seemed like endless reams in time for the July 17, 1962, edition of the *Washington Post.* I was shocked by this blatant misrepresentation. It hardly seemed worthwhile to me to fiddle with the transcript, even if you were going to publish it in the Soviet press—which they did. As a Westerner, I was still getting used to the Soviet capacity for deception. In the end, the Soviet hosts exploded at Estabrook when they received reports from Washington about what he had published. Adzhubei and Foreign Ministry spokesman Zamyatin cornered him at the farewell reception days later and accused him of singlehandedly spoiling a chance for better Soviet-American relations, a charge that today seems totally vacuous when you consider that Khrushchev was making the decision at that time to deploy missiles secretly in Cuba.

By the beginning of 1963, Ruth was approaching her due date. Since airlines generally declined to transport women later than the eighth month of pregnancy, we decided that Ruth should fly to London on British European Airways in the middle of January. For the next month, I labored as a nervous bachelor, spurred on by Bud and his wife, Christine. Finally, on January 27, 1963, Miranda was born in Norwich, not far from her grandmother's house at Hoveton-St.-John in England's East Anglia. That gave me the opportunity to leave Moscow for a few weeks to join her. I flew out a few days later on Air France bound for Warsaw and Paris. I called on my father who was then living with his third wife, Angele, at her house in Sceaux, just outside Paris.

What was unusual about this trip, however, was that I ran into Yuri Chernyakov, a deputy in the Press Department of the Foreign Ministry, at the airport before boarding. He and the Soviet delegation were on their way to Geneva for the continuing U.S.-British-Soviet nuclear-test-ban talks that had taken on new importance after the missiles of October. In the departure lounge, this tall man approached me and without prompting raised the issue of Aline Mosby's poisoning in 1961. "We were totally taken by surprise," he told me, "and we apologize to you and to United Press International." He offered no further explanation of the event, which was apparently engineered by the KGB without the knowledge of the Foreign Ministry. Normally, this taciturn man would not be speaking to such a junior member of the UPI team, and I felt uncomfortable. The conversation amounted to a friendly gesture that showed me that even a forbidding Soviet bureaucrat might harbor a real human being inside. After a few more sentences, Chernyakov walked away to the VIP area. Although we took the same flight, I did not see him again, nor did I spot him in the transit lounge in Warsaw, where we stopped briefly for refueling.

Throughout 1963, the state of Soviet-American relations had been a continually evolving topic. The missile crisis had sobered the leadership of the two superpowers, and they were now engaged in efforts to forestall any future conflict of the proportions of 1962. President Kennedy's conciliatory speech on Soviet-American relations at American University in June 1963 was so different in tone from his inaugural that it gave a boost to relations. Shortly after the crisis, the two sides began quietly working on a Moscow-Washington hotline and announced an agreement on June 20, 1963. The hotline would consist of two parts: a two-way telex line from Washington to Moscow passing through Copenhagen, Stockholm, and Helsinki. It would have a redundant component consisting of a duplex radio telegraph circuit going from Washington to Tangier to Moscow. The equipment was the same as the East German Siemens telex machines we had in our office. The Soviet "red telephone" was located in the Kremlin, while the American end was placed in the Pentagon. For the next four years, until the Middle East Six-Day War, the only thing that traveled over the line was a test message— probably of the same gravity as the quick brown fox and the lazy dog.

Meanwhile, the talks between the United States, Britain, and the Soviet Union on banning atmospheric weapon tests progressed steadily. Despite Khrushchev's complaints that verification would amount to legalized espionage, agreement was reached to monitor compliance through a complex of seismic observations and satellite reconnaissance that were termed "national technical means." For the first time since the 1947 foreign ministers' conference, an American secretary of state arrived in Moscow. Secretary

Dean Rusk participated in the final round of negotiations, while I and others cooled our heels outside the Foreign Ministry guesthouse of Spiridonovka. The agreement was finally signed on August 5, 1963, after which Rusk was invited to stay on as the personal guest of Foreign Minister Gromyko. Khrushchev even invited Rusk to fly south to Gagra on the Black Sea for an informal stay at his vacation retreat.

Suddenly, nearly a year after the Cold War's greatest crisis, relations between the United States and the Soviet Union seemed to be on an upward course. Bud Korengold flew to Gagra to record the high and mighty relaxing, Soviet style. It promised to be a unique insight into how the powerful passed the time when they were not making decisions affecting the whole world. But he got little access and recalled later, "I wound up circling around outside trying to write a lot with very little."

Despite warmth at the top, two incidents at the end of 1963 showed that the bureaucracy of hostility was still grinding. The first concerned Don Larrimore, whose Moscow assignment in 1961 had been so oddly canceled at the last moment. On the evening of August 3, 1963, *Izvestia* came out with a page 4 article charging that Don, now a UPI correspondent in Warsaw, was actually a CIA agent. "People such as he," *Izvestia* declared, "serve as the basic cells of the American espionage network. They hunt for their quarry which is later studied by others. To put it briefly, Larrimore is a recruiter." The lengthy *Izvestia* article provided many details, apparently from Soviet counterintelligence, of Don's 1956 Moscow trip. Larrimore flatly denied the spy allegations and announced that he was ready to defend himself before any court in Poland. However, UPI management insisted on recalling him. Shortly afterward, Larrimore quit UPI and went off to Positano in Italy to work on a novel. He resurfaced several years later as a writer working on a history of the Vietnam War sponsored by the U.S. Army. When I last spoke to him in 2001, he still insisted he had no connection with U.S. intelligence and asserted that the KGB had confused him with a real CIA agent named Donald E. Larimore.

The other incident of 1963 concerned an American scholar who was visiting the Soviet Union. Since Stalin's death, tourism had resumed, and the Central Intelligence Agency quietly went about asking some tourists and scholars to undertake a few low-profile jobs. The CIA had several thousand American tourists to choose from, as well as eight American professors and thirty-one graduate students who were residing and studying throughout the Soviet Union. One particularly conscientious visitor was Yale University professor Frederick C. Barghoorn, who embarked on an extensive trip to gather information on local government. He left Helsinki by train at the end of October for Leningrad and planned to return home on November 1, 1963, after visiting Tbilisi, Tashkent, Samarkand, and Alma-Ata.

On the evening of October 31, Barghoorn joined Deputy Chief of Mission Walter Stoessel Jr. at the U.S. Embassy for cocktails, then was driven by embassy car to the Metropole Hotel, where he was staying. He expected to meet Tom Orchard of the British Embassy for dinner, but the British diplomat apparently forgot the appointment; otherwise, he might have witnessed the ensuing drama. As Barghoorn got out of the car, according to his later account, an unknown person approached and thrust a roll of newspapers into his hands. No sooner had he touched the papers when four plain-clothes policemen hustled him into a waiting car and drove him off to a police station in handcuffs. He was held there for several hours before being transported to the KGB's notorious Lubyanka Prison. For nearly two weeks, the Russians remained silent. No one missed the professor until November 12, when the U.S. consul was called to the Foreign Ministry and informed of the arrest. Ambassador Foy Kohler met the next day with Deputy Foreign Minister Valerian Zorin, who strongly insisted that Barghoorn had been on an intelligence mission from the CIA. In his presentation, Zorin added three other points. He charged that Barghoorn had worked for intelligence at the U.S. Embassy in Moscow during World War II, that he had been involved in intelligence gathering after the war in Germany by interviewing Soviet refugees, and that he had fifteen photographs of rockets in his possession—inside the roll of newspapers! That evening we correspondents seized on a tiny notice in *Izvestia* buried on an inside page, headlined "Khronika" (Chronicle). Evidently, the authorities wanted to acknowledge the arrest, but in a low-key fashion.

An angry American reaction followed. Writers John Steinbeck and Edward Albee, visiting the Soviet Union, fired off protest letters to Khrushchev's son-in-law. The American Embassy announced it would boycott the celebration of thirty years of diplomatic relations at Friendship House. High American officials asserted that the incident demonstrated the need for a consular convention, and postponed the renewal of the cultural exchange agreement. Speculation spread that the real reason for the arrest was the detention on spy charges in Englewood, New Jersey, of three Soviets and an American engineer, John W. Butenko. Two of the Russians who had diplomatic immunity were released, but the third, a chauffeur named Ivanov, was detained. Barghoorn's arrest was evidently in retaliation for Ivanov.

On November 14, President Kennedy held a press conference in Washington in which he alluded to the Barghoorn case, declaring that the professor had no relationship to U.S. intelligence agencies. And the following day, Foreign Minister Andrey Gromyko summoned Walter Stoessel, the chargé d'affaires, and announced that Barghoorn would be released for humanitarian reasons. However, Gromyko insisted once again that Barghoorn had been involved in espionage, and the charges against him were never dropped.

I was on duty on the afternoon of November 16, 1963, when an embassy spokesman called about half past two to say that the Russians had decided to expel Barghoorn. Knowing this was page 1 stuff, I rushed to the telex machine to pound out an urgent story. The ever intrepid Sam Jaffe was ahead of all of us again. He had been tipped off about the release by one of his Soviet sources and withheld his scoop from us. Barghoorn was rushed to the airport by the KGB, and sent off on the evening British European Airways flight to London, which we were able to confirm by telephone. In the following days, the professor remained noticeably restrained at a press conference at Yale, never putting to rest the issue of espionage. Barghoorn died in 1991, but before his death he acknowledged to Yale historian Dr. John Bloom that in 1963 he had, indeed, been doing a favor for the CIA.

A week after the Barghoorn case, Ruth and I were marking our second anniversary in Moscow. The snow fell in lazy whorls over the capital on that November day. I was scheduled to man the desk from afternoon to midnight. It was a busy time when the Soviet Union signed a trade pact with Denmark, complained to the government of Congo about the arrest of a Soviet correspondent, and Khrushchev sounded off on a Berlin convoy crisis. Before reporting to the office, I went out to cover the opening of an American dry-cleaning plant. Moscow was very poorly equipped in those days for dry cleaning. One of the attractions of the American operation was that you did not need to adhere to the usual rule of cutting off all buttons, and you could get your clothes back the same day.

Covering dry-cleaning plants was not my idea of Cold War journalism. It took me some time to realize that the everyday problems of Russians were as fascinating to the American readership as a missile crisis. The plant was a project of Romaine Fielding Associates of Los Angeles, and the Moscow authorities agreed to buy it for $250,000 after two weeks of operation. The assignment came off as predicted. Ambassador Kohler attended the ceremony and declared the plant was "an example in the best tradition of American enterprise." After making notes and taking a few pictures, I returned to Kutuzovsky Prospekt and settled into the bureau for the night.

Darkness fell at about four o'clock that November 22, the snow turning to drizzle, wet, cold, and dismal. The evening shift started off routinely, scanning Izvestia and checking the evening TV news. Then suddenly at the end of the ten o'clock news, Moscow radio announced: "Reports by American press services say during U.S. President Kennedy's visit to Dallas an attempt was made on his life. Kennedy was seriously wounded by a firearm." I hunched over the TASS machine, absorbing new details with incredulity.

At 10:57 P.M., the radio followed up: "Just now it is officially announced, President Kennedy passed away. It is supposed the murder was done by persons of extreme right-wing elements." Moscow radio began playing Tchaikovsky's Symphonie Pathétique, normal for a dying Soviet politician, unusual for an adversary.

What would become of us next? I wondered. The first president that I had ever had any feelings for, murdered! A conspiracy? Could you believe it was a lone gunman? What would happen to the U.S. government? Within a few minutes, however, my professional cool returned, and I alerted my colleagues Danny Gilmore and Jay Axelbank, who were dining in Shapiro's apartment. I next called Malcolm Toon, the political officer of the U.S. Embassy, at home. His only comment was, "Thank you," and he hung up. The UPI office soon began filling up with members of our alliance; they stood around, glumly scanning the incoming copy. Jay Axelbank, fighting back tears, got Ambassador Kohler out of bed, who reacted by saying, "I'm devastated. I don't know what to think."

I ran over to the cavernous lobby of the Ukraine Hotel, where I found a knot of people huddled around a radio loudspeaker, curious and disturbed. A policeman dressed in a heavy blue overcoat was saying, "It doesn't matter, comrades. People come and people go, but the institutions remain the same." Most of the people I stopped on the streets shrugged their shoulders and moved on to warmer places. A garbageman, emptying trash in our apartment complex, was more thoughtful. "Is it possible?" he mumbled. "It's barbarous—Kennedy was a man of great achievement. He did so much for peace."

The three of us worked all night interviewing strangers and updating our reaction story. *Pravda*, the Communist Party daily, came out the next morning with black borders and a portrait of Kennedy on the front page. The U.S. Embassy announced that a condolence book would be set up at Ambassador Kohler's residence, and we organized ourselves to be there if Khrushchev appeared. That meant staking out Spasopeskovsky Square in the persistent rain, where the white-walled mansion was located. Finally, at half past twelve, Khrushchev showed up in a dark suit and silver tie, accompanied by Foreign Minister Gromyko, to sign the book, which was guarded by a U.S. Marine in dress-blue uniform. We learned that Khrushchev sent a message to Jacqueline Kennedy saying, "Everyone who knew him had deep respect for him and the meetings I had with him will forever be engraved in my memory." We rushed Khrushchev's words onto the wire.

When Oswald was arrested in Dallas, Bud, now a midcareer Nieman Fellow at Harvard, called UPI headquarters in New York to inform them that

Aline Mosby had interviewed Oswald in 1959 and the Moscow Bureau could provide rich background. In the confusion, New York never informed us, and the Oswald interview languished in our filing cabinets until it was resurrected for the Warren Commission investigating the assassination.

Finally, on November 25, the day of the state funeral in Washington, the superpower adversary offered an unusual tribute to the Kennedy family and the United States. Khrushchev, who had come to admire Kennedy, approved a live broadcast from Washington to be aired on Soviet television. In the 1960s, it was extremely rare that live action from the West could be seen on the national network. The funeral parade was transmitted by Telstar satellite to Western Europe's Eurovision and from there to the Soviet Union's Intervision. We watched as Kennedy's coffin was transported from the Capitol down Pennsylvania Avenue on a caisson, preceded by a black riderless horse, boots fixed backward in the stirrups, and listened to a woman announcer provide a touching commentary, unblemished by Cold War hostility. Because of improving relations after the missile crisis, the notion that Oswald might have been dispatched to kill Kennedy by the Soviet secret services was far from our minds. I wrote:

> The voice of Moscow television's woman commentator quavered, then suddenly cracked. Plainly she was choking as she spoke over the dismal tolling of the cathedral bells.
>
> "There you can see the coffin, draped with an American flag and drawn on a caisson by six white-grey horses.
>
> "Behind walks a mass of world leaders, including deputy premier Anastas Mikoyan.
>
> "Now you see inside Saint Matthews Cathedral and Richard Cardinal Cushing, dressed in red, celebrating the pontifical requiem."
>
> For the nation's millions of television viewers, this was a rare departure from the daily round of news, sports, variety, culture and propaganda.

Chapter 12

The Mystery of Mr. Khrushchev

Reporting on the unpredictable Khrushchev was one of the great challenges of Cold War journalism, requiring imagination and ingenuity. He was one of the world's most mercurial leaders, capable of rational compromise but often barely in control of his emotions as he sought to promote the forward march of communism. For politicians, diplomats, and journalists, he was a puzzle. No one could say what this powerful man really meant at any specific moment or what he might do.

Long before I went to Moscow, Khrushchev interested me. In 1956, in his famous "Secret Speech" that outlined the crimes of Stalin, Khrushchev revised Marxist-Leninist theory to admit of peaceful coexistence between capitalist and socialist states. Then in an outburst at a Polish Embassy reception later that year, he declared, "My vas zakopaem!" (We will cream you!). This statement was mistranslated as "My vas pokhoronim!" (We will bury you!) and was taken in the West as a hostile threat. What Khrushchev really meant was "We will outstrip you in our competition." Henry recognized the error and attempted to correct it, but, as journalists know, corrections never catch up with the original sensation.

Khrushchev's groundbreaking visit to the United States at the invitation of President Eisenhower in 1959 generated plenty of incidents. I heard wild stories of Khrushchev visiting a supermarket where the crush of newsmen was so great that one photographer tramped across a meat counter in a supermarket to snap a close-up. Another reportedly stepped on a tub of butter, which collapsed under his weight. I particularly admired Stu Hensley's exploit. Hensley, UPI's chief diplomatic correspondent, was always competing against his opposite number, John Hightower of the AP. They were both assigned to cover Khrushchev's trip across America, looking for diplomatic angles. On the train from Los Angeles to San Francisco the journalists got some time with Khrushchev in his carriage. As soon as it was over, they began typing up their stories, expecting to file from San Francisco when the train rolled in. Hensley told me that he was determined to beat the AP and asked a conductor where the train might slow to about twenty miles an hour. Informed of the appropriate spot, Hensley opened a train door—ah, the enthusiasm of the chase!—jumped out, and rolled down the bank unharmed. He then dashed to the nearest telephone and called UPI headquarters in New York, getting a substantial beat over his gentlemanly opponent.

Bud had his great Khrushchev scoop, too, for which he got no credit. It occurred during the first American cultural exhibit to Moscow at Sokolniki Park in August 1959. Khrushchev and his distinguished visitor, Vice President Richard Nixon, attended the exhibit together. The message of the show was that the U.S. economic system had produced a much better standard of living for Americans than the Soviet people enjoyed. Khrushchev was determined to knock down this subversive message. To cover the visit to the exhibition, the Foreign Ministry arranged for a bus to take the visiting Washington journalists to the park and bring them back downtown. Ernie Barcella of our Washington Bureau flew to Moscow especially for the occasion and was accompanied by Bud. "Fortunately, I had a ringside seat," Bud said of the event that became known as the Kitchen Debate.

> Finding myself initially on the outside rim of a half circle of officials, reporters, and photographers, I jumped the rail of one of the other rooms in the house and worked my way into the kitchen itself. There I simply sat down and took notes at the feet of Khrushchev and Nixon. At one point I became so involved that when Nixon interrupted Khrushchev in midsentence, I spontaneously spoke up and said, "Let him finish!" That made Nixon pause for a second or two, but then he went right on.
>
> The debate—if you could call it that—was at the intellectual level of two adolescents in a schoolyard poking and pointing fingers at each other and exchanging epithets of the type: "Your mother wears army shoes!" or "So's your old man!" But it became a historical event, and Nixon afterward played it for all the rough-guy propaganda value he could.

Bud took detailed notes and rushed off to the nearest two-kopek pay phone and called Henry. Meanwhile, Barcella and his competition, John

Scali of the Associated Press, got back on the bus for the tedious ride back to town. UPI's story, under Barcella's byline, reached American newspapers forty-five minutes before the AP's version. Our Washington man thus became a hero without ever putting pen to paper while the real wizard remained in obscurity. Such is the chase—exciting at the time but often of no lasting consequence.

The next year, 1960, Khrushchev made several foreign trips that yielded sensational headlines. In Paris, he stormed out of the summit conference with the United States, Britain, and France. In the autumn, Khrushchev went off to the United States, again this time to attend the fall meeting of the U.N. General Assembly. Waxing emotional during his address, he took off his shoe and banged it on the podium. Prime Minister Harold Macmillan is reputed to have interjected: "Translation please!" While the exact facts as to what happened have been disputed, the perception was that Khrushchev had acted unacceptably for a major statesman. This view persisted in years to come and fed the growing dissatisfaction of his Politburo colleagues.

In Moscow, Khrushchev tended to be a tamer figure than when he was traveling abroad. Whereas he would receive prestigious foreign journalists, he generally refused to sit for resident correspondents. The reason was that the Moscow correspondents knew too much about the local situation and were not likely to be hoodwinked by Khrushchev's charm. Nevertheless, Henry was able to obtain a formal meeting on November 14, 1957, with Khrushchev of which he was very proud. He always referred to it as "a classic, textbook interview," something that should be included in journalism textbooks.

Of course, covering Moscow was not all Khrushchev. In the 1960s, the majority of news—perhaps 75–80 percent—came from Soviet media. Since there were masses of newspapers, magazines, and literary journals, scooping up the unusual required a systematic approach. Henry organized this in an orderly way. Our translators, Arthur and Lyova, read through some ten daily Moscow newspapers every day such as *Pravda, Komsomolskaya Pravda, Izvestia,* and *Vechernaya Moskva.* When they had finished, they would turn to provincial newspapers such as *Zarya Vostoka, Turkmenistanskaya Pravda,* or *Leningradskaya Pravda,* then on to the magazines and literary journals.

Meanwhile, at Furmanova Street, Henry's wife, Ludmilla, was scouring the more exotic publications that came in from the provinces. It was through this type of sleuthing that she turned up evidence that Yuri Gagarin and Gherman Titov were part of the first cosmonaut group before they were publicly identified. We were not allowed to subscribe to more than one provincial daily newspaper and never to the evening newspapers such as

*Vechernyi Leningrad.* The reason was that the evening provincials maintained a closer relationship to their reading public than the republican newspapers and consequently were more frank about daily living conditions, which might reveal shortcomings as well as coming events.

Additionally, we cross-checked our findings with Dr. Hermann Poerzgen, Henry's old friend—who spent eleven years in Vladimir Prison during the world war—who nevertheless returned to Moscow to head the *Frankfurter Allgemeine* bureau. By the end of the morning, we would share our harvest with colleagues at Agence France Presse, our major alliance partner. The subjects that the world wanted to know about were diplomatic developments, internal Soviet politics, the quality of Russian life, scientific discoveries, and exotic items such as the Old Believers, who cut all contacts with the outside world after the Russian Revolution of 1917 and survived in Siberian forests.

By the early 1960s it was possible to have some confidential sources, who were usually connected to the KGB, the Press Department of the Foreign Ministry, TASS, or media outlets. We had no regular firsthand sources. So far as I know, we had no contacts with any leading political or scientific figures. (I believe some American academics did, however.) Everything was at arm's length. Khrushchev did have an extraordinarily gifted English-language interpreter, Viktor Sukhodrev, who worked for the Foreign Ministry. But we had difficulty contacting this amiable man, and when he appeared in public he was careful to maintain distance.

Moscow did not publish a public telephone book in those years, even though before the Russian Revolution both Moscow and Leningrad produced copious phone books. Although classified phone books existed, we had no access to them and were therefore obliged to build and maintain our own telephone files. Not that this helped much. We were forbidden by the Press Department to arrange any interviews on our own. Every interview had to be arranged through the department, which soon earned the alias the "Antipress Department."

One maneuver that helped pry out information from the system was to meet a Soviet official traveling as a spokesman for a Soviet delegation abroad or with a Soviet cultural exhibit. If one could develop a relationship with such a person, they might become useful later in Moscow. Aline Mosby encountered a young man by the name of Vladimir Krivitisky at the Brussels Fair in 1958. When she got to Moscow, he held a research job in the Foreign Ministry Press Department. He clearly liked Aline and Bud and became their "guardian angel," passing on tidbits and steering them away from trouble.

In London, Karol Thaler had a good contact named Nikolai Makarov, whom I tried to find in Moscow when I arrived but never did. Our photographer, Yuri Korolyov, had a friend at *Izvestia,* Valerii Lednev, who worked closely with Adzhubei as a deputy managing editor. Lednev would occasionally pass on to us the galleys of *Izvestia*'s front page a couple of hours before it hit the streets, thus allowing us to get a beat on a big story. Lars Bringert, a correspondent for Sweden's *Dagens Nyheter,* developed a contact at TASS who would occasionally slip him information about a coming space launch. Since Lars was a member of our alliance, we sometimes got a scoop through him. And Sam Jaffe seemed to have a wealth of mysterious sources that we could only wonder at and envy. One of them I met at a party in Sam's apartment; he was Yuri Vinogradov, a former Russian-English interpreter whom Sam befriended when he covered the United Nations.

In the months following the Cuban missile crisis, we began to hear reports that all was not well with Khrushchev. The rumors were vague, coming from Russian friends who were connected with the media and in some cases from lower-level officials. A persistent theme was that Khrushchev had behaved in an intemperate fashion at the United Nations. There were hints, too, that he was becoming increasingly impulsive, not consulting his political colleagues and undertaking fatally flawed projects, like planting corn in northern climes.

By 1962, Khrushchev did not always seem to be his old rambunctious self. He would occasionally say that he could not hold on forever to the two posts of premier and first secretary of the Communist Party. Just how much the world hung on Khrushchev's words was illustrated on the night of April 13, 1964, as he addressed a visiting Polish delegation in the Kremlin. At one point TASS stopped transmitting his speech in midsentence, and an hour-long silence ensued. Queries to TASS produced the explanation that communications *svyaz propala* (had fallen). This explanation, given in Russian, was apparently misunderstood by one German correspondent to mean that Khrushchev had "fallen dead."

At 11:53 P.M. the German news agency DPA sent out a flash stating that Khrushchev had died at 10:19 P.M. The impact was explosive. London newspapers reported Khrushchev's passing. Television in Portugal flashed Khrushchev's death. Diplomats were routed out of bed by their ministries to check the report. Like everyone else, I got an urgent callback from New York stressing the very urgent need to pin down the report one way or another. At midnight my only source was TASS. I reached a high-ranking official who gave me a firm denial in Russian that I flashed back to UPI headquarters. Within five minutes, DPA withdrew the death report, explaining it was the result of a misunderstanding. The next day I got a message from London praising me for being "as steady as the Rock of Gibraltar." DPA was not so lucky. The Foreign Ministry gave their correspondent twenty-four hours to pack up and leave, unusually harsh retribution.

Khrushchev's seventieth birthday four days later, on April 17, 1964, was an occasion to speculate again on his future. Henry wrote an analysis asserting that Khrushchev was in full control of the Kremlin that a few months later proved to be quite wrong. On September 8, 1964, Henry rewrote that original piece to read, "The mantle of power never rested more easily and securely than it does today on the shoulders of the 70-year-old coal miner Nikita Khrushchev." If anything, these pieces showed that Henry did not really have exotic sources in the Kremlin. Khrushchev's political end would come five weeks later.

At the end of September, Khrushchev departed from Moscow to spend time at his retreat at Cape Pitsunda, where he had entertained Secretary of State Dean Rusk the year before. By now Khrushchev's final overthrow on October 14 has been well described by historians. What is remarkable is that Khrushchev received a half-dozen warnings of a plot, including one reported by his son Sergei, an engineer for one of the Soviet Union's top rocket scientists. The old man, however, dismissed them all.

The launching of the world's first multipassenger spaceship, Voskhod-1, on October 12, 1964, served as a smoke screen for the hidden maneuvering in the Kremlin. As usual, Khrushchev held an enthusiastic telephone conversation from Cape Pitsunda with the cosmonauts in orbit. "I warn you," he chortled over nationwide TV, "you managed quite well with the gravity overloads during takeoff, but be ready for the overloads which we will arrange for you after you come back to earth. Then we'll meet you in Moscow with all the honors you deserve." He handed the phone reluctantly to his Presidium colleague Mikoyan, who seemed to be grabbing it away from him—and his face disappeared from TV screens forever.

We correspondents had no sources to tip us that the Communist Party Presidium (the top leadership group), under the leadership of Leonid Brezhnev, had gathered. The meeting was unannounced, and none of us chanced to pass the Kremlin to see the black limousines drive in. Increasingly irritated by Khrushchev's authoritarian behavior, they were finalizing a plan to remove him from power. Brezhnev telephoned Khrushchev at Pitsunda and summoned him back to Moscow, ostensibly to discuss urgent agricultural matters. At first, Khrushchev resisted, but finally gave in. The unexpected interruption in his vacation required him to alter a meeting with French energy minister Gaston Palewsky. He moved up his October 13 meeting with the Frenchman from 10:00 A.M. to 9:30 A.M. and broke it off after a half hour. Thus, Palewsky became the last foreign visitor to see him in power.

Once Khrushchev reached Moscow, he drove immediately to the Kremlin to face his enemies. There, speaker after speaker accused him of a laundry list of faults. His deployment of missiles to Cuba was a major topic, as well as his vast agricultural plans. He was accused of being irritable, and rude, of embarking on solutions to problems without having thought them through. By the end of the session, Khrushchev was beaten down and acknowledged some of his errors. "I am old and tired," he confided, "and I am not going to put up a fight."

None of this drama reached us, of course, but we did note something that raised questions. The Voskhod-1 flight, which had been expected to stay aloft for a week, was ordered down after only twenty-four hours. The television broadcast a puzzling conversation between the secret space chief and the cosmonaut commander, Valentin Komarov.

> CHIEF: Are you ready to proceed to the completion of that part [the descent] of the program?
> KOMAROV: The crew is ready, but we would like to prolong the flight.
> CHIEF: I read you, but we had no such agreement.
> KOMAROV: We've seen many interesting things. We would like to extend the observations.
> CHIEF: There are more things in heaven and earth, Horatio . . . We shall go, nevertheless, by the program.

Horatio? Huh? What did that mean? The Shakespearean allusion was from Hamlet: "There are more things in Heaven and Earth, Horatio, than are dreamt of in your philosophy." In retrospect, it seemed to mean: There are other considerations you don't know about, and I am not going to reveal, that are driving this decision. Nor did we guess why Khrushchev did not put in his usual call to the cosmonauts after they had landed safely.

The next day, October 14, Khrushchev again secretly returned to his accusers and told them he would accept whatever outcome they desired. The Presidium drafted a statement, announcing that he had asked to retire for reasons of health and age. Immediately following, the full Central Committee of the Communist Party convened and ratified the actions of the Presidium. Still, official silence reigned. I wrote later, "Moscow's Indian summer was at an end. Thursday, October 15, brought with it a clammy mist over the Moscow River which snakes through the city and winds under the Kremlin's ancient fortress walls. Outwardly, Moscow was quiet, just as Moscow was quiet in the eye of the storm of the Cuban missile crisis just two years ago."

On the afternoon of October 15, hints of strange happenings began to emerge. Excitement started with a telephone call that a Soviet citizen made to a London newspaper just before five in the afternoon, Moscow time. The

call was from Viktor Louis, one of a handful of Soviet citizens who were authorized to "string" for Western newspapers, in this case the *London Evening
News*. "Moscow is being decorated in preparation for welcoming the cosmonauts who come to the capital tomorrow," Louis cautiously told a
dictationist at the newspaper. "But missing from the usual portraits of
governments leaders is the well-known face of Mr. Khrushchev. Nobody
knows anything for sure, but many Russians expect either today or at the
latest tomorrow morning some explanation of a number of unusual events
now taking place." The *London Evening News* published a brief note on its
front page that afternoon titled "The Mystery of Mr. K" that rang alarm bells
around the globe.

Within minutes, the UPI Moscow Bureau was alerted to Louis's story, and
we began frantically checking our sources. We called newspaper contacts;
we telephoned the Foreign Ministry; we contacted the embassies. Nothing.
"We've got to take this seriously," Henry told us, "given the fact that this is
from Viktor. A man in his position is not going to play around with this sort
of story recklessly."

Sam Jaffe, drawing on his informants, who were amazingly more available than Henry's, outpaced us. He later acknowledged to me that he
managed to wheedle a cryptic tip from a KGB source. "Sam, someone you
know and respect is out," the source said. Sam replied, "From both positions?" Answer: "Yes." Knowing that he could be expelled for impugning
Khrushchev's authority if he was wrong, Sam contacted his New York editors with the same caution that Louis displayed earlier that afternoon. He
reached Jesse Zousmer on the ABC desk and reported, "A man I have traveled with has been demoted."

"Can I guess who it is?" asked Zousmer.

"Go ahead," Jaffe said.

"Khrushchev."

"Yes!" Jaffe replied.

Sam's scoop on this occasion was put together very much in the same
way as Henry's exclusive on Stalin's death a decade before.

As the evening wore on, Henry telephoned constantly around Moscow
for hard evidence. Experience had taught him not to jump too fast on a personnel shift. He told me later that an old Russian friend had tried to call on
him at his apartment that day to give him a beat, but he had put him off as
the day got busy. Finally, about ten that night Henry dispatched me and
Yuri Korolyov to Red Square to look at the decorations being put up for the
cosmonauts' welcome. I remember as we entered the square at ten-thirty a
huge portrait of Khrushchev hung on the Hotel Moskva. But by eleven
when we left, workmen were taking the portrait down. I quickly found a

pay phone and reported to Henry. "That's it!" he exclaimed. And within minutes—based on that sighting—he put out an urgent story announcing to the world that Khrushchev had been removed from power. Then the long wait for confirmation began.

An hour later, three minutes past midnight, the Soviet news agency, TASS, reported:

MOSCOW, October 16—Nikita Khrushchev has been released from his duties as First Secretary of the CPSU Central Committee and chairman of the Council of Ministers of the U.S.S.R. Leonid Brezhnev has been elected First Secretary of the CPSU Central Committee. Alexei Kosygin has been appointed chairman of the Council of Ministers.

It has been announced today that a plenary meeting of the CPSU Central Committee held on Wednesday October 14 considered Khrushchev's request to be relieved of his duties in view of his advanced age and deterioration of his health.

The next day, *Pravda* announced a further shakeup. My story was front-paged in the *Washington Post* on November 17:

MOSCOW, Nov. 16 (UPI)—The Soviet Communist Party leaders who ousted Nikita S. Khrushchev stripped his former deputy, his farm expert, and his son-in-law of Kremlin power today.

An official announcement said ailing Frol R. Kozlov, Khrushchev's political crown prince until felled by a stroke two years ago, was "relieved" of his place on the Party Presidium, its highest body, because of grave illness.

It said Alexei Adzhubei, the Khrushchev son-in-law and brain truster who had been fired as editor of Izvestia, has been expelled from the Central Committee for "mistakes in his work."

In the days that followed, more information leaked. A secret document was read to Communist Party cells throughout the country listing twenty-nine errors that Khrushchev had committed. Among them were charges that he engaged in "harebrained schemes" and "voluntarism." We learned of these accusations through European Communist journalists who got it from East European Communist delegations that traveled to Moscow for an explanation.

What was notable about the end of the Khrushchev era was that the transfer of power, for the first time, was bloodless. After Khrushchev disappeared from public life, Henry summed up what was on everybody's mind by telling us, "You have to think of the Presidium as a kind of 'vice-presidents' club.'

Everyone wants to be treated in a decent way, knowing what could eventually happen to them."

Naturally, story ideas began popping into our heads: How will Khrushchev be regarded now? What will his retirement be like? Will he reappear on the streets one day and make some dramatic pronouncement? Will he become an "unperson"? That term was used to describe a powerful figure who had fallen from grace and was being banished from sight. Such things happened during czarist times, too. Now, pictures of Khrushchev disappeared from bookstores; mentions of him in the press or in books were forbidden; volumes of his speeches became unavailable.

Stu Loory of the *New York Herald Tribune* added to the mystery by publishing a front-page story centered on me. He saw me jogging on Lenin Hills, where Khrushchev had stayed during the Presidium deliberations, and assumed that Henry had sent me out in disguise to scoop up news. He wove a story out of it, but there was really nothing there. I regularly jogged on Lenin Hills to relieve the tension of our busy days. UPI headquarters in New York spotted Loory's article and called for a photograph of me running near the government houses for UPI publicity purposes. On reading the New York message, Henry looked disapproving. I thought he felt upstaged, and I decided to disregard the request. Within a day, UPI New York forgot about its request.

We did get a tip, however, on March 14, 1965, that Khrushchev would show up to vote in municipal elections. I made it to the polling place in time and got him to comment, "My health is so-so, and I am living the normal life of a man on a pension." Khrushchev, accompanied by his wife, kept discreetly out of the limelight while the other luminaries voted. He would disappear for a while, but we would hear from him again.

Chapter 13

## Something Rotten

The other great challenge during my first Moscow assignment was the U.S.-Soviet space race. The Soviets had emerged the leaders of this Cold War competition with Sputnik in 1957 and continued producing spectaculars, one after another, amazing the United States. Khrushchev soon understood he had an ace up his sleeve that could frighten the West while obscuring the stunning weaknesses of the Soviet system. When he visited Washington, D.C., in 1959, he highlighted Soviet successes by presenting President Eisenhower with a metal sphere, made up of twenty-two five-cornered elements, similar to the one that his scientists had landed on the surface of the moon with their Luna-2 probe on September 14, 1959. In the ensuing years, the Russians made clear they were striving to put a man in space by launching dogs and bringing them back safely to earth. Then in 1961—that difficult first year for President Kennedy—they launched Yuri Gagarin into orbit on April 12, and Gherman Titov on August 6. These human "firsts" were supplemented by a dazzling array of space shots to photograph the dark side of the moon and to probe the surfaces of Venus and Mars.

To the world, it appeared that the Soviet Union was forging ahead. You were tempted to believe that the Russians had really succeeded in creating that "new Soviet man"—a human being content to suppress his ego for the benefit of the collective. The Soviet space program bellowed to the world that a population of new men had taken over and Russia was marching irresistibly ahead. Was it bluff? The early Soviet moon shots convinced U.S.

politicians that a technology gap had opened up, putting the United States at risk. Kennedy used the "missile gap" as a stick to beat his opponent, Richard Nixon, over the head in the election campaign of 1960. And just months after his inauguration, President Kennedy announced on May 25, 1961, the proposal to put a man on the moon "by the end of this decade." The space race between the United States and the Soviet Union had officially begun.

By the time I got to Moscow in 1961, the bureau was dealing with more than fifty space shots a year. Not all of the space shots were of first priority, of course. Some were weather or communication satellites that rated only a few paragraphs. In 1962, the Russians began their Kosmos series that masked a whole variety of purposes, from human-precursor flights to interplanetary probes and eye-in-the-sky satellites trained on U.S. military objectives. As the space race intensified, it became obvious that the program presented the Soviet leadership with a powerful propaganda advantage.

This possibility, as I observed it, was to build up achievements that could not be hidden while maintaining supercensorship on some subjects even if it spawned wild rumors, such as secret cosmonauts dying in space. Censorship imposed a heavy veil over key scientists, their places of work, the organization of the program. The Soviet media were allowed to talk about the "chief designer" or the "chief theoretician" but were careful never to identify them. They would describe in general terms only the Baikonur Cosmodrome, equivalent to the Houston spaceflight center; they identified the "State Commission" as the equivalent of NASA, releasing no details of its charter or its exact mission. The fact that the space program was joined to the military was acknowledged but not elaborated. Needless to say, the Soviet image makers assigned several Russian correspondents to write about the space program under severe restrictions. The Kremlin used TASS to make the initial launch announcement and the Novosti Press Agency to supply color, which the foreign press always wanted.

We American correspondents were never allowed to witness a launch, visit any scientific institute involved in the program, or talk to any cosmonaut, or any scientist, or any administrator other than at carefully controlled press conferences. One of the tricks that the propagandists of the Communist Party Central Committee seized upon was to break big news over the English TASS wire monitored in London by Western news agencies. Breaking news first in London forced Western media to hew closely to the Soviet releases and thereby set the tone of all subsequent reporting. An hour might go by before our London Bureau could alert us in Moscow that a new ship was circling the earth, and only then could we weigh in with background and interpretation.

It would have been helpful if we, in Moscow, had a good knowledge of physics and astronomy as well as the rich history of Russian rocketry going back to Konstantin Tsiolkovsky in the late nineteenth century. Unfortunately, none of us had a scientific background. Henry's expertise was in history, law, and diplomacy. Bud Korengold was the superb reporter, a hard-driving cultivator of sources, with a nose for news. He left in 1963, and his slot was filled on a permanent basis by Jay Axelbank, a facile writer who could spin a catchy lead out of cobwebs in a New York minute. As for myself, I had a nascent interest in science. When I was twelve, Mother gave me a blue box called Chemistry Set No. 1 for Christmas. My familiarity with chemistry increased when I began developing and printing film. In high school, I was interested in plane and spherical geometry and learned how to calculate distances between remote points using triangulation and the Pythagorean theorem.

Writing about what you don't know directly but can figure out by "triangulation" excited me. You could "triangulate" the Soviet space program by close reading of the national press, comparing what you found with the more open American sources, chatting with science attachés of Western embassies, and keeping your ears and eyes open for unexpected tidbits. When Henry's wife, Ludmilla, identified Yuri Gagarin and Gherman Titov as the first cosmonauts-to-be, the story went out under Henry's byline, leading people to believe that Henry Shapiro possessed secret sources deep inside the Kremlin.

As far as I have been able to determine, however, Henry had no "Deep Throat"—no extraordinarily well-informed official in the Kremlin or the space program. Interestingly, he did have a potential connection to a very important space scientist. A cousin of Henry's wife, Dr. Yuri A. Pobedonostsev, was one of the inventors of the Katyusha rockets, an expert on rocket fuels, and a Stalin Prize winner. Stalin had once asked him to head the rocket and space program after World War II. Years later, Ludmilla told me that Pobedonostsev declined the post, saying that he was a poor administrator and, if named, the program would fall apart. Pobedonostsev never passed on any tips to Henry, Ludmilla added. To do so would have been to violate the laws on state secrets with all their harsh consequences and would have made Henry vulnerable to charges of espionage. "Everyone attributed Henry's scoops to sources in the Kremlin," Ludmilla told me after Henry died in 1991. "People sometimes called him an agent of the Kremlin. But that was not true. He knew the system so well that microscopic changes in articles or announcements he could interpret correctly, something a person who was less familiar might not."

To illustrate his cunning, she told me how Henry wangled a onetime connection with Premier Nikolay Bulganin and Khrushchev when they visited

England in the spring of 1956. Henry had gone from the UP London Bureau to the Savoy Hotel, where the delegation was staying, and began chatting in Russian with members of the delegation. The receptionist mistook Henry for one of the Soviet guests and assigned him a room. That gave Henry an unusual opportunity to mingle with members of the Soviet delegation and get tips of coming events. Henry's Western colleagues protested madly, but to no avail.

Some years after the Soviet Union dissolved, I asked former KGB general Oleg Kalugin how he recalled Henry's relations with Soviet officials. He replied, "Relations were very friendly. They had a mutual liking and gave each other assistance. They briefed each other on what was going on. The Russians used him as a channel of information on important matters. That doesn't in any way diminish his integrity as a journalist." Kalugin added that the KGB had a code name for Henry. "But that was standard. We probably also had one for you, too," Kalugin told me.

Kalugin's remarks were borne out by what I personally observed. Henry had the respect of both high Soviet and American officials. During the world war, he developed excellent relations with Averell Harriman, then American ambassador to Moscow, and enjoyed steady entrée to the U.S. Embassy. On trips to Washington, he was occasionally received by presidents from Roosevelt to Kennedy, always eager for his views. Visiting personalities always wanted to call on him. On Sunday nights, he often played poker with senior American officials. I never saw any evidence that they suspected him of disloyalty. Furthermore, I learned that he passed on to the U.S. Embassy copies of *Sobraniye Postanovleniya*, a collection of official decrees, which ended up in the State Department library in Washington. Correspondents were allowed to receive this periodical for journalistic purposes, but the embassy, in those years, was not.

An unusual event on November 3, 1963, helped us advance our efforts at uncovering the space program. This was a wedding reception that Nikita Khrushchev gave in honor of Valentina Tereshkova, the first woman in space. Tereshkova, who flew in Vostok-6 in 1963, had fallen in love with fellow cosmonaut Andrian Nikolayev and married him. Khrushchev threw a reception in their honor, and invited a long list of space administrators, scientists, and engineers. It was also a way of giving recognition to the secret scientists who labored unnoticed by the general public, and unknown to many of their own colleagues. The guest list included representatives of AP, UPI, and a few prominent Western newspapers. At the party, the mysterious chief constructor and chief constructor of rocket engine systems were present and their identities leaked. Our colleague Ted Shabad identified the chief constructor as Sergei P. Korolyov and Valentin P. Glushko as one of the prominent missile engineers in the November 11, 1963, issue of the *New York Times*.

We duly noted these names, and added them to our files. Bud liked to call this process "saving string." By the summer of 1964, our efforts at building up the files began to pay off. I was able to pen a forward-looking article for our top European editor, Paul Allerup. It began this way:

> MOSCOW (UPI)—Will the Soviet Union give man his first chance to leave an orbiting space ship next year and take a brief walk in the cosmos?
>
> Western experts say this is a possibility if the Soviet Union succeeds in linking two orbiting space ships in 1965.
>
> Such a link-up also may involve a plan for a space-suited cosmonaut to climb briefly outside his vessel—orbiting at close to 17,000 miles an hour—to check on the docking operation.

The rendezvous concept sprang from the double flights of Vostok-3 and Vostok-4. These two spaceships piloted by Andrian Nikolayev and Pavel Popovich, respectively, were launched sequentially and chased each other in orbit in August 1962. The experiment was repeated in 1963 with the flights of Valery Bykovsky aboard Vostok-5 and Tereshkova on Vostok-6. The spaceships came close to each other, as if testing the dynamics of approaching and docking. Pseudonymous authors occasionally wrote articles that hinted that the docking of spaceships in flight would be the first step toward building an orbiting space station.

In mid-March 1965, Henry came into the office in great excitement. The Soviets, he told us, were probably going to launch a spectacular. A cosmonaut, he reported, would emerge from the ship into open space while his companion remained inside. It was not at all clear to us how the cosmonaut would do this. Henry talked about the cosmonaut being enclosed in a special capsule, possibly a minispaceship. Henry was not able to elaborate further, so in writing his advance story, I avoided specific details and focused on a coming "spectacular." How did Henry find out about this specific launch? By custom, we never inquired about each other's sources, but my guess is that Henry had friends in TASS who would occasionally slip him some of the advance details on which they had been briefed.

During the day of March 17 there were indications from abroad that something was brewing. A UPI correspondent in West Germany questioned Dr. Heinz Kaminsky of the Institute for Satellite and Space Research at Bochum. He reported that the launch "could come within the next 24 hours or within the next eight days." Breaking Soviet secrecy was becoming something of a

sport, and even Soviet journalists occasionally engaged in it. That evening a
Moscow television announcer let slip a hint, saying, "Now, a new space spectacular is expected, and who knows, it might come tomorrow." The launch
seemed timed to draw attention away from the impending American Gem-
ini launch that would put two U.S. astronauts into a three-revolution orbit.
By evening, Henry tipped me that the launch was now imminent, and I put
out a cautiously worded story aimed at U.S. morning newspapers of March
18. It began:

> 1st Night Lead Space
> By Henry Shapiro
> MOSCOW (UPI)—The launching of a new Soviet manned space spectac-
> ular can be expected within the next few days, probably before the end of
> the week, usually reliable sources said today.

The launch finally came at ten o'clock the next morning. Launches of
manned vehicles were never televised live in case something went wrong,
and we learned of it only when officially announced by TASS. In this case,
TASS released the news about a half hour after launch when it was clear that
all had gone well: "The spaceship-satellite Voskhod-2, manned by a crew
consisting of Pilot-Cosmonaut Col. Pavel Ivanovich Belyayev, commander
of the ship, and Pilot-Cosmonaut Col. Alexei Arkhipovich Leonov, co-pilot,
was launched into earth orbit by a powerful booster rocket at 10 A.M.
Moscow time on March 18, 1965, in the Soviet Union."

I refashioned the TASS announcement, and my new lead cleared the telex
machine at 10:50 A.M. (2:50 A.M. in the eastern United States). Henry phoned
in additional details from his sources, which I inserted: "Scientific sources
said during the flight one of the two cosmonauts will emerge from the space
ship in a special observation capsule." This wording gave the impression
that, indeed, the capsule would be some kind of minispaceship. The flight
was expected to last twenty-four hours. We phoned our contacts at the U.S.
Embassy, who speculated that if a cosmonaut did emerge into the vacuum
of open space, it would probably be related to an eventual linkup. That
would be a crucial operation for building a permanent orbiting space station from parts launched into orbit individually. I inserted another line: "If
a cosmonaut emerges in a 'space capsule' it will be important for a link-up,
western observers say."

About two hours later, Moscow television signaled that an important announcement was coming that would be broadcast nationally and across
Eastern Europe. Shortly after one o'clock, Moscow TV began rolling videotape. We watched in amazement as Alexei Leonov, fitted out in a bulky

space suit with an oxygen tank on his back, slowly emerged from the orbiting ship and floated away on a lifeline. The "observation capsule" that caused so much confusion was nothing more than a flexible space suit. Leonov spent a total of about twenty minutes in space, including long minutes trying to free himself from the ship and then trying to reenter it. In all, Moscow television presented about three minutes of videotape that was broadcast two hours after Leonov's completed space walk. TV broadcast the scene several more times during the day. At the request of our New York headquarters, I described the scene:

> TV viewers saw this: a visored helmet emerged from a hatch and a man wriggled out to his waist.
> He did it carefully, as if he was afraid of tearing his protective suit and losing the artificial atmosphere he carried within him.
> For the first 10 minutes he held on to the hand-rail around the circular hatch, then he balanced on his stomach, his special air-conditioning tanks strapped on his back.
> And then came the moment.
> With a flick of his silvery-gloved hand, Leonov pushed himself away . . . five, ten, fifteen feet and more.
> If the life-line had broken now he would never have returned. He would have drifted away from the ship, but still orbiting around the earth.
> He looked like an unborn baby, floating at the end of an umbilical cord in a hostile fluid.
> Scientists said the feat was strictly calculated. They said the Soviet program undertakes no spectacular risks . . . sets only moderate tasks.

Throughout the day TASS issued several announcements about the progress of the flight. The news agency reported that the spaceship would disappear from Soviet visibility from the eighth to eleventh orbit. I felt safe closing the bureau overnight, never anticipating the drama that was awaiting us when the ship was due over Soviet space at 4:14 A.M.

In the morning, anonymous flight managers announced that the flight was being extended by one extra orbit, but gave no explanation. This meant that the craft should land about twenty-five and a half hours after its initial launch time, or around 11:30 A.M. a.m. Moscow time (3:30 in the eastern United States). I stood at the ready, because bringing the flight to a successful conclusion was a critical part of space coverage. London was predictably anxious because of the one-orbit extension and began pressing to learn when touchdown would occur. Henry sent a message from his apartment shortly after eleven saying, "Please sit tight. Something expected momentarily."

Apparently, his source was telling him that reentry had started. Shortly after noon, Henry phoned me from home with the news that the cosmonauts had returned to earth safely, and I put out an urgent story based on his "informed sources."

London, however, was not satisfied. The editors demanded more details to ensure the credibility of our report. Henry asked me to send another message to London Bureau manager Danny Gilmore: "Regret unable to tell you the source." Two hours later, Gilmore sent another query. Henry replied this time, "Appreciate anxiety and we too on pins and needles. Expect announcement momentarily." But there was no announcement. Meanwhile, Don MacKay, the European radio manager in London, asked for an audio spot. I telexed back: "If want, put call through and I'll pick up if possible, but tensest now awaiting official announcement."

Usually, TASS would report the safe return within an hour, but on this occasion three hours had gone by with no news. Henry showed up unannounced at the office and retired to his back room to work the phones. We fidgeted, fearing some last-minute catastrophe. "The worst thing," Henry quipped as we waited, "is the scoop which stays exclusive." Finally, after a wait of nearly five hours, Moscow TV and radio reported:

On March 19 at 12:02 P.M. Moscow time the spaceship Voskhod-2, manned by a crew consisting of Colonel Pavel Ivanovich Belyayev, commander of the ship, and Lieutenant Colonel Alexei Arkhipovich Leonov, copilot, landed safely in the vicinity of the city of Perm.

The landing was made by the ship's commander, Colonel Belyayev, using a manual control system.

Comrades Belyayev and Leonov feel well.

The program for scientific research was completely fulfilled. During the flight a complex scientific-technical experiment was successfully carried out on the excursion into space by a cosmonaut in a special space suit with an autonomous life-sustaining system, opening a new stage in the mastery of space by mankind.

That statement grossly minimized the difficulties the crew had encountered, which we learned about only later. The phrase "using a manual control system" sounded suspicious. London began second-guessing us, asserting that something must have gone wrong and we should dig out the details. The fact that the craft put down some fifteen hundred miles off course in the *taiga*, the forest area around Perm in Siberia, and actually landed between two giant fir trees certainly suggested problems. The cosmonauts had reported their landing by radio. This news had reached editors at Moscow radio and television within a quarter of an hour, thus providing the basis for Henry's scoop. But the rescue helicopter did not arrive on the scene for two and a half hours and was unable to land because of deep snow. Conservative space officials did not want to put out an official announcement until they had thoroughly assured themselves the cosmonauts were safe.

The next day, March 20, official sources revealed that it took some four hours for local hunters and a doctor to reach the impromptu landing site. The hunters treated the cosmonauts to some refreshments in a lean-to, then made their way to a hunting lodge for the night. Space officials, operating under both civilian and military censorship, were not authorized to release negative details. Only years later did it become known that Korolyov extended the mission by one full orbit when ground control discovered the automatic landing system had failed. This is what required Belyayev to guide the ship down manually. Equally serious, Leonov's flexible space suit expanded like a balloon once he entered the vacuum of space, and he was forced to reduce its bulk by depressurizing so he could crawl through the airlock into the safety of the spaceship.

The London Bureau was pleased with our performance on this story, and both Allerup and Gilmore messaged congratulations. Henry replied graciously this time: "Multithanks and following local practice reciprocal cheers for the applauders. Happy testify Nick's trooper like work and immense contribution with only two of us on deck."

The two cosmonauts next appeared briefly on March 21 at Perm Airport as they traveled back to the Baikonur Cosmodrome. Leonov told the television cameras, "I did not experience fear, only the sense of the infinite expanse and depth of the universe. I could see everything very clearly. Then I constantly felt the presence of people on earth and the presence of the ship's commander." The following day more details of the landing leaked out during a press conference at Baikonur, but Belyayev sought to tamp down suggestions of danger. "Everything functioned irreproachably," he declared, amply illustrating that paradox of censorship that untruths, after they become known, undermine all credibility.

On March 23, Communist leader Leonid Brezhnev and his colleagues led a traditional Red Square welcome for Leonov and Belyayev. I handled the story from touchdown at Vnukovo Airport to windup on Red Square. For four hours without stop, I composed and pounded out running copy, reloading twice with new developments. My last lead moved easily from the triumph in Red Square to an angle likely to catch the eye of American editors:

bulletin

3rd lead space

moscow, march 23 (upi)—communist party chief leonid i. brezhnev, at a mass welcome-home rally for russia's two new cosmonauts, announced today soviet volunteers are ready to fight for north vietnam.

brezhnev converted the red square meeting into a major denunciation of u.s. policies as cosmonauts alexei leonov and pavel belyayev stood quietly beside him.

"the soviet union is already taking the necessary measures for aiding in strengthening the defense potential of the democratic republic of vietnam," he said to the wild cheers of thousands.

further, he said, soviet citizens "are expressing their readiness to take part in the struggle of the vietnamese people for freedom and independence."

(more) (nd-hs) d1536

Looking over those yellowing "takes," I am proud of the way I assembled the coverage from television and Henry's phoned-in reports. I saved the dispatches, thinking they would help get me a serious job with a serious newspaper sometime in the future. Today I realize the only thing the copy proved was that I could compose as fast as a telex machine could run. That was a good skill to have because in Washington, where I was soon to begin reporting, dictating finished copy off the cuff after a major press conference was de rigueur.

About six months later, on January 14, 1966, tragedy hit the Soviet space program. *Pravda* announced in a brief obituary that Sergei P. Korolyov had suddenly died. His identity as the chief constructor was now officially confirmed. A few days later he was buried with full honors under the Kremlin wall behind the Lenin Mausoleum. It turned out that Korolyov had been one of the early rocket enthusiasts of the 1920s and as a young man had even met with Konstantin Tsiolkovsky, a self-taught scientist who died in 1935 and is now universally regarded as the grandfather of interplanetary exploration in Russia. In the 1930s, Korolyov ran into serious trouble during the Stalinist purges when his colleague Valentin Glushko denounced him, under duress, for having illicit ties with German rocket scientists. Korolyov was arrested and sent to work in the Kolyma labor camp, where he endured inhuman conditions in the far North. When World War II broke out, he was recalled with other prisoners to work in an aerospace design bureau run by the secret police. After the war, he was called on by Stalin to take charge of the Soviet rocket program. A man of iron will, Korolyov managed to push the bureaucracy toward developing long-range, multistage missiles that could be used for both military and civilian purposes. Throughout the

1950s and into the 1960s, it was Korolyov who conceived and administered a program to use multiengine, multistage missiles to reach the moon, Mars, and Venus, and eventually to carry men and women into orbit.

According to family members and colleagues, Korolyov worked unceasingly, paying little attention to his health. From injuries he suffered at Kolyma, he lost teeth and injured his jaw so that he could not fully open his mouth. He suffered a heart ailment, and in his last years he developed colon polyps. On January 14, he checked into the Kremlin hospital to have the polyps removed. The minister of health, Boris Petrovsky, an accomplished surgeon, decided to undertake this relatively simple operation himself. But in removing the polyps, Petrovsky discovered that he had misdiagnosed the extent of Korolyov's condition, and massive cancer had invaded the abdominal area. His choice was to complete the polyp removal and schedule a more invasive procedure for later. Instead, he continued working, despite the misgivings of the anesthesiologist. Suddenly, he was faced with massive hemorrhaging that he could not stop. Out of desperation, he summoned his archrival, Professor A. Vishnevsky. "Wash up," he said when Vishnevsky arrived, "and help me." Vishnevsky quickly examined the patient and left almost immediately, declaring, "I don't operate on corpses." Korolyov died on Petrovsky's operating table.

In the closed environment of the Soviet Union, such details were kept from the Soviet public. Only thirteen years later did the true story leak through an article by an immigrant doctor, Vladimir Golyakhovsky, published in the Russian émigré newspaper *Novoe Russkoye Slovo* on October 21, 1979. Such delayed disclosure spawned all sorts of rumors detrimental to Soviet prestige.

It also promoted the "we-they" mentality of the Cold War: we are open, reasonably honest with transparent motives; they are secretive, devious and probably covering up evil intentions. Those of us who lived in Moscow in the long term easily fell into "we-they" suspicions. Frankly, we cultivated the notion that there was something abnormal about the Soviet Union. "They can put men in space, but they can't build a reliable elevator," we joked. Some even adapted the Shakespearean line, "There's something rotten in the state of Denmark." Looking back on those days, I would say there were at least three negative elements about the Soviet Union that weighed heavily on us: heavy militarization of the economy deprived citizens of consumer goods; the notion of building a new, more just society was fading fast; and, finally, fear and paranoia were holding Soviet society together.

One of the most obvious failings of the unbalanced economy was the grain failure of 1963. In the nineteenth century Russia was an exporter of grain, and the black earth region of the Ukraine was often called the "breadbasket of

Europe." Collectivization of the agriculture, which Stalin ordered at enormous cost, had not made Soviet farms either efficient or productive. In 1963, the grain harvest was so bad that Moscow was forced to buy massive amounts of wheat from Canada and the United States. In Moscow and other cities, bread was rationed. Pea flour was substituted for white and brown flour, making for coarse, tasteless loaves. People lined up for them, I among them.

From time to time, I would speak with embassy political officer Richard Davies, who was happy to treat me like a student studying an authoritarian government. He taught me that the nation of 270 million was run by a minority political party that listed 18 million members. These 18 million elected a congress every five years of about 5,000 members, which elected a central committee of about 500 members. The Central Committee produced the policy-making Politburo (under Khrushchev it was called the Presidium) of about 15 members and the Secretariat of about 10 members to execute political decisions. "When you look at the Soviet economy you cannot help but see that they are putting major effort into guns and not into butter," Davies said. "Eighty percent of the economy goes into military in one way or another. They really don't give a damn about the consumer."

There were plenty of examples of government disdain for the citizen. The most obvious was the poor quality of goods and the billions of dollars of shoes that had been warehoused because they could find no buyers. Food displays in Moscow stores were pathetic in their variety and assortment. Muscovites willingly conceded that the many types of sausages available before the Second World War had now declined to one or two sorts. Availability in provincial cities was worse. On domestic Aeroflot flights, the pilots and crew were ostentatiously served their meals before the passengers, with the aroma of hot food wafting through the cabin. The crew, after all, were working, whereas the passengers were considered freeloaders.

If you examined your apartment closely, you would find sloppy workmanship everywhere. There were hardly any correct right angles. Every joint was slightly off. Sometimes the floors of different rooms were on different levels. I was struck by how shoddy Soviet brickwork was, especially compared to the eighteenth- and nineteenth-century brickwork visible in London. It didn't take much guesswork to realize why your Soviet staff was always interested in knowing when your next trip abroad would be. That would be an opportunity for them to ask for presents—perfume or, better still, long winter tights for women, heavy parkas for men.

Undoubtedly, one of the Soviet leadership's great concerns was youth. Over the decades, they had marshaled young people into youth organizations that had the double purpose of producing a cheap labor force and pro-

moting suitable candidates for the Communist Party. Small children became "Octobrists," junior schoolchildren became "Pioneers," and high
school students became members of the Communist Youth League, or Kom-
somol, which served as a pool for replenishing party cadres.

By the mid-1960s, it was clear that young people were aching with dissatisfaction. The creation of the Moscow youth café Aelita was one bureaucratic attempt to find a way to keep young people off the streets. I once
picked up a young woman on the road from Vnukovo Airport, and all she
wanted to talk about was the latest fashions in the West. On a trip to
Leningrad, Ruth spotted a fashion magazine that featured drawings of
models who were dead ringers for the chic Jacqueline Kennedy. When we
would comment on this consumer hunger, Henry would recall the fervor
for building communism in the 1930s. But he noted that the builders had yet
to see results in their lifetime. If you scratched a bit, you could see that the
1960s generation doubted that it was going to have the things Khrushchev
talked about—an apartment for every family, good health care, affluence in
the stores, "a chicken in every pot."

On June 7, 1963, Henry wrote a "curtain raiser" on a Central Committee
meeting beginning June 18, 1963. "Their goal," he wrote, " will be to rekin-
dle the revolution and the moral spirit of the 1917 Bolshevik Revolution in
a country they fear has started to grow fat, happy and complacent with success. In the 46 years since the czars were overthrown in Russia, the U.S.S.R.
has gradually changed from a nation of revolutionaries willing to fight and
die for their beliefs to what could almost be called a society of bourgeois,
middle class communists." Needless to say, neither that party meeting nor
any other succeeded.

Fear was also an important part of life in Moscow and much of the Soviet
Union in the 1960s. Paranoia particularly affected foreign correspondents.
We sometimes learned that one of our Soviet staff had been called to a KGB
office and questioned about us. Although such conversations might begin
with routine matters such as whether the employees were getting fair treatment, not infrequently questions turned elsewhere. Were the bourgeois employers anti-Soviet? What seemed to interest them? What stories was
*Gospodin* (the prerevolutionary word for "Mister") working on? What tasks
did he assign? Would those tasks blacken the image of the Soviet Union?

There were some unsettling abuses by the KGB. One of the most sensational incidents involved a technician who was sent to Moscow to check for
"bugs" in the West German Embassy. He was something of a trickster.
When he found a hidden microphone, he would send a high-voltage charge
through it to the other end, causing a severe shock in the ears of the monitor. In September 1964, we learned that a West German technician was

flown suddenly out of the country. No one in the West German Embassy would reveal the details. Years later, we discovered that KGB agents injected technician Horst Schwirkmann with mustard gas in the legs as he stood in a church at Zagorsk.

It was hard for us to judge to what extent such paranoia existed within the Russian population. There were severe barriers preventing us from getting to know even a few of the millions of citizens who surrounded us. We got hints that the KGB was watching who consorted with whom. I remember trying to make contact with Russian skiers at the country retreat Peredelkino one winter, but no sooner did I open my mouth than they fled. Similarly, when I fell into conversation with a Russian woman at the Chekhov Museum in Moscow, she quickly declined my offer to meet again. "Not the right moment for that," she said and scurried off. One brave young boy I encountered would call me at the office, and then suddenly stopped and disappeared from view. In the course of my first Moscow assignment, Ruth and I were able to make only two Russian friends outside the office. One was Leonid Kogan, a freelancer for Radio Moscow, who on occasion invited us out to his room in the country after wheedling permission from his bosses. The other was Yelena (Lena) Yurieva, a Russian-English translator for the Japanese newspaper *Mainichi* who later got a rare accreditation from the Foreign Ministry to string for the Women's News Service and the Religious News Service in the United States.

By the spring of 1965, I had worked for three and a half years in the Moscow Bureau and was beginning to tire. I had been in Europe since 1957, and it seemed to me that the time had come to go home. At the beginning of the year, I began putting out feelers, first to the *New York Times* and later to the *Washington Post*. I didn't get very far with the *Times*, but in the late spring Russell J. Wiggins, the executive editor of the *Washington Post*, arrived in Moscow, and I made my pitch to him. Meantime, UPI offered me a spot on the London general desk, and in mid-May 1965, Ruth, Miranda, and I flew westward for what we thought was going to be pleasant family life in England.

Chapter 14

Whose Side Are You On?

In London I was awarded banker's hours and a 40 percent salary increase from $100 to $140 a week in recognition of hard work in Moscow. We bought a run-down Georgian house on Gibson Square in Islington for the equivalent of fifteen thousand dollars (five thousand pounds) and began remodeling it. I would arrive at Bouverie Street about ten in the morning and work until six, editing international copy. Compared to Moscow, the setting in London was luxurious and the workweek had dwindled from six days to five.

By July, however, word came from foreign editor Phil Foisie that the *Washington Post* was welcoming me back and offering a job on the foreign desk in September. I grabbed the opportunity while agonizing over how to resign from UPI. It was going to be difficult. I walked into Paul Allerup's office and explained the situation with tears in my eyes. I was remembering the good times, suppressing my frustration over the "worst company to work for." He was not impressed. He asked me to name my last day so I could be swiftly replaced. Crestfallen, I slunk out of his office.

In September, I flew to Boston for a few days in New England, then took the overnight train to Washington. Reporting to work at the *Post* filled me with enthusiasm. I was assigned by Phil Foisie to work under the supervision of assistant foreign editor Anthony Astrachan, who seemed to know everything, especially how to bargain for better play of foreign stories in the newspaper. Internal newspaper politics was something completely new to

me. I soon learned that the significance of a story and its play was never obvious, and that its final display and headline in the pages were the result of
considerable horse-trading. The desk work was not something that I took
to naturally. I felt much more comfortable in the role of reporter, talking to
people, thinking up angles, uncovering facts, and fashioning them into
readable stories. When I broke my left arm by tripping over a dog while
jogging, Foisie and Astrachan assigned me to the copy desk for extra practice in writing headlines. They did not bother to explain that they were unhappy with my work, and I did not catch the hint. Under the scrutiny of
taciturn editors who had served decades on the copy desk, I scribbled with
my right hand, tried to catch mistakes, attempted to size stories to specified
lengths. I found no joy in this technical work, and I was not good at it. I
came to hate this nighttime world of ink-stained wretches, far, far from the
Cold War.

Toward the end of December, Ben Gilbert, now a deputy managing editor, called me to his office. I thought I was going to hear good news. But to
my astonishment, Gilbert began, "Your work on the foreign desk has not
been satisfactory. You don't have the skills that we need in a deskman. There
really is no future for you here." He paused while I absorbed the shock, then
resumed, "Given that we have known you since you were a copyboy, we are
not going to throw you out tomorrow. But you should begin thinking about
your next move. We'll give you time and some help. We can arrange for you
to go to New York and have an interview with the folks at *Newsweek*. Maybe
they could find a place for you."

I was stunned, especially since this happened just days before Christmas. We had been planning for Ruth's mother, Molly, to join us in Washington for the year-end celebrations. A few days later, Ben Bradlee, the
*Post*'s hard-charging editor, called me to his office and asked for my letter
of resignation. I complied, but also demanded the full dismissal pay that I
was entitled to. The episode embittered me. My enthusiasm turned to
anger. I continued as best I could—determined, rebellious, withdrawn. I
traveled to New York for a fruitless interview with *Newsweek* and spent
much time thinking of alternatives . . . maybe postgraduate work at the
London School of Economics, maybe living in our house in London, maybe
work as a stringer for the *New York Herald Tribune* in Europe, maybe even
going back to UPI.

In August 1966, I got a call from Roger Tatarian, now managing editor of
UPI, responding to my appeal for help. He offered me a place in the Washington Bureau, and I crawled back. Bureau manager Grant Dillman assigned me to the general desk under the direction of day editor William
Umstead. The atmosphere in the Washington office once again proved that

the company hired "only the nicest people." Bill Umstead, whom I soon began calling "Uncle Bill," took me under his wing. We lunched frequently together at Sholl's Colonial Cafeteria, a dollar-a-lunch joint near McPherson Square, and he stimulated me with tales from American politics and history.

After six months on the desk, bureau manager Dillman summoned me in March 1967. "Go over to the State Department and help out Stu Hensley," he said matter-of-factly. "Don May is quitting." Changes in these key positions did not seem to trouble Dillman much; there were always plenty of people wanting to move up. Don May, Hensley's number two, had decided to leave for the Center for Defense Information and presumably a better salary. While on the desk, I had conversed with him often by phone and, through him, built up my fantasies about the glorious world of diplomacy that I lusted after. I learned much, much later that Dillman was acting on a Tatarian suggestion that I might one day become Moscow Bureau chief, and it would be good if I got some domestic experience covering foreign affairs.

During the Cold War, the State Department was a prestige assignment, and the "regulars" who covered this bureaucracy at Twenty-second and C Streets, Northwest, were reputed to be among Washington's best. Leading the regulars were two titans, referred to by diplomats as "Hensley and Hightower." The two names had a ring to them that suggested some kind of top-drawer firm specializing in diplomatic reportage. They were, more precisely, my UPI colleague Stewart Hensley and John Hightower of the Associated Press. Hensley had graduated in journalism from the University of Missouri in 1934 and got his start with newspapers in New Mexico and Texas. In 1941, he joined the U.S. government's foreign-radio monitoring service as a news editor but jumped at the chance to become a war correspondent in 1944 by joining United Press at age thirty-one. In early 1945, he was dispatched to the China-Burma-India theater and worked out of New Delhi. At war's end, he was reassigned to Washington but sent back temporarily to India to recover one hundred thousand dollars in arrears from the Indian government. When he succeeded doing what many thought impossible, he returned to D.C. to write dispatches for UP's Asian clients.

Even before he was named chief diplomatic correspondent in 1958, he had made a name for himself through grit and imagination. In 1951, he obtained the terms of the Japanese peace treaty hours before they were made public at the conference in San Francisco. His prowess in the diplomatic world led United Press to assign him regularly with White House correspondent Merriman Smith to cover all of the president's overseas forays. In a trip to Chile, the UP duo gave running coverage of President Eisenhower's motorcade through Santiago, soundly beating the AP. They did this by outfitting "Smitty" in the press car with a walkie-talkie connection to

Hensley on top of a high-rise, who dictated to New York on an open phone line.

Stu's AP competitor was no less impressive. John Murmann Hightower, a graduate of the University of Tennessee, became a reporter for the *Knoxville News-Sentinel* before joining the Associated Press in 1933. He came to Washington in 1936 and was assigned during World War II years to the Navy Department. He began covering the State Department regularly in 1944 and attended all the major international conferences until his retirement in 1971. Hensley and Hightower looked for all the world like diplomats themselves. As was common for newsmen in those days, they dressed like the people they were covering: well-tailored gray suits, cuff links, elegant watches. They knew the nuances of diplomatic lingo such as "frank discussions" (meaning sharp and usually fruitless exchanges) as well as the purposeful omissions. They were both reassuring and threatening to diplomats. High officials could count on them to get the story right, but they worried that the two would unmask any inept dissembling. "You damn well better get your story straight before you face Hensley and Hightower," they would say.

I had first encountered Stu in 1958 when Tatarian got me a summer job taking dictation in the Washington Bureau. Stu, six feet two, with horn-rim glasses, was a child of the Depression and would hold on to his job for life. He was gentle with UP deskmen, even when they woke him up in the middle of the night, but tough on quavering officials. He knew how to cajole and to provoke. I remember him declaring disingenuously at a press conference, "I'm just a country boy from Colorado, and I don't get what you are saying!" He once insulted a secretary of state by asserting, "Where I come from that statement would be called a lie."

When I was still on the general desk, I once filled in for Hensley at a late-night briefing with Secretary of State Dean Rusk. Returning from an overseas trip, Rusk summoned reporters to his office late one Sunday night. I remember nothing of that meeting, but I'll always recall the thrill of being taken seriously by America's top diplomat. That night I sensed that this son of a Russian immigrant was moving out of the mongrel's doghouse and into mainstream America—and not just the mainstream, but into the inner circle of an elite group of Washington journalists.

Going to cover the State Department in the mid-1960s was like entering the Foreign Service itself. Not everybody took to the beat easily because there was no action to observe, no heated public debates, no screeching takeoffs of fighter planes, only rambling conversations with anonymous officials. Security for us was minimal. Regulars got passes to park in the department's basement with high-ranking officials. We had the run of the building; we ate with country desk officers in the department cafeteria, knocked on the doors of any office, telephoned officials from our cubicles in the press room, buttered up their secretaries with compliments and presents so we could reach taciturn officials in extremis. We had free access to the seventh floor, where secretaries of state maintained their elaborate offices decorated with antiques dating back to the founding of the Republic.

The official spokesman, Bob McCloskey, held one briefing every day at noon and showed up, too, on Saturday mornings. This was an opportunity for him to make the announcements that the department considered important, to answer questions, and to give informal guidance to the regulars, which included Lew Gulick and Endre Marton of the Associated Press, Marvin Kalb of CBS, John Scali of ABC, Richard Valeriani of NBC, Bernard Gwertzman of the *Washington Star* (and later the *New York Times*), and Murrey Marder of the *Washington Post*.

One of the first things that any new correspondent had to learn were The Rules under which diplomats and White House officials shared information. Diplomats were willing to talk because, like the police in any U.S. state, they needed media help in certain situations. Sometimes they wanted to float a trial balloon; sometimes they wanted to alert Congress informally to an impending initiative; sometimes they wanted to prepare the public, or a foreign country, for an earth-shattering development.

The Rules had been evolving since President Franklin Roosevelt held his first press conference in the White House on March 8, 1933. Relations in those days had been strained since November 20, 1921, when President Warren Harding incorrectly described to reporters in the Oval Office how the projected Washington Naval Limitation Treaty would apply to Japan. Six hours after his misstep, the White House was forced to issue a correction, and, subsequently, presidents insisted on answering only questions submitted in advance. Roosevelt decided to try a more relaxed style. He explained to White House reporters that he had gotten on well with newsmen in the past. Henceforth, he would be willing to brief them in the same way he had as secretary of the navy and governor of New York:

I see no reason why I should not talk to you ladies and gentlemen off the record. . . . I don't want to be directly quoted. . . . [T]here are two other matters we will talk about: The first is "background information," which means material which can be used by all of you on your own authority and responsibility and must not be attributed to the White House. . . . The second thing is the "off the record" information, confidential information which is given only to those who attend the conference. . . . I want to ask you not to repeat this "off the record" confidential information either to your own editors or associates. . . . [T]his is only for those present.

That was the beginning of the rule that today is called "on background." It has evolved since FDR's description. Today, information given "on background" may be used in full but should be attributed only to "officials" of a specific government department. It is supposed to be paraphrased and no part enclosed in quotation marks. Thus, one is well within The Rules to report: "State Department officials disclosed today that the United States may call for the resumption of the nuclear-test-ban talks next week."

A derivative of "background" is "deep background." This was—and still is today—information conveyed by an authoritative figure but not attributable to any official or government department. Rather, the information must be presented on the correspondent's own personal authority. Deep background grew out of World War II, when military commanders wished to surface some piece of information but did not want the source to be traceable. It produces such labored constructions as: "It is understood that the United States may call for the resumption of the nuclear-test-ban talks next week."

Deep background got a boost from Ernest K. Lindley, a columnist for *Newsweek,* when he went to work for Secretary of State Dean Rusk in 1961 as a media adviser. Lindley would leak information to former colleagues on the condition that the source remained a mystery. "I enforced this requirement rigidly," Lindley once explained to a group of us. This shadowy practice, referred to at the State Department as the "Lindley Rule" was adopted hook, line, and sinker by Rusk in briefing the regulars whom he regarded as an extension of his personal team.

Finally, "off the record" information was considered the equivalent of the top-secret classification on government documents—to be used only as a tip. Stu had developed such trust among American officials that they would confide the most sensitive items to him. He once told me, "I would never repeat such stuff, and certainly not to my wife, Bunny. You don't want to burden your spouse with keeping a secret, especially since you know how women are inclined to gossip." Unlike classified information, off-the-record disclosures have no "sell-by date"; it is unclear when such information may eventually be made public, if ever. In twelve years? Twenty-five? Fifty?

The Rules go to the heart of independence in American journalism. Without them, much of what the press writes or broadcasts would amount to authorized press releases. The Rules permit reporters to probe behind the scenes and obtain information that explains context and motivation without publicly embarrassing the source. Members of a new administration often have no idea of the nuances involved and sometimes get into hot water when they fail to make clear on what basis they are talking. Professor Richard Pipes, a Harvard historian who went to work on President Reagan's National Security Council, caused a flap in March 1981 when Jeff Antevil of Reuters quoted him *on the record* as saying that Nixon's "détente" with the Soviet Union was dead and there was no use talking to Moscow. He said further that the Cold War would end only when the USSR fell apart. That created the impression that the Reagan administration planned to subvert, weaken, or destroy the other superpower. In his memoir, *Vixi,* Pipes says he thought he was speaking off the record, and acknowledged that he had never heard of the "background" or "deep background" rules when he left Cambridge to go to work in Washington.

I arrived to take up my new assignment during the final phase of the Vietnam War. I soon learned that Secretary Rusk maintained close relations with the "firm" of Hensley and Hightower. If Rusk could inform them first of a major event, he could shape coverage across the United States and even influence the way the *New York Times* presented the news. This intimate relationship was similar to the way TASS would first break space spectaculars out of London. Hensley recounted to me how Rusk called him and Hightower to the State Department in the middle of the night of November 23–24, 1964. The United States had airlifted Belgian paratroopers in C-130s to Stanleyville, the Congo, to save a thousand Europeans and Americans who were threatened by rebels in Katanga Province. Rusk invited the pair to the Operations Center on the seventh floor to listen to radio reports direct from U.S. diplomats in the field. On that occasion, Hensley and Hightower were lapdogs, although I have no doubt that if something had gone wrong, they would have reported it. It is hard to imagine such close cooperation between the media and officialdom today.

Another incident is engraved on my mind. In June 1967, Soviet Premier Aleksei Kosygin was visiting the special session of the U.N. General Assembly following the Six-Day War between Israel and the Arab countries. The United States was anxious to use the occasion to promote arms limitations with Moscow. The immediate issue was how to arrange a meeting because neither side wished to be seen as supplicant. President Johnson refused to go to the United Nations to meet Kosygin, and Kosygin refused to come to Washington to meet the president. For a while, it appeared the superpowers would miss this opportunity until Hensley caught Rusk on a sidewalk outside the United Nations and lobbed a question to the usually reserved secretary of state: "You'll find a way to meet, won't you?"

Rusk remained his Buddha-like self. Then he smiled slowly and winked. On the basis of that wink, buttressed by a history of mutual trust, Hensley put out an urgent story that the two sides were reaching agreement on a place to meet. This was the same journalistic dynamic that motivated Henry Shapiro to announce the fall of Khrushchev in 1964 on the basis of a portrait being removed from its public place. A strong hint, backed up by knowledge and confidence.

In the 1967 case, President Johnson was furious over the disclosure and exerted heavy pressure on UPI management to retract the report. The top editors grilled Hensley mercilessly, but he refused to change a comma. The story stood. Shortly afterward, the White House announced that President Johnson and Premier Kosygin would meet at a point halfway between Washington and New York—Glassboro State College in southern New Jersey. That was a typical Hensley scoop, but it took its toll. An alcoholic, Hensley fell off the wagon during that summit meeting. I can see him now, staring grimly at his typewriter, pumping out copy and stubbing out his cigarette butts on the beautifully varnished floor of the basketball court, which had been turned into a press room. The next morning, I got a call at six at the Tudor Hotel in New York, informing me that Hensley had collapsed from drink on the floor at UPI headquarters in the *New York Daily News* building and would I please get him out before top management arrived. I succeeded, but only just. Glassboro State College, rumors had it, demanded ten thousand dollars in compensation from the U.S. government for its ruined basketball court.

One Friday afternoon at the height of the Vietnam War, Dean Rusk scheduled one of his Lindley briefings. We convened in the aftermath of the "Tet offensive" in early February 1968 during which Communist uprisings in scores of towns across South Vietnam gave the impression that the United States and South Vietnam were losing the war. This particular Friday was special: it was February 9—Dean Rusk's fifty-ninth birthday. To mark the occasion, Bernard Gwertzman of the *Washington Star* bought a bottle of twenty-five-year-old Chivas Regal, Rusk's favorite scotch, and presented it to him on behalf of the State Department Correspondents Association.

Among the attendees were Marvin Kalb of CBS, Murrey Marder of the *Washington Post,* John Scali of ABC, Richard Valeriani of NBC, myself, and a handful of others. As the briefing got under way, the conversation turned to the Tet offensive, whose military significance Rusk minimized. The effect of that Vietminh offensive on us correspondents was similar to the shock (I remembered this from schoolboy days in France) in May 1954 when the North Vietnamese defeated the French at Dien Bien Phu. John Scali recalled later:

It was the Friday afternoon after the Tet offensive. The Vietcong had managed bombings and violence in 101 places in South Vietnam—at a time when we were quote winning the war unquote. They had invaded the

U.S. Embassy grounds. General Westmoreland came up with the story that it was a big, failed offensive—consequently a big American victory. An interesting way of looking at it. The fact that the Vietcong were able to coordinate that many places meant something significant.

I asked Rusk something like, "Do you think the Tet offensive was a major defeat for the Viet Cong, and a victory for us?" He replied, "Most certainly," and he repeated the Westmoreland line.

Scali pressed Rusk to say the United States had suffered an intelligence failure. Why did the United States not have better information of the coming attack? Why had it not been able to respond more effectively? Rusk, who was constantly suffering from a low-grade fever in his last year in office, became increasingly annoyed. He insisted that the United States must prevail against the Vietnamese Communists. "Don't you realize," he snapped angrily, "that none of your broadcasting companies are going to be worth a damn unless we succeed in Vietnam?" Finally, no longer able to control his irritation, Rusk blurted out, "Damn it, John, whose side are you on?"

For a moment, we all fell silent. Rusk was charging disloyalty, maybe even treason. And this was the same John Scali who had been covering the State Department since 1945 and who in 1962 brought Rusk a secret proposal from the Soviet Embassy for ending the Cuban missile crisis. For Murrey Marder, more than for anyone else seated around the desk on which the Treaty of Paris was signed in 1783 (ending the American War of Independence), the outburst had meaning. He wrote on the front page of the *Washington Post,* on the following Sunday, February 11, 1968:

> The stress of high tension is showing through the top layers of Washington officialdom as the Vietnam war rolls through its most acute, testing stage.
>
> It is damn-the-dissenters and damn-the-questioners mood. To a degree unusual for Washington even at times of great stress, those who seek even querulously about proclaimed accomplishments are encountering, on occasion, outbursts in place of explanations.
>
> One official, noted for supreme aplomb, startled a group of newsmen who asked if there had been an intelligence failure in detecting the Communist city offensive, by counter-asking, "Whose side are you on?"

In writing that story, Marder violated The Rules. He had not presented the incident on his own authority but sourced it to an official, presumably a high one. Furthermore, he had used a direct quote that was supposed to be off-limits under either background, deep background, or the Lindley

Rule. Years later, Marder explained to me that he always saw two perils in Lindley. First, it shifted responsibility for the accuracy of the information from the issuing official to the correspondent, and, second, the correspondent could never really know whether he had been lied to. "I always reserved myself the right to use a quote if the information was such that you could not paraphrase it," Marder told me. "Rusk's quote, 'Whose side are you on?' was the perfect example. You could not paraphrase that, and I must say I did enjoy upsetting the applecart!"

Rusk, in his memoir, *As I Saw It,* criticized the national coverage that Marder's report generated and noted that "the media treated the remark as if I had raped the Vestal Virgins." Despite Rusk's outburst, there were no harsh consequences for Marder from the administration. And his colleagues supported him. Bernard Gwertzman complained bitterly about the slipperiness of "deep background." He noted that Defense Secretary Robert McNamara would brief Pentagon regulars on "deep background" on Wednesdays, and Rusk would do the same on Fridays. And there was no way to signal to readers where the information was coming from and what institutional bias it carried. In his recollections, Rusk softened his comment about Scali by noting that when the newsman was later appointed U.S. ambassador to the United Nations in 1973, "I had good fun reminding him that he was going to be asking many people, 'Whose side are you on?'" What none of us knew at the time was that the habitually gracious Rusk called Scali to his office shortly after the flare-up and apologized in private.

With the election of President Nixon in November 1968, the ground rules began evolving once again. Nixon was determined to be his own foreign-policy architect and maintained tight control over major events with the help of Dr. Henry Kissinger, his national security adviser. The man whom Nixon appointed to replace Rusk, William P. Rogers, attorney general under Eisenhower, had no real experience in foreign affairs. Rogers felt insecure facing State Department correspondents and tried to avoid press conferences. He did, however, make one concession to the regulars by allowing them to travel with him in his jetliner on overseas trips.

Early in the administration it became clear that the White House intended to do the managing of relations with the Soviet Union and Communist China. Here was an opportunity to play Moscow off against Beijing. One of the key players was Kissinger, the Harvard professor who had taken a two-year leave of absence to serve the president. At the center of power, Kissinger made clear that if there was to be any leaking of information, he would do the leaking. Naturally, he hid behind The Rules to afford the administration "plausible denial" if matters got out of hand.

Embarrassment was something that Nixon's closest advisers, Haldeman and Erlichman, were concerned about. Kissinger, for all his charming wit, had a pronounced Germanic accent that could prompt unfavorable comparisons to the mad scientist played by Peter Sellers in the movie *Doctor Strangelove*. In the early months of the administration Kissinger wrapped himself in "background" and "deep background." On April 4, 1969, the Overseas Writers, a group founded in 1921 at the Versailles Peace Conference, convened to hear Kissinger outline the new administration's foreign policy. My notes show that Kissinger spoke on that day under the Lindley Rule. As Kissinger's influence grew, he invented his own tag: "a senior administration official." It was not long before foreign diplomats in Washington knew whenever this phrase appeared in print that Kissinger was talking.

The year 1971 proved to be a time of exceptional maneuvering. With the help of the government of Pakistan, Kissinger flew secretly to Beijing to lay the groundwork for President Nixon's breakthrough visit to Communist China in February 1972. The United States had begun to play the China card in its relations with the Soviet Union. At the end of the year a burgeoning crisis loomed. India and Pakistan had gone to war over the disputed territory of Kashmir. The Soviet Union lent its support to India, while the White House worried about its friend Pakistan. Returning December 14, 1971, from a meeting between President Nixon and French president Georges Pompidou in the Azores, Kissinger gave correspondents on *Air Force One* a briefing that contained a pointed threat at Moscow. Unless Moscow withdrew its support from India, "a senior administration official" said, President Nixon would cancel his summit meeting in Moscow with President Brezhnev. Ben Bradlee, editor of the *Washington Post*, saw the reports flowing on the wires of the Associated Press and United Press International and asked Don Oberdorfer, his foreign affairs correspondent, to find out who had given the briefing. Oberdorfer, who had not been on the trip, called a contact at the White House, who confirmed the briefer was Kissinger.

Bradlee was incensed. He and his colleagues had wanted for some time to dismantle The Rules. They detested the fact that officials could hide behind such attributions as "usually reliable sources" or "informed sources," escaping any iota of accountability. Bradlee recalled the case of Secretary of Agriculture Orville Freeman, who let an official read his report to Congress "off the record" on one occasion when he fell ill. The report was made public the next day. "It was ridiculous," Bradlee recalled. "What the hell did Agriculture have that was secret? So that, I think, put us on our toes."

In the 1971 case, the administration was issuing a threat but obscuring how seriously it should be taken. "We had been discussing this problem," Bradlee told me years later. "Wasn't there something we could do to stop this goddamn practice?" Bradlee figured that all important observers, foreign and domestic, knew well enough who the briefer was. It was only the American public that was left in the dark. Bradlee decided to use this incident to launch a major assault on The Rules. At his command, the *Washington Post* identified Kissinger. In a page 1 story, Stanley Karnow began his second paragraph, "The warning was contained in a background briefing given by presidential adviser Henry A. Kissinger to a pool of reporters who accompanied Mr. Nixon on his return from two days of talks with French President Pompidou in the Azores." Adding insult to injury, the *Post* also published a photograph of Kissinger standing between Nixon and Pompidou at the farewell ceremony.

Predictably, there were angry reactions. Some colleagues complained to Bradlee about this blatant violation of The Rules. The Nixon administration retaliated by not inviting *Washington Post* correspondents to official functions. But Kissinger never complained, Bradlee told me. "So we said, let's see if we can't make some improvement in the situation."

Bradlee next instructed his reporters to protest any briefings by administration officials that were held "on background." They were to take the floor at the start of each briefing and demand to know why the briefing could not be "on the record." When the briefer refused to go on the record, the *Post* correspondent would walk out. During those years, I had my doubts that this strategy would work. Although The Rules were undoubtedly being abused from time to time, they did serve a useful purpose. As it turned out, Bradlee's attack put the *Washington Post* at a disadvantage. Its reporters would have to quiz other reporters who attended the briefing about what had been said. Murrey Marder protested to Bradlee, noting that foreign governments would say nothing to reporters unless the source was disguised. Bradlee tried to counter these difficulties by enlisting Abe Rosenthal, the editor of the *New York Times,* to his cause. Rosenthal, who had spent many years covering diplomats at the United Nations and abroad, declined to go along. So in the end, Bradlee's campaign failed. "We struggled more or less manfully and then finally abandoned it," Bradlee told me later. "The reporters said that it made their jobs impossibly hard. Occasionally, you could get great cooperation from your colleagues who agreed with you, but often you wouldn't."

Ironically, the man who would destroy "deep background" would be grateful for the sleight of hand it provided some six months later. In the midst of the Watergate scandal of 1972, Bob Woodward informed managing editor Howard Simons that he had a source inside the administration who had access to many White House operations and the shenanigans of the Committee to Re-elect the President. The source could comment on the administration's efforts to manipulate the 1972 elections in Nixon's favor. However, this source insisted on conditions even more stringent than "deep background." No contact by telephone. Summons only by visual signal—moving a red flag from the front of Woodward's balcony to the back. Meet at two in the morning in an underground parking garage to help guide Woodward's inquiries while offering only a minimum of substance.

Such help proved invaluable as the *Washington Post* unmasked the malfeasance of Nixon officials. The source turned out to be the number-two man at the FBI, Mark Felt, whom Woodward had met accidentally as a junior naval officer, carrying papers from the Pentagon to the White House. Woodward cultivated Felt assiduously at the start of his career as a reporter on a community newspaper. Years later when Watergate broke, Woodward pressed Felt into service with the promise that the *Post* would never reveal his name during his lifetime. In June 2005, however, Felt's family disclosed his identity. Interestingly, Katharine Graham, owner and publisher of the newspaper, did not wish to know the identity of "Deep Throat" during the Watergate episode, and managing editor Howard Simons was never informed by Bradlee. Simons, however, nicknamed Woodward's mysterious source "Deep Throat" after a porn film of that time . . . and the name stuck.

In war or peace, The Rules are an essential part of American journalism, even though they are regularly abused. The George W. Bush administration, for example, violated The Rules in 2004 when White House spokesman Scott McClellan revealed the contents of a background briefing by terrorism expert Richard Clarke. In that briefing, which took place in August 2002, Clarke played up the administration's alleged concern about terrorism. However, after he retired, Clarke told the 9/11 Commission that the administration had really been ignoring the terrorist threat. In 2002 Clarke was a propagandist for the administration who could not be held accountable. In 2004, after he retired, he offered the more truthful account. Clarke's 2002 version was what Bradlee was complaining about—tendentious official information without accountability.

Chapter 15

Dancing with Spooks

In 1968, a year after I went to the State Department, an old friend from
Moscow turned up in Washington. Sam Jaffe had completed an assignment
as ABC bureau chief in Hong Kong and now was hoping to follow reporters
such as Marvin Kalb of CBS covering "Foggy Bottom," the apt nickname
used in Washington to describe the State Department. ABC management,
however, did not see Sam's future that way. Perhaps they thought he needed
to get back in touch with American grass roots, or perhaps they had other considerations. In any event, they offered him an assignment covering Capitol
Hill. Sam, not intrigued by American politics, brushed it aside. ABC did not
appreciate his refusal and began sending him out as a general assignment reporter to such events as the annual Cherry Blossom Festival. Frustrated and
upset, Sam made the fatal mistake of quitting without another job in hand.

So began Sam's seemingly endless search for work either as a broadcaster
or as public relations man. Once in a while he got some freelance assignments; on occasion UPI would ask him to cover the U.N. General Assembly.
One summer in 1974 he even got the chance to report for UPI from Communist China, which was then opening up to the outside world after President Nixon's historic trip to Beijing in 1972. None of these jobs led
anywhere, and suspicions began to circulate among editors in Washington
and New York that Sam's passion for covering Communists was more than
just personal ambition. After a while Sam decided that the intelligence community was conducting a whispering campaign against him.

As Sam appeared less and less in the Washington journalistic community, old friends either forgot or abandoned him. This was not our case, however. Ruth and I went regularly over to the house that he and his wife, Jeune, had bought in the Maryland suburb of Bethesda. Jeune, who was very good with flowers, started a floral business, and later, when I became president of the State Department Correspondents Association, I would occasionally ask her to arrange flowers for luncheons we held for international politicians and diplomats. When I got interested in beekeeping in the early 1970s, Sam and Jeune urged me to put a couple of beehives on their land.

"Nikolini! Nikolini!" Sam would greet me with a mischievous grin as I arrived with bee veil and other equipment for the bees. Sam was always uncannily charming. He had incredible "people skills" that allowed him to enter easily into contact with total strangers and get them talking as if they had known each other for a long time. On the other hand, Sam had no pretensions as a researcher and was only a fair political analyst.

Sam stood about five feet eight, with russet hair and a bushy mustache. Born in California in 1929 of a Russian Jewish father, he went to work as a reporter for the *San Carlos Courier-Bulletin* at eighteen. A year later he got a job with the San Francisco Bureau of the International News Service but quit to join the marines, serving as a combat correspondent in Korea from 1950 to 1951. He liked to recall that his uncle Sam Jaffe worked in Hollywood and starred in a dozen films, including *Gunga Din*. During the McCarthy era, Sam Jaffe elder was blacklisted as a member of the Hollywood Nineteen who would not cooperate with the government. This family background plus a strong desire to succeed in television probably inspired Sam to take an interest in those nations that could threaten the United States. He jumped at the chance to hobnob with foreign diplomats after the marines by taking a job as a radio newswriter at United Nations Radio, and shortly afterward joined *Life* magazine, and later the *Nation*.

Whenever Ruth and I visited Sam and Jeune we easily lapsed into Moscow nostalgia. As often as not he would blurt out his troubles while helping Jeune arrange and transport flowers. He spoke with emotion, and it was difficult to make sense of what he was saying; his thoughts tumbled out in a disorganized way. "Kislov! Kislov!" he would mumble. "It all began with Slava Kislov!"

Kislov? Who? It was decades later that I found out that Sam began to run into trouble in Moscow immediately after the Cuban missile crisis in 1962. His exclusive that Kremlin hawks had opposed Khrushchev's agreeing to President Kennedy's public formulation on ending the confrontation did not sit well with the Communist Party's image makers. In their eyes, any Soviet concession announced by American TV diminished the authority of the

Soviet government. I now know that Sam's difficulties began to accumulate on October 29, 1962, the day after the missile crisis ended.

That evening Sam attended National Independence Day at the Turkish Embassy. Ruminating later, Sam told me that he met *Life* photographer Stan Weyman as well as members of the Press Department of the Soviet Foreign Ministry at that reception. As the celebration wound down, Weyman suggested that this little group, which included a Russian woman Sam was squiring about, retire to the *Life* apartment. The guests drank at Weyman's until well past midnight, when one of the officials left and Sam offered to drive the second ministry representative and the lady friend home. That was typical of Sam: his willingness to put himself out for others was what helped him make friends everywhere.

After dropping off the second press official, Sam began driving back to his Kutuzovsky Prospekt apartment through an unfamiliar part of Moscow. Suddenly, the car hit an unmarked pothole and blew out the two front tires. Sam, divorced at the time, asked his woman companion, Galya, to go to a nearby telephone booth and report the accident to the police while he went off in search of help. Glancing over his shoulder, he noted a KGB "tail" following him. Nothing to be done but to act normally. By three in the morning Sam managed to change the tires with help from two milimen and several passersby. Galya, however, did not return, and not knowing what to do, Sam went home without her. "At seven thirty the next morning, I got a hysterical call from Galya, who reported that she had been seized by two men as she left the phone booth and was carted off to a police station," Sam would relate. There, he said, she had been interrogated throughout the night by KGB officials, who accused her of being a prostitute and breaking a promise she made in 1959 not to associate with foreigners. In those Cold War days, Soviet national newspapers seemed to delight in attacking Western correspondents and portraying them as hopeless drunks who behaved in boorish fashion.

The KGB men warned Galya that the government newspaper, *Izvestia*, would attack Sam if she did not cooperate and desist from hanging around foreigners. What to do? Sam never explained to me why he did not seek advice from the "dean" of Western correspondents who had many years of experience with Soviet dirty tricks. Possibly Sam did not want to reveal his private life to Shapiro, but it is also possible that the thought never crossed his mind. Where to go for advice if you ran into trouble could be a difficult question, as I myself was to find out years later. In this case, Sam decided to call the informant who slipped him the scoop about Khrushchev. During the Cold War, strange as it seems, such sources sometimes acted as "guardian angels," helping their Western contacts out of unforeseen crises. After all, Western contacts were potential conduits of scarce gifts for wives or mistresses.

Sam told me that his source was Yuri V. Fedorov, whom he had met in early 1962 when the Soviet official had accompanied the Soviet Children's Art Exhibit to New York. Fedorov not only was a senior editor of the APN news agency but also held a position with the KGB, not an unusual combination at that time. Fedorov told Sam he would look into the situation. By the afternoon of October 30, Fedorov was able to inform Sam that a nasty article was being prepared, not for *Izvestia* but for *Komsomolskaya Pravda.* He added that if Sam could break free from his work that afternoon, he could arrange a meeting with a deputy editor and perhaps they could work something out.

Sam agreed, and on the way to the restaurant Fedorov revealed that the man they were about to meet was not really a *Komsomolskaya Pravda* editor but another KGB operative with authority to order up, or cancel, smear jobs against Westerners. Fedorov introduced Sam to a KGB man named Vyacheslav Kislov, or "Slava" for short. As they began to talk, Kislov berated Sam for revealing the dispute between Khrushchev and the Kremlin hawks. He also criticized one of our colleagues, Whitman Bassow of *Newsweek,* recently expelled for reasons unclear. After unloading these charges, Kislov then made nice, suggesting that he and Sam meet from time to time. What it came down to was this: "Trust me. I'll help you get reliable inside information. Others won't be able to match what I can do for you. And, by the way, maybe you could help me, too, occasionally." Pretty much the same pitch that Vadim Biryukov gave to me.

This good cop, bad cop routine was a prelude to entrapment, and Sam sensed he was being set up. He decided to relate the incident to the embassy's minister counselor, Boris Klosson, as well as to the embassy's security officer. This latter official asked Sam to write a memo, dated November 5, 1962, which he filed in the embassy archives with a copy to the Department of State. Two weeks later, on November 20, John F. Reilley, deputy assistant secretary of state in Washington, forwarded this same memo to J. Edgar Hoover, director of the FBI, with a cautionary note that Sam Jaffe, ABC bureau chief, might be slipping into the arms of the KGB in Moscow. This Reilley memorandum, which none of us knew about, would pop up at odd times in the future when questions were asked about Sam's behavior.

On reflection, I think that Sam was taking the sorts of risks that ambitious journalists take all the time. Moscow correspondents worth their salt all had relations with KGB officials who masqueraded as newsmen. The issue was what kind of relations. How deep? How compromising? Informing the embassy seemed reasonable enough, although I doubt that Sam ever foresaw that his account would lie fallow for some time and then begin circulating in the U.S. bureaucracy, spreading suspicions about him.

"I'm fascinated with the Communists," Sam used to say. He sensed that cozying up to Russian, Chinese, and North Vietnamese officials would allow him once in a while to pry out some extraordinary material that would make a splash for his news organization and further his career. As a relatively young journalist for the *Nation*, he experienced the exhilaration of getting a big exclusive at the Bandung Conference of 1955 when he pulled off an interview with Chinese premier Zhou Enlai. When he worked in New York in the 1950s, he spent hours at the U.N. bar drinking Bloody Marys and consorting with all manner of diplomats.

Sam's modus operandi in New York came to the attention of the FBI soon enough. As early as 1952, its special agents made contact with him and asked that he inform them of conversations he might have with Russians. A memo, dated December 9, 1960, from the FBI field office in Manhattan to Hoover shows that Sam worked as an FBI informant after he joined CBS. During 1960, for example, he made regular reports to the FBI, apparently without serious remuneration. This memo notes that he was paid the paltry sum of $4.70 on April 11, 1960, apparently for expenses. Later, the FBI gave Sam a code name, Harry Hines, which he was to use in reporting to an FBI representative in Paris when he passed through on leave from Moscow. Sam would say, "I did this because I knew the risks I was taking and I wanted to cover my ass." It was more a question of protection than patriotism, I suspect. In any case, the FBI was pleased with his contribution. The December 9 memo also states, "To date, informant has proved to be reliable and he has shown no signs of instability."

In those Cold War days the alliance between the Soviet Union and Communist China seemed to threaten the very heart of Western civilization. Intelligence agencies were seeking every possible source on Russian political and military developments. After Stalin's death in 1953, the agencies began recruiting travelers of all sorts—tourists, academics, newsmen, diplomats—to undertake minor reconnaissance in Russia, checking out the location of objects of interest, photographing them, asking questions. Sam confided to me that he had been approached by the Central Intelligence Agency. "A CIA official promised that if I agreed to cooperate, CBS would hire me and I would be sent to Moscow." He added, "I refused that offer, but got hired by CBS anyway in 1956."

Because of the difficulty of developing human spies in the Soviet Union, the Central Intelligence Agency pushed forward with high-tech methods. One such tool was the U-2 reconnaissance plane, capable of flying at altitudes above sixty thousand feet, far above the maximum altitude of Soviet antiaircraft rockets. (Commercial jetliners, by comparison, usually fly no higher than forty thousand feet.) I remember Stu Hensley telling me that the U-2 was the product of a secret unit of the Lockheed Corporation known as the "Skunk Works." It was the brainchild of Clarence L. "Kelly" Johnson and amounted to an ultralight airframe powered by one jet engine, capable of rising to extreme altitudes, taking pictures, and scooping up electronic emissions.

An "Open Skies" proposal was one of the confidence-building initiatives that President Eisenhower had put forward at his summit conference with Khrushchev in Geneva in 1955. But the Soviet leader had immediately denounced it as legalized espionage. No matter, the next year the United States began sending U-2 planes along Soviet borders to capture elint (electronic intelligence) signals and eventually began cruising over Soviet territory with impunity. These black single-seater aircraft were invisible to the naked eye but detectable by radar. Accordingly, Soviet engineers went to work to develop high-altitude rockets that could bring them down. I remember Yuri Korolyov telling me in later years in Moscow that the Soviets accidentally shot down several of their own planes as they tried to perfect the anti-U-2 missile.

Finally, on May 1, 1960, the Soviet rocket forces succeeded in exploding a SAM-2 missile by the tail of a U-2 over Sverdlovsk as pilot Francis Gary Powers guided it on a course from Peshawar, Pakistan, to Bodø, Norway. Powers succeeded in freeing himself from the plane as it spiraled downward, parachuting to the ground safely, where he was immediately captured by local residents. Four days later, on May 5, Khrushchev announced in Moscow that defense forces had shot down a U-2 spy plane in what he called "an aggressive provocation" by American hawks who wanted to wreck the May 16 summit with President Eisenhower and British Prime Minister Harold Macmillan. At the Paris meeting, Khrushchev demanded that Eisenhower stop further U-2 flights and apologize. Eisenhower refused, and the summit collapsed. Khrushchev walked out of the conference, blasting the United States and canceling Eisenhower's planned trip to Russia.

The next big event in the deteriorating relations between Moscow and Washington was not long in coming. Powers's espionage trial was announced for August 17, 1960, in Moscow. At CBS headquarters in New York, editors pushed ahead with plans to cover this major event. CBS maintained a permanent office in Moscow headed by Marvin Kalb. CBS editors thought he should have additional help, and Sam seemed a logical choice because of his many contacts with Russian diplomats. In early August, a CBS assignment editor pulled Sam over and announced, "You're going to the Powers trial in Moscow."

CBS made the travel arrangements, while on August 9 and again on August 11 Sam was invited out to lunch with representatives of the CIA. Jay Reeves, the CIA representative in New York, and a psychiatrist asked Sam to undertake a few tasks during the assignment. First, they asked that Sam avoid referring to Powers's mishap as a spy flight but rather call it a reconnaissance mission. Presumably, the CIA men thought this was a more neutral term. Second, they asked Sam to be on the lookout for evidence that Powers had been brainwashed. And, finally, they asked that if CBS succeeded in interviewing Khrushchev, would Sam ask a question that would cause the Soviet leader to comment on Soviet relations with China and Mao. Reeves recorded the three assignments in a memo that the Jaffe family eventually obtained through the Freedom of Information Act.

On August 12, Sam went to Idlewild Airport (later renamed John F. Kennedy Airport) and boarded a Sabena airliner to Brussels, where he was to catch an Aeroflot flight to Moscow. To his surprise, he found on board Powers's wife, Barbara, her mother, and Powers's American attorneys. He quickly took a seat beside Barbara Powers, and before long they began drinking heavily as they flew eastward. Their arrival in Moscow turned into a media circus. Bud Korengold recalled that Barbara Powers had an exclusive arrangement to provide *Life* magazine with pictures. As she walked from the plane to the terminal, AP correspondent Stanley Johnson tried to disrupt the arrangement by positioning himself in front of Mrs. Powers to block the photographers' view. Korengold, who was there to file a report, snap pictures, and take newsreel shots with a 16-millimeter camera, dodged from left to right in search of a good angle. "On the spur of the moment," he related, "I rushed up to [Johnson] and gave him a hard kick in the shins. He hobbled off in pain, and I was able to film."

Kalb, who also went to the airport to record the scene, remembered that the Powers delegation flew in on a special flight from Brussels. "Sam arrived with the Powers family, and they were the only ones on the plane. I had the impression it was a special plane sent for them. Sam was part of the official family and stayed with them all the time."

In our conversations, Sam always seemed surprised at the treatment he got in Moscow. "They put me up in the Sovietskaya Hotel on the same floor as Barbara Powers! I have no idea how this happened, but it sure was a great entrée to Barbara." His colleagues also found this arrangement suspicious. "We always assumed," Bud remembered, "that the CIA thought Sam had some special tie to the KGB because he had been extremely friendly with Russians he covered in the United States. We also assumed that the KGB thought he had some special ties with the CIA for the same reasons and played along by arranging for him to stay in her hotel. I always had the impression that even Sam was bewildered a bit by all of this but simply went along."

Declassified documents now show that the Soviet side, indeed, considered Sam to be linked to the CIA and sent to keep an eye on Barbara Powers. They were assigned the same rooms that Richard Nixon and Pat Nixon occupied a few years before at the Sovietskaya Hotel, which was generally reserved for important foreign guests. Journalists covering the trial were housed in the center of town near the House of Trade Unions, where the purge trials of the 1930s took place and where the Powers trial was to be held. At the trial, Sam was given a seat with the Powers family and did not have to cover the proceedings from the press gallery with other correspondents.

Arriving in Moscow, Barbara Powers, twenty-five, made clear that she wanted to meet with her husband as soon as possible, and preferably before the trial. "He's the most wonderful man I've ever met," she declared, even though her relations with Powers were extremely rocky at the time. She confided to Sam that she suspected her husband of philandering while he was assigned to reconnaissance flights out of Turkey. On the eve of the trial, August 16, Barbara Powers tried to communicate with her husband by telegram. When she received no reply, she began drinking with Sam. In the early hours of August 17, according to Sam, she asked him to take her to Lubyanka Prison. "I got a taxi and we drove down to the prison, which is located in the center of Moscow," Sam told me. "We stood there with Barbara crying. Everything was locked up, and we eventually returned to Barbara's room."

On return to the United States, Sam reported to the FBI. An FBI memorandum recorded that melancholy moment outside the prison:

> There she told the informant that she was not in love with her husband and did not have any intention of staying in the Soviet Union. Barbara Powers grabbed the informant and started kissing him, but he repelled her. He told her that she could not talk that way and could not divorce her husband at this time. He told her that she would be accused of "deserting a sinking ship" and that she should not even mention this.
>
> The informant said that on this occasion, he could have been intimate with Barbara Powers, but that he was not. He said that on many occasions when he was in Barbara Powers' company, she was in her pajamas, and he could probably have been intimate with her if he so desired, but at no time was he intimate with her.

During the 109 days of pretrial interrogation, Powers declared that he was a mere technician who flew over the Soviet Union on orders from the CIA, turning switches on and off that activated cameras and other electronic equipment. He said he was sorry for what he had done and agreed to plead guilty. The trial turned out to be a 3-day show during which the real defendant was the United States and its policies. Powers duly pleaded guilty and professed remorse. He was sentenced to 10 years' imprisonment and carted off to Vladimir Prison, a hundred miles east of Moscow. In the end, however, he did not serve out his term. He was exchanged on February 10, 1962, on the Glienicke Bridge connecting East and West Germanies for Rudolf Abel, a Soviet spy sentenced to 30 years in the United States.

Given these dances with spooks, it's not surprising that Sam got off to a fast start when he became the first ABC bureau chief in Moscow. He recorded in his diary on November 29, 1961, several days after he arrived in Moscow, "Everything is going along splendedly [sic]. Even Henry Shapiro admits he's never seen the cooperation that's been given me."

In the coming years, Sam would establish an admirable journalistic record. He became known for a series of impressive scoops as an ABC correspondent. He was the only American newsman to report Khrushchev's difficulties in acceding to President Kennedy's public offer on the Cuban missile crisis; he was ahead of us all in reporting Professor Barghoorn's expulsion from Moscow in 1963; he was the first American to report Khrushchev's overthrow in 1964. We assumed that Sam was getting his information from KGB-connected sources, but we did not know who they were. Still less did we know what FBI documents now reveal—that the infamous Kislov had asked him to report regularly on the American ambassador's Friday briefings and to bring him back from the United States a special present that he described as a "mini-phone-recording machine."

As time went on, however, Sam's successes with the Russians began to raise questions among his colleagues. The official memoranda that the Jaffe family has been able to extract from the government show that by 1965 Moscow-based colleagues were occasionally reporting to the U.S. Embassy that Sam's behavior seemed suspicious or inappropriate. I remember Sam telling me that he once pretended to be the American ambassador when police found him sitting drunk in his car, which had broken down on a Moscow street at night. He told me, too, which American colleague he suspected of bad-mouthing him at the U.S. Embassy.

Ironically, by 1965 Sam was falling from grace with the Soviet side as well. In late September 1965, the Soviet Foreign Ministry ordered his expulsion. The occasion was an ABC report that described infighting in the Kremlin between General Secretary Leonid Brezhnev and Premier Aleksei Kosygin a year after Khrushchev's ouster. All of us correspondents were on the lookout for such tensions because it did not seem that the Communist Party could be headed by two coequal leaders. One surely had to win out, as was demonstrated by the way Khrushchev gained full control over Premier Nikolay Bulganin in the immediate post-Stalin years. The story that caused Sam's downfall, oddly enough, was not developed by Sam but rather by John Scali, the ABC diplomatic correspondent, who broadcast it from Washington.

What the Foreign Ministry held against Sam was that he did not, from their point of view, actively rebut Scali's infighting broadcast. In fact, Sam did file reports for ABC Radio, knocking down the Scali story. The Foreign Ministry considered that insufficient, and gave him one week at the end of September to depart. The order was directed against Sam as if officials felt he had betrayed them personally. Although the ministry did hold up the visa of Sam's replacement, they took no action against the ABC bureau, which remained open and staffed with local personnel. Sam's replacement, George Watson, did eventually arrive.

For Sam, the expulsion was less traumatic than it might have been. As America's involvement in the Vietnam War deepened, ABC had already decided to transfer Sam to Hong Kong to keep watch over China and its involvement in the conflict. Hong Kong was also a point from which Sam, with his talents at getting along with Communist officials, might find a way to get to Hanoi and report on the North Vietnamese side in the war. American diplomats and British officials immediately began watching Sam's activities in Hong Kong with more than just a casual eye. Once again, Sam became active in making contact with journalists of the Communist Chinese news agency Xinhua as well as with disgruntled Soviet sailors. The American Consulate in Hong Kong received a notice from the State Department in late December 1965 that Sam would probably be issued a visa to visit North Vietnam, and in July 1966 ABC's Washington Bureau asked the State Department to validate his passport for travel to Hanoi. On this venture, however, Sam lost out to Harrison Salisbury of the *New York Times*, who managed to get permission to visit the North Vietnamese capital in 1967, to the consternation of critics in Congress.

In May 1968, Sam, his wife, Jeune, and their two daughters, Deborah and Leah, were transferred to Washington. Within a year Sam quit ABC and began casting around for a job; he even approached President Nixon's spokesman, Ron Ziegler, for work at the White House. Without hope of steady work, he turned his energies to routing out rumors, speaking on news shows from time to time, seeking documents from the CIA and the FBI to clear his name . . . and drinking.

In these efforts, he succeeded with the Central Intelligence Agency. He received a letter from CIA director William Colby dated November 24, 1975, that stated, "We have no evidence you have ever been an agent of the Soviets or other foreign intelligence services." In a second letter dated May 10, 1976, the CIA added, "Official records provide no indication that you have ever been an employee or agent of the CIA."

He was not so lucky with the Federal Bureau of Investigation. The FBI pointedly refused to offer him a similar letter. In their files was an undated memorandum, classified secret, that reads: "Soviet defector Yuri Nosenko has advised that Jaffe was recruited by the KGB in about 1962 while he was in Moscow through his relationship with a Soviet female." Sam's role was to pass on to the KGB any information concerning Americans living in Moscow, a CIA official who had close contact with Nosenko told me in 1976.

In 1978, as I was working in the State Department press room, I got a telephone call from Yuri Nosenko totally out of the blue. He was calling, he said, to warn me about Premier Kosygin's son-in-law Gherman Gvishiani, in whom I was taking an interest at the time. Nosenko asserted that Gvishiani was a KGB agent and that I should be careful. I took the occasion to ask him about Sam and his possible ties to the KGB. Nosenko replied, "We considered him a good friend, an asset," or words to that effect. Looking back on that telephone call, I must say I am astounded that Nosenko called or even figured out how to call me. At this remove, I would be inclined to suspect my memory was playing tricks on me, but Jeune noted my conversation with Nosenko in their family diary. Forty years later, former KGB general Oleg Kalugin told me, "Sam was approached by the KGB, and he agreed to cooperate. But we always suspected he might be a CIA agent."

With the help of the American Civil Liberties Union, Sam sought to force the FBI through court action to give up key documents relating to him under the Freedom of Information Act. The FBI responded by filing papers with the U.S. District Court stating that there was "no doubt" an unnamed foreign intelligence agency "regarded him as their agent," even though he may not have realized he was used by them. In 1984, U.S. District Court Judge Barrington D. Parker, dealing with the complaint, studied the extensive records and issued an opinion saying that the FBI had no grounds for questioning Mr. Jaffe's patriotism.

Sam struggled on, never succeeding in completely clearing his name during his lifetime. Weakened by emphysema, drink, and frustration, he died in Jeune's arms early on the morning of February 8, 1985. He was buried in Arlington Cemetery six days later as a former marine combat correspondent. I was then on my second assignment in Moscow, this time for *U.S. News and World Report,* and sent my fond recollections to the family. But the words that really stood out came from Ted Koppel of ABC, who offered these thoughts in his eulogy: "When I was beginning my network career with ABC in the early 1960s, Sam was what I wanted to be. He personified the foreign correspondent: tough, aggressive—always seeming to know a little more than he told, in a profession whose practitioners often seem to tell more than they know."

Chapter 16

America, 1970

A year after Richard Nixon became president, I was assigned to guide a group of high-level Soviet journalists and academics around the United States. They were seeking information for journalistic purposes, but some of them were of such status that whatever they uncovered was likely to be passed on to influential players in the Soviet government. I remember Grant Dillman summoned me from the State Department to his office on December 31, 1969. "Would you be willing to be an interpreter-escort for a group of Soviet journalists visiting the United States?" he asked. "It's a return visit for the American Society of Newspaper Editors, which visited Russia earlier this year. They'll be coming in mid-January."

I glanced at the clock; it read 10:58 A.M. "When do you want an answer?" I inquired, thinking he would give me at least a few days to think it over.

"Right now!" Dillman frowned.

Why the rush? Was this a loyalty test to see how high I could jump on a moment's notice? I thought to myself that ASNE president Norman Isaacs had probably queried Julius Frandsen, UPI vice president for Washington, about recruiting a Russian-speaking guide and had passed the request on to Dillman, who in the rush of daily news forgot about it until the year was almost over. Isaacs, whom I knew personally as the executive editor of the *Louisville Courier-Journal,* had probably been calling, trying to find out what had happened to his request. This irritating rush was typical of wire-service journalism.

I realized the potential of such an assignment immediately, but I had reservations. I had a lot on my mind as 1969 came to a close, not least the birth of Caleb, our son, on December 1 and the extra help Ruth was needing. Although my Russian was good now, I did not feel that I could competently handle such varied subjects as diplomacy, dairy farming, cinema, economics, and who knows what else would come up on the trip around the United States. I feared, too, that I would have a blood pressure attack during the tour for eleven demanding Soviet editors. Nevertheless, within seconds I agreed. "I'll do it," I told Dillman, without revealing my concerns.

The group was to arrive in New York on January 19, 1970, for a twenty-three-day trip, almost exactly a year after President Nixon took office. Isaacs, who had led an ASNE delegation to Russia in the fall of 1969, would take care of the itinerary, hotels, and transportation. He hadn't thought much about the language problem, however. I contacted him and persuaded him that it would be a good idea to employ a professional interpreter as well. He called around and finally settled on Ross Lavroff of Arlington, Virginia. Ross, whose original name was Rostislav N. Lavrov, was born of Russian parents in a World War II refugee camp and later immigrated to the United States. He was exquisitely bilingual and was employed by the State Department as a contract interpreter in the U.S.-Soviet strategic-arms talks.

On January 19, he and I set off from Union Station in Washington to meet the group at Kennedy Airport. I carried a secret flask of vodka to nip on if stress became unbearable. No sooner did we get on the Metroliner than Ross dropped a bombshell. He had decided within the past few hours to divorce his wife. He said he had taken on this job "because I need the bread." I hid my worries that he might be so distracted that he would become unreliable. In the end, he turned out to be totally professional. "Language fluency," he conceded, "is not the only thing that makes a successful interpreter. You need to know the subject matter well, and often you'll find that the vibes you give out are equally important."

Norman Isaacs and Alexander Yevstafiev, press attaché of the Soviet Embassy, joined us when the blue-and-white Ilyushin 62 jetliner set down at JFK. We packed the delegates into a bus and headed off toward the Algonquin Hotel in Manhattan. Head of the delegation was Lev N. Tolkunov, a member of the Communist Party Central Committee and chief editor of the Soviet government newspaper, *Izvestia*. His number two was Enver E. Mamedov, first deputy chairman of the Soviet Radio and Television Committee, a very influential government broadcaster. Accompanying the delegation as interpreter was Gans A. Vladimirsky, who had been educated in New York high schools when his father worked for Amtorg, the Soviet trade mission, in the 1920s before diplomatic relations were established.

Once we reached the hotel our first task was to reduce the itinerary from the twenty-three days Isaacs had envisaged to eighteen. Why eighteen? Because that was the amount of time Isaacs's delegation had spent in the Soviet Union in the fall of 1969, and Tolkunov, who appreciated the niceties of power in Moscow, insisted on "reciprocity." Equal treatment in all things was the constant goal of the Soviet leadership in the latter part of the Cold War. It revealed, I thought, an abiding defensiveness, even an inferiority complex. Tolkunov immediately insisted that a planned trip to Hugh Hefner's Playboy enterprises aboard his Bunny jetliner should be eliminated as frivolous and inappropriate. "Look how he wields that blue pencil," quipped one of the editors as Isaacs rewrote the schedule. "That's the mark of a true editor!"

Meetings with members of Congress such as J. William Fulbright, Charles Percy, Mike Mansfield, and Gerald Ford were welcomed; appointments too with Henry Kissinger, Nixon's national security adviser, and Secretary of State William P. Rogers were confirmed. "We're here for business before pleasure," emphasized one of the Muscovites. ASNE actually gave the visitors a gift of appointments outside the framework of reciprocity because in Moscow the highest official the Americans met was Nikolai Baibakov, a deputy premier and director of the central planning agency, Gosplan.

After a relaxed morning the next day, the program began in earnest. First was lunch with the top leadership of the Columbia Broadcasting System. Here the conversation centered around Vice President Agnew's attacks on the media, and the concerns that it created among national broadcasters. The afternoon was filled with discussions at McKinsey and Company about the latest American management techniques, a subject of major interest to the Russians, who were experiencing increasing difficulties throughout the 1960s with worker discipline and productivity. The day wound up with a large reception in midtown Manhattan at the Soviet Mission to the United Nations.

On January 21, we lunched with editors of the Associated Press before catching a subway to City Hall for a meeting with Mayor John V. Lindsay. The Russians, who were used to the marble stations and speedy service of the Moscow metro, were taken aback by the shabbiness of the New York subway. It was bitterly cold, and our train was twenty-two minutes late. You could feel the frustration rising. "When was this metro built?" one of them asked incredulously. "They began tunneling at the end of the nineteenth century," I replied, hoping that would explain some of the differences with the Moscow metro, which was built in the 1930s. This transportation experience made them skeptical of Mayor Lindsay's claim that New Yorkers could get to work in fifteen to twenty minutes, even though they were charmed by the mayor's WASP-ish manners.

At the end of the meeting, it seemed to me that the visitors were reverting to "we-they" mode. An important element here was that both sides possessed widely differing facts about any particular issue. Furthermore, the American media, with their multiple voices, different angles, and opinions, confused the Russians, who often could not sort out the wheat from the chaff. That's why on-the-ground explorations by Russians to America and Americans to Russia could be helpful, although such expeditions often reinforced existing prejudices. In this case, the mayor's chauffeur, who drove some of us back to the Algonquin, validated the editors' skepticism. "New York," he said, "does not spend enough on services." The editors nodded in approval.

In the evening, I suggested that we walk the several blocks from the Algonquin at 59 West Forty-fourth Street to the *New York Times* at 229 West Forty-third. The traffic was heavy in the gathering dusk, and the biting cold made the expedition tedious. Tolkunov, who walked with a limp from World War II injuries, admonished me. "You should know that some of us were wounded in the war, and we find it difficult to walk so far." It was becoming clear that the delegation expected to be delivered to meetings in comfortable style. Eventually, we arrived and were whisked up to the boardroom on the fourteenth floor of the *Times* building, where the editors fell into serious discussions with the *Times* men about the American economy and U.S.-Soviet relations.

We flew to Chicago on January 22 for a quick look at the Midwest and a meeting with Mayor Richard J. Daley of Chicago. Ironically, the elevator proved less than an orbital missile and got stuck between floors from overload. It seemed like hours before help arrived. We suffered in silence. I learned on that occasion that some of the editors suffered from heart conditions and other infirmities; I could see sweaty brows and anguished expressions. Finally, we were set free and went in to confront the mayor. The editors fired questions to Mayor Daley about the troubles that erupted at the 1968 Democratic Convention, and he parried their thrusts. He acknowledged shortcomings, including racial tensions and substandard housing. The Russians were not impressed. "He's obfuscating and evading the issue," one of them whispered to me.

The chemistry of the delegation was now becoming clearer. Tolkunov was the statesman, the elder above the fray. Mamedov, who had been instrumental with his wife in promoting a friendship society dubbed the Institute of Soviet-American Relations, was the hatchet man, as would become clear later. Another member of the "senior circle" was Professor Alexander N. Yakovlev, deputy chief of the Propaganda Department of the Communist Party Central Committee. Yakovlev had studied at Columbia University as an exchange student during the 1958–1959 academic year (along with Oleg Kalugin, later a KGB general) under the first U.S.-Soviet cultural agreement since Stalin's death. Three years after our trip, he would be sent to Canada as ambassador, where he would serve a full ten years. Eventually, Mikhail Gorbachev plucked him from Ottawa to be one of his most extraordinary brain trusters. On this journey, however, Yakovlev kept to the elders, and I don't remember ever seeing him display anything but the most orthodox Communist views in public.

We took our first train trip, leaving Chicago for Milwaukee, on January 23. The train was clean, the ride smooth and on time. A bus met us and whisked us to Mayor Henry W. Maier. By now the delegation had loosened up. Tolkunov asked Maier how old he was. "I'm fifty-one," he replied, and a common bond was struck. The Russians were clearly impressed with this provincial city. They commented on the industriousness of the natives, and wished them success in their goal—which some thought patently absurd— of becoming "the greatest city in the world." We lunched at the *Milwaukee Journal,* then visited a farm where Tolkunov famously held a lamb in his arms for a local photographer.

January 24: Back in Chicago we got an introduction to Operation Bread-basket, where the Reverend Jesse Jackson was pushing a voter registration campaign in a large, darkened auditorium. An official explained that many thought Reverend Jackson was likely to become an important national po-litical figure. I'm not sure how much the Russians were able to take in other than to experience the energy that Jackson exuded. It was impossible to in-terpret during the performance. "I understand English pretty well," said Genrikas Zimanas, editor of the *Tiyesa* newspaper of Soviet Lithuania, "but I couldn't understand a word that Jackson said."

After the Jackson meeting, we moved to the office of the *Chicago Defender,* the historic black newspaper, for lunch. The editors asked pointed ques-tions about America's racial problems, which our hosts dutifully answered without conceding too much. They, in turn, threw back questions about dis-crimination against Jews in the Soviet Union. That was the first telltale sign of the buffeting we were to take as the trip progressed. The defensiveness of the editors on this issue began to show through. In the end, I wondered if both sides were talking past each other.

In the afternoon, we left O'Hare Airport for a flight to the West Coast. Getting on the plane, I sent a note to the pilots to welcome the guests over the cabin loudspeaker. They did so, but there was hardly a reaction from the

editors. The rest of the passengers shrugged off the news that they were flying with card-carrying Communists and potential enemies. We arrived in a
slight drizzle, exhausted but delighted to taste the mild sea air.

On Sunday, January 25, we spent a relaxed, quiet day. We got up late and
made a tour of the Bay Area Rapid Transport System. The foremen who
guided us handed out hard hats. The editors were tickled with the white
headgear and delighted to learn that the BART architects incorporated some
crowd-control features from the Leningrad subway. Their mood seemed to
lighten.

We drove next to Sacramento for a meeting with Governor Ronald Reagan on the twenty-sixth. Henry Shapiro, who was vacationing in the area,
joined us to schmooze with the senior editors who, he figured, could eventually become his best sources in Moscow. That was typical of Henry's
savoir faire, always looking for new avenues to information. Once assembled, the delegation was taken aback by seeing Reagan limp into the room,
complaining that over the weekend he had been "fighting" a new horse at
his ranch and that the horse won. Much of the conversation revolved
around Reagan's transformation from Democrat to Republican, leading editors to wonder whether the two political parties were either converging or
the system was a sham. It's fair to say that none of us in that room suspected
that Reagan would be elected president of the United States in 1980 or that
he would come to my rescue fifteen years later when I ran into trouble in
Moscow.

In the corridors, I did pick up warnings from state officials that we might
face a demonstration by Jewish protesters later in the day. I didn't see there
was anything I could do about it, and kept the threat to myself. The dinner
at the San Francisco Press Club began calmly enough. But as the evening
progressed, pickets gathered outside and began denouncing discrimination
against Soviet Jewry. To defuse the situation, I urged a quiet talk between
Ephraim Margolin, one of the demonstration leaders, and three editors. The
conversation was subdued and dignified. But suddenly word reached us
that demonstrators were waving placards on which the hammer and sickle
were juxtaposed with Nazi swastikas. The crisis worsened when we discovered that someone had padlocked the press club door, blocking our exit.

The editors were furious. They called the placards "a desecration of our
flag!" One editor shouted in my direction that he had lost sixteen members
of his family during the Nazi invasion. Enver Mamedov collared me and
shouted, "You colluded with those demonstrators! You knew about the
demonstration in advance and did nothing to stop it!"

Now I really could feel my blood pressure rising. At that stage in my career, eight years after becoming a copyboy at the *Washington Post,* I had only

a hazy notion of what the First Amendment actually states and to what extent local officials respect its words. That kind of ignorance on my part seems strange now, but, in the event, I began winging it: "In this country there is freedom of expression and the right to demonstrate publicly so long as it is peaceful," I said. Then I took the jump: "There is nothing anybody can do to turn off the demonstration. Not even the president."

That clearly did not satisfy Mamedov. He challenged me, saying he had been on a previous trip to the United States during which his guide, Harrison Salisbury of the *New York Times,* acted decisively. "When things got out of hand, he knew where to call! And another thing," Mamedov continued, "what has happened is an insult to us personally and to the dignity of our nation. We'll probably cancel the rest of the trip and fly back to Moscow!"

I had no answer to that. But the next thing I did was to run down a flight of back stairs and send an urgent message to Isaacs suggesting a telegram of immediate regrets. I even included some groveling language that I thought would satisfy my inquisitor. Isaacs rejected my text, but responded swiftly with his own. At breakfast the next morning, I found the editors passing around Isaacs's telegram with smiles on their faces. Crisis resolved.

Paradoxically, as crises will do, this incident brought some of us closer together. I even joked with one of the editors that I was preparing a humdinger of a demonstration when we got to Washington. Igor Geyevsky, of the newly established Institute of the USA and Canada, offered this ditty about the American guide:

>    Mr. Nik—bol'shoi shutnik
>    On burovik—i gluboko pronik!
>
>    (Mr. Nick is a big joker
>    He is a driller, and bored in very deep!)

One of the problems I kept having on this trip was organizing the reception at the next stop, in this case Los Angeles beginning on January 27. The editors begged me to have a basket of fruit and bottles of mineral water in their rooms. Mineral waters like Evian and Pellegrino were not yet very well known in the United States at the time, and often our guests arrived to find gallon jugs of some local spring quite distinct from the Narzan or Borzhomi waters they were accustomed to in the USSR. They did not hide their irritation.

One of the highlights of the visit to L.A. was the RAND Corporation, supported by the U.S. Air Force to produce classified analyses of current situations. The editors seemed to think that they would be shown amazing technology but instead found a modern office building staffed by well-educated analysts who talked volubly about current topics. They went away feeling that RAND was not what it was cracked up to be.

A dinner party in Hollywood hosted by Jane Fonda and Steve McQueen, however, delighted them. Jane Fonda charmed Yakovlev and A. I. Lukovets, deputy editor of *Pravda*, with stories of her trip to Russia five years before. The three came to the conclusion that America suffers from the "scramble for the almighty dollar" and that Russians, who own less, possess more in the quality of their friendships.

From the West Coast we flew to New Orleans on January 30, where we arrived to a new crisis. More Jewish demonstrators were decrying the fate of their coreligionists in the USSR, and now anticommunist Cubans joined the mix. They began protesting Moscow's support of Fidel Castro. At dinner in International House, we were suddenly panicked by word of a bomb threat, but after fruitless inspection of the building by police, we carried on without incident. After the bomb scare, the New Orleans police assigned several plainclothes officers to our group. They accompanied us everywhere: as we toured the city, as we walked down the streets, as we shopped for such exotic items as lightweight fishing tackle, Scotchguard upholstery, and . . . swizzle sticks. I was appalled by the police presence because I thought it gave a poor impression of public safety in the United States. But, to my surprise, my reaction was wrong. The editors were delighted that the New Orleans police treated them with the respect they obviously felt they deserved.

From New Orleans we flew to Washington, D.C., on February 1, where we were greeted at National Airport by old friend Bob McCloskey, official spokesman of the State Department. These next days were moments of heavy diplomatic soundings. Several black Cadillac limousines were put at our disposal to drive us to Capitol Hill for meetings with key senators, then off to the State Department and White House. Secretary Rogers received us in his elegant seventh-floor offices, and Henry Kissinger gave us a half-hour seminar on foreign policy and U.S.-Soviet relations in the West Wing of the White House. The Russians were impressed by Kissinger's calm dissection of world problems, and noted his Germanic accent. They correctly concluded that power in American foreign policy resided more with Kissinger than with Secretary Rogers.

On the morning of February 4, the mild thaw that greeted us a few days before suddenly turned into a blinding snowstorm on the day of our departure for New York. At five in the morning I got word that our ten o'clock flight had been canceled, and we made a fast switch to the 7:30 A.M. Metroliner. As we arrived at Union Station, Ambassador Dobrynin drove up in his limousine to say his farewells. The remaining hours of the editors' stay would be devoted to shopping and visiting with New York–based Soviet correspondents.

Departure day, February 5, came none too soon. I was exhausted and slept badly that last night at the Algonquin. Breakfast brought the final crisis: Student Struggle for Soviet Jewry threatened a new demonstration that could complicate our departure for the airport. I hastily arranged a meeting between Jacob Birnbaum of Student Struggle and Zimanas. Other editors refused to join this successful defusing operation.

As we left for the airport, I asked the visitors what they would take away with them. The consensus was that America was racked with internal problems, principally race and inflation. They suspected that the federal system was incapable of dealing with them and what was needed was a stronger central hand. On U.S.-Soviet relations, they believed major differences divided the governments in Moscow and Washington, but that the American people were curious, hospitable, and wanted to live in peace. They found some hope that relations could be improved, if there was sufficient will on both sides.

Such views were not surprising. We all view the world through our own cultural framework, and we are maddeningly slow to challenge the stereotypes we grow up with. What were the Soviet stereotypes of the United States in 1970? The United States was a powerful and dangerous nation, dominated by a military-industrial complex, and run on a day-to-day basis by a small group of people known as the "ruling class." According to this Marxist view, the "middle and petty bourgeoisie" were constantly struggling to make ends meet. All large business corporations were "monopolies" regulated only by greed. The United States was an imperial power, openly hostile to the Soviet Union, and filled with contradictions that had the potential of undermining its strength. Importantly, the United States was obsessed with expanding its global influence to the disadvantage of developing nations that Moscow tried to defend. This was particularly true of America's "adventuristic course" in Vietnam.

I tracked what the journalists wrote on return to Russia to see if the trip had somehow influenced their views. Igor Geyevsky published an academic piece in the August 1970 issue of *SShA, Politika, Ekonomika i Ideologiya*, journal of the Institute of the USA and Canada. It reflected little of the trip and concluded that President Nixon's policy was to court the right wing of the Republican Party, which would lead, in his opinion, to instability and turmoil. Yakovlev devoted a few pages thirty years later in his memoir, *Whirlpool of Memory*, to our odyssey. He had kind words for the meetings with Fulbright, Rogers, and Kissinger and was clearly attracted to Jane

Fonda, who later tried unsuccessfully to track him down in Moscow. Most notable to me was Yakovlev's appraisal of the United States, which displayed how much his orthodox Communist views had evolved and softened as a result of his decade in Canada. He wrote, "No matter how you regard this country, in all fairness, you have to recognize that the United States is an effective stabilizer in our unsettled world although it often makes irritating mistakes." Yakovlev added that America caused him to worry, too. "It seems that they don't know their future, or maybe they don't want to know what reserves of strength they possess. I'll be very happy if I am mistaken in my doubts and presentiments."

Tolkunov kept his promise by publishing a two-part series, "America Today," beginning on February 28, 1970, in *Izvestia* and one hundred pages on the trip in his book *Myths and Reality*, published a year later in 1971. How well did Tolkunov break away from the devil's view in addressing his readers, which included key figures in the Soviet leadership? His was a mixed picture, I thought. At first glance, it looked as if Tolkunov had dictated a long memorandum to an associate who did additional research and came up with a draft. I believe *Izvestia*'s Washington correspondent, Melor Sturua, also added important insights for his top editor. Much of Tolkunov's language was the usual Marxist terminology of the time. I found it interesting, however, that he recognized the stereotype problem when he noted that Americans tended to push their conception of the world on others without recognizing that there might be totally different social systems and views. In other words, he acknowledged that problems of understanding arise from the differing perspectives of other nations.

Tolkunov noted that the Vietnam War was causing an unacceptable level of casualties in the American body politic and was turning into a major domestic issue with which the Nixon administration was going to have to deal. I thought him perceptive in seeing there remained many influential Democratic politicians, notwithstanding the loss of the 1968 election to the Republicans, who would take advantage of any political mistakes by the Nixon administration. Specifically, he had kind words for Senator J. William Fulbright (D-AR), whose views differed sharply from the administration's. Despite the fact that America's "imperialistic course" had given birth to major problems in U.S. political life, Tolkunov did not foresee a collapse of the two-party system so different from the Soviet party structure.

I was surprised that he did not place more emphasis on the meetings with Kissinger and Rogers. These conversations were "on background," but that would not have excluded some description of these political personalities. And why should a Soviet editor abide by American "background rules" anyway? From private conversations, I knew that the editors were convinced that Kissinger was the center of foreign policy power, not Rogers. Yet this impression did not come through. And although Tolkunov and his research assistants did considerable scouring of the files, the series reflected no hint of Nixon's 1967 *Foreign Affairs* article that foreshadowed a U.S. rapprochement with Communist China to the disadvantage of the Soviet Union.

Finally, I was disappointed by Tolkunov's interpretation of the Jewish demonstrations that upset our peace. The protesters, I thought, wanted to pressure Moscow to allow Soviet Jewry greater religious freedom or a chance to emigrate. Tolkunov avoided all meetings with Jewish activists and was content to interpret the demonstrations as actions to divert public attention from Israel's settlements in the occupied territories. So the stereotypes asserted themselves after all. And I wondered whether political leaders, deeply involved in day-to-day decisions, can ever really shake off the conventional wisdom that they bring to power and accept unfamiliar, contrarian views.

As the delegation departed on that February day in 1970, one editor ruefully conceded to me, "We don't have a picture of America. Perhaps we have the approaches to a picture of America." After eighteen days in the United States, we were not much closer to understanding the same facts that we had viewed together. Such intensive travel does plant seeds, however, and these may flower at some point in the future. That was illustrated most dramatically by Yakovlev, who eventually abandoned his orthodox Communist views to become a driving force for freedom of expression and democratic values during the Gorbachev years.

My grandfather General Yuri N. Danilov with Czar
Nicholas II during World War I. *Left to right:* General
Danilov, Czar Nicholas II, chief of staff General N. N.
Yanushkevich, and Grand Duke Nikolai Nikolayevich
Romanov. (From illustrated magazine at the time)

Soviet diplomat Semyon Tsarapkin accepts the copper Ibis stolen by Harvard students from the top of the Lampoon Building in Cambridge, Massachusetts, as a prank. *Left to right:* Michael Maccoby (Harvard '54), Ambassador Semyon K. Tsarapkin, George Abrams (Harvard '54), at the Soviet Mission to the United Nations, New York, 1953. (Photo by John Loengard of 20 West Eighty-sixth Street, New York, NY 10024)

Double-decker London bus that Oxford University students drove to Moscow, September 1959. Curious passersby gawk at the vehicle. (ND archive)

With newspapers, I take a break from the international conference on Laotian neutrality. Geneva, 1961. (ND archive)

*Left to right:* Lyova (translator), Henry Shapiro, Jeune Jaffe *(partially hidden),* Ruth Daniloff, Christine Korengold, Nick Daniloff, Jay and Mary Axelbank, June 1963. (Courtesy of Robert J. Korengold)

Red Square farewell: UPI correspondent Bud Korengold and his wife, Christine, leave the Soviet Union after a four-year assignment. *Left to right:* Nick Daniloff, photographing; Lev Shtern, translator; Tonya ("significant other" of Yuri Korolyov); Christine Korengold; and Bud Korengold. (ND archive)

At the John Steinbeck press conference in Moscow. The UPI photographer taking pictures is Yuri Korolyov. (ND archive)

I cover Soviet leader Nikita Khrushchev at the Embassy of Nepal, 1963. (ND archive)

I question Soviet leader Nikita Khrushchev face to face. (ND archive)

UPI chief diplomatic correspondent Stewart Hensley adjusts his radio telephone while covering President Eisenhower's trip through South America in 1960. (Courtesy of William Hensley)

Sam Jaffe of ABC in Moscow. (From Jaffe family collection)

Dr. Goldfarb and his wife, Iliya, entertain
the author in their Moscow kitchen.
(ND archive)

Close-up of Decembrist revolutionary Alexander
Frolov. The watercolor is preserved today at the
Pushkin Museum in Moscow. (ND archive)

I take notes in Shushenskoe, place of exile of Alexander Frolov in Siberia and also the place of exile of Vladimir I. Lenin, some fifty years later. Museum director Yuri A. Ivanov *(smiling)* and historian Dr. Ludmilla Sisoyeva *(reading documents)*. (ND archive)

At Frolov's grave in Moscow in winter. (ND archive)

Confrontation over the Atlantic Ocean: U.S. F-14 Tomcat
fighter, based on the USS *Nimitz*, tails a Soviet Tu-95 "Bear"
long-range intelligence aircraft during 1980 NATO exercises.
(Official U.S. Navy photograph)

The *Looking Glass* plane, an airborne command post that can assume control of U.S. strategic missiles should SAC underground command posts be knocked out by Soviet nuclear attack. The aircraft is an EC-135, the military version of the Boeing 707. (Photo by Strategic Air Command)

Inside the *Looking Glass* plane. (Photo by Strategic Air Command)

Diplomatic editor Joe Fromm conferring with John Law, *U.S. News and World Report* correspondent for the Middle East. (Courtesy of *U.S. News and World Report*)

I work in the press room of the Iceland summit conference
between President Reagan and Soviet leader Mikhail Gorbachev. Reykjavik, Iceland, 1986. (ND archive)

White House meeting, October 1986. *Left to right, facing camera:* Vice President Bush, Nancy Reagan, President Reagan, and Nick Daniloff. *On couch, backs to camera, left to right:* Miranda, Caleb, and Ruth Daniloff. (Official White House photo)

Beside the grave of Benjamin Pierce, a Revolutionary War soldier, in Chester, Vermont, 1989. (ND archive)

Nick Daniloff as a professor of journalism at Northeastern University, September 1999. (Photo by Denis Van-
dal of Northeastern University)

# Chapter 17

## Good Snoop, Good Gossip

Despite my work with the Soviet editors for which I received high praise from the top brass, all was not well. This was odd because no one criticized my work directly, and it was only after the editors departed that I learned of an undercurrent of dissatisfaction directed at me. Confusing the issue still further, Roger Tatarian asked me to come to New York to discuss the possibility of replacing Henry Shapiro as manager of the Moscow Bureau. This was one of a series of invitations to better jobs that started coming my way, as people outside of UPI began to notice what I had been doing. George Packard, managing editor of the *Philadelphia Bulletin*, for example, had suggested to me that I join his newspaper. I worked out a proposal that asked for an increase in salary, but our negotiations went nowhere.

When Roger called, I thought I glimpsed an opportunity to get my salary raised from twelve thousand dollars a year to something like twenty thousand. At the time, Hensley told me he was making about twenty-five thousand. When I put my figure to Roger, he gracefully told me the request was far too high. I was not too disappointed. Frankly, my life had changed. Ruth and I had come to like Washington, we had bought a house, and our family was growing, with Caleb's birth in 1969. My thoughts of replacing Shapiro were now eclipsed by the hope of replacing Hensley. When the Moscow deal did not work out, I told colleagues that UPI management refused my salary suggestion. UPI management, for their part, let it be known that I had refused their offer. This breakdown gave rise to bad feelings, especially among those who expected me to be the next Shapiro.

A further turn in the situation occurred when Julius Frandsen, spotting a takeout on the Soviet economy in the *Wall Street Journal,* asked me to do a similar report for UPI. I agreed, but then could not get it started. I dawdled and eventually forgot about the request. Months later, I began hearing veiled remarks that Dillman was displeased with me. I decided I had better find out what was wrong, and we agreed to sit down to lunch on February 23, 1971.

Dillman was not someone to trifle with. As a young man of twenty-one in 1939, he joined the *Columbus (Ohio) Dispatch* and later, in 1943, landed a job with the Columbus Bureau of United Press. Mitral valve disorder prevented him from joining the navy in World War II, and he transferred to the Washington Bureau of UP in 1945, working his way steadily up the ladder until his retirement as a vice president in 1983, forty-one years later. To him, it seemed to me, experience trumped everything, including youth, energy, and, most certainly, academic knowledge. Dillman was frequently praised as a fair but demanding manager. "I thought he was a great editor," recalled Helen Thomas, White House bureau chief for UPI when Dillman died in 2001. "He was tremendous in the slot. You could get a flash like the Kennedy assassination, or when Nixon resigned, and you have to make crucial decisions. He rose to every occasion and was cool under fire."

Despite all that, I always thought there was something odd about Dillman, as did other members of the bureau, who started a secret newsletter called *Grant's Tomb.* Dillman spent the majority of his time inside the bureau riding herd on every aspect of coverage. It struck me as peculiar that he rarely went out to meet the politicians and news makers. I suspected he harbored an inferiority complex beside these highly educated overachievers and made up for it by throwing his weight around the office. Incidentally, Marlin Fitzwater, who later became the respected press spokesman of Presidents Reagan and Bush the elder, recalled his own fractious encounter with Dillman in the mid-1960s. Fresh out of college, Fitzwater came to the UPI Washington Bureau, looking for any job. Dillman brushed him off and told him to go back to Kansas and get some experience.

Within the bureau, Dillman would more than occasionally ogle the young women dictationists—sexual harassment in those days was not an issue—then take them out for coffee at a downstairs eatery called Bassins. What went on at those encounters I never knew. In later years Dillman became a strong supporter of Helen Thomas, naming her chief White House correspondent for UPI and pushing her for membership in select associations such as the National Press Club and the Gridiron Club. Yet at times Dillman could act unfairly, erupting in a rage, firing a reporter over a trivial matter, and then reinstating him the next day.

Dillman began our lunch with an apology. He told me that management had always thought I would be in Washington only temporarily before heading back to Moscow, and therefore he had never given me any clear instructions as to how I should work. "You're trying to mimic Hensley too much," he said. "Let him cover the big stories. Your role is to go out and find the unusual stories that others overlook, stories that can get good play." He went on to say that Frandsen thought I did not approach my work with enough curiosity and urgency. "A good journalist must be a good snoop and a good gossip," Dillman emphasized.

I defended myself, saying that often the desk was not moving quickly many stories that I had spent considerable time developing. Clearly, we were not going to come to an understanding on that point.

Then came Dillman's death blow. He raised my failure to deliver on Frandsen's special request. "When your boss asks you to do something, and you don't attack it for months and months, you're just no damn good." He grimaced, and that was that. He was right, of course, and I slipped away from the hour-and-a-half lunch humiliated. Within a short while, however, I researched the Soviet economy story and delivered. But the damage was done.

Taking Dillman's "snoop and gossip" advice to heart, I began reaching outside the State Department to develop offbeat international stories. I came up with a number of features I took pride in: a report on the State Department operations center, the tale of an émigré doctor at George Washington University Hospital who went back to China to learn acupuncture, and the story of Dr. Armand Hammer who, years later, would play a role in my own life.

Dr. Hammer was in the news those days because he had concluded a mammoth eight billion–dollar fertilizer contract with the Soviet Union, one of the biggest in foreign trade. I knew little about Hammer, although he had been mentioned occasionally in the Soviet press during my first Moscow assignment. Born in 1898 in New York City, he was the roughly the same age as my father and had gone to Russia in 1922 just after the Bolshevik Revolution. During that first visit as a youth of twenty-three, Hammer met Lenin. I thought that talking to Hammer would give me some new insights into U.S.-Soviet relations and even into the beginnings of the Soviet state.

At my request, Hammer invited me to his Watergate apartment for several chats. A stocky man with tortoiseshell glasses, he had graduated from Columbia University College of Physicians and Surgeons in 1921 while simultaneously managing his father's small pharmaceutical lab. "When I graduated," he said with unnerving confidence, "the business was so successful that I found that I had made enough money to retire, and I thought I would never need any more money."

He went on to describe how he journeyed to Russia after graduation with help from Ludwig Martens, the unofficial Soviet representative in New York. They traveled together to the Urals, where he confronted the devastating results of famine and civil war. He saw threadbare survivors stacking corpses like cordwood behind railroad stations and starving children whining for food outside the carriages of their special train. "How much grain do you need to save the population of this district in the Urals?" he asked Martens. The official replied, "A million bushels would take care of the population until the next harvest."

What Hammer told me next made me feel like an insignificant actor in a world of giants. "I've got a million dollars," my tape recorder caught him saying. "I'll buy a million bushels and ship it on credit, provided that every ship that comes with grain you load with something I can sell in America to pay for the grain." The deal was struck, and when Lenin learned of it, he summoned the youth to the Kremlin and offered to make him one of the first foreign concessionaires under the New Economic Policy.

I marveled how Lenin thus launched Hammer's fabulous career as an international businessman and couldn't help asking his impressions of the Soviet leader. "He made a very good impression on me," Hammer recalled, "and when he talked about the plight of the children as a result of the civil war, tears came to his eyes. He seemed a very warm person." Admittedly, at the time of our interview in 1973, Lenin's role in the brutal repressions that established the Soviet state and his involvement in the assassination of Czar Nicholas II and his family had not yet become common knowledge. Hammer had reacted like the quintessential businessman happening upon a good deal. At the end of our initial interview, I decided to test Hammer's language ability and switched suddenly to Russian. He stumbled with a heavy American accent, then saved himself with a bit of disarming humor. He described the factory meeting he had addressed in the Urals after his first grain deal was concluded. He spoke, in his newly learned Russian, of a freighter plowing across the Atlantic, bringing a cargo of grain and salvation. At the end, he was heavily applauded. Afterward, he expressed surprise to Martens that the meeting went so well. His handler replied, "They were polite. Actually, they didn't understand a thing you said. They thought you were speaking English!"

Truth to tell, after twelve years with UPI in Europe and Washington, I believed I had now learned everything that wire-service journalism could teach: persistence in routing out facts, skill in interviewing, speed in composition (including off-the-cuff dictation), how to cultivate sources, and more. It was easy to continue for a wire service like UPI, which was so paternalistic it was not going to fire a below-par employee who had years of service. To do something different was to take a risk. My academic leanings were now seriously tugging at me, and in my spare time I began writing a history of the Soviet space program. Washington seemed like a good place for that kind of research. The air force had established a research group at the Library of Congress that was engaged in meticulous reading of Soviet open sources on space exploration. There were many experts, including Charles Sheldon of the Library of Congress, who were willing to share their knowledge. I would spend weekends at the library reading Russian materials, sometimes going for only a short period of an hour or less just for the sake of "discipline." After four years of part-time work, Alfred Knopf of New York published my book *The Kremlin and the Cosmos* in 1972. It was a critical success, but failed to win back the five thousand–dollar advance. At least I had proved to myself that I was a substantial snoop who could bring a project successfully to completion.

The year 1972, of course, was a major turning point in international affairs, and the Washington Bureau of UPI was deeply engaged. Kissinger's secret trip to Beijing in the fall of 1971 led to President Nixon's dramatic announcement that he planned to go to the Chinese capital to reorient America's relations with the People's Republic of China. The visit meant that the United States was moving away from its support of the Republic of China on Taiwan, something highly resisted in conservative quarters in the United States. Playing the "China card," which the administration often denied it was doing, put relations with the Soviet Union into a new triangular power play.

The Washington Bureau geared up in a major way for the coverage of the Nixon trip. Assigned to the adventure were Helen Thomas, chief White House correspondent, and Stu Hensley. Hensley, now seriously suffering from emphysema, was outfitted with a portable oxygen pack in a brown leather case that made him look like a deep-sea diver. Devotion to duty was not something Hensley lacked, even as his health declined.

The Washington Bureau's schedule was turned on its head because of the twelve-hour time difference with China; most staffers came to work late in the afternoon and worked through the night. I was shifted from the State Department to the bureau and reported for work on the desk at midnight until eight in the morning. Surprisingly, I found I could work throughout the night and exist with as few as three hours of sleep during the day.

Nixon's trip awakened enormous enthusiasm among journalists. I saw China as a new outlet for my own ambitions and began following Chinese affairs with growing interest. I decided to apply for a Nieman Fellowship at Harvard University so I could study Chinese history, politics, and language. The Nieman Fellowship program, created in 1938 by the family of Lucius

Nieman of the *Milwaukee Journal,* offered journalists a chance to take a mid-career break to refresh their minds. I recalled that Shapiro once told us that the foundation reserved two of twelve spots for representatives from the Associated Press and United Press International and that he himself had been a Nieman Fellow from 1954 to 1955, after Stalin died. I asked Hensley to write one of my recommendations. His letter of January 25, 1973, sang the praises that I could never hope to get from Dillman. One phrase I cherished: "Daniloff at present is at what I would describe as a 'take-off point' in his career. He has done an excellent job for UPI but his true potential is yet to be realized." In May 1973, the Nieman Foundation informed me that I was accepted for the academic year beginning that fall.

My project was to look at the Cold War from a new perspective: the People's Republic of China. I made up my mind, too, to study Mandarin Chinese in the hopes of eventually getting a Beijing assignment. In the fall, Ruth and I packed up our family, Caleb and Miranda, in our VW Bus and drove up Interstate 95 to a small basement apartment I had managed to rent in Cambridge. Under the direction of Dr. Jim Thomson, a China expert and former staff member of the National Security Council in the Johnson administration, all of Harvard's resources were open to us. Ruth and the other wives were granted the same privileges as the fellows, and during this year made a major leap forward in her efforts to become a writer, publishing in the *Harvard Magazine* and elsewhere.

My study entailed a graduate seminar on Chinese contemporary politics run by Ross Terrill, an Australian expert on China who was attracting considerable attention because of his firsthand knowledge of the mainland. Thomson also encouraged us to teach, and shortly I began giving newswriting lessons to Milton Chen, an undergraduate of Chinese extraction who went on to become an expert on children's television at KQED in San Francisco and later executive secretary of the George Lucas Foundation.

All of us were pushed by Thomson to stray from our official projects and seek out new fields. I was lucky to win a trip to Germany to examine NATO deployments, as well as a visit to Japan and to the European Community in Brussels. In Cambridge, I started going to the Harvard Law School to hear lectures by Professor Jerome Cohen, head of the East Asia Studies Center. One night he included me in a group of students at his home to hear a "mystery guest" on China and international law.

The guest turned out to be John Downey, a former CIA agent, now a student at the Harvard Law School. He had been shot down while on a secret mission, penetrating into Communist China on November 29, 1952, in a C-47. In those years, the CIA was infiltrating agents into both Communist China and the Soviet Union. On this 1952 mission, the pilot and copilot were killed, but Downey and another CIA colleague, Richard Fecteau, survived to be captured, tried, and imprisoned. Over the years, Downey has been reluctant to reveal the details of the abortive mission, but that night in Cambridge he spoke nonstop for more than three hours. As a "Dillman snoop," I thought I had better take notes. Of course, since Downey was speaking off the record, what he was saying would be unpublishable under Washington Rules. But we were not in Washington, and, furthermore, secrets get declassified in most countries after twenty-five to seventy years. Now, more than thirty years later, the time has come . . .

What struck us all that evening was how well Downey had adjusted to his new life as a forty-one-year-old law student. (He has since become a judge in Connecticut.) Sipping a beer beside the fireplace, he professed no bitterness over twenty lost years that he asserted benefited no one. A heavy-set man with glasses, dressed in tweeds, blue shirt, and red tie, he spoke with an impish sense of humor. We soon realized that the evening was, in part, a way for Downey to say thanks to his Yale classmate, who had never forgotten his college friend and pushed the Nixon administration to rescue him.

Downey's odyssey began during his senior year at Yale, when he and Cohen attended a session by a CIA recruiter. Downey joined the agency; Cohen went to law school. Downey recalled that the CIA told him that if he ever got into trouble during an operation to expect no help. "You're on your own," he was told. John Downey was eventually assigned to a secret program for inserting Chinese from Taiwan into mainland China to undermine the regime of Mao Zedong, who came to power in October 1950. On the night of November 29, 1952, a C-47 piloted by Robert C. Snoddy and Norman A. Schwartz was to fly from Korea to Japan, passing briefly over a pickup point in northern China to retrieve one of the infiltrators. As the C-47 prepared to depart, a call went out for a volunteer. Standing on the tarmac, Downey spontaneously agreed, at the very last moment, to go.

It was a daring mission. Before departure, the would-be rescuers received a radio message in Morse code, verified as authentic by the telegrapher's personal key touch, reporting all was ready. The infiltrator would be suspended in a sling from a "clothesline" strung between two sturdy posts. The C-47 would fly in low and snatch the "clothesline" and radio operator with a grappling hook. Downey and Fecteau would then haul the agent into the slowly flying plane.

Everything seemed to be going fine, up to the time we hooked the agent and started winching him in. Then as the pilot nosed the C-47 up, all hell broke loose. The Communists began firing with small arms and machine guns. The plane started losing altitude, the nose came down as if someone had turned off the ignition, and we plowed forward for the longest time through treetops. I dove for a sleeping bag and came through almost without a scratch. When the plane came to a stop, Fecteau and I got out and wondered what we should do next. We never saw the pilot or copilot again.

Only Downey and Fecteau survived the crash, and the two were immediately surrounded by local Chinese. It turned out that the infiltrators from Taiwan had been captured long before, and the radio operator who had sent the "all ready" message was operating under Communist control. Chinese counterintelligence had turned the rescue attempt into a trap. For the next two years, Chinese interrogators questioned Downey and Fecteau separately. The two never had a chance to coordinate their stories. Downey said he insisted that he was a civilian working for the Department of Defense and therefore could expect to be treated as a prisoner of war. However, this cover story was blown by the fact that he was wearing civilian underwear beneath army fatigues. On the sixteenth day, he acknowledged he actually worked for the Central Intelligence Agency. He tried to resist, but as the questioning wore on, he occasionally stumbled.

> I tried to hold back at first. I pretended that I thought I was in Korea. All the time I was trying to save what I could. I tried to delay. But they managed to scare the living Jesus out of me, and I could see no end to the interrogation.
>
> From the interrogation I got feedback which I thought meant that Fecteau was talking a lot. It later turned out that Fecteau had given the Chinese the names of his college football players as CIA agents. I sometimes had trouble remembering the stories I had made up to divert the interrogators.

Downey and Fecteau were put on trial in October 1954. Downey recalled that he was given ten minutes to confer with a defense lawyer before the trial. The lawyer pleaded for leniency, noting that Downey was repentant and, in any case, was only a small cog in President Truman's "imperialist machine." This was essentially the same defense that Francis Gary Powers put up during his trial in Moscow six years later and for which he received a ten-year sentence. The Chinese court sentenced Downey to life imprisonment and Fecteau to twenty years. Downey remembered,

> I was expecting to get a ten-year sentence, particularly since the Chinese made such a point of leniency if we showed a repentant attitude. When I was sentenced to life, it was a complete revolution in my expectations. I

was really depressed when I went back to my cell that night. And I said to myself, "Do you realize, old buddy, you've just been sentenced to life imprisonment?" I had this vision of myself as an old gray-haired man, speaking broken Chinese, shuffling about the prison, sweeping up.

How do you survive in prison when there seems to be no way out? As I was to learn later myself, you say that no matter how bleak the situation, things can change overnight. After sentencing in November 1954, a tough-looking interrogator asked Downey if he had anything more to reveal. As an incentive to talk, the interrogator asserted that living conditions could be improved, although, of course, there could be no change in the sentence. "His suggestion had an opposite effect on me," Downey chuckled during that Cambridge encounter. "I then felt sure that something was up—that there was hope." Though he did not know it, the Chinese made a number of subtle gestures to the Eisenhower administration aimed at improving relations. In August 1955, they freed the crew of a B-29 bomber shot down on January 12, 1953, on a leaflet-dropping mission near the Yalu River during the Korean War. Downey recalled that six months earlier in 1954, he and Fecteau were put in the same cell as the crew of the B-29 and its commander, Colonel John Arnold. "That has got to rank as one of the real thrills of my life. We had a ball!"

But the joy soon faded. In 1959, the Chinese authorities ordered Downey, Fecteau, and an English-speaking Chinese prisoner to form a group to study Mao's thoughts. "I was scared to death at first," Downey admitted. "I thought I was going to be brainwashed, and turned into some kind of robot." But it didn't work out that way. In self-defense he claimed to believe some of Mao's reflections. The study group was ordered to work six hours a day, six days a week. At the same time, Downey hung on to some semblance of his own identity. As a Roman Catholic, he was allowed to keep a Bible, which he read an hour a day and foiled every attempt to take it away. "I hung on to it like a talisman, and when I was released, I put it aside, and, you know what," he gasped, "I never really missed it."

As time wore on, Downey was supplied with many of the world's literary classics, which he read with enthusiasm. He was even allowed to receive some American communist publications and was able to keep up with many events in the United States. He began studying Russian with a Chinese prisoner but resisted learning Chinese. "After being sentenced, I was pretty turned off on everything Chinese. To begin studying Chinese was sort of like giving up. It meant admitting there was no future."

In 1966, when the Cultural Revolution began, prison conditions turned upside down. "All of the honchos of the prison staff were overthrown,"

Downey continued. "Some of them were thrown out of their administrative posts and made to carry night soil. The food really became crud, and all the amenities were curtailed."

Still, there were a few breaks in routine. In 1970, two Vietnam-era pilots—Captain Philip E. Smith, shot down in 1965 over Hainan Island, and Lieutenant Robert J. Flynn, shot down in 1967 over southern China—were thrown in for a while with Downey and Fecteau. Five times during his lengthy prison term, Downey's mother was allowed to come to China quietly to visit him. And at one point, the Chinese even took him for a six-week tour of China, including visits to Wuhan and Hangzhou. The authorities explained these excursions by saying, "When you go home, you'll be able to tell of the achievements of China."

The Nixon administration, moving to shift diplomatic recognition from Taiwan to mainland China, kept pressing for the release of these two prisoners at Professor Cohen's insistence. The stumbling block was the Chinese demand that the United States acknowledge publicly that Downey and Fecteau were spies employed by the Central Intelligence Agency. Throughout most of their incarceration, the United States denied that link. Finally, at a January 31, 1973, press conference, President Nixon admitted that the pair had been CIA employees. And on March 13, 1973, Downey was freed, allowed to walk across a bridge leading into the British colony of Hong Kong.

Beijing was easier on Fecteau: he was released one year before completing his twenty-year sentence, in 1972 in connection to Nixon's trip to China. Twenty-six years later, in July 1998, Downey and Fecteau received public recognition of their secret service when they were awarded the CIA Director's Medal. And Downey even returned to China in 2002—fifty years after the C-47 crash—with a U.S. military team seeking full details of the deaths of Snoddy and Schwartz.

A prisoner who lives through twenty years of prison or a correspondent who observes fifty years of history is sure to appreciate the irony of life. Neither nations nor individuals have permanent enemies, only permanent interests. And the overwhelming interest of men and nations is to survive.

## Chapter 18

## Au Revoir

On returning to Washington from the Nieman year, I joined a small crowd of guests in the East Room of the White House to witness one of the most bizarre farewells in American political history. It was the morning of August 9, 1974, the day after President Nixon announced he was going to do the un-precedented—resign the U.S. presidency. He gathered his cabinet members, friends, supporters, and White House staff to say "au revoir," not really a farewell, but as he put it, "we'll meet again." The moment was heavy with emotion and more than a few tears.

Nixon addressed the crowd, standing behind a podium, against the back-ground of the American flag and battle standards, surrounded by his im-mediate family, wife Pat, his sons-in-law and their wives, David Eisenhower and Julie, Ed Cox and Patricia. The scene was illuminated by piercing lights, and we were viewing a public man shorn of the smiling mask he put on for official appearances. I knew something about that mask. I once surprised Nixon unexpectedly as I came to work one morning through the northwest gate on Pennsylvania Avenue. He was walking briskly from the White House to the Executive Office Building, surrounded by his bodyguards. "Good morning, Mr. President," I greeted him politely. He barely glanced at me, as if I was an unwelcome presence, continued walking at a fast pace, without so much as a reply.

On August 9, Nixon spoke awkwardly, slowly, in a quavering voice, often on the verge of cracking. We could only guess how much he had personally suffered during the final days as he struggled with the decision to resign. Commenting on his extraordinary leave-taking, he told his supporters, "We don't have a proper word for this in English. A better word is 'au revoir.'" His emotion had not been obvious the night before when he addressed the American people over national television. On the evening of August 8 he laid the blame for the crisis, not on Watergate or the subsequent cover-up. He never mentioned Watergate by name, although he did admit to making some unspecified mistakes. The blame, he explained, lay with the loss of political support in Congress. It seemed to me that what he was doing was casting his fall into the dynamics of the European parliamentary system, where a vote of no confidence is always a possibility but not necessarily a personal disgrace.

On this morning-after, Nixon avoided face-saving and allowed himself to devolve into self-pity. "I'm not a wealthy man," he confessed, "and I'm going to have difficulty paying my taxes." Then at another point, he fumbled in recalling a citation from Theodore Roosevelt and interjected, "I kind of like to read books. I'm not an educated man, but I do read books." And finally he came around to his parents, to his father, a poor lemon farmer in California, and to his mother. "My mother was a saint. Nobody is going to write a book about her, but she was a saint."

Throughout this emotional performance, Pat Nixon stood next to her husband, choking back tears. She was, after all, being evicted publicly from the White House. The president never mentioned her or other members of his family, never offered them a word of comfort. Later he would say that if he had, Pat might have completely broken down. Finally, when he came to his last words, he implored his guests never to give up, never to give in to hate, because if you do, you have lost.

He and his family then moved out to the waiting marine helicopter on the south lawn to fly to Andrews Air Force Base and on to California in the *Spirit of '76*. Lingering in the doorway of *Marine One*, Nixon turned to the crowd, waved lustily, his mask now firmly back in place, his arms high over his head, his fingers in two V signs. Then he was gone, and an hour and a half later, at noon, Vice President Gerald Ford was sworn in as the thirty-eighth president. At the same time, Nixon, flying over Missouri, turned invisibly from president of the United States of America to private citizen. At the White House, all reminders of Nixon, all framed photographs of the thirty-seventh president, all mementos of his presidency, disappeared from the walls in an operation that reminded me of the Soviet practice of turning a disgraced politician into an "unperson."

Why I was present at this leave-taking was the unlikely outcome of office politics when I reported for work in Washington after the Harvard year. Nieman curator Jim Thomson had warned us we would face frictions, even conflicts, when we resumed work. We would be forced to wear "a hair shirt," he predicted, before we regained acceptance. Even so, I did not expect the brutality with which my bureau chief greeted me when I went back on July 1. I found Dillman feisty and aggressive.

In my absence, UPI had been hit by a strike that had radicalized management and workers. During the strike, the Washington Bureau stopped covering the Pentagon, and no client complained, Dillman said. He said he had drawn up a list of reporters whom he would be glad to get rid of and announced that I was on that list. "Actually," he went on, "we were all hoping that you would quit while you were up at Harvard and go into academic work. You're better suited for that than journalism." He paused. Then he drilled me with steely eyes. "Hensley and Jim Anderson have the State Department covered, so there's nothing for you there." He paused, letting the tension mount, then concluded disdainfully, "For the moment you can work on the desk."

That was the beginning and end of the encounter. I fled as fast as I could and dissolved in tears somewhere on Pennsylvania Avenue, not far from the White House. How could he be so unfair? The pain lasted for days, then suddenly without warning, Dillman called me on July 6 with this bombshell: "Gene Risher has quit his White House job." I waited for the next sentence. Dillman continued, "Get your ass over to the White House and help Helen cover the Nixon story." I was stunned. How could the boss denounce you one day, then turn around completely and offer you a part of one of the biggest events in American political history? Why not assign a worthier candidate and send the mediocrity off to fill his hole? Was this simply deplorable management? Or the turbulence of a passive-aggressive personality?

The next day Helen herself called me from Key Biscayne, where she was covering the wounded president. "I'm delighted you're coming to help me," she said according to a note I made in my journal for July 7. She promised to relay her enthusiasm to Dillman, too.

Working with Helen Thomas was a treat. She introduced me to the inner workings of the press corps that covers the president. Reporting from the White House is often considered the pinnacle of a Washington journalistic career, or at least a stepping-stone to even more important positions such as anchors, commentators, and editors. The reality of presidential coverage, however, is far from glamorous. Depending on the administration, White House officials may be difficult or only somewhat less difficult to reach and interview. Presidential spokesmen may be forthcoming or reticent. At the height of the Nixon crisis, I remember spokesman Ron Ziegler getting increasingly short with the press and losing credibility daily. The atmosphere in the White House press room was corrosive to an extraordinary degree.

"What lies are you telling us today?" was a comment occasionally hurled at Ziegler before the fall.

Journalists have very limited freedom at the White House; they are essentially at the disposal of the president. The assignment requires long hours of unproductive waiting. Quarters in my day were cramped. The press room was housed in the part of the White House that contained a swimming pool during the Johnson and previous administrations. The room, as I came to know it, was divided into three parts: an auditorium for press conferences behind which were the tiny cubicles of the Associated Press and United Press International, and some further space in the back for a few lucky journalists. In this "way back" was a staircase leading down to an underground bunker where television companies maintained their booths.

Helen, who started covering the White House during the Kennedy administration, was a daunting model to emulate. She came to work about six and left late. After fifteen years at the White House she developed a skeptical view of power and its temptations; she believed officials were usually hiding something, and she didn't mind demanding that they confess. Even so, she preserved a human touch and never descended into rudeness. Helen fought hard for women's equality with men and was devoted to the American idea of the melting pot. She decried the ethnic divisiveness that she saw sprouting in the United States. Her parents had immigrated to the United States from Lebanon and Syria, and she proudly declared, "I am an American, not an Arab American."

Helen was born in Kentucky and grew up in Detroit. As a high school student she became enthralled with journalism, and later graduated from Wayne State University. She came to Washington in the summer of 1942 after graduation and worked briefly as a waitress before getting a job as a "copyboy" for the *Washington Daily News* at $17.50 a week. Later, she moved to United Press, where she got an "inside" job writing early-morning radio copy. In time, she was assigned a regular beat—the Departments of Justice and Health, Education, and Welfare. During the presidential campaign of 1960 she covered Jacqueline Kennedy, and when Senator John Kennedy won over Richard Nixon, she moved to the White House to cover the new administration. I found Helen extraordinarily diligent, with a special ability to make friends and cultivate sources. Helen was a vacuum cleaner, sucking up pinpoint details like the color of a necktie, the tone of voice, hesitancy in answering questions that suggested something was being hidden. All these observations added credibility to her reports.

An enormous amount has been written about the demise of Richard Nixon and probably none better than *Final Days* by Bob Woodward and Carl

Bernstein, who had initially uncovered the Watergate affair, and by Jonathan Aitken, a member of the House of Commons in London, in his biography, *Nixon*. There is little that a journalist who was assigned temporarily to the White House can add except, I think, for one thing. I covered the fall of Nikita Khrushchev in Moscow in 1964 and the fall of Richard Nixon in Washington ten years later. In both cases, deeply human considerations involving face-saving, secrecy in decision making, news that was too hot to control, public reassurances, and justifications before history imposed themselves in similar ways on two extremely different leaders of two extremely different political systems.

The first stage of collapse—I'll call it "Heading for Divorce"—began many months before the actual resignations. In Washington, the discomfort began with the arrest of the Watergate burglars on June 17, 1972, and their trial in early 1973. The situation worsened on March 23, 1973, when one of the convicted intruders, James McCord, wrote Judge John J. Sirica that the burglary was executed under political pressure. In May 1973, the Senate Watergate Committee held nationally televised hearings during which former presidential counsel John Dean described the cover-up as a "cancer growing on the presidency," followed a few days later by Alexander Butterfield's revelation that Nixon had a voice-activated recording system in the Oval Office that had captured innumerable conversations with his official visitors. This led to the appointment of a special Watergate prosecutor, Archibald Cox, whom Nixon fired months later, along with Elliot Richardson, the U.S. attorney general, on October 20, 1973. The "Saturday Night Massacre" alerted the nation that something very suspicious was going on.

Cox was replaced by a Texas lawyer, Leon Jaworski, who the White House hoped would go easier than his predecessor but who plunged forward with his investigation with unrelenting energy. Nixon resisted the continuing demands for tapes by asserting they were covered by "executive privilege"—the argument that a president must have the ability to conduct his business in private; otherwise, no one could trust the presumption of confidentiality of important conversations in the Oval Office. Nixon and his lawyers tried various forms of persuasion: releasing edited typescripts of the tapes, releasing selected tapes, allowing certain senators the right to listen to certain tapes. From a variety of sources, Jaworski suspected that the tapes of March 21, 1973, held the crucial information that he sought.

In Moscow, a decade earlier, this first stage of falling began in earnest as a result of the Cuban missile crisis of 1962. It built upon growing criticism of Khrushchev's leadership style within the Soviet elite, such as the shoe-banging incident at the United Nations in 1960, his ill-thought-out agricultural experiments, his intemperate attacks on dissident artists, his occasional foul language in public, his increasing tendency to make important decisions without consultation. His effort to counter these ills by intimidating the United States through secretly deploying medium-range missiles in Cuba cured nothing. It only exacerbated the situation.

We correspondents in Moscow picked up rumors that the Communist chief might retire around the time of his seventieth birthday, in 1964. We prepared for any development, and when the TASS wire stopped transmitting a Khrushchev speech in the Kremlin without explanation in April, some correspondents flashed the false news that he was out. In or out? That was a continuing question. Ambassador Foy Kohler reportedly messaged the State Department that there was no really credible threat to Khrushchev's position. And Henry Shapiro filed a dispatch to UPI on September 8, 1964, a month before the fall, that assured readers that Khrushchev was solidly in power.

The second stage—"Alarm Bells"—sounded loudly enough for Khrushchev during the summer of 1964, although we foreign correspondents had no clear knowledge of them. He received several hints that dissatisfaction was growing to the point that his position was threatened, but he dismissed them out of hand. The warnings have now been well documented by Professor William Taubman in his excellent biography, *Khrushchev*. During that summer, Rada Adzhubei, Khrushchev's daughter, received a telephone warning from an unidentified woman who wanted to warn her of the plot. She refused to receive her. Khrushchev's son, Sergei, an aerospace engineer, received a hint of the plot from a bodyguard in September and reported it to his father. Again Khrushchev refused to credit it. Finally, Leonid Brezhnev, the number-two man in the party, summoned Khrushchev to return from a Black Sea vacation ostensibly to discuss agricultural policy, but in actuality to face the showdown.

In Washington, "Alarm Bells" were ringing loudly by July, as if announcing the denouement of a Greek tragedy. During his summit meeting in Moscow in June, Nixon had been unable to convince Soviet leader Brezhnev to include a line in their final communiqué stating that their personal relationship had helped ease tensions between the superpowers. More ominous, Turkey, taking advantage of what looked like American weakness at the top, invaded Cyprus and set up a Turkish Cypriot government on the north of the island against the wishes of the United States. It was beginning to look like Watergate was undercutting American power in international affairs.

On July 24, 1974, the U.S. Supreme Court ordered Nixon to turn over sixty-four tapes subpoenaed by the special prosecutor. In the ensuing days, more incriminating information was released by the Senate Watergate Committee, and the House Judiciary Committee began to discuss articles of impeachment. Yet Nixon, like Khrushchev, tried to brush these alarms aside. Spokesman Ronald Ziegler said the president was convinced he had not committed any impeachable offense. Correspondents covering Nixon's stay at his California home, La Casa Pacifica, wrote of the aura of unreality that surrounded the president.

At the White House press room a number of us wondered whether Nixon would try to defy the Supreme Court. Hours went by after the Court's decision. Recalling how the authorities placed Washington under curfew with armed soldiers on the streets following the killing of Martin Luther King in 1968, we speculated that the president might try military force. I imagined the 101st Airborne Division descending on Washington and setting up machine-gun nests at key points. Later, we learned that Defense Secretary James Schlesinger had similar thoughts and took steps to prevent the execution of any unconstitutional military order emanating from the commander in chief. After an eight-hour wait, Nixon stated he would comply with the Supreme Court order.

Stage three—"Decision to Resign"—was reached in secret in both Washington and Moscow. Following Brezhnev's telephone call of October 12, 1964, Khrushchev flew to Moscow the next day, cutting short a previously scheduled meeting with Gaston Palewsky, French minister of atomic energy. The meeting was announced by TASS as if nothing unusual was happening, and it carefully remained silent about Khrushchev's secret return to the capital. From the airport, he went directly to confront his colleagues in the Presidium of the Communist Party, rather the way Nixon found himself about to confront impeachment by the House of Representatives. Khrushchev lost his fight in the Presidium, and the case was then referred to the Central Committee. That could be viewed as the equivalent of a U.S. Senate trial of an impeached high official. The Central Committee voted against Khrushchev, who declined to fight back because, as he admitted, he was old and tired.

Throughout this dramatic series of events, Moscow was unusually calm. A lovely autumn was beginning; the air was clear and soft; the mushrooms were plentiful. Not a word of political events appeared in the media. Instead, all eyes were focused on the flight of Voskhod-1, which was recalled early from its mission. The flight commander, Valentin Komarov, on receipt of the descent order, protested mildly in a conversation broadcast nationally over the radio.

In Washington, the moment of decision came during the week beginning Monday, August 5, 1974. We journalists now expected an announcement of resignation and were looking everywhere for signs of it. On the weekend before that Monday, I had been sent to cover Nixon's quiet stay at Camp David in the Catoctin Mountains outside of the capital. Coverage was a joke, since we correspondents were holed up in a motel at Thurmont, Maryland, at the base of the mountains, far from the president. We could observe nothing. We even failed to spot the marine helicopter that flew into Camp David from Washington and learned about it only later when White House spokesman Jerry Warren called us at Thurmont to say that Nixon had summoned two speechwriters, Ray Price and Patrick Buchanan. On the basis of that meager information, I filed an urgent story, as did the Associated Press, that Nixon had reached a decision and was agonizing over how to announce it. What the decision was, however, remained unclear, and no one dared to go so far as to suggest that the president had made the fateful decision.

On the next day, Tuesday, August 6, I attended a photo opportunity at the start of a cabinet meeting in the White House at which Nixon piqued everybody's interest with these words: "I've called you to discuss a subject which is on everybody's mind . . ." At this point I prepared to bolt to the UPI cubicle, only to hear Nixon complete the sentence: "the economy and inflation." I wrote at the time, "I saw a man who appeared relaxed, good humored, serene. He radiated confidence . . . or, I should say, he wore a carefully contrived mask. He was determined that the business of government should go on as the House of Representatives pursued its constitutional process. And he would not resign. Not resign, not resign, his aides kept saying until Wednesday, August 7."

On that Wednesday Nixon finally made the decision to resign in secret. He met with three congressional leaders, Senator Barry Goldwater, Senate minority leader Hugh Scott, and House minority leader John Rhodes. Emerging from their meeting, they told White House correspondents that they had outlined the growing pressure in Congress for impeachment or resignation but stated that the president had not disclosed what he intended to do. Nixon also met with Rabbi Baruch Korff, leader of the National Citizens' Committee for Fairness to the Presidency, on both Tuesday and Wednesday of that week. I caught Korff leaving the White House on Wednesday; he told me that the president's predicament was sad, and unjust, but I would have to draw my own conclusions about resignation. About ten-thirty that night we spotted Henry Kissinger's black limousine parked in the White House driveway. What Kissinger's limousine meant we could not guess at the time, and no one would say. Now we know from Woodward and Bernstein's *Final Days* that Nixon had summoned his secretary of state, informed him he was resigning, and asked that the two of them get on their knees and pray.

The intense pressure surrounding such historic moments meant that it would be humanly impossible to keep the decision entirely secret until the official announcement. Thus, in Moscow as in Washington, another stage revealed itself—"The Unmatchable Exclusive." In an earlier chapter, I have described how Victor Louis, a correspondent for the *London Evening News,* and Sam Jaffe of ABC scooped the rest of us with their special access to word about Khrushchev's resignation. In Washington, a White House staff member unexpectedly met an old journalist friend as they rode home on a late-evening bus. The official was exhausted but talkative and told his friend that Ray Price had been writing the resignation speech but was having difficulty getting the wording right. The journalist, working for the *New York Daily News,* flashed the news to his desk when he got home, and it made the late four-star edition of the newspaper. The *Providence Journal* also printed a quote from a confidential source on August 8, before any decision had been announced, saying, "I can tell you that the decision is irrevocable. The President has come to the conclusion that the national interest may best be served by his resignation, irrespective of the mammoth injustice committed against him that has prompted this painful decision on his part." The quote had the ring of truth; I guessed it came from Rabbi Korff, a resident of Providence, speaking to his hometown newspaper.

In both capitals, these scoops sent the rest of us seeking high and low for confirmation. I've written how I spotted Khrushchev's portrait being taken down from the Hotel Moskva. In Washington, I caught Defense Secretary Schlesinger emerging from a meeting at Blair House on Thursday morning, August 8, and asked if the reports of resignation were "pure bunk." He declined to answer. But another reporter, following up quickly, threw out a parallel question heading in the same direction: would Schlesinger serve as defense secretary in a Ford administration? Schlesinger replied, "That would be a decision that Mr. Ford would have to make." A quasi-official confirmation!

Stage five: "The Official Announcement." In Moscow, the Communist Party issued this laconic statement through TASS:

A plenary meeting of the Central Committee of the CPSU was held on Oct. 14. The meeting granted N. S. Khrushchev's request to be relieved of his duties as First Secretary of the CPSU Central Committee, and chairman of the Council of Ministers of the U.S.S.R. in view of his advanced age and deterioration of his health.

The plenum of the CPSU Central Committee elected L. I. Brezhnev First Secretary of the CPSU Central Committee.

In Washington, Nixon planned a personal appearance on national television. But before the appointed hour of nine o'clock, he told his chief of staff,

Al Haig, that he wanted to walk around the White House grounds without running into anyone. Haig instructed his deputy, Major George Joulwan, to secure the grounds. Joulwan passed on the order to the Secret Service, which locked reporters in the White House press room and ordered officials not to leave their offices without offering the slightest explanation. In the press room, black humor set in; we joked that soon the lightbulbs would drop from their sockets, and we would all be exterminated by Zyklon gas. Meanwhile, Nixon walked alone from the residence to the Executive Office Building to meet with congressional leaders before the televised address.

His performance was more personal and more instructive than the Moscow announcement, but the purpose was the same. The chief must step down for an objective and acceptable reason. No acknowledgment of wrongdoing. Stress on continuity of government. The world is reassured.

But there is more to come in what I would call "The Morning After," stage six. In Nixon's case it was the extraordinary parting in the East Room on August 9, 1974. In Moscow, two days after the resignation, *Pravda* began publishing the accusations against Khrushchev that explained the reasons for the ouster. He was accused of "hare-brained schemes" and "armchair methods." New words were invented such as *voluntarism* and *projectorism* that capture the essence of his management: making unilateral decisions like a dictator. These explanations were expanded further in a secret briefing paper circulated to Communist Party cells throughout the country.

The final, seventh, stage was "Le Retour," or "We Do Meet Again." President Nixon retired to La Casa Pacifica in California and set about penning his memoirs, *RN*. He continued to write, producing a half-dozen more books, giving advice on U.S.-Soviet relations and other political matters. At his death in 1994, Nixon received an outpouring of national attention. In Moscow, Khrushchev and his immediate family were similarly concerned about history's judgment. His son, Sergei, began helping him write his memoirs. In death, Khrushchev regained a measure of recognition when he was buried in a prominent Moscow cemetery, his grave marked by an unusual black-and-white monument, signifying achievements and mistakes, designed by a Moscow artist whom he once publicly chastised.

In the end, both Khrushchev and Nixon returned from the wilderness as literary creatures. The world took note, and history began to judge them.

Chapter 19

Adventures with Kissinger

To my amazement, by October 1974 I had managed to earn my way back into Dillman's grace as a result of our Nixon coverage. I say "amazement" because once you make a bad impression in journalism, it is nearly impossible to overcome it. Helen Thomas liked to say, "You're only as good as your last story." And our last stories on the Nixon crisis had been very good. I would have been happy to continue covering the Ford White House with Helen, but Dillman announced that the European news editor, Dick Growald, would be leaving Frankfurt, West Germany, to take my place on Helen's crew. As a consolation prize, he said, "Go up to the Hill and cover foreign affairs from the Senate and the House. From time to time, I'll see if I can send you on a trip with Kissinger."

On this one, Dillman produced. Shortly, he assigned me to the trip Kissinger was planning to Moscow and Southeast Asia at the end of the month to lay the groundwork for a summit meeting between President Ford and Leonid Brezhnev at Vladivostok in November 1974. This was a delicate moment in U.S.-Soviet relations when Kissinger hoped to repair foreign policy after the disaster of Watergate. The sides had reached two important agreements in 1972: the Anti–Ballistic Missile Treaty and an interim agreement limiting the development of strategic armaments. The interim agreement was to be replaced by a strategic-arms-limitation accord dubbed SALT-II. The accords lay at the heart of what President Nixon called "détente," a French word suggesting a relaxation of tensions between superpowers.

For me, this assignment was much more than a reward for a job well done at the White House. It was a chance for me to reassess Soviet-American relations after nine years away from Moscow and to cover the extraordinarily high-profile secretary of state and his special relationship with the press. I was looking forward to seeing what fruits the Nixon-Ford policy of détente had brought to the lives of ordinary Russians. I had noted that a number of Soviet leaders, including Petr N. Demichev, a top leader charged with cultural affairs, had called for "sharpening the ideological battle," as Western influences seeped into the Soviet Union. I was anxious to reacquaint myself with old friends with whom we had made only fleeting contact since our departure from Moscow in 1965.

On the night of October 22, I joined fourteen correspondents at the State Department to be bused out to Andrews Air Force Base. Our first stop would be Copenhagen and then on to Moscow and Asia. On arrival in the Danish capital early the next morning, we were hit with startling news—Strobe Talbott, diplomatic correspondent of *Time* magazine (later top adviser to President Clinton on Russia), was forced off the party because the Soviet Foreign Ministry denied him an entry visa. No explanation was given. The news put us correspondents in an angry mood. We wrote a letter of protest that was distributed worldwide by AP and UPI. Meantime, Strobe dutifully left the Kissinger delegation and arranged to rejoin us in New Delhi several days later.

During the three-hour flight from Copenhagen to Moscow, I let my mind wander back over the many times Ruth and I had spent with two Russian friends, Yelena (Lena) and Zinovy Yuriev. In the early 1960s, it was unusual for foreign correspondents to develop much of any relations with Soviet citizens. Russians were scared to have anything but the rarest contact with Westerners living in Moscow. Lena was different; she seemed fearless and approachable. Her father had been a Communist Party official in Leningrad before the Second World War and had represented the interests of the German airline Lufthansa. During the Great Terror, he had been arrested on charges that were probably trumped up. Lena learned years later, during Gorbachev's glasnost era, that her father had been tortured horribly during interrogations. He had been severely beaten, and blinded. Her mother had been shipped off to a labor camp as an "enemy of the people." Lena had been dispatched to central Asia, where she was raised as an orphan. She returned to Moscow after the war, entered the Institute of Foreign Languages, and became an expert in English, which helped her land a job as secretary-translator to the Moscow Bureau of *Mainichi*, the Japanese newspaper chain.

Lena was full of energy and imagination; her character was irrepressible. I guessed that she thought the Soviet system owed her a serious recompense for all the hardships she had endured. She soon became a master fixer, using her uncanny ability to smile, flatter, and, ultimately, persuade and conquer. By offering small presents at strategic moments, she pushed her agenda along. It did not take her long to begin stringing for the North American Newspaper Alliance (NANA) and to wheedle permission from the Soviet Foreign Ministry to serve as an accredited correspondent for the Religious News Service, a specialized American agency. As such she was able to move freely in the circle of foreign correspondents in Moscow, striking up friendships with both British and American reporters. We often wondered if there was a quid pro quo: freedom to wheel and deal while reporting from time to time to the authorities.

Her husband, Zinovy, was unusual, too, although in the 1960s he preferred the shadows to the light of foreigners. He was employed by the humor magazine *Krokodil,* and focused on writing satirical pieces about situations abroad. We often referred to him as the foreign editor of that magazine. Zinovy had an encyclopedic knowledge of American history and proved over the years to be a very sober, hardheaded observer. His English was even better than Lena's. He was a voracious reader of books and magazines in English and reveled in using the latest idiomatic expressions. Sometimes, however, his reading would not guide him to the correct pronunciation, and he would stumble over an adjective like *poignant,* sounding the *g* rather than softening the *n.* In the 1960s, we would spend long hours with the Yurievs, sometimes at country dachas, sometimes in their city apartment. We felt we were privileged being let into a part of the Soviet world that foreign correspondents rarely entered.

One evening in the mid-1960s, we were invited to a birthday party for the Yurievs' older son, Misha, who had just turned five. This was the first family celebration we had ever been invited to in a Moscow flat filled with friends in a holiday mood. These were not dissidents, not people willing to risk their livelihoods, just people brave enough to spend an evening with a couple from another world. The evening unfolded with good food, excited conversation, and a sparkling show of talent. Each guest had written a song or poem and tried to outdo the previous performer. We returned in the early hours to our apartment feeling that we had been initiated into the hidden world of ordinary Soviet life.

Another secret moment came to mind, too. The Yurievs had invited us to a dacha owned by *Literaturnaya Gazeta* in the forest outside Sheremetyevo Airport. The atmosphere was one of nineteenth-century Russia, a row of wooden cottages, huddled in snow at -20 degrees, surrounded by tall pine trees. No modern conveniences, no running water, buckets from a well where ice had to be cracked in winter. We skied along trails for hours as jetliners landed and took off over the evergreens. I could feel their pride about these airliners, which were symbols of modernity and progress, evidence of Russia advancing in the world. As an American with Russian roots, I felt a bit sentimental, too; their love of country was infectious.

"Understand," Lena would say, "in the nineteenth century Russia was a great country. It was one of the most influential European powers. And now in the twentieth, we are again a great and important power—a superpower, a major force in the world." That evening we retired to the cozy kitchen, around a potbellied stove. Lena put on a large pot of soup. Suddenly, there was a knock at the door, and a tall man in a rough sheepskin coat entered, asking in accented Russian if he could borrow some salt. That was unusual because the cottage was located in a zone closed to foreigners. Lena hunted through the kitchen shelves, and produced a can of English Cerebos salt. The tall man's eyes lit up. He thanked her and vanished out the door.

"You know who that was?" Zinovy asked us. We had no idea. "He goes by the name Malcolm Frazer; he is an Englishman." He paused, and we waited in anticipation for the explanation. "His real name is Maclean, Donald Maclean, the diplomat who defected from England in 1951 along with Guy Burgess."

We were taken aback. We glimpsed Maclean again the next day. An interview with Maclean in 1964 would have been a surefire story for both the British and the American press. Not much was known about his life as a defector, working at a Moscow policy institute. But we restrained ourselves. I had to weigh the benefit of a brilliant scoop against a long-term relationship with Lena and Zinovy. We did not want to do anything to harm them or draw undue attention to our hosts, who had invited us into an area where foreigners were barred. Of course, we wondered how Lena dared invite us into this closed zone. We decided she was an irrepressible risk taker.

As I dreamed of old times, my thoughts also turned to Yuri, the UPI photographer, and Tonya. It had been easier to keep in touch with Yuri because of his connection with UPI. In 1973 he had accompanied Leonid Brezhnev to the United States for his summit with President Nixon. Yuri and I had both been assigned to cover that conference and flew together on the press plane to California. On the return flight to Washington, the press plane inevitably turned into a flying party well lubricated with alcohol. Booze, and the promise of more booze, was something that unlocked many doors in the Soviet reality. When Bud and Christine Korengold were leaving Moscow in June 1963 after their three-year assignment, Yuri, Tonya, Ruth and I, and our translator, Lev Shtern, gave them a rousing send-off from Red Square. They were to drive from Moscow to Paris in their VW Bug, and to wish them well Yuri uncorked a bottle of champagne as we stood by the GUM department store opposite the Lenin Mausoleum. We all quaffed down a glass and poured the remains over the front of the car. At that point, two policemen arrived from nowhere and announced they were going to arrest our colleague. Yuri, who held an accreditation from the Ministry of Internal (Police) Affairs, protested and dashed off to telephone some mysterious personage. Shortly, the policemen received a message by radio and backed off. We were impressed.

When we touched down at Vnukovo-2 Airport, the field used by official government delegations, a high-level party of Soviet greeters welcomed the secretary of state and whisked him into town in a black limousine. We correspondents boarded a bus that chugged us to the Intourist Hotel, opposite the Kremlin. From the start, it was clear that this was not going to be a jolly visit. The hotel personnel were sullen and made clear they expected us to respect their rules, however unreasonable we might find them. "Be sure to hand in your keys when you go out of the hotel. If you don't, you'll be fined," warned the doorman. "All women to be out of your rooms by 11 P.M.," one of the floor attendants told us. That did not prevent a female voice from calling my room invitingly at midnight one night when the only thing on my mind was completing my file for the day.

The official representatives were grim, too, apparently miffed by the protest we had launched from Copenhagen. When we arrived the next morning at the Kremlin, they set a limit of ten correspondents for our group of thirteen to witness the first minutes of the meeting between Kissinger and Brezhnev, claiming that the room was too small to accommodate a larger group. We argued with Vsevolod Sofinsky, former Soviet ambassador to New Zealand and now the chief of the ministry's Press Department. But it was to no avail. At last, he announced that the meeting was under way, and we were all excluded. In later meetings, we were reluctantly allowed to witness the start of talks and then left to fend for ourselves.

During Kissinger's lengthy meetings in the Kremlin we correspondents had little to do, and I put my reunion plans into action. I decided against telephoning Lena and Zinovy and, instead, took a taxi to the Sokol metro station in the northern part of the city where they lived. In nine years, I had forgotten exactly how to find their apartment building but slowly reoriented myself enough to find their street named after the Romanian Communist Party leader Gheorghe Gheorghiu-Dej, without having to ask anyone for directions or give myself away as a foreigner. I finally discovered No. 3, identified the right stairway entrance, and made my way uncertainly up to the third floor, constantly looking over my shoulder to see if anyone had spied me entering the building. Feeling guilty, as if I were committing some unknown crime, I rang the bell and within seconds saw an eye at the peephole in the padded brown leather door that swung open.

Lena instantly recognized me and pulled me into the apartment from the dimly lit landing. Closing the door tightly, she gave me a big hug. "*Skol'ko zim, skol'ko let?* How many winters, how many summers have gone by since we last saw each other?" we greeted each other. Zinovy padded out from a back room in slippers, and we excitedly began exchanging details of our personal lives as I handed over a few presents I had brought with me. I was astounded to learn that Misha, who came into the kitchen, had been admitted to Moscow State University to study physics even though he was only fourteen.

Soon we were sitting around the kitchen table as Lena unearthed vodka and a variety of *zakuski,* appetizers of pickled cucumbers, tomatoes, sour cream, caviar. Before long, the conversation turned to the state of Russia and Soviet-American relations. Moscow authorities had reluctantly approved an open-air exhibit of nonconformist artists in September, then used a bulldozer to break up part of it; finally relenting, they allowed a token display to continue.

I noted that in the West that word *détente* was used to suggest a general relaxation of tensions. I said that the U.S. Embassy now had two display cases with information about America in front of the building, unthinkable a decade ago. I recalled too that a decade earlier, only two hundred Russians, old and infirm, were allowed to emigrate to the West each year; now the figure was up to two thousand. Was there really a relaxation in tensions?

Zinovy was quick to comment. "Your 'détente' is only an accommodation between our two governments. Our government needs trade, technology, wheat, consumer goods. Your government wants to stabilize the arms race which our leaders are pushing. Don't expect any easing up at the level of ordinary people here. To the contrary. Our leaders will tighten the screws because they won't want any Western microbes to take hold and undermine their system."

Lena jumped in too:

Sure we live better. Take the apartment. It used to be considered luxurious. Now it is considered to be a normal-size apartment. But it really bugs me that I can't travel abroad. I don't have any hope of ever leaving the country.

It's not that I don't like Russia—I couldn't live without it. And I could travel the length and breadth of the Soviet Union and see many, many interesting things. But I know I can never leave. Living here is like living in a cage.

That image of a prison stuck in my mind. I tried to protest that change was in the air. It might take time, but things were moving. "Compared to pre-revolutionary Russia, your country has developed a lot."

Zinovy, irritated, interrupted. There were always two yardsticks for assessing Russia, he said: Russia compared to prerevolutionary Russia and Russia compared to the West. In the former case, progress in 1974 compared to 1914 was clear enough, but not in the latter. In many ways, Russia was still a developing country. The Soviet leadership always wanted to compare the Soviet Union with the United States, always tried to make out that the Soviet Union was on a par in all things with the West. The equivalence related more to military and industrial strength, not to freedom of expression, human rights, or the dignity of individuals.

After hours of conversation, I finally pulled myself away, determined to write that Nixonian détente, rather than leading to a relaxation in the lives of ordinary Russians, was doing the opposite. As Kissinger completed the groundwork for a Ford-Brezhnev summit, the Ministry of Foreign Affairs announced a reception for the secretary's party at Spiridonovka, the ministry's guesthouse. Cruising among the many guests was Vadim Biryukov, whom I was startled to see. I remembered how in the 1960s he tried to warn me off Lena on the grounds that he, Vadim, could be a much more reliable source for me. Going over to him, I posed that question that agitated many of us: "So why did your government deny Strobe Talbott a visa?"

Biryukov frowned somewhat menacingly. "He knows perfectly well," he replied. "Go ask him yourself." When I recounted the incident to Talbott after he rejoined the party in New Delhi, he, too, declined to elaborate. Years later, I learned that the Khrushchev family had wanted to get their father's manuscript out to the West, where it would not be buried or covered up. Through a roundabout series of connections, the family secretly made contact with *Time*, which arranged for the Khrushchev tapes to be translated, edited, and published. Talbott played a major role in doing the translation. The publication of the memoirs angered the Kremlin leadership and landed Talbott on its blacklist for several years. The tapes are now preserved at Columbia University in New York.

It was another two years before I returned to Russia, again accompanying Kissinger on strategic-arms negotiations. Shortly before leaving in January 1976, Dillman amazed me by sending a congratulatory note describing me as both "a superb news craftsman" and "a truly good human being." What a turnaround!

This trip would prove an excellent example of the relationship between America's top diplomat and his traveling scribes, as well as our tense relationship with the top Soviet leaders. At ten on January 21, we were bused from the Intourist Hotel to the Kremlin, where we assembled noisily in a corridor within the Council of Ministers building. Joining us was a group of Soviet newsmen and photographers, including our UPI photographer, Yuri Korolyov. We were reminded by both U.S. and Soviet officials to make no tape recordings and to treat Brezhnev with respect. This caveat grew out of our aggressive posturing in 1974 when Talbott was bounced from Kissinger's trip. We now know that by 1976 Brezhnev's health was so bad that he had difficulty functioning.

Shortly before eleven, Brezhnev, dressed in a blue suit, blue shirt, and red-patterned tie, entered the room and moved to a central spot behind the long conference table covered in green baize. Scooping up color for my report, I noted portraits of Marx and Lenin on the paneled walls, bottles of Coca Cola and Russian mineral water on the table. We journalists, Russians and Americans, slowly took places in a line facing the conference table opposite the Soviet leader.

"This is a linkup between Soviet and American journalists, like the linkup of Soyuz and Apollo," Brezhnev announced cheerily, referring to the recent rendezvous of two superpower spacecraft. We shifted nervously, awaiting Kissinger's arrival. My colleagues were often pressing me to throw out a few opening questions in Russian, an obligation that made me extremely nervous. I glanced around at our side and spotted Murrey Marder of the *Washington Post,* holding a notebook on top of a folded newspaper beneath which, hardly visible, was a mini–tape recorder already running in defiance of the day's rules. Finally, Kissinger entered the room, and the performance got under way. "You look much younger," Brezhnev said, welcoming Kissinger. "You look very well," the secretary of state replied.

Then Brezhnev turned to Kissinger and patted him about the stomach with his outstretched hands, a gesture so human and so unofficial it stood no chance of being reported in the Soviet media. "I'm getting fat," Kissinger quipped. I turned in Yuri's direction and saw he was snapping away, knowing exactly what Western media wanted.

"Comrade Leonid Ilyich," I interrupted in Russian. "Can you assess the current state of U.S.-Soviet relationships?"

"It's hard for me to evaluate," Brezhnev replied. "It's up to what nice things Dr. Kissinger has to say."

At this point, Kissinger broke in. Glancing at me, he quipped, "I hope he is friendlier in Russian than he is in English!"

I tried a second question, according to the transcript that I wrote, based on Marder's secret recording. "What are the chief subjects of your talks? Will Angola be among the subjects?" We had come to Moscow at a time when the Soviet Union was supplying weapons to Marxist rebels in that country, a development that was causing hardliners in Washington to criticize the Ford administration for being soft on the Soviet Union. "I have no issues about Angola," Brezhnev replied. "It is not my country."

Kissinger, realizing that the conversation was taking a dangerous turn, immediately replied for the benefit of politicians back home, "It will certainly be discussed."

The Russians tried to deflect the negative drift. Foreign Minister Andrey Gromyko reminded the audience, "The agenda is always adopted by mutual agreement." Kissinger parried rather sternly, "Then I will discuss it!" To which Brezhnev countered, "You'll discuss it with Sonnenfeldt [Kissinger's aide Dr. Helmut Sonnenfeldt]. That will assure complete agreement. I've never seen Dr. Kissinger have a disagreement with Dr. Sonnenfeldt."

At this point, the Soviet officials, sensing the give-and-take was getting out of hand, began gesturing that it was time for the journalists to leave. Indeed, Kissinger in his memoir, *Years of Renewal*, noted: "By thus publicly rubbing our noses in our defeat in Angola, however self-inflicted, Brezhnev destroyed whatever sentiment was left in the United States for agreements with the Kremlin."

As we scuffled down the stairs to the waiting bus, I was hardly thinking about my role as provocateur, or Brezhnev's incapacities. Rather, I wanted a photo scoop for UPI. Yuri sidled over and slipped me his film of the Brezhnev stomach pat. I stuffed the roll in my coat pocket and rushed back to the UPI office. The picture hit: it was prominently published in the next issue of *Newsweek*. I got the credit because Yuri never wanted to be identified. It's no good being a cobblestone in a parquet floor, he liked to say. As we emerged from the building, I could also sense Yuri's delight at seeing me after a long absence. He promised to drive me to his dacha that evening for a vodka-soaked reunion.

Yuri picked me up in his green Zhiguli for the drive out to the writers' colony of Peredelkino around six o'clock. The last time I tried to go there in 1974, the hotel refused to supply me with a car and driver on the grounds that Peredelkino was located in a zone closed to foreigners. The Soviet Union had instituted a system of closed zones during the Second World War to protect military objects, and many of them remained closed throughout the Cold War. As we drove along the Minsk Highway, Yuri and I chatted about many things that had transpired since we last met. I said, "I suppose I should not have sent you that telegram, signed 'Krokodil,' telling you I was coming." "Doesn't matter," he replied. "They delivered it anyway." Yuri, his wife, Tonya, and I had nicknames for each other drawn from a

Russian children's book. It all started as a joke and somehow lived on. I was Uncle Crocodile (Dyadka Krokodil); he was Uncle Alligator (Dyadka Aligator), and she was Auntie Giraffe (Tyotka Jirafika). There was nothing sinister about it, but counterintelligence at the International Telegraph Office probably imagined these names were coded messages.

Some forty minutes later we were driving down the dark alleys of Peredelkino, surrounded by tall pine trees, to his country house on Dovzhenko Street. Yuri shared a cottage with a neighbor who lived on the second floor who was known to work for the KGB. Even though I visited the place over many years, I never laid eyes on this shady person and never had a clear idea what Yuri's real relation was with him. I guess Yuri had a relationship with the KGB, but I never knew for sure. The cottage was surrounded by a ten-foot-high fence that blocked the view from the street of the garden inside. You entered through a solid double gate leading directly into his one-car garage and workshop. Yuri had collected a full complement of hand tools that he used to repair his car and the Evinrude outboard engine that he had acquired on a trip abroad. Viewing this collection of instruments certainly gave you the impression that his personal enjoyment was more important to him than Marx or Lenin, or his relations with the police.

As we entered the house through an enclosed porch, Tonya hailed us with greetings and hugs. Within minutes, Yuri was opening a chilled bottle of vodka while Tonya and Yuri's daughter, Lena, were placing hors d'oeuvres—baby mushrooms soaked in brine, red and black caviar, lightly salted cucumbers, various types of bread—on a low coffee table. He raised a toast to the lost years, and we got down to the serious business of catching up. I always liked the Russian style of going around the table, asking each guest to offer a toast. The practice engaged each participant and put a premium on wit. I knew I would have to watch it because Yuri's capacity for vodka far exceeded mine.

"You know," he asserted, "the Japanese have invented this new pill which will take away entirely the smell of liquor on your breath."

"So you have a supply with you for this evening?" I asked.

"No, unfortunately, I used them all up. But we Russians have other means. Raw potatoes. Just eat a raw potato before getting behind the wheel."

Our conversation that evening ranged widely, but we finally came to the inevitable political roundup. When I first met Yuri in Geneva in 1960, he loyally defended the Soviet system while pursuing the pleasures of the West. During the Second World War, he had been an eighteen-year-old aerial photographer and had since developed into a celebrated photojournalist.

"I get the impression you are far more critical of Kremlin policies today than you were just a few years ago," I ventured.

"Right," he replied. "You know people in this country have absolutely no interest in Marxism-Leninism. They want to live a decent life. And those old farts in the Kremlin, what they're really interested in is their warm armchairs. They have no interest in the rest of us. So it's up to us, to make out as well as we can."

As it was getting late, I proposed one of our traditional private toasts that we would rehearse whenever we met for a blowout. "I raise my glass against all shitfaces! *Protiv vsekh shitfeisov!*" Russians love to incorporate English expressions into their speech, and this line had grown spontaneously out of our evenings in the 1960s at Tonya's in-town apartment. On parting, Yuri said he was too drunk to drive back into town and I should return by car with his daughter.

We drove out to the Minsk Highway, which was lit only by the lights of passing cars. Within minutes Yuri flagged down a driver who was willing to take us. "Keep your mouth shut," he warned, "and don't open it until you reach the hotel." Lena and I got into the backseat, and we were off. I felt totally conspiratorial moving out of a secret world into my public one.

As Kissinger's visit moved toward its conclusion, I managed to call Lena from a public phone booth. She instantly recognized my voice and answered, "Will you drop by?"

I started to say, "I'm here until Friday . . ."

"Will you drop by?" she insisted hurriedly. "Eight o'clock, Friday?"

"Good," I replied, continuing the conversation with several questions. But she hung up abruptly without saying good-bye, sending a chill over me.

On the evening of January 23, I gathered the presents I had brought, a few of the latest hit books and some clothes for Lena. I hailed a cab and, as last time, left for the Sokol metro station. I found the apartment building without difficulty this time, and entered the inner court where a child was plaintively crying, "Mama! Mama!" I pushed on without discovering what was wrong, found the entrance, and climbed the stairs. I passed an old woman coming down and wondered if she recognized me as an outlander. Foreigners were always easy to identify in those days by the shoes they wore, or the frames of their glasses. The woman disappeared out the stairwell door without a word. Again, I began feeling awkward as if I were committing a terrible infraction. This was *strakh*—Russian fear—the sort people complained was lodged in their genes.

On reaching the apartment, I felt slightly reassured. The brown leather padding on the door to apartment 34 had been redone in red leather, a sign of increasing affluence. It was now a bit after eight. I rang the bell three times, the usual signal among Russians that a friend had arrived. The door opened, revealing a boy in his early teens dressed in what looked like gray pajamas.

"Is Lena here?" I asked, surprised.

"No," the youth answered without hesitation.

"But this is house number 3, apartment 34, isn't it?"

"Yes."

"And Lena lives here?"

"Yes," the boy replied. Suddenly, I realized I was speaking to Yura, Misha's younger brother. I had not recognized him at first. I had last seen him ten years ago when he was only three. Now he was a teenager accustomed to the peculiar restrictions of Moscow life. I got the sense that he knew I was coming.

"When will she be back?" I continued.

"Not until late tonight. But come in." Once I was inside, he explained, "My mother wanted to avoid you. She got a call from a certain Biryukov who told her that you were coming with the Kissinger party and that she should not meet you, or else . . . She said you know Biryukov."

I was shocked. This was exactly the sort of problem you never wanted. A feeling of helplessness compounded my fear. I struggled for words, "But how have you all been?"

"Okay," Yura answered. "But Mama has had a difficult time with the KGB. About a year ago she was summoned and told to stop contacts with foreigners. The name Rick Smith was mentioned." (That was a reference to Hedrick Smith of the *New York Times* who had gone to see her on my recommendation.)

I marveled at Yura's self-possession. He spoke quietly, not nearly as nervous as I. "What do they hold against her?" I managed to get out.

"There was a suggestion of espionage," he offered.

"Espionage? What sort of espionage?"

"I don't know," Yura continued. "But it's sad, particularly when there were those agreements in Helsinki." He was referring to the Helsinki Final Act of 1975, signed by the Soviet Union, Canada, and the U.S. and European governments. It recognized postwar borders in Europe and encouraged greater East-West communication.

"I understand," I said. "It's clear. But apart from that, how have you all been?"

"Good enough. Misha is working in a laboratory. My father is writing a lot. Mother is a part-time correspondent for our Novosti news agency." He made a gesture with his hand to indicate that he thought the apartment was bugged. He glanced through the peephole in the door. During our conversation the phone rang twice, and twice he replied matter-of-factly, "He is not here." I could only wonder who that *he* was supposed to be.

"And how is Auntie Ruth?" This was his first question, and it seemed to break the tension of our meeting.

"Fine," I answered. "She is writing a lot. Miranda is grown up; our son is six. He is well, very energetic. Look, I have some presents for you." I fished in the bag I was carrying and handed them over. Then it was time: I wanted to emerge onto the streets before some arrest team showed up, if they were going to show up. "Ruth hugs you all," I said, "and you know we love you; we wish you well."

We hugged, and I slipped away in silent outrage. What a terrible way to live, to grow up! I decided to calm myself by walking back to the Intourist Hotel, a long distance away. I strode quickly along the Leningradsky Highway, past the in-town Aeroflot Terminal, past the green and white Byelorussian Railway Station, down Gorki Street, glancing frequently over my shoulder but never spotting a "tail." It took a full hour and a half before I reached the hotel in time for a late-night briefing by Dr. Sonnenfeldt on the nine hours Kissinger spent with Brezhnev. As I wrote my story for UPI late that night, thoughts kept swirling in my head, thoughts about "détente," about the tensions of Soviet life, about genetic fear, about Biryukov. I was so troubled by the encounter with Yura, I wrote a lengthy account in my diary for January 23, 1976. I never anticipated, however, the fate that awaited Biryukov in post-Soviet Russia.

Flying back to Washington from a Kissinger foray was always exhausting but stimulating. This time we flew first to Brussels so Kissinger could brief NATO foreign ministers on the strategic-arms talks and then on to Spain. In Madrid, Kissinger signed a four-year defense treaty that brought the new post-Franco government into close alliance with the United States. Then we took off from Torrejon Air Force Base and headed out across the Atlantic.

It had become something of a tradition on the homeward flight for Kissinger to invite correspondents to join in a ninety-minute graduate seminar on international affairs topped off with cups of champagne. These sessions, unlike his background briefings during a mission, were off the record. Since the roar of the engines was roughly equivalent to a roomful of humming vacuum cleaners, it was often difficult to hear, and he permitted tape recorders. To ease the noise problem further, we devised a seating plan by which we would rotate around him, briefing by briefing, like moons revolving around the sun.

Generally, we addressed him as "Mr. Secretary," although some preferred "Henry." When Kissinger had been appointed secretary of state in 1973, one

White House reporter had asked him, "How should we address you now? Doctor? Mr. Secretary?" He had replied with an impish grin, "Your Excellency will be sufficient." I favored formality over false intimacy.

Kissinger, the former Harvard professor, enjoyed these exchanges and seemed to draw energy from his captives who were neither peers nor subordinates, nor under any obligation to agree with him. For his part, Kissinger was extremely frank in those pre-Internet days, except when he wanted to hide some vital detail. He sometimes would get so enraptured that he would make imprudent comments. It soon developed that he had a low opinion of most world leaders. "Most of them you would not want to meet at a cocktail party," he said. "What you're really interested in is their power, not their intellect. There are exceptions, though—Mao Zedong, Zhou Enlai, Charles de Gaulle, and Michel Jobert." His opinion of the Soviet leadership was at the bottom of the scale; on one occasion he called them "shits." He observed that Brezhnev did not become top dog by being a "choirboy" in a system that had no procedures for an orderly transfer of power.

Kissinger explained to us that he considered the Soviet leaders the "greatest chiselers" among all his negotiating partners. In my notes from the 1974 trip to Moscow, I wrote:

> Usually, he says, he prefers to give the straight U.S. position and thereby over months build up a reputation as being scrupulously honest. The Russians must always bargain down. This results in both sides coming to the table with high opening positions and a variety of fall-back positions.
>
> On the World War II Lend-Lease debt, Kissinger said he opened with an outrageous figure which sent Brezhnev into a fit. However, subsequently Kissinger dropped the figure by $10 million a throw till they settled at a figure $35 million above what was acceptable to the United States. Brezhnev was able to claim a triumph to his Politburo members.

An example of Soviet stubbornness directly affected an acquaintance of mine, Professor Woodford McClellan, and his Soviet wife, Irina. A historian of imperial Russia at the University of Virginia, Woody had fallen in love with her during a research trip to Moscow in 1974. They were married there only to find that the authorities would not let Irina emigrate to the United States. Nor would they approve a visa for Woody to visit her in Moscow. Their struggle for reunion continued for several years. The Soviet security police even tried some dirty tricks, sending Irina doctored pictures of herself, supposedly making love to another man, and demanding a six thousand–dollar bribe for permission to leave the country.

Woody exposed the situation publicly and appealed to the State Department and members of Congress for help. He asked me, too, if I could talk to Kissinger, which I did on the homeward flight in 1976. Kissinger reported that Foreign Minister Gromyko asserted that Soviet counterintelligence believed the marriage was fictional and actually a CIA ruse to create a channel into the KGB. The KGB asserted that Irina possessed secret information from her work at the Moscow Institute of International and Economic Relations (IMEMO), something that both she and Woody denied. Eventually, the Soviet side allowed Irina to leave for the United States after a wait of several years.

We traveling correspondents were sometimes accused of becoming far too close to Kissinger, in essence acting as his surrogate spokesmen. I disputed this charge at the time, but what is clear is this: in the 1970s, before cell phones and the Internet, Kissinger held an advantage over us when we were airborne because he had a monopoly of information. We all knew that. I tried to level the field by taking with me copious files and interrogating our local bureaus. That helped but did not completely undo his advantage.

I thought my friend Bernie Gwertzman summed up the relationship very well. He said on one occasion,

> In the role of supplier of information, Mr. Kissinger has often been maligned. He is portrayed as a manipulator, dispensing to the "puppets" of the press only that which furthers his ends. This is only partially true. Like all officials. Mr. Kissinger does "declassify" what he thinks helps him out. But he is not by nature able to control himself that well. He cannot just reveal this much and not any more. He is a very talkative man, who when the mood strikes him is apt to go far beyond what he intended. His anecdotes are often earthy, his language crude, and his portrayal of the world leaders embarrassingly frank. Away from Washington Mr. Kissinger is particularly voluble.

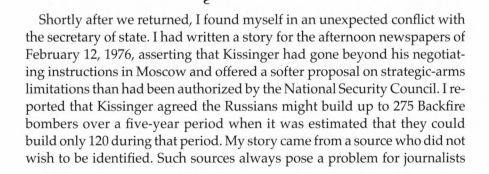

Shortly after we returned, I found myself in an unexpected conflict with the secretary of state. I had written a story for the afternoon newspapers of February 12, 1976, asserting that Kissinger had gone beyond his negotiating instructions in Moscow and offered a softer proposal on strategic-arms limitations than had been authorized by the National Security Council. I reported that Kissinger agreed the Russians might build up to 275 Backfire bombers over a five-year period when it was estimated that they could build only 120 during that period. My story came from a source who did not wish to be identified. Such sources always pose a problem for journalists because they escape accountability. In this case, the source had flagrantly manipulated me.

Kissinger's spokesman, Robert Funseth, called as I was struggling to write up the congressional reaction to Kissinger's press conference earlier in the day. "Can you see the secretary at five-thirty this afternoon?" he asked.

"Yes," I replied and hung up. I did not wait to find out what this was about. I dutifully tanked across town from the Hill to the State Department and was ushered into the outer office of the secretary of state at the appointed hour.

In a few minutes, an angry Kissinger appeared. "Mr. Daniloff, I want to talk to you off the record about a story you have written on the UPI wire. It asserts that I exceeded my negotiating instructions during my January trip to Moscow, and offered a softer proposal to Brezhnev on limiting strategic armaments than authorized." Kissinger disputed the facts I had cited, and threw out some new figures that I had difficulty grasping. I defended the story by saying I had tried to check the accuracy of the report by calling officials at the State Department and also at the Arms Control and Disarmament Agency, but they had been unhelpful. They were probably not high enough to be fully informed, and I had decided to trust my source. I suspected Kissinger guessed who my source was and denounced the story as "a malicious lie."

"Mr. Daniloff," he looked at me sternly, "you are a receptacle into which garbage has been poured!"

For a moment, I was silent as I realized that I had been used by my source for political reasons. Then I asked what he would like done. He suggested a follow-up story written "off the record." I replied I could take no corrective action off the record. He asked, "How about on 'deep background'?" I replied I did not feel I could do anything on that basis either. I added that I would keep his explanation for personal edification and would use it if a suitable occasion arose. He replied he would not feel cheated and arranged for me to get an immediate briefing from his counselor, Dr. Helmut Sonnenfeldt.

Reflecting on this incident at the time, it seemed to me that Kissinger had handled his problem in a civilized manner, calling me to account but supplying me with useful information for future use. I never detected any measure of retribution. Kissinger was well aware of the need to have an honest relationship with the press. He once remarked, "If you mislead the press consciously once, and you're caught at it, your credibility is destroyed forever."

That remark stuck in my mind, and in June 1976 I submitted an article to the *Foreign Service Journal* criticizing Kissinger's handling of the press. I focused on several incidents when he had been deceptive: once in October 1973 when he flew secretly to Moscow, but more important in February 1974 when he left for Syria on a "shuttle diplomacy" mission. Israel had refused to participate in negotiations unless Syria first produced a list of Israeli prisoners of war. Kissinger led correspondents to believe he was flying to Syria to obtain the list when, in actuality, he already possessed it. When Kissinger later acknowledged the true facts, Bernie Gwertzman said to me, "It may sound naive, but I was shocked and had trouble sleeping that night. It meant that if Kissinger could lie once, he could lie again. My gripe was that he shouldn't have said anything."

On June 16, 1976, I was invited to a breakfast with Kissinger organized by Dick Growald, who had replaced me two years before at the White House. Also attending at the State Department were Grant Dillman, UPI vice president Robert Page, foreign editor Walter Logan, and foreign affairs writers Jim Anderson and Henry Keys. As the breakfast in the James Madison Room broke up, Kissinger pulled me aside and thanked me for sending an advance copy of my article, which he said was "reasonably fair" although "not exactly flattering." He rebutted my suggestion that he had lied, saying that he had been sworn to secrecy by the Israelis.

"Mr. Secretary," I replied, "if you ever lie and you are discovered, it will never be forgotten or forgiven."

"But I disclosed it myself!" he countered.

"It doesn't matter. You will be perceived as capable of lying."

"So what should I have done?"

"You should have said firmly, 'This situation is far too delicate for me to comment further.'"

His last words to me were, "Maybe you are right."

To the dismay of many, the frictions between press and politicians will continue forever. In a democracy, after all, the press is supposed to assess critically the public actions of official people. Many of these assessments will be worthy, but some will be frivolous. Journalists are right to be skeptical of authority. Officials know this and sometimes even joke about it. As Kissinger once remarked about the incessant quibbling of journalists, "If we achieved the millennium of peace, there would still be a credibility gap because you guys would assert it was only good for 999 years!"

# Chapter 20

## The Devil's Details

When Dillman assigned me to cover foreign affairs from Capitol Hill in the fall of 1974, I had no idea what I was getting into. Like my colleague Sam Jaffe, I understood little about the workings of the U.S. Senate or the House of Representatives. I imagined that Congress was a cacophony of domestic political concerns that often frustrated the policies of the executive branch. Steve Gerstel, chief of UPI congressional correspondents, welcomed me to my new assignment and gave me a tour of the Capitol and the Senate press gallery.

The press gallery is located on the second floor of the Capitol, alongside the Senate chamber. It has a double swinging door that leads directly to the public gallery above the seat of the president of the Senate (that is, the vice president of the United States). From there you have a splendid view of the senators' antique mahogany desks arranged in a semicircle. The Associated Press and United Press International both had an area perhaps thirty feet long and ten feet wide along the length of the gallery. Our space abutted the wall of the Senate chamber, while the AP's was across the aisle by windows looking out on the north side of the Capitol. Each one of these areas was equipped with fax machines and typewriters, soon to be replaced with first-generation computers.

Gerstel explained to me that much of my work would be to attend committee hearings, especially those of the Foreign Relations and the Armed Services Committees, and to report on new twists in administration policy

226

and the evolving criticism from opponents on the Hill. I would be responsible, too, for covering confirmation hearings, the passage of authorization and appropriation bills, particularly those relating to foreign aid and defense, and other issues that might affect the international posture of the United States. "Get to know the key senators and congressmen," Gerstel counseled. "Better still, get to know the key aides of the key senators."

The first senator I reached out to was J. William Fulbright, who would be leaving the Senate at the end of December, having been defeated for reelection by Governor Dale Bumpers of Arkansas. There were reasons I bothered with a lame duck. For one thing, Fulbright was well known on the international scene; he might have become secretary of state under Kennedy had his southern origins not aligned him with the segregationists of the Deep South. He had been chairman of the Foreign Relations Committee since 1959 and had guided the controversial Tonkin Gulf Resolution through the Senate in 1964, giving President Johnson what was later called the "functional equivalent" of a declaration of war against Vietnam. Within a year of that achievement, Fulbright felt he had been misled by the administration about what really happened in the Tonkin Gulf and developed the gravest doubts about the war in Vietnam.

Beginning in January 1966, he had held televised hearings on Vietnam to educate the public. In those days, I was working unhappily on the foreign desk of the *Washington Post*, and I would trudge up to the hearing room in the mornings to view the show before reporting for work downtown later in the day. The hearings infuriated President Johnson, who questioned Fulbright's loyalty and occasionally referred to him as "Senator Halfbright." I thought those hearings raised most important questions about a war that I did not believe in, and I looked on Fulbright as one of the courageous men of Washington, possibly one of the wisest I might ever meet.

In seeking to interview the Arkansas Democrat, I was also guided by Stu Hensley's observation that insights into policy decisions leak out over time through the reminiscences of public men. I hoped to learn from Fulbright more about the political maneuvers of the Senate and the role it plays in forming U.S. foreign policy. And, on another level, I was fascinated by this man, once a Rhodes Scholar, once the president of the University of Arkansas, who had created a mighty international exchange program that carries his name to this day. Back then, I admit, I still thought that knowledge and wisdom resided largely in universities. I was curious to find out how Fulbright's respect for education had influenced his public life.

We met for the first and only time on my birthday, December 30, 1974, in Room 1215 of the Dirksen Office Building. I found the senator in a relaxed mood, dressed in a three-piece suit, surrounded by packing cases. In writing this chapter, I was struck by how amiable Fulbright was to this totally un-known reporter and how he deprecated himself as an old "fuddy-duddy" in need of a rest. He had been offered a number of positions, including the am-bassadorship to the United Kingdom or a regular consultant's job to the State Department, all of which he had turned down. In his day, he had often con-sulted with journalistic luminaries such as Walter Lippmann and James Res-ton of the *New York Times*. Now that he was on the way out, this encounter must have been for him no more than a fleeting annoyance. "I need a sab-batical to regain a sense of perspective and to sort out the issues which have been troubling us," he told me as we got started.

In interviewing a celebrity, there are always two and a half questions to ask: What was your biggest achievement, and how do you see the future? The throwaway half, which the cunning Hensley taught me as an insurance policy against a critical editor, who might have questions you had not thought of, was this: Is there anything you would like to say that I have not asked?

When prompting him to talk about his proudest moment, I expected Ful-bright might say that during the Vietnam War he had stood up for truth, de-nounced the arrogance of power, and dissented against his own government. I had also heard from Gerstel that he probably felt that the Fulbright exchange program was his high mark, and, indeed, he was quick to proclaim it as his monument. What really surprised me was that an event as far back as 1901 inspired him. It was the indemnity that China paid the United States for the damage done to U.S. property in Shanghai during the Boxer Rebellion and was used to bring Chinese students to study in the United States. Why not use the proceeds from the sale of U.S.-supplied equipment to the Allies in World War II to finance an exchange of scholars and students? Foreign students would come to the United States and American scholars would go abroad using these foreign moneys. Each set of scholars and students would explain their societies to the other, thereby contributing to world understanding and strengthening world peace.

The program began with a brief amendment to the Surplus Property Act of 1944. It was passed almost unnoticed by Congress but was subsequently improved and amended by the Fulbright-Hays Act in 1961. During the Mc-Carthy era, Fulbright worried that the program might be denounced as abetting the Communists more than aiding the United States, and he sought to counter that perception. In the first thirty years of the act, Fulbright told me, 150,000 people had participated in the exchange in one way or another. He estimated that in 1974 there were 20 chiefs of state who had been "Ful-brighters," as well as 250 cabinet officers and legislators in different parts of the world. In this way, the Fulbright program had surpassed the scope of the scholarship program that English imperialist Cecil Rhodes had envisioned to bring leadership talent to Oxford at the start of the twentieth century. "I think of these alumni scattered across the world, acting as knowledgeable interpreters of their own societies; as persons equipped and willing to deal with conflict or conflict-producing situations on the basis of an informed determination to solve them peacefully; as opinion leaders communicating their appreciation of the societies which they visited to others in their own society," he said, quoting from a comment he inserted in the *Congressional Record* of December 19, 1974. It was easy to agree.

And the future? On that December afternoon, Fulbright saw China and Mexico as major long-term issues emerging in the twenty-first century and the unsettled Middle East as the world's most volatile danger. He clearly had sympathy for the plight of the Arab nations and what he took to be the aggressive posture of Israel. At a speech at Westminster College (where Churchill had decried the "Iron Curtain" descending over Europe in 1946) Fulbright on November 2, 1974, laid considerable blame on Israel for complicating efforts at a peaceful resolution. "Unfortunately, neither the Israelis nor their uncritical supporters in our Congress, and in our media, have appreciated what is at stake. Endlessly pressing the United States for money and arms, and invariably getting all and more she asks, Israel makes bad use of a good friend." Not a comment to please the Jewish lobby.

One area where Fulbright disappointed me was in his assessment of Soviet-American relations. In earlier years he had tried to reduce the funding for the Voice of America and Radio Liberty as outmoded propaganda weapons in the era of détente. I knew from my Moscow experience that these radio stations were very important channels of alternative information for the Soviet people, largely deprived of reliable information on international affairs during the Cold War. Fulbright seemed to accept that the Nixon administration's détente was going to result in a general relaxation of tensions between the superpowers. Perhaps he had been misled by the address Leonid Brezhnev made on national television when he visited Nixon in Washington in July 1973 and on national television declared the Cold War over.

Wise men are not necessarily wise on every subject. They are not infallible, and the journalist must assess critically whatever they say. I believed I knew the Soviet-American equation better than Fulbright as a result of my years in Moscow and my trip there with Kissinger that fall. The U.S.-Soviet relationship was always one of hardball, more so after the Cuban missile crisis that caused the Kremlin to accelerate its nuclear missile program. Efforts to limit or reduce nuclear armaments required carefully thought-out compromises that would not give away precious advantages. Fulbright did not

involve himself in the details of weaponry and looked askance at his colleague Senator Henry Jackson (D-WA), who continually pushed the administration toward a harder line. "He has no trust, no confidence in the
Russians," Fulbright said. "When he talks about the Russians—they're like
the burglar who goes along hotel rooms, testing every door to see if he can
get in. I shouldn't be talking about my former colleague, but there's no secret about it."

Jackson and his colleague in the House Charles A. Vanik (D-OH) had succeeded in passing one amendment that would create a major hurdle to the
improvement of superpower relations. This addition to the Trade Act of
1974 would force the Soviets to allow much increased Jewish emigration if
they wanted to benefit from favorable trade terms with the United States.
And the senator from Washington had dogged Kissinger to take a tougher
stance. "I think Congress has put extremely serious obstacles in Secretary
Kissinger's way in this interference with détente, and in their complete and
unrestrained support of Israel," Fulbright sighed.

Coming to the end of our meeting, I skipped the "Hensley throwaway"
and veered off on a far-out question intended to provoke a spontaneous response: "Is man really rational enough to control his destiny?" I ventured.

Fulbright shot back with a touch of irritation, "It's no good my thinking
in those terms. That's for the philosophers—Immanuel Kant or Oswald
Spengler. Man in politics has to assume it is possible. The alternative is that
there is no use trying."

At this point, I blurted out, "But I thought you were a philosopher!"

"Whatever made you think that?" Fulbright countered, a rising inflection
in his voice, as if this was a novel—and preposterous—proposition.

"Well," I began, not knowing exactly how I was going to bat back, "you
have a long interest in education. You've been to some of the citadels of
great thinking. In your own public life, it seems to me, you've always maintained a high standard of principle and credited human reason with a great
deal."

"It's my hope," Fulbright replied. "It's a hope and I believe it is possible,
and the probability varies from time to time. The exchange program is one
of the things that makes me think that gradually there is building up a cadre
of people who would be willing to cooperate."

As I concluded our conversation and started for the door, Fulbright called
after me, "There is always hope. I'm sure the world has felt there were in-
soluble problems. But one way or another, it muddles through."

One thing I realized from the Fulbright interview was that congressional
correspondents and congressmen are organically tied to one another. The

journalists constantly want information for good stories, and the congress-men constantly crave publicity. The search for national name recognition was especially true of members of the House who had to run for reelection every two years. Since senators faced elections every six years, they were a little less hungry. But anyone who aspired to the presidency knew very well how important access to publicity was.

Fulbright was replaced as chairman of the Senate Foreign Relations Com-mittee by Senator John Sparkman (D-AL), a seventy-five-year-old southern gentleman. A man of considerable reputation from the Deep South, he be-lieved that the committee's rightful role was to advise the full Senate and to be generally supportive of the administration's views in foreign affairs. Under Sparkman, the committee lost luster. It was not until Senator Frank Church, an energetic forty-nine-year-old Democrat from Idaho, replaced Sparkman in 1978 that the committee once again became a major source of information. Church had a vision for the Foreign Relations Committee: he saw it as a center for study of the long-term international interests of the United States, especially China.

Looking over my interviews with Church, I was struck by another in-sight. Political decisions, even highly controversial ones, pale with passing years, but personal motivations hold their attraction. A good way to begin any interview, I concluded, was to go for biography. On one occasion, I started an interview with Church this way: "I thought we might begin with a few personal questions. I read somewhere that you became interested in politics when you were a teenager."

"I became interested in politics even before that, in elementary school," Church replied with his famous smile. "At the time I was in the fourth or fifth grade. I suppose that was the result of the fact that my father constantly talked politics at home, although he had a very low opinion of politicians. When Dad didn't have his friends to discuss politics with, he discussed them with me. He liked to argue, and to accommodate him, I had to find out what the other side of the case was."

Church went on to explain how, coming from a Republican family, he turned into a Democrat. He recalled that his father was a staunch Republi-can who hated Roosevelt. "I used to go to the Carnegie Library, which was just a block away, and read up on political history. In the process I discov-ered that the Democratic Party played a role much more to my liking throughout most of our history. So I converted myself into a supporter of Roosevelt."

In high school, Church became fascinated with Senator William Borah, who chaired the Senate Foreign Relations Committee in the 1920s and had opposed the League of Nations. "Borah was something of a boyhood hero to me, and I followed his career, read his speeches, admired him greatly. Because he was a senator, I wanted to be one. Because he was chairman of the Senate Foreign Relations Committee and had great influence on foreign policy in the 1920s, I wanted one day to follow in his footsteps."

Church's views were far more internationalist than Borah's, in part because of his military service in China during World War II. He joined the army in 1943 after a semester at Stanford University and was discharged from the service three years later. On return to the United States, he resumed his education, eventually attending Harvard and Stanford Law Schools. He married Bethine Clark in 1947 and shortly faced a serious bout with cancer, which he overcame. Despite his illness, he maintained an unusually healthy appearance. In fact, his energy, youthful looks, and winning smile sometimes caused him embarrassment. After he was elected to the Senate in 1956 at the age of thirty-two, he gave up wearing blue suits, the uniform for the teenage boys and girls who served as Senate pages. Chuckling, he explained his sartorial decision to me: "I gave up those suits when an older woman in a Senate elevator mistook me for a Senate page!"

The year after I started covering the Senate—the year 1975—would prove to be a challenging one for the senator from Idaho. This was a year of great scandal at the Central Intelligence Agency because of illegal domestic spying, plots to assassinate foreign leaders, and other violations of its charter. Senate majority leader Mike Mansfield picked Church, an experienced committee chairman, to head the Senate's investigation of the CIA. This assignment would give him excellent publicity, but at the same time force him to submerge his presidential ambitions until the inquiry was completed. By then the presidency would elude his grasp.

On March 10, 1975, I hustled over to Church's hideaway office in the Capitol to interview him about the investigation. We settled into overstuffed chairs, he handed me a Coke, and I chatted with him as easily as with Fulbright, if not more so. In the course of an hour, he predicted the probe would be difficult to contain, widen, and touch many agencies besides the CIA, but he hoped it would reach a conclusion by the end of the year. That night I wrote in my diary: "Interestingly, he claimed not to be polarized by intelligence, in fact, reflected a middle view. He seemed to be saying that the CIA should not be destroyed, that some provision for covert actions should be maintained. As to assassinations, he was quite clear: 'We will have to get to the bottom of those accusations. No element of the U.S. government is authorized to commit killings.'"

I soon found out that reporting on foreign affairs involved far more than consorting with legislators whose views reinforced my own. An equally important technique was to cultivate aides with contrary views, assistants to congressmen whose party did not control the White House. Gerstel was right: congressional aides were sometimes more important than their principals and had an incentive to leak. Their "deep background" tidbits were like termites, aimed at undermining the positions of the administration, and very often produced excellent stories.

Since I was always interested in the U.S.-Soviet equation, it was inevitable I would eventually meet one of the most informed sources who was frequently called the "Prince of Darkness." This assistant turned out to be six years younger than myself, heavier set, with jet-black hair, and, like Mephistopheles, inescapably charming. He got his nickname for helping Senator Jackson push the Nixon and Ford administrations to adopt sterner positions toward the Soviet leadership than they were inclined to at first. He was a man with an exceptionally clear mind, who could explain strategic issues with precision and detail, and always seemingly calm, unemotional, rational. This was Richard Perle, whom I came to respect for his high intelligence, although I disagreed with many of his views.

I first glimpsed Richard in 1972 when he substituted for Senator Jackson at a briefing for journalists on the shortcomings of the projected Interim Agreement on Strategic Arms known as SALT-I that President Nixon was seeking. Later, in 1972, he drafted language for Senator Jackson's famous amendment to the 1974 East-West Trade Act that demanded free emigration from any communist country before the United States would grant normal trading terms (most-favored-nation status). This action, which became known as the Jackson-Vanik Amendment, required the Soviet Union to allow some seventy-five thousand Jews to emigrate annually. When it was adopted, I doubted that it would have a beneficial effect because such an overt intrusion into Soviet internal affairs was likely to elicit a strongly negative reaction. Moscow coughed heavily, but swallowed. Time proved me wrong.

Although I disagreed with Richard on some issues, we would meet happily enough at the permanent investigations subcommittee office of the Senate Government Affairs Committee of which his senator was a member. I soon learned that Richard had the deepest suspicions of the Kremlin's motives, which were hidden behind the opaqueness of the Soviet system. "The devil is in the details," Richard would repeat over and over again. Particularly at issue throughout the mid-1970s was the controversy over the new Soviet Backfire bomber that Kissinger had sought to limit during his 1976 negotiations in Moscow. The Russians asserted that the Backfire was designed for regional conflicts in Europe. But experts like Perle noted that it was capable of aerial refueling, which could give it intercontinental range. Therefore, they argued, it could be used against the United States on one-way missions with recovery in Mexico. Richard went further. The Backfire, he insisted, could also be used for suicide missions against the United States. "You've got to be rigorous about those details," he would say.

He learned his rigor from Albert Wohlstetter, a specialist from the RAND Corporation in Santa Monica, and kept in touch with him as he completed his B.A. at the University of Southern California. In fact, Wohlstetter introduced Perle to Senator Jackson when he was completing his master's degree at Princeton. The senator, delighted with this clearheaded young man, asked him to join his staff in 1969, and he served for eleven years. With Richard's help, Senator Jackson was often successful in slowing down the administration, thereby complicating Kissinger's negotiating trips to Moscow. Despite such irritations, Kissinger described Perle as "one of the ablest geopolitical minds" he had encountered in Washington.

I liked Richard so much I came to consider him a friend. I believed he understood Soviet intentions better than the Democrats. After the Cuban missile crisis, the Democrats took this view: The Russians, like us, want to survive, and they want to ensure the survival of their children and grandchildren. They are intelligent people, and they understand that the two superpowers must do all they can to avoid another missile crisis. Furthermore, the missile crisis showed that when it comes to looming catastrophe, reality trumps ideology. The trouble with this argument was that the Soviet government was not elected by the people but was co-opted from the ranks of the Communist Party. Once in power, the leaders were not subject to serious checks and balances, and often it appeared that they were more interested in preserving their own positions than the fate of the nation. The Democrats, in my view, also did not appreciate how great a part fear and secrecy played in Soviet life, nor to what extent the Soviet economy had been put at the disposal of the military.

The gross domestic product of the Soviet Union in the mid-1970s was probably less than half that of the United States, yet somewhere between 15 and 30 percent of its GDP was destined for military purposes. The equivalent figure for the United States was about 3–5 percent. Decades of isolation from the West also made it difficult for Kremlin leaders to understand the political reactions in a democracy. Their facts, their ideological cast, were so different from ours that I wondered whether Politburo members could really comprehend the information that Ambassador Dobrynin sent them, and how accurate was Dobrynin's information, for that matter?

On one occasion Ruth and I invited Richard to a small dinner at our house in Washington to meet my old acquaintance Yuli Vorontsov, now deputy chief of mission of the Soviet Embassy, and his wife. I imagined that these two political players would talk and develop a useful back channel. To my surprise, the two circled each other throughout the evening, never addressing the other. This kind of standoffishness repeated itself a few years later when Ambassador Dobrynin invited Jackson to visit Moscow. When the senator declared that he would meet with academician Andrey Sakharov and other dissidents in Moscow, the Soviet Embassy withdrew the invitation.

On August 7, 1975, I called on Richard when Senator Jackson was out of town. He led me into the senator's office, announcing cheerily, "Well, détente's dead!" Then he stretched out on the red leather couch and ticked off his criticisms of the administration's Russia policy. The Soviet leaders, he said, were pursuing an aggressive arms buildup and were not constrained by the SALT-I agreement, they had increased the number of espionage agents in the United States, and they were pouring money into Portugal, seeking to cause disruptions in the Western camp.

When I asked him what was the alternative to getting along with the Russians, he conceded that a modus vivendi had to be found. If Jackson were elected president, he said, his administration would undertake a thorough review of U.S.-Soviet relations. An attitude tougher than the Nixon-Ford-Kissinger approach would be hammered out. "It wouldn't be Cold War," Richard predicted. "We would call it Cold Peace." Later that summer Richard addressed a class I was teaching at American University on foreign policy and the press. I noted in my diary on August 20, "This was the last day of my class, and Richard Perle was the guest speaker. He argued brilliantly, as he always does, about the failure of detente. . . . Richard also cited numerous examples of Kissinger blatantly lying in his dealings with Congressmen and their aides. He insisted that Kissinger squandered U.S. negotiating power. He felt that Kissinger would go down in history as not a very great statesman."

And here I return to my February 12, 1976, story reporting that Kissinger had disregarded his negotiating instructions in his January 1976 meetings in Moscow. Yes, it was Richard who leaked that to me on "deep background." Looking back on that incident, I see that I had been manipulated by Richard and his hardline friends to undermine the SALT-II treaty, then under negotiation. My story quoted "informed sources" but gave no hint of the political direction from which the sources were coming. This was the sort of distortion that the deep-background rule could permit, a problem that caused a major debate among journalists at the start of the twenty-first century.

When Jimmy Carter was elected president in 1976, I thought Perle, nominally a Democrat, would be a natural candidate for the staff of the National Security Council. But Dr. Zbigniew Brzezinski, Carter's national security adviser and a hardliner when it came to the Soviet Union, did not recruit

Perle. When I inquired into that, I was told that Perle was regarded as a leaker, and not likely to be loyal. On December 4, 1977, the *New York Times* ran a full column describing Richard as a "hardline zealot" from the point of view of the Carter administration. He responded by telling the newspaper, "I really resent being depicted as some sort of dark mystic, or some demonic power. All I can do is to sit down and talk to someone." Richard acknowledged to me that these criticisms "put a ceiling on how high I can rise. But then, I am not all that ambitious." In moments of frustration, he claimed he would resign and open a restaurant specializing in egg dishes.

Perle's fortunes changed with the election of Ronald Reagan as president. He became assistant secretary of defense for international security policy, 1981–1987, during which time he articulated numerous criticisms of Soviet policy and Western weakness. Under President George W. Bush he became a member of the Defense Policy Board, an advisory committee for the secretary of defense on policy. Perle was occasionally criticized for ethical lapses, and resigned the chairmanship of the board while remaining a member. Much later, Perle, a backer of the war in Iraq, became disillusioned with the Bush administration for its incompetent execution of the postwar period in Iraq. For me—and I think for all would-be journalists—the influence of the "Prince of Darkness" is a stunning example of how intelligence, expertise, calm presentation, and skill in dealing with the media can actually make a nation shift course.

Chapter 21

The Rogue Elephant

By the end of 1974, the United States was in turmoil. The Watergate scandal had dealt a serious blow to the presidency, and President Ford was attempting to calm the political situation with honest talk and a controversial pardon for Nixon. Abroad, Ford sought to stabilize Soviet-American relations while the war in Vietnam dragged on. I watched as a frustrated Congress threatened to cut off funds for military operations (no, not Iraq yet!) in Cambodia and passed the War Powers Act, limiting the president's ability to commit troops abroad. And to top off these crises, the CIA emerged as a rogue agency out of control.

Yet this was also a period when the CIA was successfully recruiting dissident Russian scientists and conducting a few unusual operations against the Soviet military that few people knew about. One evening in the first half of March 1975, my colleague Danny Gilmore rushed into the Senate press gallery in full exuberance from a briefing with CIA director William Colby and a dozen mainstream journalists. In conspiratorial tones, Danny swore me to secrecy. "Colby summoned us about a crazy operation," he confided. "He wanted to persuade editors to hold back because the story is so sensitive. But now he's worried it's going to break. If it does, we can go with it."

In 1975, it was most unusual for the director of Central Intelligence to summon journalists to his office, even though the CIA had slightly lifted the heavy veil that surrounded it since I applied unsuccessfully in the 1950s. In the immediate post–World War II years, secrecy was so tight that the CIA's actual location was hidden from view. When you drove up, you saw only a sign that announced the Bureau of Public Roads. Since most Washingtonians knew where the spy headquarters was located, CIA chief James Schlesinger eventually acknowledged the inevitable by putting up a CIA marker in 1973 beside the Public Roads sign.

Creeping "openness" had progressed to the point that the agency employed a public affairs officer whose usual duty was to say, "No comment." I once arranged an unclassified briefing on the Soviet space program through the spokesman. On that occasion, Angus Thuermer (a former correspondent for the Associated Press) even gave me a tour of the agency's library where American spies had deposited a rich lode—telephone books from almost all important cities of the world. Telephone books are rich in resources: they often contain street addresses as well as telephone numbers, locations of important institutions, advertisements, and unexpected miscellaneous information—good stuff for espionage.

"So what was this briefing about?" I pressed Danny.

He lowered his voice. "The navy located a Soviet sub which sank in the Pacific back in 1968 with all hands aboard. And guess what?"

"Well," I continued, "they must have figured they might be able to extract something out of it. If they could find it."

"Right," Danny continued. "And the CIA conceived a project to raise the whole damn thing using a specially constructed ship. But the sub broke apart in the process, and they were only able to retrieve a section of the bow."

"So what did they find?"

"Colby didn't want to get into that. He seemed to be confirming details which some other journalists had dug out. Some documents, some bodies. And guess what? They buried the bodies at sea according to the Soviet naval manual! Not only that, but they filmed the whole ceremony. Getting that film would be a hell of a scoop!"

I stored that knowledge in my head, thinking that one day I would unearth that film, and eventually I did. In the spring of 1974, much attention had been focused on a strange-looking ship called the *Glomar Explorer* whose declared purpose was to mine seabed minerals, especially manganese nodules in the Pacific Ocean. The ship was constructed at the Sun Shipbuilders and Drydock Company in Chester, Pennsylvania, but to reach the Pacific, where the minerals abounded, it had to sail around South America because its beam of 116 feet was too great for the Panama Canal. In June 1974, the *Honolulu Advertiser* noted the ship's arrival at Hawaii, but, of course, we in the Senate press gallery paid no attention to that.

The *Glomar* was specially built to salvage the Soviet diesel-powered submarine that had sunk in the North Pacific on April 11, 1968. The Soviet boat was a Golf-class sub, built in 1958, that carried three nuclear-tipped missiles and a dozen torpedoes. Its recovery could give the United States excellent insight into the state of Soviet technology and possibly yield valuable code books, decoding machines, and transmission devices. Soviet rescue ships had searched in vain for the sub but had not been able to locate it. The U.S. Navy, however, was luckier. Its underwater listening devices in the Pacific, known as Sea Spider, had detected several explosions and were able to determine the sub's coordinates in the area of 180 degrees east longitude and 40 degrees north latitude, about one thousand miles north of Midway Island. But there was a major problem: the sub lay partially buried on its starboard side in very deep water—three miles below the surface.

To raise this sunken vessel demanded a huge commitment that would eventually cost between $350 million and $500 million. The challenge was to construct a grappling hook comparable to a giant steel hand, 180 feet long and 50 feet wide, weighing 2,150 tons, and fitted with eight fingers, or claws, that could burrow under the sub's hull to grasp it securely. The *Glomar Explorer* had to be so maneuverable that it could hover over the optimal spot in the ocean despite rough swells and heavy wind, never straying more than 150 feet from the target area.

The salvage ship arrived on-site July 4, 1974, just as President Nixon was returning from his last summit conference in Moscow with Brezhnev. In early August, the crew aboard the *Glomar Explorer* began lowering the giant hand on a three-mile-long string of connected pipes similar to those used in deep oil drilling. The hand was nicknamed "Clementine" after the miner's lament "My Darling Clementine." As the recovery crew positioned Clementine by remote controls, the heavy device unexpectedly banged against hard rock beneath the sandy bottom, apparently causing hairline fractures in three of the eight claws. Checks through underwater television cameras revealed no obvious damage. Eventually, the crew succeeded in burrowing the claws under the submarine. Then, the *Glomar*'s cranes applied 17 million pounds of upward thrust, and the sub broke loose. After forty-eight hours, the *Glomar* had raised the boat a single mile off the ocean floor when suddenly the hairline fractures split open and four-fifths of the carcass broke away, falling back into the deep. The crew managed to hold on to a 38-foot-long bow section and succeeded in landing it aboard the *Glomar*.

As the men began dissecting the bow, notably radioactive, they were astounded to hear the flash from Washington on August 8 of Nixon's resignation. Still, the work went ahead. The men recovered two torpedoes, a valuable journal by one of the officers on the weaponry, and several naval reference books. Because water pressure at 16,500 feet is 4 tons per square inch, a great deal of the finds were grotesquely compressed. The investigators noted poor metallurgical work on the ship's hull and wasteful use of precious metals. But they failed to recover the most important targets: code books, code machines, any of the three missiles or their nuclear warheads, navigation guidance systems, or communication devices.

Among the discoveries were the corpses of three twenty-year-old submariners—Viktor Lokhov, Vladimir Kostyushko, and Valentin Nosachev—which had been cushioned by mattresses as the boat sank. Also in the bow they found the partial remains of three others, for a total of six bodies from a crew of approximately eighty. The CIA, anticipating human remains, had made provision to bury them at sea with full honors in the age-old tradition of mariners. That might calm any uproar should Moscow decide to make an issue of the salvage operation.

Accordingly, seventy-five members of the crew gathered in the *Glomar's* hold around a boxlike vault, painted red, eight feet square and four feet deep, fitted with six interior shelves. One by one, the corpses in body bags and covered by a Soviet naval ensign, were placed on the shelves. Six crew members in white uniforms, caps, and gloves stood by the steel vault as a chaplain conducted the service against a backdrop of the American flag and the Soviet naval ensign affixed to a bulkhead. After the U.S. and Soviet national anthems, the chaplain intoned as an American interpreter arduously rendered the words into Russian:

> In a very real way this ceremony has resulted from the continuing contention between our two nations. . . . The fact that our nations have had disagreements does not lessen in any way our respect for these men and the service they have rendered. . . . As long as men and nations are suspicious of each other, instruments of war will be constructed and brave men will die, as these men have died in the service of their country. . . . May the day quickly come when men will beat their swords into plowshares and spears into pruning hooks, and nations shall not rise up against nation; neither shall there be war anymore.

An eyewitness described the final moments: "The forward crane on the starboard side of the ship hooked the metal box and lifted it out of the hold. At first it stubbornly refused to sink, but after a few minutes it had partially filled with seawater and begun to settle. When loosed from the crane's cable by a crewman's jerk on the releasing pelican hook, the red box with bodies of six Russian sailors finally sank beneath the swells."

It was twilight on a calm sea, September 4, 1974, some ninety miles southwest of Hawaii. Eighteen years later on November 12, 1992—after the Cold War ended—the then head of the CIA, Robert M. Gates, visited President Boris Yeltsin in Moscow and presented him the naval flag used in the ceremony and a videotape that was subsequently broadcast on Russian television. The CIA was happy to send me a copy of the videotape in response to my Freedom of Information Act request.

Disappointed that a major part of the submarine had eluded them, the project managers wanted to return in the summer of 1975 to recover the remainder. Thus, maintaining deep secrecy was imperative. However, within six months details of the first mission began to leak. On February 7, 1975, the *Los Angeles Times* published a four hundred–word front-page story revealing that the CIA was seeking to raise a Soviet submarine but incorrectly locating the effort in the Atlantic Ocean. The *Times* attributed the story to "local law enforcement officers" who were investigating a burglary into Howard Hughes's Summa Corporation in Los Angeles on June 5, 1974. During that burglary, several footlockers of documents had been stolen, including a secret memorandum about the *Glomar Explorer* project. Immediately notified, Colby sent agents to talk to the *Times* editor, who agreed to downplay the story in later editions by moving it to page 18 in the hopes that the Soviet Embassy would not notice.

I was intrigued at the time—and even more so today—that Colby had been willing to share details with journalists. He could have taken the traditional "no comment" stance. It turned out that three weeks after the *Los Angeles Times* published its February 7 report, *Parade* magazine editor Lloyd Shearer contacted Colby about pictures his magazine had obtained of the *Glomar Explorer* as it plumbed the ocean site. Colby reportedly told Shearer, "You are on to something very, very delicate. This one I really would like you to sit on." Shearer replied, "Can you turn off all the sources who have it? Do you think you can sit on it?" Colby promised, "I will try like hell."

In the days that followed, Colby began an extraordinary campaign to restrain the press by appealing to editors' patriotism. He felt obliged to do this since the United States, unlike Britain or Russia, has no official-secrets act forbidding journalists from disclosing national secrets on pain of criminal prosecution. He contacted Katharine Graham of the *Washington Post*, editor William F. Thomas of the *Los Angeles Times*, publisher Arthur Sulzberger and Sy Hersh of the *New York Times*, *Time*, and *Newsweek*. As Colby tried to persuade, he was inevitably forced to share some essential details, but all agreed to self-restraint so long as the story remained under wraps.

On March 17, 1975, *Parade* editor Shearer sent another message to Colby that the story was now "all over" the National Press Building. On March 18, 1975, he got word that columnist Jack Anderson might be on the verge of divulging the details. Colby and Thuermer rushed all over Washington in search of Anderson but failed to find him, and Anderson broke the story on two evening broadcasts over the Mutual Radio Network. Anderson's angle was not that the CIA had achieved an extraordinary coup, but that the agency was trying to suppress news of a $350 million fiasco. "I don't think the government has the right to cover up a boondoggle," Anderson said later. "I have withheld other stories at the behest of the CIA, but this was simply a cover-up of a $350 million failure—$350 million literally went down into the ocean." A boondoggle? It seems likely to me that Colby may have downplayed whatever success the CIA actually achieved to dampen negative reactions from Moscow. Salvaging another nation's warship, according to maritime law, was, after all, plain and simple robbery.

The *Glomar Explorer* issue was only one of the cascading challenges that Colby faced in his two short years as director, from 1973 to 1975. Since the end of World War II, the United States had been countering the international communist threat not just with military force but also with aid for the Third World, support for dictatorial regimes that sympathized with the United States, and the special resources of its secret agency. The CIA's armory included traditional espionage, exotic technology, and infiltration of disinformation into foreign and American media. This infiltration began to unravel by 1967 when the antiestablishment magazine *Ramparts* published a major article on CIA funding of the National Student Association through dummy foundations. The agency's effort had been to provide support for articulate American students to travel abroad to Soviet-sponsored youth conferences and challenge communist propaganda. The public disclosure of this secret support produced shocked reactions throughout Washington.

By the summer of 1971, popular opposition to the Vietnam War was spreading distrust of the administration, too. In June of that year, the *New York Times* and other newspapers published a secret Defense Department history of American involvement in Vietnam known as the Pentagon Papers. The U.S. Supreme Court upheld the newspapers' right to publish by a vote of six to three, humiliating the Nixon administration. The White House reacted by undertaking a vigorous effort to plug future disclosures and brought the leaker of the Pentagon Papers, Dr. Daniel Ellsberg, to trial. However, the treason case against him collapsed when it was discovered that two White House agents, with help from the CIA, had broken into the offices of Ellsberg's psychiatrist to steal material that might impugn his character before the jury.

At the end of 1972, Nixon shifted CIA director Richard Helms to the ambassadorship in Iran and named James Schlesinger, a White House budget official, to replace him. Schlesinger was so appalled at the misuse of CIA resources in the Ellsberg case that he ordered an internal investigation. Dubious actions in the post–World War II years were compiled into a lengthy report that became known as "The Family Jewels." The new director began cleaning house by dismissing officials who had participated in the abuses. Schlesinger had served only four months when President Nixon shook up his national security apparatus in May 1973 and transferred him to head the Defense Department, naming Colby, chief of clandestine services, as the new CIA chief.

Colby knew from his confirmation hearings in July 1973 that Congress recognized the agency was in deep trouble. If the "Family Jewels" report ever became public, it would cause a major crisis; furthermore, questions about CIA infiltration into the media continued to circulate widely. That fall an invitation from the *Washington Star* may have stimulated Colby's damage-control skills. He was invited to an editorial luncheon at the *Star* by editor Newbold Noyes. The session was held under the "Lindley Rule" (no attribution for anything that might be written) in the editor's private dining room. Toward the end of the encounter, assistant managing editor David Kraslow asked Colby if the agency had ever used journalists under cover and, in particular, if it had ever employed anyone from the *Washington Star*. Colby promised to look into the issue.

After weeks of silence, Kraslow asked diplomatic reporter Oswald Johnston to follow up. Johnston called the CIA and got a big surprise. The CIA spokesman invited him for a rare one-on-one meeting with Colby at Langley headquarters. The surprise deepened when Colby outlined with utter frankness the extent of CIA infiltration into the American media. Thirty-six journalists working abroad, he said, were on the CIA payroll as undercover informants. Five full-time staff correspondents of mainstream American news organizations were being phased out for fear of their being exposed. The CIA chief, respecting promises of anonymity, declined to identify any of the journalists. Johnston published these revelations on November 30, 1973, in an article that remains to this day one of the most authoritative accounts of the situation. Clearly, Colby had concluded the best way to proceed was to seek understanding from Congress, the media, and the public through candor while protecting the deepest secrets such as names, budget figures, and current operations. Within months, however, the situation turned even more dramatic.

Details of the "Family Jewels" report leaked at the end of 1974 to Sy Hersh, possibly from disgruntled officials who had been fired by

Schlesinger. Hersh alerted Colby and arranged to meet with him on December 20, 1974. The director was willing for two reasons: he respected Hersh for having sat on the *Glomar Explorer* story for more than a year at Colby's request, and, more important, the *New York Times*'s anticipated revelation of "The Family Jewels" called for a most careful reaction.

On December 22, 1974, the *Times* published a page 1 story headlined "Huge C.I.A. Operation Reported in U.S. against Anti-War Forces, Other Dissidents in Nixon Years." Colby declined comment for the record, but Hersh got many of his details from the director on "deep background." Hersh's story stated that the CIA had maintained files on some 10,000 Americans who opposed the war in Vietnam, and had engaged in illegal wiretapping, mail openings, and break-ins since the 1950s.

The details unleashed the expected firestorm. President Ford, seeking to dampen the issue, quickly created a blue-ribbon investigating panel under Vice President Nelson Rockefeller. This was, in effect, an executive body investigating executive misdeeds. It was not likely to put the scandal to rest. Congress launched its own investigations that eventually involved dozens of committees, but principally the special panels of the House and Senate. My acquaintance Senator Frank Church, named to head the Senate Select Committee on Intelligence, wasted no time in denouncing the CIA as "a rogue elephant rampaging out of control."

During the next two years, Colby and other CIA officials were constantly traveling to Capitol Hill to answer questions in public and private. Colby took the attitude that nothing should be hidden from Congress. The congressional investigations disclosed that the CIA had operated mail-intercept programs between 1953 and 1973 in New York, San Francisco, New Orleans, and Hawaii that violated federal criminal laws on obstructing the mail. In the last year of the program, operatives examined 2.3 million letters in transit between the United States and the Soviet Union, photographed the covers of 33,000, and opened 8,700. The CIA had responded to a request from President Lyndon B. Johnson to determine if the Soviet Union was prompting the anti–Vietnam War disorders. Under a program called CHAOS, the CIA developed computerized files on more than 300,000 persons and organizations with possible foreign contacts, among them files on 7,200 American citizens.

During the Cold War, Washington had been beaming alternative news and popular music into the Soviet Union through Radio Free Europe and Radio Liberty, services partially financed through the agency. The CIA had been secretly financing many cultural activities such as the National Students Association and the English literary magazine *Encounter* and distributing anticommunist books through the Praeger publishing house in New

York. The agency had set up front foundations through which to dispense moneys for other anticommunist activities and to acquire 40 percent of the *Rome Daily American* newspaper.

The superpower conflict occasionally generated Soviet defectors to the United States who brought with them valuable information about Soviet society, its economy, and its military. Usually, these defectors were debriefed, given new identities, and inserted into American society with modest benefits. But Yuri Nosenko suffered a crueler fate. CIA counterintelligence suspected he was a "plant" who was specifically sent to spread false reports within the intelligence community. He was held in solitary confinement in a small, damp cell for three years before the authorities decided to release him.

Among the most sensational disclosures were reports that the CIA had been involved, either indirectly or directly, in assassination plots aimed at eliminating Congo leader Patrice Lumumba, President Rafael Trujillo of the Dominican Republic, President Ngo Dinh Diem of South Vietnam, Chilean army chief General Rene Schneider, and Cuban leader Fidel Castro. The hearings revealed that the CIA had sought help from mobsters to kill Castro, and had contemplated finishing him off with poisoned cigars. At one meeting, Senator Church dramatically displayed an assassination dart gun that the CIA had developed but never used. We learned, too, from congressional sources that technicians at the U.S. Embassy in Moscow had succeeded in monitoring radio telephone conversations between Soviet leaders as they drove in limousines through Moscow. That disclosure ended one of the few means of listening to the conversations of top Soviet leaders.

These revelations made for exciting journalism. The hearings also demonstrated that an open society like the United States finds it hard, perhaps impossible, to tolerate an agency that must sometimes operate with the greatest stealth. Early in the congressional hearings, I observed the CIA chief at close range. After sitting through two and a half hours of Colby's testimony before the Defense Subcommittee of the House Appropriations Committee, I was astounded by Colby's openness. I wrote in my journal on February 20, 1975:

> Colby made an impression of great candor within the limits which he felt constrained to maintain. His effort is to salvage a pretty badly damaged CIA and to preserve as much as he can. Probably he wants to preserve CIA ability to conduct covert operations abroad and much of its traditional activities. But he has to reckon with the current public uproar and he has to consent to a new and more vigorous system of oversight. It is ironic that the CIA has at its helm today a man who grew up in the agency and has no independent standing. This is not a man with a big outside reputation. This

is a working stiff who has had thrust upon him great political responsibilities which were not all evident when he first became director.

As 1975 progressed, my thoughts often focused on the CIA and the press. Since the Second World War, the agency had developed covert relationships with hundreds of journalists. That had been tolerated into the 1960s. Danny discovered that the CIA had paid some journalists to make trips to Eastern Europe and report back on assigned subjects. We learned, too, that the CIA used its journalistic ties to insert disinformation about Soviet intentions in overseas publications. Such stories were occasionally picked up by Western wire services and transmitted back to American media. This phenomenon was known as "flowback" and clearly violated the spirit of the law under which no American propaganda was to be aimed at the American public. The CIA had arrangements with top management of some television networks to pick up unused video footage (outtakes) that might serve intelligence but was not deemed newsworthy. Once in a while, the CIA persuaded newspaper managements to hire CIA staffers and train them as journalists. The *Louisville Courier-Journal* complied, and we "Unipressers" in London wondered if Larrimore's work was part of the same pattern.

During the congressional investigations, Colby acknowledged in general terms some of the agency's ties to journalists. Colby named no names, just as he declined to identify reporters for the Johnston interview. The journalists, after all, had been promised "perpetual anonymity." On one occasion, Colby was willing to say for the record, "Over the years . . . we have worked with these people to help us on our foreign intelligence responsibilities. In some cases, they can provide us information that we ask them about; in some cases they can make contact with people that it is difficult for an official of an embassy or an American mission abroad to be in touch with."

Colby's frankness bothered the White House. President Ford's displeasure became clear on November 2, 1975, when he announced a major shakeup of his national security apparatus. He fired Colby (who continued to serve until January 30, 1976) and ordered Kissinger to give up his post of national security adviser, which he had held simultaneously with the position of secretary of state. Ford named George H. W. Bush, then the U.S. representative in China, to take over the CIA. One of Bush's first actions was to stop the secret hiring of mainstream journalists while allowing contacts with freelancers overseas.

What was the best way for the Ford administration to handle this intrusive questioning into intelligence operations, stonewall or cooperate? Kissinger and Ford favored reluctance. Colby's position was odd, I thought, because a man whose career had been heavily in clandestine operations could have been expected to favor silence. Was it because he was trained as a lawyer at Columbia University and practiced law before he joined the CIA? Did he feel his Senate confirmation hearings in 1973 obliged him to be open? When I asked Thuermer in 2005 about it, he replied only that Colby kept his motivations "close to his vest." The best explanation, I think, comes from Colby's memoir, *Honorable Men:*

> My strategy quite simply had been to be guided by the Constitution and to apply its principles. This meant that I had to cooperate with the investigations and try to educate the Congress, the press, and public, as well as I could, about American intelligence, its importance, its successes and its failings. The Agency's survival, I believed, could only come from understanding, not hostility, built on knowledge and not faith. And I thought this could be done without exposing the true secrets that needed to be kept, the names of the Americans and foreigners who worked with us under cover, and the sensitive technologies that could easily be made useless if revealed to the intended targets.

I concluded that journalists should be able to talk to whomever they wish, whenever they wish. But they should never be used to carry out operational activities—paid or unpaid. That was why I refused to help FBI special agent John T. Field in 1969, who wanted me to put specific questions to diplomats I knew in the Soviet Embassy. I believed I could not do that if I wanted to preserve my journalistic and personal integrity. Secret ties between secret services and newspeople would eventually become known and undermine media credibility. What if a journalist came across information critical to national security? Or if an intelligence officer asked casually if I knew something about X, Y, or Z? That was a conundrum. On balance, I believed that doing a favor for the government was sometimes permissible but only in very special cases.

In the spring of 1978, William G. Miller, staff director of the Senate Intelligence Committee, invited me to testify before the Church committee. On May 3, I joined Dan Schorr, then of CBS News (today a commentator on National Public Radio), and Jack Nelson of the *Los Angeles Times* in assessing legislation the panel was drawing up on CIA-media relations. We all insisted that journalists should have the right to talk to whomever they wish, and we opposed a rule that would require the CIA to report to Congress all journalistic contacts. Dan Schorr strongly opposed the use of any person connected with the media—administrators as well as editorial employees, foreign media as well as American—as agency assets. Any contact with the media he saw as the thin end of a wedge that would only deepen with time.

248 Of Spies and Spokesmen

For my part, I told the senators, I would be relieved to know in the future that the Central Intelligence Agency had severed all relations with journalists. That would make me feel safer, I said, if I was working in a hostile country. Dan Schorr dismissed my observation as naive. "I am not impressed with the argument that categoric legislation is needed to keep the Soviets from making propaganda hay by labeling American journalists as CIA agents," he told the senators. "They will in any case make their accusations whenever it suits their purposes." A decade later, I learned how right he was.

Chapter 22

## The Infamous Zone

One of the great debates of 1977 and 1978 concerned the future of the Panama Canal and the U.S. colony that surrounded it. As correspondents covering Congress, my UPI colleague Cheryl Arvidson and I were well placed to follow the Carter administration's controversial efforts to turn the canal over to Panama. At one point our disclosures about drug dealing among the Panamanian leadership brought us into a bruising conflict with the White House and its extraordinary efforts to control our reporting.

The fifty-mile waterway across the Isthmus of Panama had a long, tumultuous history. Its completion by American engineers just before the First World War was an extraordinary achievement that conservatives across the country compared to the landing of men on the moon in 1969. By the mid-1970s, it had become clear that the canal was becoming an international problem because of rising nationalism in Panama. The canal could be closed down at almost any time by Panamanian saboteurs as a way to force the United States to abandon the Canal Zone and the canal that divided Panama in two.

President Carter made the achievement of two new Panama Canal treaties a top priority of his administration along with completing strategic-arms limitations with the Soviet Union and reaching full diplomatic relations with Communist China. The fate of the canal resonated across America throughout 1977, especially in the heartland, where many articulate citizens were demanding that it remain solidly in American hands.

Cheryl Arvidson, who had grown up in Iowa, was particularly sensitive to these concerns. She had joined the Des Moines Bureau of UPI in 1969, and her aggressive reporting helped her become bureau chief within a year. Cheryl was well acquainted with the full range of Iowa's problems, its politics and government at all levels, and understood well the mentality of middle America. Like me, she believed that turning the canal slowly over to Panama was in the U.S. interest and would guarantee stable operations for world shipping long into the future.

She became interested in the canal story when a commanding Republican figure, California governor Ronald Reagan, declared early in the national debate, "What in the world are we doing—negotiating a giveaway of the canal to a Marxist military dictator? We bought it, we paid for it, it is sovereign U.S. territory, and we should keep it!" The adamant opposition in Iowa unnerved Cheryl, who told me, "I had been home visiting family in Iowa in the late summer and appeared on a talk show on WHO Radio, ostensibly to discuss Washington news and media coverage. The host opened the phone lines, and I found myself bombarded with callers saying, 'Why are we giving away our canal?' I was stunned—honestly, every caller was on that kick."

Canal negotiator Ambassador Ellsworth Bunker offered an opposing point of view, based on the canal's physical vulnerability. "We are negotiating," said the elderly diplomat, "because we see a new treaty arrangement as the most practical means of protecting our interests. The real choice before us is not between the existing treaty and a new one, but rather between a new treaty and what would happen if we should fail to achieve a new treaty." Throughout 1977 negotiators Bunker and Sol Linowitz pushed forward energetically to the dismay of much of the nation. On September 7, 1977, the United States and Panama signed two new treaties: one on the permanent neutrality of the waterway, the second that would hand over the running of the canal to Panama in stages over the next twenty-two years and dissolve the Zone. At one minute past midnight on December 31, 1999, the canal would become Panamanian, and the northern and southern parts of the Republic of Panama would be reunited. What was left, and what interested Cheryl and me as journalists, was how the administration would get the U.S. Senate to ratify the two treaties.

By the fall of 1977, it was obvious that the administration faced an uphill battle to win the necessary sixty-seven votes—two-thirds of the U.S. Senate—a very high threshold under any conditions. Treaty opponents intensified their efforts to reject the treaties at the start of the new year. The most outspoken leaders were Senators Jesse Helms, James Allen, and Robert Dole. As the public debate progressed, information began to surface that the family of Panamanian president Omar Torrijos had been engaged in drug trafficking to the United States. Torrijos's brother Moises, for example, had been indicted by a U.S. court, and an effort to arrest him in 1972 failed. The Carter administration was aware of these accusations, but judged them peripheral to U.S. long-term interests. Conservatives angrily asserted that the Panamanian leadership was so corrupt it could not be counted on to enforce the terms of any treaty. Staff aides to conservative congressmen hinted darkly that the administration was so fearful the two pacts might be turned down that it was withholding incriminating information.

My own view was that the United States could not adequately protect the canal from sabotage or terrorism. Therefore, I approved of the administration's efforts. At the same time, as a journalist, I believed that all derogatory information should be disclosed so that no unexpected surprises would arise. By January 1978, Cheryl and I began picking up suggestions on Capitol Hill that the White House had been misleading the Senate. Our information came principally from two sources; one we nicknamed the "Gold Watch" because of the pocket watch he wore on a gold chain, and the other the "Cute Little Fella" because of his good looks and military bearing. They were agreeable individuals, often seeking us out, speaking knowledgeably and with enthusiasm for their cause, but always on "deep background."

Their importuning set Cheryl and me to work. We soon learned that the White House had consulted with Senate majority leader Robert Byrd and minority leader Howard Baker and that a decision had been made to supply the Senate Select Committee on Intelligence (the same committee that investigated the intelligence community under Senator Frank Church) with relevant information relating to what was becoming known as the "Panama drug connection." What heightened our energies was an account from our two sources that on October 7, 1977, the Drug Enforcement Agency (DEA) had spent a weekend reviewing its files and selecting pertinent documents for transfer to the committee. Furthermore, the sources told us that they had received a phone call from a "high DEA official" that some documents had been removed, possibly destroyed, and rerouted to the office of Attorney General Griffin Bell.

For several weeks we pounded the spokesmen of the drug agency and the Department of Justice for comment on this allegation. After much insistence, we received a statement from DEA spokesman Robert Feldkamp that all "relevant documents" had been forwarded to the committee. In the post-Watergate era of suspicion of government, we took that word *relevant* to mean that some documents had, indeed, been withheld. We intensified our inquiries, found additional sources who raised alarms about the integrity of the Panamanian government, and obtained a number of documents, including some confidential testimony that had never been released. Finally,

after two months of digging, we composed a newsbreaking three-part series on the drug connection, which began:

> Since 1971 the U.S. government has received a stream of allegations link-
> ing Panama's Supreme Revolutionary Leader Gen. Omar Torrijos, his fam-
> ily and associates to drug trafficking, a UPI investigation has disclosed.
>   The allegations—some from officials, others admittedly secondhand—
> come from informants, drug pushers and agents. They are in the files of
> the Canal Zone government, the Drug Enforcement Agency, the U.S.
> Army, the CIA, and congressional committees.

The series described how the U.S. government had tried to arrest General
Torrijos's brother in 1972, detailed various aspects of the smuggling operations, and pointed out that President Carter had ordered the files turned over
to the Senate, but the issue was so contentious that not all files had been made
available and some might have been hidden in Attorney General Griffin Bell's
office or, worse still, "may have been destroyed." We clearly needed comment from White House officials, but we did not want to give them much
time for fear they would think up some clever way to block our series. The
fairness of this short-response-time approach should be questioned. On
Wednesday, February 15, I sent a letter to White House spokesman Jody Powell asking for an on-the-record meeting. On that same evening of February 15,
the Washington Bureau moved the series by national wire to all clients, without White House comment, for publication several days later, beginning on
February 19, a Sunday. Publication was timed to precede a rare closed session
of the Senate scheduled for Tuesday, February 21.
    Several days later, on February 18, I received an agitated call from Pow-
ell, summoning me and Cheryl to his office, adding that there were serious
issues and we should bring our bureau chief, Grant Dillman, along. White
House spokesmen do not usually involve themselves so blatantly in Washington journalism, and newspapers from Washington to California were
quick to denounce this assault on freedom of the press. As it turned out,
Powell's attack on our personal integrity was more brutal than those of
Dean Rusk against John Scali in 1968 or Kissinger's against me in 1976. The
meeting in no way resembled the genteel manipulation by CIA chief
William Colby to bend the media to his aims in 1975, but I must also say the
interference was far less acute than the controls Moscow ordinarily imposed
on its own media.
    Since what went on during that four-hour meeting at the White House
has never been published, I offer this account based on Cheryl's "morning-
after" memo, the two tapes I recorded during the meeting, the "sanitized"

transcript the White House supplied, and my own notes. The meeting began in Powell's office in the West Wing promptly at 2:30 P.M. Powell, an assertive spokesman (actually, some might say an aggressive alpha male), greeted us from behind his broad mahogany desk. Two officials whom we had never seen before sat to one side on a couch and chair. They were Phil Jordan, special assistant to Attorney General Griffin Bell, and Robert Beckel, deputy assistant secretary of state in charge of helping the proposed canal treaties through the Senate. Of all the Carter bureaucrats, they were the only ones who had attended all decision meetings involved in turning over Panama drug documents to the Senate committee.

We sat facing Powell, Dillman to the left, Arvidson in the middle, and me to the right. Powell attempted to set a reasonable tone, offering us refreshments from a six-pack of Cokes, and asserting he sought no confrontation. Cheryl recalled that a framed copy of the First Amendment, hanging on the wall behind his desk, gave her some comfort. Powell urged that we speak informally about the administration's concerns and then move on to any on-the-record statements we might request. Sweetness and light did not last long, however.

It quickly developed that the third section of the series was the nexus of their concern, specifically our report that not all documents had been turned over to the Senate committee and that some had been removed, possibly secreted in Bell's office, or even destroyed. In increasingly heated tones, Powell challenged those sentences. "No administration in the history of this country has busted its butt to give the United States Congress the sort of information we gave them," he blustered. "We had people working their ass off. We went through every possible thing we could get our hands on! It is probably an undertaking that is unprecedented. And here we have—based on some jackass up there in the Senate with a vested interest in attacking the credibility of these people—a background statement which he is not even willing to take credit for himself that he lays off on somebody else in DEA, and all of a sudden we are faced with these damn innuendos!"

Beckel rushed to Powell's support. "This is a pretty serious thing, and I can promise you if you really look into this carefully that what people did was the best effort that I've ever seen in an administration-wide effort to provide information."

The attorney general's man homed in on the suggestion that documents might have been destroyed. "I totally deny that on the record," Jordan shouted, "as the only person receiving those documents in the attorney general's office . . . and you have put that on every fucking wire service in the whole country! I really resent it because you are impugning the attorney general of the United States!" Then he hammered us: "I'm putting you on notice right now: if you run it with a denial, you may not have avoided a lawsuit."

Dillman remained impassive, saying nothing. But Cheryl, who had done the bulk of the reporting on that part, rushed to defend, citing our numerous efforts to elicit clear statements from the Justice Department and the DEA.

Powell counterattacked, denouncing our sources as antitreaty opponents who were hiding behind "deep background" formulations like "UPI has been told . . ." He challenged Cheryl to say whether she understood where these sources were coming from and demanded that their political bias be clearly underlined in each part of the series. She flatly refused to answer, and that infuriated him. He jumped out of his seat and lunged at her as if ready to strike, crashed over an ashtray on the floor, and burst out the door shouting, "I can't deal with her!" Jordan, a look of frustration on his face, muttered under his breath, "Goddamn it! How can you get through to these blockheads?"

Shortly, Powell returned somewhat sobered, and we began again in a calmer mood. Much of the ensuing conversation centered on the transfer of documents from the DEA to the Senate Intelligence Committee and how we had obtained our details. Cheryl reported that our two sources had said that documents were removed, and, when pressed, acknowledged they knew this because a high official in the DEA had so told them. Powell pressed further: "Removed and not returned?"

As the conversation proceeded, Beckel and Jordan explained that pertinent documents had been removed, copied, and returned to their original files. None had been destroyed, they insisted. A misunderstanding seemed to have occurred, but where? Had the high DEA source misinformed, or misled, our two sources? Or had our sources misunderstood the high official when he said documents had been "removed"? Or did we misunderstand our sources when they repeated the verb *removed*? That point was never clarified and practically exhausted us all. As we all began to tire, Powell called for a breather and offered all of us a "real drink"—Scotch or bourbon? The officials accepted; the journalists did not.

What became clear was that sources could easily disguise identities and political orientations by speaking on deep background. Powell came back again and again insisting that what sources tell you almost certainly carries a political bias; working documents (unless generated by biased sources) are more trustworthy. "Most of your stuff does not come from documents that you examined," Powell asserted. "Most of it, particularly the outrageous, comes not from documents but from what people said." He and Jordan asserted that our source, the "Cute Little Fella," was actually the son of a navy admiral from North Carolina, active in politics, whose family was known for its arch-conservative views. We declined to agree, but Powell was correct. He went a step further and pronounced our whole series as "crap, irresponsible," and not worthy of UPI journalism.

From a reporter's point of view another thing became obvious: the federal government is such a complex organization that it is difficult for a journalist to pinpoint on short notice the officials who are truly in a position to comment or elucidate a sensitive subject. The officials in this meeting acknowledged that the Drug Enforcement Agency and the Department of Justice had been cautioned to provide only minimum comment in response to drug-trafficking allegations. Jordan conceded we had difficulty getting a reasonable comment and added almost apologetically, "What you've been getting is like a pinprick around the edges of the process."

After we had been arguing for some two hours, we finally got down to the business of going through the three stories in detail. Because we had been constantly going on and off the record, Powell called in a stenographer to make sure we all recognized the changes. For the most part, the adjustments corrected the language describing the transfer of documents to the Senate and added on-the-record statements by Powell in appropriate places.

As we neared the fourth hour, Powell summed up: "It would be a great shame if the treaties which are in the best interests of the United States, not just this year but well into the next century and perpetuity, are rejected with all that portends, because of arguments about matters which I would suspect in the year 2000 will be lucky to be a footnote in history." Throughout, Dillman, whatever his failings as a manager of people, played a moderating role, never raising his voice and projecting an air of calm reasonableness under fire. Both Cheryl and I were glad he had managed to defuse this crisis. Afterward, Dillman justified the changes by telling the *Washington Post* on February 21, "Portions of the original were unfair to the White House after hearing Powell."

Our series was immediately revised and redistributed over the UPI national wire for publication as originally planned, beginning February 19. On February 21, the Senate went into a rare secret session to consider the drug connection. At the end of two days of debate, the senators voted to publish the transcript of their deliberations. Cheryl and I were pleased to see that the Senate debate added nothing to our series that was published in the *Washington Star* and other newspapers across the country.

The fate of the treaties was still uncertain. According to our notes of February 18, there were fifty-four senators in favor, twenty-six against, and twenty undecided. The administration revved up its lobbying effort and quietly accepted the inevitability that amendments, reservations, and understandings would be added to the treaties, something that President Wilson tried to discourage during the 1920 debate over the League of Nations treaty that the Senate rejected. A month later, on March 16, Senate majority leader Robert Byrd scheduled the vote on the Neutrality Treaty for four o'clock. Several hours before, Byrd invited a small group of us to his ornate chambers for a briefing that I recorded in my journal:

> He sits, dressed on this day, in a very dignified black, three piece suit. His wavy gray hair is swept back; his eyes somewhat distant; his mouth, pursed in a rather rooster-like expression. He faces a portrait of General Stonewall Jackson which bears the notation "Class of 1878."
>
> In the beginning, Byrd begins, there were only 25 senators or so who supported the Panama Canal treaties. But in the last few weeks, despite all the educational efforts, the vote seemed to stick at 59–60 in favor. The week before the final vote, Byrd convened a series of undecided senators in his office. In 10 years of working in the Senate leadership, he says, he has found that if you can sit people down and talk with them you can generally find a solution.
>
> Four P.M.: The Senate has filled to the brim. The negotiators Bunker and Linowitz are in the galleries. The last hour is filled with opponents' and proponents' arguments. Byrd is the last to speak. He is eloquent, quoting from Daniel Webster, recalling Roman history, and reciting Shakespeare: "There is a tide in the affairs of men, which taken at the floor leads on to fortune . . ."
>
> The balloting goes swiftly. Senator Gaylord Nelson renders the 67th vote, and Byrd holds off to vote last. It is 68–32; the treaty is ratified. Soiled by reservations, perhaps, but ratified.

The second treaty detailing the staged process of turning the canal over to the Panamanians was brought up for a vote a month later, on April 18, 1978. Compared to the first vote, this one was prolonged and anticlimactic. Senators Abourezk, Hayakawa, and Cannon raised last-minute objections. Senators Long and Scott quarreled over whether to prolong the vote by another forty-five minutes. The entire roll of one hundred senators was called three times. Senator Jackson was late getting to the floor, and his vote in favor was number sixty-six. Byrd, who had planned a rhetorical summation as last time, hurried to cast the sixty-seventh vote, ensuring the ratification but torpedoing his final flourish. A few minutes later Senator Clifford Case ambled in and cast the sixty-eighth vote. The second treaty, like the first, passed, sixty-eight to thirty-two.

Byrd's masterful performance in securing passage for these two treaties impressed me; his high-flown rhetoric underlined the high drama of political life, so different from the backstairs maneuverings of pinstriped diplomats. Several days after the vote, I persuaded the majority leader to explain his skills to me. And for the next seven hours on that Saturday we talked and talked while he took phone calls, put off intruders, and attempted to work. Days later I penned a feature article (a "personality spotlight," or "perspot," in UPI lingo) on Byrd that began like this:

WASHINGTON (UPI)—Shy young Robert Byrd pumped gasoline, cut meat, and welded ships. He dreamed of becoming an architect and spent 10 years earning a law degree. Now he is the man who, if anyone, "runs" the U.S. Senate.

There is no way to avoid a Horatio Alger tone in describing the early life and public career of the junior senator from West Virginia, elected leader of the Democratic majority and the key figure in the epic struggle for ratification of the Panama Canal treaties.

A few days after the successful conclusion of the treaty battle, Byrd sat down in his Capitol office to talk about his journey from "grinding poverty" of a coal town boyhood to his present position of national power.

Byrd was in a reflective mood. "Seldom does the majority leader have the responsibility of getting out front too far," he admitted. "Usually, it's the committee chairmen who deal with the substance. But this was a great national issue. These were treaties which were going to have a profound effect on our relations with Latin America, and they were treaties which were not supposed to be ratified."

Byrd confessed he was always cautiously optimistic but conceded his optimism was based on faith and his intuitive sense of the Senate. "When the chips are down and the votes are cast on a matter of this importance," he said, "the Senate is going to do the right thing."

Recalling my conversations with Senators Fulbright and Church, I decided to dig into his past, which was about as removed from mine as it could be. Robert Carlyle Byrd was born November 20, 1917, in North Wilkesboro, North Carolina, and within a year lost his mother to the worldwide influenza pandemic. He was raised by an aunt and her coal-miner husband in West Virginia. He tended his aunt's pigs, learned how to butcher, learned how to play the violin, learned how to weld. Later, in World War II when he was grown up and married, he moved his family to Baltimore, where he worked as a first-class welder on Liberty ships. "It was during that time that my interest in world affairs developed more and more. And I must say my suspicions developed too as I watched how our ally, the Soviet Union, acted."

He got into politics on the prompting of a friend and was elected to the West Virginia House of Delegates in 1946. That friend gave the neophyte, who could barely speak in public, a bit of sage advice. "Take that fiddle," Byrd quoted him, "and make it your briefcase. Use that fiddle. That will be your entrée. Get yourself a speech. Study up. And once you get in, tell them what you stand for." One of the things he stood for in his early days was the Ku Klux Klan, which he took to be a respectable fraternal organization not involved in lynchings or other criminal affairs. "It was a mistake," he agreed during our talk, "and I can't go back now and change the pages of history."

Byrd was elected to the U.S. House of Representatives in 1952 and to the U.S. Senate in 1958. His ambition and leadership talents shone from the beginning of his entry into national politics. As a member of the House, he began studying for a law degree at American University at night. But he could read law only in alternate years because he had to run for reelection every two years. Nonetheless, he succeeded in winning his law degree on the same June day in 1963 when President Kennedy made his famous speech on Soviet-American relations and was crowned with an honorary doctorate. Byrd sat back in his chair and chuckled, "Kennedy quipped to me: 'It took you ten years to get your degree, and I got mine in thirty minutes!'"

The drama of the Panama treaties and our controversial series had a few pleasant postscripts. For one thing, Dillman extended to Jordan the unusual courtesy of looking over the revised series, and he came away satisfied. On leaving the bureau, he commented, "I came out of this much less afraid of dealing with the press. Despite the heat, nothing was personal." UPI was satisfied, too. Cheryl and I received praise from top UPI editors. Ron Cohen, the deputy bureau manager, wrote me, "Your professionalism showed through from Day One. We never were beaten on a major development, the logs [daily usage reports] were good throughout, and you, as usual, were a pleasure to deal with." Frank Bartholomew, UPI chairman of the board emeritus, wrote that our series represented "our reportorial highlight of 1978 to date in my book; possibly because I know Panama, the background and the personalities involved."

What a relief! After all the mud that Dillman used to hurl my way, I now was beginning to feel that I was making it. I had reason to believe I really was going to get to the top.

Chapter 23

War Machines

The next year of 1979 was the season of my military education as a journalist. It began when I started digging into six cardboard boxes my grandfather spirited out of Russia when the White counterrevolution collapsed in
1920. They had lain unopened for fifty years in a barn belonging to one of
my American aunts in New Hampshire. My father ignored them, Baboota
never mentioned them, and no one knew what they contained.

Inside the cartons, I found my grandmother's passport, issued by the
Donetsk authorities in 1920, Russian émigré recollections published in Paris
in the interwar period, and typewritten flyers composed by Baron Pyotr
Wrangel, one of the last counterrevolutionary generals, announcing the
seaborne evacuation of 150,000 from the Crimea to Constantinople. There
were no Bolshevik documents, but I did unearth my grandfather's unpublished account of the fall of the Romanov dynasty. Suddenly, I realized I was
holding in my hands a chapter that went a long way toward answering my
question of why a czarist general would abandon Russia's Western allies
and help the Bolsheviks sign a separate peace with Germany in March 1918.

This chapter begins with General Danilov's recollection of a telephone
call on the night of February 24, 1918, from the War Ministry in Petrograd.
He and my grandmother Baboota had been out for dinner, and when they
returned, another call came in about ten-thirty. Baboota, protective of her
husband, urged him to ignore it. "My wife's request that I not go to the telephone, motivated by her fear for me, I thought rather mean-spirited, and I

stepped up to the telephone so I could find out what was wanted of me," the general wrote.

On the other end of the line was General Potapov, asking my grandfather, living in retirement, to join the Soviet delegation that was leaving that very night for Brest Litovsk to sign a separate peace with Germany. The general's reaction was instantly negative. He replied that he was uninformed about the two previous rounds of negotiations, and, furthermore, his own view was that a separate peace would mean abandoning the French and British allies and was not in Russia's interest. The Russian army was in a state of collapse after Lenin's famous Decree No. 1 calling for peace and his subsequent orders eliminating ranks and medals of distinction. Discipline was evaporating; units were breaking up; troops were deserting.

General Potapov was not to be put off. He explained that Russia, after the revolution of November 7, faced a most difficult situation. The Germans were advancing steadily through the Ukraine and the Baltic states, and soon would be within striking distance of Petrograd. Berlin had announced an ultimatum on February 21 under which hostilities against Russia would be stopped if Russia ceded Ukraine and the Baltic states and renounced imperial ambitions in Persia and Afghanistan. For these concessions, Russia would be allowed a buffer zone around the capital of Petrograd. General Potapov said the General Staff hoped that military experts might persuade the Germans to soften their demands. He identified Rear Admiral Altfater, Colonel Angodsky, and Captain Lipsky as the experts who would be leaving on a special train. General Potapov added that the military experts would take no part in signing any government document—Lenin's representatives were being sent for that.

Holding the telephone in his hand, my grandfather wavered and finally agreed to join the expedition against his better judgment. So began what was probably one of the most difficult assignments my grandfather undertook for Russia. In a short while, a car from the War Ministry whisked him to headquarters, where he found the department in chaos. Instead of being greeted by an impressive doorman decked out in medals, he found soldiers lounging on the wooden benches of the entrance hallway, talking loudly, and blowing clouds of smoke into the air. The carpet leading up the stairs was covered with February's filth, the hallways littered with cigarette butts. One high official, with a bandage on his face where he had cut himself while shaving, had apparently been summoned to take Danilov's place if Grandfather could not be found.

During the car ride to the railroad station, Danilov implored his military colleagues to act as one and refrain from giving separate opinions. No sooner had the train pulled out of the station about one o'clock on the morning of

February 25 than the military experts met with the Soviet delegation. The official delegates included Grigory Sokolnikov, a revolutionary who had shared Lenin's exile in Switzerland and would become Soviet ambassador to Great Britain before being purged in the 1930s; Grigory Chicherin, an intellectual, expert on military and diplomatic history, and lover of Mozart who would later become Soviet foreign minister; and Adolph Yoffe, from the Social Revolutionary Party, who participated in the previous rounds of negotiating and would become Soviet ambassador to Berlin, committing suicide in 1927. "All these personalities I was seeing for the first time," Danilov recalled.

> At the start of the meeting, it fell to me as senior among the military experts to articulate our common view that conducting separate peace talks with our military adversaries, and concluding a separate peace, was not in the interests of Russia and was not called for by the circumstances. We did not consider ourselves authorized to sign any government document, and we would limit ourselves to explaining to the responsible part of the delegation the meaning and significance of the German demands.

The military experts then went down the German demands, point by point, explaining the consequences that each would entail. Russia would be twice damned, they said, for bowing before the enemy and for forsaking its allies. The wisdom of a separate peace had been bitterly disputed by some of Lenin's colleagues, particularly as the German terms constantly hardened. Leon Trotsky, commissar for foreign affairs who headed the Soviet delegation during the second phase of the talks on December 27, 1917–February 10, 1918, walked out, declaring that Russia would leave the war no matter what the Germans demanded and would pursue a "no war–no peace" policy.

On February 21, 1918, the Germans issued their ultimatum calling for an agreed peace within three days of the arrival of the delegation. Lenin consulted with the top Communist leadership, but Trotsky continued to oppose a separate peace on these terms. Finally, Trotsky relented, and the separate peace policy was approved on a 7–6 vote. Next Lenin took the issue to the Central Executive Committee, where the vote in favor was 116–83, with 26 abstentions.

The journey to Brest Litovsk turned out to be an arduous one. At one stop, the train was approached by a group of Russian officers who implored the military experts to explain to them what to do in the face of advancing German armies and the efforts of the Petrograd government to sue for peace. At another point, the military experts pressed the Soviet negotiators to abandon the separate peace policy because of the continuing German invasion and the possibility of carrying out guerrilla counterattacks.

But Lenin, having won backing from his cohorts, was now unyielding. "You must not waver in signing a separate peace," he telegraphed the train. "That would be impermissible." Not realizing how difficult the physical journey had become, Lenin was worried that something had happened to shake their resolve, Chicherin would later write in his memoirs. Sokolnikov, in an account published in the 1920s, described how the delegation had to abandon the first train at Pskov because of a bombed-out bridge. Crossing the frozen river in the dark of night, the travelers took refuge in a building beside the tracks and awaited another train. A German guard unit was quartered inside, and Sokolnikov marveled how the unit's sergeant kept emphasizing that he was not an "enemy."

Danilov's description of this moment was heartrending. The Russian military experts, dressed in civilian clothes, huddled exhausted in the middle of the room and tried to sleep sitting up. The German noncom and his troops made do along the walls. "His subordinates, youths exhausted by their duty, were less interested in the unknown visitors and preferred sleep," wrote my grandfather. "The measured breathing and quiet, tired, snoring soon echoed from all corners of the room that was crammed with people. This monotonous picture was occasionally broken by the sudden cry of one of the sleeping men, or the periodic preparations for the next watch. Thus, with the exactitude of mechanical clockwork, in the fourth year of the war, this officer would go about his duties. As a former army commander, I looked upon him with a feeling of deep envy."

Finally, on February 28, the mission arrived after a two-and-a-half-day trip. The experts, in the course of the trip, had telegraphed the War Ministry in Petrograd about their failed efforts to convince the Soviet representatives not to sign the peace and asked for a return statement of support for their opposition. None came. On arrival at Brest Litovsk, the military experts sought to emphasize their opposition by distancing themselves from the Soviet delegates. They declined to leave their carriage until the Soviet delegates had disembarked, and demanded assurances from the German station commander that they would not be photographed, or filmed, leaving the train. At the talks, the military experts insisted on sitting at some remove from the Soviet delegates.

Lenin's representatives were determined to carry out Lenin's orders, but to signify their disgust at humiliating terms, they categorically refused to go through the proposed agreement article by article. Rather, on March 3, 1918, Sokolnikov signed the treaty and denounced it at the same time.

For General Danilov, the treaty was more than he could tolerate. The Bolshevik government asked him next to take command of the western front, but he declined. A few days later, Adolph Yoffe brought him an order signed by Lenin, naming him to a high post in the War Ministry. Again he declined. To put a stop to these entreaties, Danilov persuaded the War Ministry to relieve him of all further obligations. Still, even after this, Lenin sent word, asking him to become chief of the all-Russian General Staff. That was the final straw. "Circumstances came to our help," he concluded, "and we traveled on one of the [Ukrainian] Hetman's trains in great comfort to my native Kiev where I settled as a private citizen."

After reading these unique recollections, I felt I had found the answer to my question of why an opponent would join the Soviet delegation. General Danilov's decision was motivated by a sense of duty acquired through thirty years of service to Russia. He differentiated between the government and the state. Governments come and go, but the state remains, and there was no certainty in 1918 that the new Communist government would survive for very long. Throughout his account, there was a sense that General Danilov fully realized the burden that he was undertaking, one for which he could be attacked in future years. "I took upon myself the heaviest obligation—to participate in the developing disgrace—in the hope of bringing strong help to Russia. I did not feel I could wash my hands of it."

The Brest peace did not last long. The Bolshevik government abrogated it within nine months after revolution broke out in Germany, and Berlin, in turn, sued for peace. Meanwhile, Danilov, now a private citizen, served briefly as one of several directors of a newly formed bank until civil war engulfed the Ukraine. He then joined the White counterrevolutionary movement and actively worked for Lenin's overthrow. When he judged that the White generals' efforts in the Ukraine were failing, he embarked for Japan in a desperate effort to join the independent Russian government set up by Admiral A. V. Kolchak in Siberia. However, Kolchak was captured by the Reds and executed before Danilov could arrive. My grandfather then sided with General Pyotr Wrangel, who led the last resistance to the Red Army. When Wrangel's forces were forced out of the Crimea, Danilov left Russia in the seaborne evacuation to Constantinople. The general eventually settled in Paris, where he served as Wrangel's unofficial and unpaid "ambassador" as my father and uncle began their new lives in the United States.

Six years after the Brest debacle, General Danilov sent my father a photo of himself dated August 29, 1924, with this touching message on the back: "Russia and America (USA) are two countries which should happily join each other in your heart. Love the latter and guard sacredly everything good which the former gave you even though it is far away but eternally yours." When I wrote my father fifty years later in 1979 asking for details of the general's life, he answered promptly and congratulated me on taking an interest in our superpower adversary. But he added in passing, "My personal interest in Russia and things Russian is nil." Evidently, my father took about as much notice of his father's advice as I did of my father's.

I regarded Serge's disdain for Russia as cultural suicide. Yet it was understandable. November 7, 1917, had robbed him of his country and forced on him the necessity of reinventing himself as an American. My view was different. I was not touched in a personal way by the Bolsheviks' seizure of power, and I was intrigued by the society they had erected. In 1979, the Soviet Union was a nuclear superpower to be reckoned with. No one guessed it would fall apart within a decade. My job, as I saw it, was to understand its hidden mechanisms, to enlighten myself, and, I hoped, to inform the public.

One of the continuing issues I followed as a Cold War journalist was the effort to limit strategic weapons that by 1979 threatened to bankrupt both the Soviet Union and the United States. These talks had a long history that went back at least to the 1967 Glassboro summit between President Johnson and Prime Minister Kosygin. At that meeting Defense Secretary Robert McNamara persuaded Kosygin that building defensive weapons only stimulated the other side to build greater offensive weapons. When President Nixon was inaugurated in January 1969, he began a review of the strategic arms and concluded in 1972 restrictions on antimissile defenses, known as the ABM Treaty, and temporary limitations on offensive missiles, known as SALT-I. This latter treaty was highly criticized by Senator Henry Jackson for codifying a Soviet advantage in offensive missiles.

After SALT-I, President Nixon and General Secretary Brezhnev launched the SALT-II negotiations that were continued by President Ford after Nixon's resignation in 1974. When Jimmy Carter won the 1976 election, he placed a high priority on SALT-II. By the spring of 1979, now nearly a decade after the superpowers had begun negotiating, a complex agreement began to emerge. Both sides would be limited to equal ceilings of 2,250 strategic weapons composed of land-based, sea-based, and bomber-based missiles beginning January 1, 1982. This would require the Soviet Union to reduce its inventory of 2,500 by 250 strategic missiles, whereas the United States could, if it wished, increase its stable from 2,060 to 2,250. A number of equal sublimits, applying to both sides, would restrict the number of multiple warheads each category of missile could carry.

Additionally, the Soviet Union agreed to limit production of its Backfire bombers, which the U.S. military considered capable of attacking the United States, to no more than 30 a year. And the U.S. Air Force was permitted to built one new strategic missile, the MX, to replace its land-based Minuteman missile force. Both sides agreed to exchange detailed data on their strategic arsenals, agreed to a Standing Consultative Committee to resolve disputes, and planned to begin a new round, SALT-III, to agree on more extensive reductions.

On April 19, 1979, Richard Perle and I took a walk around the Capitol to talk about the emerging accord. It was a symbolic day: the Capitol was in full glory, surrounded by flowering yellow and red tulips. But despite the sunshine, an unpleasant wind was blowing. Perle confessed that he felt embattled. The agreement, he asserted, was flawed because its cuts were insufficient, allowing the Soviet side too much "throw weight"—the payload its heavy missiles could hurl at the United States. "I know about 12 reporters covering SALT," Perle lamented, "but there will be 180 covering the hearings and the debate in the Senate. They've never heard of me. When they do, they'll think I'm crazy or paranoid." He made clear that conservative senators would work hard to amend the treaty to further restrict the Soviets, just as they amended the Panama Canal treaties. The Soviet Union was not Panama, however, and I doubted Moscow would allow itself to be toyed with in this manner.

On May 9, 1979, Secretary of State Cyrus Vance and Defense Secretary Harold Brown announced at the White House that the two superpowers had finally completed the SALT-II treaty. The U.S. military was far from enthusiastic. The Joint Chiefs of Staff gave only lukewarm support, and Lieutenant General Edward Rowny, military expert to the talks, declined to attend the signing scheduled for June in Vienna. General David Jones, chairman of the Joint Chiefs, insisted on a 5 percent increase in the U.S. military budget for his support. When I neglected to mention General Jones's demand for the budget increase in a story I filed for UPI, he called me to complain from his limousine on his way to Andrews Air Force Base for a physical examination.

On announcement of completion, I rushed over to the law offices of Paul Warnke, who had been the chief negotiator for much of the negotiations, for comment. He was finishing a telephone interview with a British correspondent in London on the very subject. When he saw me in the doorway, he turned to his law partner, legendary Washington power broker and former secretary of defense Clark Clifford, and introduced me. "Clark, you know Nick Daniloff," he said, as if I were a Beltway celebrity known throughout the nation. I'm sure Clifford had not the slightest idea who this interloper was, but he nodded amiably in the manner of the high and mighty in Washington.

More useful was a beef Stroganoff–and–noodles luncheon with Carter's national security adviser, Dr. Zbigniew Brzezinski, on May 23. Seated around the small table in Brzezinski's West Wing office were Joe Fromm of *U.S. News and World Report*, Hedrick Smith of the *New York Times*, and Bob

Pierpoint of CBS. This get-together was typical of sophisticated press man-agement in Washington. The conversation turned into a *tour d'horizon* fo-cusing largely on SALT-II, which Brzezinski predicted the Senate would eventually ratify. Among the forward-looking issues was Afghanistan, which Brzezinski described as slipping rebelliously out of the Soviet orbit. We asked what the United States would do if the Soviet Union intervened militarily but got no clear answer. I wonder now if Brzezinski was already contemplating an opportunity in central Asia to exploit against Moscow. "It would be a major concern" was his only answer.

The persuasion lunch ended on a light note. Brzezinski revealed he had drafted a joke communiqué for Carter and Brezhnev at the Vienna summit calling for a *deterioration* in U.S.-Soviet relations. He had shown it to Carter, who had scrawled jokingly across the top: "It's OK with me if it's OK with you. JC." Brzezinski asked that we not write about this at the time. But three decades later it reveals a human element of relations at the top.

Dillman assigned me and Helen Thomas to cover the summit in Austria, which would be held on June 14–18, 1979. I reflected on the similarities between Russia and Germany in 1918 and Russia and the United States sixty-one years later. The leaders of both eras were seeking a political accommodation, while military experts went along only reluctantly. In both cases, civilian authority ruled and the military submitted. On the eve of Carter's departure for Vienna, Senator Jackson blasted the SALT-II agreement as insufficient and accused Carter of appeasing the enemy, much as Russian military officers in 1918 resisted Lenin's concessions to the Germans.

Covering a summit meeting of the world's two greatest leaders is far less glorious than one might think. Such encounters are highly choreographed. I have saved lists upon lists of the minute-by-minute movements of the prin-cipals, detailed arrangements for journalists, assignments for pool reporters who glimpse the start of a meeting and then leave. Journalists do not attend the business sessions that are held behind closed doors. They wait for official announcements, speculating on the meaning of the slightest departure from the official schedule. If they are lucky, they may get a leak from an official they have assiduously courted. If they get tired of waiting, they play cards hour after hour, do crossword puzzles, or doze. The closest approach to the meat du jour comes at an open press conference of the official spokesman, pri-vate briefings for the favored few, or the final signing ceremony.

In Vienna, there were several moments that caused a momentary stir. Brezhnev, who had been in declining health since the mid-1970s, stumbled as he walked down steps and fell into the outstretched arms of President Carter. This unexpected embrace sparked comments that the vigorous American president might be falling under the influence of the ailing Russian bear. And another curious moment: Approaching the signing of SALT-II, Brezhnev declared, "God will not forgive us if we fail to complete this agreement." This comment by one of the world's top atheists sparked heated discussion among journalists as to what Brezhnev could possibly mean. Soviet officials explained their leader was simply trying to speak in terms Americans might understand. Another moment that I savored came at a joint briefing by White House spokesman Jody Powell and Soviet Foreign Ministry spokesman Leonid M. Zamyatin. A Canadian journalist demanded to know the state of health of the Soviet leader. This drew a spirited defense by Zamyatin, who asserted (falsely, as it turned out) that Brezhnev was in possession of his full faculties and doing extremely important work. "He has no complaints about his health. Reports in your press on this matter are nothing but speculations." This exchange prompted a Soviet journalist to ask Powell, "Would you mind telling us about the political health of President Carter?" Carter had been dealing ineffectively with an Arab oil embargo and double-digit inflation. Powell parried the *Izvestia* reporter's thrust with a dollop of humor. "About the same!" he retorted. I admired that repartee and adopted it for myself on more than one later occasion. Sixty-five minutes after the signing on Monday, June 18, *Air Force One* lifted off for Washington so Carter could address a joint session of Congress that same evening.

UPI asked me to produce a "stem-winder" on the coming Senate debate. (That journalistic term means a complete report from A to Z and comes from the notion of winding a watch to full capacity.) On return to Washington, I solicited views from key aides of liberal and conservative senators. Richard Perle and I met on July 2, and he remarked that liberals such as Frank Church and Alan Cranston were experiencing trouble in their home districts for being too liberal. Only a few moderate senators had come out in favor of the treaty. Perle was jubilant. "Well," he greeted me cheerily, "it's all over. The treaty can get through the Senate only with amendments."

In the ensuing months, the Senate Foreign Relations and Armed Services Committees took long hours of testimony from administration officials. From the start, it was clear the Senate would add amendments, and, indeed, Senator Joe Biden (D-DE) opened the debate at the Foreign Relations Committee with a series of reservations crafted to hijack the amendment fever to the administration's advantage. By autumn, my Soviet contact Dr. Georgii Mamedov (son of the infamous Enver Mamedov of my 1970 tour around America) was reflecting Moscow's exasperation. "It will be no tragedy if SALT is rejected," he told me on October 8. "Our military aren't all that happy with SALT. They don't like the limits on multiple warheads, they don't like to have to dismantle 250 missiles, they don't like the fact that

SALT has spawned a new arms buildup in the United States and has not re-strained U.S. programs."

SALT-II was never ratified. The failure came not from killer amendments by Senate opponents but from the Soviet invasion of Afghanistan. We now know from declassified documents and Soviet memoirs that KGB chief Yuri Andropov was deeply worried about U.S. intentions in central Asia. A crucial meeting in Brezhnev's office on December 8, 1979, including Andropov, Foreign Minister Andrey Gromyko, Defense Minister Dmitry Ustinov, and top ideologist Mikhail Suslov, outlined these concerns. This inner circle of the Politburo concluded that Afghan president Amin intended to improve relations with the United States to the detriment of the Soviet Union. Amin's actions might give the United States an opportunity to promote a "new Great Ottoman Empire," eventually capturing the Soviet Turkic republics of Uzbekistan, Tajikistan, and Turkmenistan. They worried, too, that if U.S.-Afghan relations improved sufficiently, the United States might deploy nuclear-tipped Pershing missiles on Afghan territory that could threaten the Soviet space center at Baikonur and other military targets. Over the objections of chief of staff Marshal Nikolai Ogarkov, the inner circle decided in favor of invasion on December 12, 1979. They believed that invasion was justified, given the geopolitical threat to Soviet central Asia, even if that meant sacrificing SALT-II. In any event, the terms of SALT-II could be respected without formal ratification so long as they seemed mutually beneficial.

Having covered Congress for five years, I decided I should get a better understanding of the military aspects of the U.S.-Soviet relationship. So without agonizing, I asked Dillman to let me cover the Pentagon, probably an unwise career move because military news in peacetime is never soaked up by the mainstream media the way conflicts between Congress and the administration are. The public is little concerned with the details of weapons acquisition, and only sporadically interested in the spiraling defense budget. But I had two questions for which I sought answers. How open or closed was the U.S. military? And what was our open society doing to ensure the nation survived a nuclear attack from the Soviet Union?

This time, Dillman gave me no grief, probably because our Pentagon correspondent had recently quit, and off I went to cover the War Machine. As an arena for journalists, the Pentagon was vastly different from the Congress and more like the State Department bureaucracy. Reporters, including those from the Soviet Union and other areas of Eastern Europe, once accredited, got ready access to the five-sided building and were allowed to roam freely through the miles of concentric "rings" that make up its interior. At the very center was, and is, a small garden and café where we would occasionally go for lunch. Inside the Pentagon, most of the space was open except for special areas such as the quarters of the Joint Chiefs of Staff, its operations center, the Defense Intelligence Agency (DIA), and special project offices. Reporters had access to the official Pentagon telephone book and could make appointments with civilian or military personnel of the army, navy, and air force who might be willing to talk. The marine corps was located in another building, near Arlington National Cemetery.

My defense colleagues were as impressive as those who covered the State Department. In August 1979, the *Armed Forces Journal* published a ten-page takeout on the reporters who regularly covered defense. Largely in their forties and fifties, they had both university education and experience. Most notable was the "dean," Fred Hoffman, then fifty-six, who had covered the Pentagon for the past eighteen years for the Associated Press and knew the place inside out; others were Charlie Corddry, a former UPI colleague, a 1941 graduate of American University, now writing for the *Baltimore Sun,* and Ken Bacon, at thirty-four a ten-year veteran of the *Wall Street Journal* who would eventually leave journalism to become the Defense Department's spokesman in the 1990s. While the AP-UPI competition operated here as everywhere else, we were all generally civil and helpful to each other. The regulars organized breakfast meetings with top officials such as the chairman of the Joint Chiefs, the chief of research and development, or individual commanders when their exploits projected them into the news. Listening to the tapes I made of these "background" sessions, I can report that our questioning was informed, and most interviewees were forthcoming.

I soon discovered that a military establishment has two important characteristics. First, it has secrets that it is intent on preserving. These secrets relate largely to advances in equipment and technology, methods and sources of intelligence, and critical operations. Second, an army is a microcosm of society at large. It reflects the strengths and weaknesses, the openness and frankness, of people in everyday life. So, to my first question: It seemed to me that an unexpected catastrophe would tell you a great deal about the openness of the U.S. military. Do officials report the unpleasant truth, or do they try to cover it up? On my watch as a Pentagon correspondent (and later as a Moscow correspondent in the 1980s), I witnessed several catastrophes, including the military attempt to rescue fifty-three American diplomats, seized as hostages in Tehran.

Throughout the late 1970s, U.S. relations with Iran had been in turmoil, although the United States had not always recognized it. President Carter, in a famous toast at a New Year's gala in Tehran in 1977, had praised the shah and his country as an "island of stability." But all was not well. The shah had spent billions of dollars on modern weaponry and developed a vicious secret police called the Savak to keep his population under control.

Resentment against police brutality was growing, and Iranian religious leaders added to the unease by condemning the shah's "Westernizing" efforts. Unable to spread economic development evenly about the country and unwilling to expand democratic freedoms, the shah's regime collapsed in revolution, and he fled on January 16, 1979.

Nine months later, on November 4, 1979, radical students invaded the U.S. Embassy and seized the diplomats, vowing not to relinquish them until the United States returned the shah for trial in Iran. The Carter administration refused, declaring that the students had violated diplomatic convention, and insisted on the release of the American captives. When the students, under incitement from Ayatollah Khomeini, refused to comply, the question arose as to what to do next. President Carter pledged the safe return of the American hostages, but the months dragged by without resolution.

We now know that within a week of the students' takeover, the top leadership of the U.S. military began studying how the hostages might be plucked from the embassy that had become their prison. The Joint Chiefs of Staff began planning a rescue operation that went through several permutations and numerous rehearsals in the Arizona desert. But the long distances involved to reach the embassy deep within Iranian territory made any operation a high-risk affair.

Speculation abounded that the United States would organize a rescue such as the Israelis had performed at Entebbe International Airport in Uganda in July 1976 to save their citizens from a hijacked airline and the Germans accomplished in Mogadishu in October 1977 in a similar incident involving a Lufthansa plane. Since any operation would take time to organize, the White House and defense spokesmen did all they could to cast doubt on dramatic scenarios. The hostages were never forgotten, however, as Ted Koppel of ABC reminded viewers every night of their unresolved fate, on his late-night program that eventually became *Nightline*.

A secret rescue mission that evolved in the next months called for eight large Sea Stallion helicopters to fly from a U.S. aircraft carrier in the Arabian Sea some five hundred miles at a low altitude of several hundred feet. (The navy was reluctant in those years to allow a billion-dollar aircraft carrier to enter the Persian Gulf, which would have shortened some of the distances.) These craft would land at a spot named Desert I some two hundred miles southeast of Tehran, where they would be joined by C-130 transport aircraft for refueling. Assuming that a minimum of six of the eight helicopters were operational at Desert I, they would fly on to a spot outside Tehran named Desert II. From there an assault force of some ninety men would be bused in the dark of night to the embassy, storm the building, disable the captors, and lead the hostages to buses that would transport them to a nearby stadium. A separate operation involved breaking into the Foreign Ministry, where the top U.S. diplomat, Bruce Laingen, was being held. The helicopters would land in the stadium, retrieve the hostages, and fly them to an airfield outside Tehran, where C-141 transport planes would have flown in secretly, and airlift them out of the country. It was an extremely bold, complex plan with a high risk of failure.

To execute the rescue, obviously, required the strictest secrecy, beginning with several rehearsals in the deserts of Arizona. Among the daring undertakings—and these were accomplished successfully—was the insertion of secret agents in Tehran to scout out the embassy building, the Foreign Ministry, and the stadium and organize the buses with the help of friendly Iranians. The plan called for a secret small plane to fly to Desert I in advance of the rescue attempt to test the hardness of the landing site and to install landing lights that were successfully turned on by remote control at the very moment the helicopters and refueling planes were arriving.

Months went by with no results through diplomatic contacts and little expectation of a happy ending. On April 24, 1980, I was scheduled to meet with Secretary of Defense Harold Brown for my first one-on-one interview with him. Before the four-thirty meeting, I left the building briefly to organize my thoughts in the fresh air and returned to find one of Brown's aides, Colonel Don Wakefield, beckoning me to hurry. "Brown's appointments have all been pushed up," he explained. As we approached Brown's office (officially designated as 3E880), I caught sight of the secretary striding out the door, glancing at his watch, and muttering something under his breath without catching my eye. We entered his office and settled down on a coach only to learn a few minutes later that Brown had called from the White House to say he would not be back. I left and called our White House correspondents about Brown's presence in case that might tip them to some kind of breaking news. I then completed my day's work and went home expecting nothing further.

At one-thirty in the morning, the UPI bureau roused me in great excitement to say that a rescue attempt had been made in Iran but ended in disaster. The White House had telephoned a press release to the Washington offices of UPI and Associated Press around one o'clock stating that President Carter had canceled the rescue because of "equipment failure." The brief statement added: "During the subsequent withdrawal of American personnel, there was a collision of our aircraft on the ground at a remote desert location in Iran," and eight air force men had been killed. The UPI bureau was now screaming for details.

I had no special source for this kind of emergency, so I followed the time-tested UPI dictum: "Go to the scene!" The scene in this case was Secretary

Brown's office, where I arrived around a quarter after two. I found several other "regulars" already in the outer office, but no reportable news. About two-thirty, General Jones, chairman of the Joint Chiefs, emerged from the inner sanctum and greeted us smartly with a "Good morning, gentlemen" and disappeared. I noted later in my journal, "Disaster hung heavily over this dramatic event. Nonetheless, as the morning hours dragged on, the Marine secretaries served us coffee and generally treated us with an easy deference which is all too often missing in dealings between the press and officialdom."

At seven President Carter addressed the nation over national television and took responsibility for the failure. The military then began releasing details in a controlled manner. At noon, Secretary Brown and General Jones called a press conference to release a prepared statement. Eight helicopters, they explained, had launched from the aircraft carrier USS *Nimitz* on the night of April 24 in the Arabian Sea and flown, undetected by Iranian radar, to Desert I. In accordance with agreed-upon instructions, the commander of the assault team, Colonel Charles Beckwith, recommended calling off the rescue attempt when it became clear that three of the eight helicopters that had left for the Iranian rendezvous either dropped out in a sandstorm or were otherwise disabled. Thus, only five, not six, were operational. Beckwith was given a chance to second-guess the situation and push on despite this unexpected problem, but he refused. His abort recommendation went to higher commanders and on to President Carter, all of whom agreed by a quarter of five, which is about the time I glimpsed Secretary Brown leaving his office. A successful withdrawal at this stage would have allowed for another attempt later. However, in preparing to depart in pitch darkness, the rotor blades of one helicopter struck a C-130 tanker on the ground. Both craft burst into flames, and eight air force men burned to death.

The reporters now began hurling their questions, and it soon became clear that restraints—call it censorship, if you will—were in force. Neither Brown nor Jones would identify the dead servicemen (standard procedure) until the families had been notified. They refused to name the military units involved. They declined to say how many people had participated in drawing up and executing the plan. They released no details concerning how the hostages were to be sprung from the U.S. Embassy or anything that was to happen after Desert I. They would not say whether the United States might plan another rescue mission. A few days later, on May 1, Colonel Beckwith met with a group of us defense journalists, and he, too, declined to answer such questions. When he hesitated for a moment, an aide urged, "Colonel, we had better not get into any estimates."

The media were still hungering for details, of course. From a political operative's point of view, especially one critical of the administration, this created an opportunity. A day or so later, there appeared on my desk a plain brown envelope containing a report titled "The Iran Rescue Mission" and classified "top secret." It was a hastily prepared document on the short-comings of the mission, stating that the helicopter force ran into two un-predicted dust storms over the Iranian desert; one helicopter returned to the carrier, and two others suffered mechanical failures. The report strongly suggested insufficient planning and insufficient equipment. I surmised this report was a gift from the Gold Watch, hoping again to generate anti-Carter publicity. However, since the report contained new details, I quickly re-ported its contents. I got a scoop and some personal publicity. But I must note that if there was any glory in this scoop, it was diminished by the fact that I was blatantly used again for a political purpose. And in the heat of the chase, I did not recognize that I had been manipulated—hardly an ideal sit-uation for an "independent" reporter but, sadly, not unusual for inside-the-Beltway journalism.

Some of my most rewarding work as a newly minted Pentagon corre-spondent was visiting military and naval installations throughout the United States. These trips put me in touch with top commanders in all the services, and with the men and women of the all-volunteer military. A trip I made in February 1980 to missile and bomber sites in Montana, Nebraska, and Colorado revealed to me some of the strange mechanisms of the Cold War that I had no idea about and the general public still less. Many of these focused on the extraordinary efforts the United States made to ensure that a national government would survive a Soviet nuclear attack and would have enough surviving missiles to retaliate.

At Offutt Air Force Base, home of the Strategic Air Command, I learned about the early warning systems that would give advance notice that a So-viet missile attack had been launched. These systems included a string of radars across Canada called BMEWS and infrared sensors on satellites con-stantly looking for the hot exhaust of flying Soviet missiles. If the United States detected and confirmed a launch of incoming missiles, the president of the United States would have between fifteen and thirty minutes to con-sider his retaliatory moves.

A key piece in this arsenal was a Boeing 707 outfitted to serve as an aerial command post. It was known as the *Looking Glass* and came into service on February 3, 1961. It was called *Looking Glass* because it mirrored the nation's ground-based command and communication systems for strategic missiles. For twenty-nine years of the Cold War, a *Looking Glass* plane was constantly in the air, twenty-four hours a day, 365 days a year. The Soviet Union, too, created a similar flying command post to take over communications if a U.S.

nuclear attack knocked out its ground-based systems. The *Looking Glass* was taken out of continuous airborne service on July 24, 1990, and rebased on land on twenty-four-hour-a-day alert. What struck me as fantastic was that crew members were issued black patches that they were ordered to wear over one eye in the event of a nuclear attack. This was to guarantee that pilots and crew members would have the use of the other eye if they were blinded by the searing light of an atomic explosion.

During the visit to Offutt, I interviewed General Richard Ellis, commander of the Strategic Air Command, who described to me a Cold War minuet involving American strategic bombers and Russian submarines. When Soviet nuclear submarines approached the United States too closely, the general told me, the air force would worry about a possible launch against U.S. ground-based missiles from these subs. The concern was that sub-launched missiles would give the United States only a few minutes to consider retaliation (as opposed to the fifteen to thirty minutes in a strategic missile attack). As a warning to Moscow, the Strategic Air Command would raise the alert level of U.S. B-52 bombers that were capable of taking off on short notice to bomb targets in the Soviet Union. This heightened readiness would be picked up by Soviet electronic intelligence, and the Defense Ministry in Moscow would quietly take the hint. Usually, Soviet submarines would shortly veer away from U.S. shores.

I learned, too, from the general's aides that the air force maintained three presidential command planes, known collectively as the "Doomsday plane," at Andrews Air Force Base outside of Washington, D.C. These planes, outfitted with the latest electronic equipment, could weather the electromagnetic pulse of a nuclear attack and survive as a command post. They could also communicate easily with the *Looking Glass*, if need be. In emergencies—nuclear or nonnuclear—the president and his closest associates could be whisked by helicopter to this white Boeing 747–200, as indeed happened with President Bush after the terror attacks of September 11, 2001, in New York and Washington.

Of course, the president had the use of several underground command centers in the vicinity of Washington, D.C., too. Although not advertised, you could hardly be unaware of them if you lived in the capital city during the 1970s. On December 1, 1974, a TWA passenger plane crashed into Mount Weather near Bluemont, Virginia, causing the media to regurgitate details of several hardened complexes that had been completed in the early 1960s. White House correspondents had been invited to visit the Mount Weather facility after the missile crisis of 1962, and reported that it contained a "war room," sophisticated communication equipment, and an underground reservoir, and could accommodate up to two thousand top officials. Officials figured that in a nuclear attack, it would be vital to maintain contact with the public. Releasing critical information to the AP and UPI first, rather than television, was the time-honored method of getting word out to the public in those days. Therefore, a limited number of White House journalists were approved to join the government's survival team. They were told to keep their mouths shut and, in the event of a crisis, not to bring their families.

My next stop in February 1980 was to the headquarters of the North American Air Defense Command (NORAD) and its operations center inside Cheyenne Mountain. We entered this cavernous redoubt through a twenty-five-ton steel door and tunnel halfway up the granite mountain. Inside I found a dozen three-story buildings sitting on giant steel springs that were supposed to survive the turbulence of a nuclear attack by rocking a foot in any direction. The command post monitored satellite and radar signals of a nuclear attack against the United States and also tracked some five thousand satellites and pieces of space debris that might fall out of orbit and strike the surface of the planet.

Brigadier General John Budner, head of NORAD's operation center (also called the "mayor of the mountain") assured me that this command post could survive a nuclear attack if it did not take a direct hit. I was ready to believe him; how could I check anyway? But what really stunned me was his account of an incident on November 9, 1979, when duty officers believed the system was signaling a massive nuclear attack from Russia.

General Budner explained that his computers were being modernized, with Honeywells replacing the older Philcos. "For reasons of economy," I quoted him in a UPI story February 15, 1980, "we bought a computer system in which tests are conducted with the operational system on line. A technician inadvertently caused a transmission of 5–6 minutes of test data that indicated a major raid in progress. The people down the line weren't expecting a test, and this came like a bolt out of the blue."

The situation was quickly diagnosed and covered up; the American public remained ignorant. The general continued, "The missile warning officer immediately said, 'This can't be real.' When we analyzed what was happening in the next minutes, we noted that the launch sites and times simply did not coincide with the known locations of Soviet submarines or land-based missiles. Also, we had no infrared or radar confirmation." Duty officers in the Pentagon in Washington immediately sensed a false alarm because U.S.-Soviet relations had not plunged to a clearly dangerous state. But in those five to six minutes, the "Doomsday plane" took off without the president, and ten tactical fighters launched from the northern United States and Canada. Strategic bombers remained on high alert, but were not ordered to scramble. "The military looked at it this way: when in doubt, get airborne," General Budner explained.

Moscow's elint (electronic intelligence) picked up the November false alarm, the general revealed, and General Secretary Brezhnev sent a sharp note to President Carter, urging him to make sure such an error never happened again. There was an upside to this incident, the general added. "We got words of concern from the president, the secretary of defense, and the Joint Chiefs, and we have had lots of help ever since. It made a lot of people aware of what we do out here."

Researching my notes, I am struck by the fact that any number of accidents could have occurred during the forty-five years of the Cold War, setting off an uncontrollable catastrophe. I am thinking of trivial events, rather than such major challenges as the secret deployment of missiles to Cuba. What might have happened if a flight of geese across the BMEWS line was mistaken for a nuclear attack? Or what if some other high-tech failure occurred, or some totally unpredictable, unimaginable, ununderstood calamity transpired? The Cold War may have drifted toward stability between the Cuban crisis of 1962 and SALT-II of 1979, but the peril of planetary holocaust clearly struck the top leadership of Moscow and Washington. Defense experts in the United States worried about this. Years later members of the Soviet General Staff acknowledged at a press conference I attended in Moscow that they, too, were concerned about accidental nuclear war. With the collapse of the Soviet Union in 1991, that threat diminished. NORAD's day-to-day operations were transferred to Peterson Air Force Base in Colorado Springs in 2006, and "The Mountain" was put on standby.

This tenuous equilibrium among adversaries during the Cold War has yet to be duplicated in today's war on terrorism. Perhaps it never will be. Today's conflict is not war between nation-states that want to survive but war between states and terrorist cells, uncontrolled by any central authority, that are ready on occasion to commit crime or suicide to further their cause.

Chapter 24

Russia in 1981

In January 1979, Joe Fromm, an international affairs editor of *U.S. News and World Report*, began inquiring if I would be interested in joining the magazine to work on foreign affairs. I first met Fromm in London when I was a student at Oxford. In those days, he had suggested that I join the London Bureau, an offer I declined because I thought UPI would give me a broader background for the future.

Now *U.S. News and World Report* was calling again. This serious newsmagazine appealed to some two million middle-aged, college-educated readers living mostly in middle America. Its distinctive style was to analyze events, stress the "why" of journalism's five *w*'s (who, what, when, where, and why), and project developments in the future. The magazine specialized in Q-and-A interviews and pro-con opinion pieces, and offered a very popular page titled "News You Can Use," a section that highlighted innovations readers could use in their daily lives. The editors' overall philosophy was conservative, prodefense, anticommunist, probusiness, and somewhat alarmist when it came to the superpower confrontation. President Kennedy once described the magazine as *U.S. Blues and World Abort.* Soviet propagandists called it simply the "loudspeaker of the Pentagon" and assumed its correspondents were linked to the Defense Intelligence Agency as well as the CIA.

I was interested in Joe's inquiry because I felt I had learned about as much as possible from twenty years with the wire service, and the time had come to do something more analytical. Furthermore, I was flattered to receive a feeler from Bob Semple of the *New York Times*, who was drawing up a list of possible correspondents for the *Times*'s Moscow Bureau. Pursuing these two opportunities was going to be exciting.

I had the greatest respect for Joe, who had gone to Chicago at seventeen to take a job with the *Chicago Sun*. He quit journalism at the start of World War II to volunteer in 1942 as an ambulance driver with the British Eighth Army in North Africa, and later as a captain in the Indian Army. After the war, in 1946, he joined *U.S. News and World Report* and was dispatched immediately to Tokyo to cover the Far East. In 1956, after seven years in Tokyo, he was transferred to London, where he worked as the European editor for eighteen years before returning to Washington. As a leading correspondent, Joe was deeply involved in reporting the Communist takeover of China, the confrontation with the Soviet Union, and the postwar rebuilding of Japan, Germany, and Western Europe.

He was a small, conservatively dressed man, with a trimmed mustache, piercing eyes, and an avuncular sense of humor. Standing all of five foot four, he was deceptively powerful; with a strategic turn of mind, he saw events and their implications in global terms. In digging out facts, he was tireless. Once he got his teeth into a story, like a Jack Russell he would not let go. He would shake, pull, squeeze until he was satisfied there was no more to be pulled out. Then he would sit down at his computer, compose effortlessly, laying out future consequences that often escaped me. Behind his back, Ruth and I called him fondly "the Terrier."

Joe suggested that if things worked out, I might be his assistant in Washington. That appealed to me considerably since it would require no wrenching family moves. Miranda was now sixteen and preparing for college, while Caleb was ten and going to a nearby public school. Between March and September I met with Joe and the top editors of the magazine on several occasions, and took a week off from UPI to do a test run at *U.S. News*. I was given a guest office, instructed on the computer system, and sent out on an assignment relating to NATO. Throughout the week I interviewed sources at the West German Embassy and elsewhere, then set about producing a lengthy piece for Joe. Some days after I handed it in, Joe called to say that the piece was not satisfactory but not to get discouraged. There might be other opportunities, specifically the Moscow Bureau, where the resident correspondent, an old Asia hand by the name of Pepper Martin, was retiring. Finally, in late September, Joe called to announce that the deal was struck. I informed Dillman on September 30 of my desire to resign. My decision was greeted with graciousness by my UPI superiors. President Rod Beaton and editor in chief H. L. Stevenson wrote me that I had been "an outstanding Unipresser," said they greeted the news with sadness, and wished me good luck.

The only thing left to do now was to wind up my assignment at the Pentagon by informing officials there and my colleagues that I would be leaving at the end of October. The Pentagon press corps duly took note and, in a humorous mood, drew up fake "discharge papers" that said:

> This is to inform all concerned that the above individual, Civilian No Class Nicholas Daniloff, is honorably discharged from the Pentagon Press Corps on this day 31 October 1980. Pending reassignment to the Siberia Press Corps, Mr. Daniloff will hereby be assigned to the Moscow Press Corps. In fact, he is the Moscow Press Corps. With this discharge, Mr. Daniloff no longer is afforded the courtesy owed a member of the Pentagon Press Corps. Be it known that Mr. Daniloff no longer will be allowed to walk through the Pentagon corridors in any state of undress.

The "order" was signed by Fred Hoffman of the Associated Press, who titled himself "Acting Despot."

Going to work for a newsmagazine from a wire service required a careful adjustment. The AP and UPI specialized in digging out the facts and presenting them to readers and editors in a balanced way. Their goal was truthfulness, speed, and neutrality since they sold their services to publications with widely varying political views. *U.S. News,* by contrast, wanted its reporters to weigh events and make judgments. They wanted a clear theme to run through each article and did not seek colorful writing. "Dare to be dull" was a maxim occasionally repeated in the magazine's corridors. When it came to the Soviet Union, the editors encouraged highlighting all the failings of the Soviet system.

Fromm explained that when a situation contained positive and negative aspects, the writer had to decide which was dominant and significant for the future. "Don't confuse the reader with qualifications, especially at the beginning of the piece," he advised. "You're telling the readers what is important and what to expect in the future. If you feel you have to moderate the theme, put the qualifications in down low." Interpretive reporting made it difficult for some wire-service hires to make the adjustment, and some good UPI and AP men failed miserably at the magazine. I also struggled with this problem, too, but over the months I began to grasp the logic of the *U.S. News* approach.

One of the first projects that I worked on at the end of 1980 was a lengthy takeout on the status of communism around the world. This was a Joe Fromm brainchild from the start, and he relied on another correspondent,

Stew Powell—soon to be named London bureau chief—to be the writer. When completed, it ran as the cover story of the December 22, 1980, edition and painted a picture of a crumbling ideology and inefficient economies from Cuba to Eastern Europe, Russia, China, and Africa. Regarding the USSR, the theme was "more guns, less butter." It noted that so many resources were going into the Soviet military that 262 million ordinary citizens were condemned to a life of scarcity, corruption, and unhappiness.

The four thousand–word cover story was titled "Twilight of Communism?" and its message was summed up in an early paragraph: "Indeed, what emerges in the view of many Western analysts is a portrait of communism in bankruptcy, a system ill-equipped to build or manage a modern economy. The communist empire that emerged from World War II steadily unravels, with more nations emulating the independence of Yugoslavia." The question mark in the title was vital and intentional. We weren't affirming that the end of communism was near and thus the end of the Cold War, just hinting that it was around the corner. In retrospect, the piece was one of the few early insights into the coming collapse of the Soviet Union. Joe Fromm sensed what most Sovietologists missed.

On December 4, foreign editor Roy Hansen wrote the Soviet Embassy requesting a correspondent's visa for me as Pepper Martin's replacement. Weeks of worrying silence went by, making us all wonder if some unforseen objection had arisen. Finally, in mid-April the visa came through, and I prepared to leave toward the end of the month. The magazine's editor in chief, Marvin Stone, summoned me to his office. Stone, who had impressive credentials from the Korean War, running the International News Service bureau in Tokyo, and writing on national security issues at the Pentagon, was a tough-minded, controlling administrator. He radiated little warmth, and I found it difficult to guess what was really on his mind. When he read a piece by Ruth in the *Washington Post* about the delays with our visas, he became upset. He asked for Ruth to check with him in advance before publishing further articles, "giving me the subject matter, proposed title and place of publication." I think this was not so much male chauvinism (although it looked like it) as his desire to protect the Moscow operation from a silly misstep. Maintaining a bureau in the Soviet capital was an expensive proposition because of the need for Soviet support help, correspondents' hardship pay, and benefits for dependents. Ruth and I agreed, of course, to Stone's request, but the incident left a sobering, not to say bitter, note.

Before I left for Moscow, Stone invited me and top editors to lunch. As soon as we sat down at Il Giardino, he made certain that I understood my responsibilities. I was to work aggressively and report details unavailable to daily publications such as the *New York Times* or the once-over-lightly reports of the wire services. He made clear he did not consider that the emergence of political dissidents, however courageous, had much appeal among Soviet citizens and therefore was unlikely to result in the overthrow of the Kremlin leadership or the development of Western-style democracy. And he added a phrase that I remember clearly to this day: "I hate the Russian Revolution," he announced, emphasizing the verb *hate*. "I believe everything bad that has happened in the last forty years flows from that revolution." I assumed his experience in the Korean War underlined his view. Staring at me intently, he continued, "When you get to Russia, observe closely and report accurately. If you are expelled for telling the truth, I won't be unhappy." If he wished me good luck, I don't remember it.

In truth, there were two issues that troubled me about the coming assignment, and they were quite different from Marvin Stone's concerns. Two years before, in 1979, the Soviet Union had revised its nationality laws to state that anyone born in Russia had Soviet citizenship. Could I have received Soviet citizenship through my father, who was born in St. Petersburg in 1898? Officials at the U.S. State Department urged me to discuss this with the Soviet Embassy in Washington. I thought better of that idea, and resolved to ignore the potential problem. The other concern had to do with espionage. I knew very well that a number of American journalists had been accused of spying over the years and were expelled from the Soviet Union. I definitely did not want that to happen to me. As a precaution, I wrote my Washington lawyer, Cathy Douglas, early in 1981, "I can state categorically that I have never been employed by U.S. intelligence or anybody else's intelligence agency." Having dealt with those two matters, I was ready to depart.

I arrived in Moscow on the evening of April 21, 1981, having left family and Jack Russell terrier Zeus to follow in the coming weeks. Pepper Martin, then in his seventies, was glad to see me and anxious to leave what had been an aggravating two-year assignment for him and his wife, Lee. His good humor was reflected in the telex message he sent Roy Hansen:

413216 usnwr
item one
roy: nick and jet lag just linked in peaceful bedtime lullaby. eye booked to depart late sunday april 26 and arrive washington late afternoon april 28 stop this gives nick time to clean apartment so dog will feel at home. no difficulty about introducing nick to moscow stop he knows everybody although brezhnev gromyko suslov are not readily accessible for your photo promotion purposes stop. will do best we can dash like volga boatman stop otherwise all technical problems of handling problems are under control regards pepper.

Early days are always consumed with housekeeping issues, leaving little time for stories of substance. The bureau was located at 36 Leninskii Prospekt, a short walk from the Leninskii Prospekt metro station, with its grandiose statue of cosmonaut Yuri Gagarin. The correspondent's apartment was located on the floor below the office. What was unusual about the bureau was that it was located in an entrance solely dedicated to foreigners in a building that was otherwise completely Russian. Our entrance was populated by East Europeans and Arabs; we were the only Americans. Unlike the "diplomatic ghettos" at Kutuzovsky Prospekt and "Sad Sam," it had no police protection. That meant that any Soviet citizen could enter the building without being challenged, and a number of them did discover my office, usually to my regret.

As I look over those initial files of April, May, and June 1981, I see that what concerned us all was whether the Soviet Union would invade Poland to put down the rising independence movement, whether the Reagan administration would respond positively to Leonid Brezhnev's peace blandishments after the invasion of Afghanistan, and whether the Kremlin was up to no good in the Middle East after a visit to Moscow by Jordan's King Hussein. Another major preoccupation closer to home was the imminent arrival of our Jack Russell terrier aboard a Soviet airliner from Washington. Ruth and Caleb were to follow later by train from Paris.

For my driver, Boris, and secretary, Valentina, the arrival of Zeus became their major concern. Zeus was scheduled to depart from Washington aboard Aeroflot flight 318 on the evening of April 27. "A dog is a full member of a family," Boris said understandingly. "May God grant that everything turns out right." On this assignment, Boris did a fine job. At two o'clock on April 28, we drove the office Mercedes right onto the tarmac at Sheremetyevo Airport and parked it at the nose of the blue and white Ilyushin 62 that had just landed. When Zeus's cage was lowered out of the hold, I noted that the water in his pan was frozen—not a good sign. Suddenly, Zeus caught sight of me, shivered, coughed, and jumped with joy. We searched in vain for the airport veterinarian, who apparently had abandoned her post and driven back to town without completing the usual formalities.

During the next weeks, *U.S. News* agreed to run a piece describing how I found life in the Soviet Union twenty years after my first assignment for UPI. In this "self-interview" I attributed the questions to the magazine and supplied the answers. The trick was to develop a natural flow of observations. The article, called "Life in the Soviet Union: A Reporter Returns," ran on July 13, 1981:

*U.S. NEWS AND WORLD REPORT*: What were your first impressions on returning to Moscow?

DANILOFF: There were pluses and minuses. On the plus side, people are better dressed, and displays in the shop windows are more attractive. The restored churches are beautiful. There are more passenger cars on the streets. One major difference: the Soviet people are more polite in public than they were twenty years ago.

But I also have some negative impressions. Supply of fresh produce is erratic, and many ordinary goods are devilishly hard to get. The Russians still seem to be in the Dark Ages when it comes to credit. Did you know that checkbooks are rarely used? Bills have to be paid in cash, or by bank transfer, which requires a written letter. One senses the heavy hand of authority that does not like to admit it can make a mistake. The Soviet press still is stuffy.

Q. Are Russians suspicious of foreign correspondents?

A. It is much easier for a foreign reporter to work in Moscow than it was 20 years ago. The Soviets have come to realize the advantage of getting a better press in the West by being a little more helpful. Moreover, Moscow is a far more open city. Soviet officials are more direct, more polite, less insistent in spouting a propaganda line.

One interesting point: Twenty years ago, the Moscow telephone system operated without a public telephone book. You simply had to keep a list of the numbers you wanted to call. In the mid-1960s, the Soviets finally published a volume giving the numbers of public institutions and organizations. A four-volume edition giving numbers of home subscribers came out in the early 1970s. However, there is still no equivalent of the American phone book or the Yellow Pages. Another difference: Public telephones cost 2 kopeks a call (2.8 cents), but have no coin return.

Q. Are American and other foreigners still kept under surveillance by the Soviet secret police?

A. In the Western community, defense attaches seem to be the most closely watched. It is not unusual for them to be openly trailed as they make their rounds. Stories abound about Western apartments being wired, telephones being bugged. Some diplomats say secret microphones have been placed in automobiles, or even frequently worn clothing. But surveillance of foreign journalists is unobtrusive, and reporters tend to shrug it off.

Q. Have you found many changes in Moscow itself?

A. Moscow has grown enormously and now is home for 8 million people, up from over 6 million in 1960. The city fathers are appalled that everybody wants to live here, and an effort is being made to limit Moscow in size. Industry is being moved outside the city, and satellite towns are being thrown up. Construction is going on almost everywhere. According to officials, nearly half of Moscow's population has moved into new apartments in the last 10 years. Yet there still is a housing shortage and wretched communal apartments still exist, where families have only one or two rooms and must share kitchen and bathroom facilities with other families.

The American presence in Moscow is more noticeable than before. Street stands sell Pepsi-Cola, with signs in Russian and English. Many Russians wear jeans, some with T-shirts and sweat shirts that have American slogans or writing on them. The American Embassy flies a flag continually; a display case outside the embassy currently has a picture exhibit of contemporary American sculpture.

Another impression: Moscow makes a big effort to keep itself cleaned up. Street sweepers are out by 7 A.M. brushing off the sidewalks. Despite that, some inner court yards are a mess, and recently completed buildings are left with trash and building materials scattered about.

Q: What about the political atmosphere?

A: Twenty years ago, Nikita Khrushchev was boss. He followed the repressive Stalin days, and under his rule a thaw began. Khrushchev brought a sense of hope and excitement and urged the nation to overtake the U.S. in many spheres by 1980. Those were the heady days of sputniks and Yuri Gagarin's manned flight.

The excitement of those days is gone, replaced by Leonid Brezhnev's stable, but somewhat monotonous administration. Khrushchev, who died in 1971, is reviled by some Soviets for economic shortcomings that still exist. But he is praised by others for easing political controls and for denouncing Stalin's personality cult.

Q: Do Russians feel freer today than in the 1960s?

A: Clearly, they feel freer. In the 1960s, you could still feel the effects of the Stalin terror. You might strike up a conversation with a stranger, only to be told that you could never meet again because it was too dangerous. The authorities would warn off people who telephoned you, particularly if they were not authorized to meet foreigners.

Such fears still exist. People want to get on with their personal lives without getting into trouble. Being discreet about whom you meet continues to be important. People talk cautiously on the telephone and use code words if they think the conversation is being bugged.

But I am struck at how freely Muscovites talks among themselves. No holds barred in small, private groups. I would say such discussions are just as frank, just as probing as you would find in an American setting.

Another intriguing phenomenon is the free-swinging ways of Soviet youth. A very lively movement of folk singers has grown up that the authorities want to control but don't know quite how to go about it. The unofficial bards draw huge crowds across the country—I've been told that upwards of 200,000 have assembled on occasion—to listen to and tape the songs. And some of the verses are quite sharp, from a political point of view.

Q: Are Soviet travel restrictions as tough as before?

A: Khrushchev complained in his memoirs that the Soviet leadership did not trust the Russian people enough to allow them to travel freely abroad. Under Brezhnev, travel restrictions have been eased slightly. Soviets may go abroad on official business or on preplanned group or individual tourist trips. They also may travel on invitations from relatives or institutions abroad.

Russians still complain that predeparture screening by the authorities is humiliating. Nonetheless, more Russians are traveling abroad than before. A top Soviet travel official recently claimed that "millions" of Soviet people go abroad every year. Still travel abroad is nowhere as open or easy for Russians as for Americans.

Q: Do many Soviets want to emigrate, to leave for good?

A: In the past 10 years, more than 250,000 out of a population of 262 million have emigrated legally. Moscow Radio recently claimed that 98.4 percent of those who apply to leave are granted permission. The remaining 1.6 percent are turned down on national security grounds.

What the authorities usually gloss over is how arduous the emigration process is. After Soviet citizens make their applications, they often lose their jobs or are demoted. They never know when a decision will be made. Some youths with military service are told they know defense secrets and must wait 10 years; others are told to wait five years.

Authorities seem to be distressed at the fairly large number of people with useful skills who have left, and are moving to cut back the flow. Making emigration an increasingly difficult process is one method. Requiring an invitation from a close blood relative abroad is another.

Q: Are the Soviets really suffering from what Secretary of State Alexander Haig calls "spiritual exhaustion"?

A: I do sense a malaise among Muscovites. But it is not an exhaustion which borders on collapse. The enthusiasm to remake the world according to the precepts of the Russian Revolution has been largely lost. People here want to live better, more fulfilling personal lives. It's instructive to see with what tender, loving care car owners wash and repair their autos on weekends.

I suspect the malaise is related to the fact that people are living better than 20 years ago—and their expectations are higher. There is frustration because many economic and spiritual needs are not being satisfied. But there is no doubt that if the nation were in real danger, the Kremlin leadership could rally the vast majority of Soviet people to the defense of the homeland.

Q: What are the spiritual needs you say are not being met?

A: One senses here a search for something beyond production quotas, ideological goals, even consumer consumption. A Russian confided to me: "You know, our youth simply do not believe in the ideology of our leadership any more."

There is also a renewed interest in Russian roots, the czars, even in the brief democratic period from 1905–1917. A group called the Committee for the Preservation of Historic Monuments has lobbied with partial success for the restoration of Russian Orthodox churches.

Q: What about economic needs?

A: There are shortages of fresh produce and meat that would be considered intolerable in the West. One Russian said to me: "I don't understand what has gone wrong. In the last century, Russia used to be a major agrarian state, exporting its excess grain to the rest of Europe."

Moscow is quite well supplied, and if you look long and hard you will probably find what you want. But that is a big "if." It will cost you time and money. An American student who is studying here told me: "Products are there, but never when you want them. That forces you to take advantage of anything that comes along, buying up lots and lots of oranges, say, if you see them being sold."

About 2 million people move in and out of Moscow every day. Thousands of these people from the provinces who have come to get basic supplies. According to travelers I have met, European Russia seems to be worse off than the Central Asian republics. Among the scarcest items are good meat and fresh vegetables. Milk and eggs are sometimes hard to find. Bread and cheese seem plentiful.

Q: If goods are in such short supply, how do people manage?

A: Friends and contacts become the key to survival. Knowing how to give an appropriate "present"—basically a bribe—develops into an art. Meantime, abuses of all kinds occur in the economy as a whole. There is black marketeering and hoarding. Salespeople keep goods under the counter for their friends. Underground businesses spring up.

Q: Would it help for the government to introduce rationing?

A: After 36 years of peace, nationwide rationing would be a heavy embarrassment and probably would be an administrative nightmare in a country of this enormous size. But some items are being rationed in a few regional districts and towns. I hear of one town where residents are limited to one chicken a month. Also, a crypto-rationing system already exists in Moscow.

Q: What do you mean by "crypto-rationing"?

A: The higher your rank, the better your access to goods. Government workers and people employed by large institutions can order through special bureaus attached to their offices. Diplomats, who are granted a very high status by the authorities, buy special coupons for foreign currency and may shop at reasonably well-stocked foreign-currency supermarkets.

Q: Doesn't the average Soviet citizen resent these perquisites being given to the privileged few?

A: Undoubtedly. But that's where friends and bribery come in. These days it's not how rich you are but whom you know.

Q: Does the Soviet press give an accurate picture of events outside Russia—for instance, in Poland or Afghanistan?

A: The press here has published a lot about events in Poland. Some accounts are more truthful than others, and if you are a careful reader, you can get a fairly good idea of what is happening. The Soviet media try to give the impression that Western "reactionaries" have been fomenting trouble in Poland and that Communist Party stalwarts are doing their best to get the situation under control.

You have to remember that Soviet authorities view the press in quite a different way than Americans do. The press here is one of the instruments of power. It is not a tool for disclosing the truth. Here's how Pravda describes the role of the press: "Soviet journalists see to it that the printed word is of maximum use to society, inspires the people to fresh achievements."

Q: Are you saying the Soviet press misleads people?

A: I am saying that the press often does not tell the whole story. It tries to project the impression that Soviet policies are developing successfully. It criticizes shortcomings in the implementation of plans but on the whole it tries to put a positive gloss on events. The fact that vital facts of information are omitted means that ordinary Soviets and ordinary Americans end up with very different perceptions of the same event.

Take Afghanistan: Americans believe that the Soviets are worried about growing rebellion south of their border, invaded Afghanistan, killed President Amin and installed a puppet ruler, Babrak Karmal. The Soviet perception is that the Kabul government, troubled by resistance to the Afghan socialist revolution of 1978, called for help. The Soviet Union, after much deliberation, responded. The death of Amin resulted from a firefight precipitated by Amin's personal guard once Soviet troops arrived.

When you press well-informed Soviet scholars or officials, you get a further refinement that does not appear in the press. Their view: The Soviet Union is a great power, and it had to protect its citizens who were being butchered in Afghanistan. The invasion has absolutely no implications for Western access to Persian Gulf oil. Moscow is not so stupid as to try to seize control of oil fields there and end up in a deeply serious confrontation with the West.

Q: Does the ordinary citizen know about the Soviet military buildup that caused so much concern in the West?

A: The average Soviet is profoundly ignorant of the details of military deployments that are openly discussed in the West. The Soviet press simply does not report such military secrets as the deployment of 250 SS-20 missiles, many aimed at Western Europe, or the SS-19s that are zeroed in on U.S. missile sites. It ignores the Soviet naval buildup. Instead, it asserts that a rough military parity has been attained between the U.S.S.R. and the Atlantic Alliance countries. It tries to shift the blame for the arms race on the West by saying that if Soviet forces are being "modernized," it is only because of the relentless acquisition of new weapons by the Western side.

Q: Has the country's increased military strength made the Russian leadership more confident or adventurous?

A: Some officials undoubtedly are cocky. They say with barely disguised glee that the "ideological struggle" between Communism and the Western democracies will continue. They show no sign of scaling back assistance to such groups as the Palestine Liberation Organization, which they claim are seeking "national liberation."

But I see a continuing caution by the highest leadership. They are old, experienced men, whose memories of the horrors of World War II still are vivid. In those years, Russia truly was in grave danger. About 10 percent of the population was killed. The Nazis roamed over the western part of the country plundering and killing. The only thing comparable in U.S. experience was the devastation which occurred in the South during the Civil War.

Q: Do Soviets feel a sense of inferiority toward Americans?

A: To some extent, although they won't admit it. Surprisingly, Russians have a great affinity to Americans. In fact, I would say Russia is far less anti-American at the grass roots than many West European countries. I would qualify this only by noting that the recent plunge in U.S.-Soviet relations has led to some recent anti-American outbursts.

Russians, like Americans, think big. They are open and friendly on a personal level. It's not unusual for a Russian to say to an American: "Why can't we get on better? We have so much in common. We've never fought each other, and there is no reason we ever should."

Q: How do Soviet leaders assess U.S.-Soviet relations?

A: The Kremlin leadership, I believe, is alarmed by the Reagan Administration. They are trying to determine whether Washington's harsh rhetoric is just talk or evidence of a war policy. They see danger signals: Secretary of State Haig said at his confirmation hearings that there were some things worth fighting for. That sounded to Soviet leaders like a war call. The Kremlin also is following very closely the Reagan administration's call for a military buildup.

The Soviet leaders doubt that the U.S. genuinely desires to renew arms-control negotiations. But they say the Soviet side is ready, even anxious, to get talks going.

Q: What course do you see the Soviets taking in the months ahead, particularly in relations with the U.S.?

A: The Russians will continue to pursue what they regard as their vital interests—but they will seek to avoid an eyeball-to-eyeball confrontation with America. They will remain in Afghanistan, walk a tightrope in Poland, and try to expand their influence in the Mideast and Africa.

They will encourage other countries to pressure the U.S. to resume the arms-control dialogue. And they will get quite nasty from time to time as they try to convince the world that it is the United States—not the Soviet Union—that is promoting international terrorism.

But in the end, I expect that the Soviets will welcome a sincere American offer to resume negotiations and will back away from confrontations with the U.S. on every level.

Chapter 25

The KAL Shoot-down

"Brezhnev is dead! Brezhnev is dead!" Someone was shouting through the bedroom door. The startling news threw me into an instant sweat. It was November 11, 1982, and I was in France, far from the action, with no easy way back to Moscow. Caleb and I had taken advantage of the November 7 revolutionary holidays and were visiting my elderly Russian relatives Vladimir and Olga Matousievich. Volodya, as we called him, had been forced by the Russian Revolution to emigrate to Paris in the 1920s, where he had entered the wine business. In recent years, Olga had been anxious to develop relations with their American cousin-once-removed who was taking an interest in their abandoned Russia. We had come to visit them at Cognac, where Volodya, now the childless proprietor of a small vineyard and chateau, was producing an excellent cognac. It was Volodya banging insistently and shouting in his adopted French, "Brezhnev est mort! Brezhnev est mort!"

That's how I learned that the eighteen-year regime of Leonid Ilyich Brezhnev, seventy-six, had finally come to an end. Brezhnev's demise was not exactly unexpected. It was obvious his health was declining, and by the end of the decade he was reduced to reading his public statements in an uncertain voice. On one occasion in Tashkent in 1981, his aides handed him the wrong speech, and he began reading it until they realized their mistake and handed him the right one in midstream, to the embarrassment of the whole nation. To have him die while I was away was one more unexpected difficulty in this father-son outing. Five days earlier on arrival at Charles de Gaulle Airport, my Soviet multiple-entry visa had slipped out of my passport and disappeared. I had no legal way back to Moscow. Of course, I had immediately telephoned Ruth, who had remained in Moscow and informed the Press Department of the Foreign Ministry. Alexander Voznikov, head of the section dealing with American reporters, had been reasonably sympathetic and promised to instruct the Soviet Embassy in Paris to issue a replacement, available no one knew when.

After Volodya's announcement, Caleb and I rushed for the next train back to Paris, spending the night at my father's house in the Paris suburb of Antony and arriving early the next morning at the Soviet Embassy. That day, Friday, November 12, was the magazine's drop-dead deadline; I had no more than twelve hours to get back to Moscow and think up some kind of article for the magazine. Caleb and I called in at the Soviet Embassy but found it bedecked in black as officials attended a memorial service for the fallen leader. It took strenuous efforts on my part to rouse a grumpy consul, who reluctantly fished about for the new visa. When he finally handed me the document, we rushed by limo at ninety miles an hour to the airport, where we managed to board an Air France flight with only minutes to spare.

*U.S. News* had prepared plenty of advance material in the event that the Brezhnev years would come to an abrupt end. Such occurrences usually happen at the most inconvenient moments, like Saturday or Sunday night. Ruth, knowing the magazine's demands as well as I, had already pitched in. Without a signal from me, she had performed as my alter ego, filing a report on the apathetic reaction of ordinary Muscovites. The only thing left was to write an analysis about what could be expected in the weeks ahead. By eight o'clock Moscow time, after the three-hour flight from Paris, I was back in the office and telexed my analysis by midnight, or four o'clock Washington time.

Yuri Andropov's emergence as number one several days later was a surprise to foreign correspondents. We thought his secret-police background would prevent him from reaching the top post. As it turned out, his Politburo colleagues concluded he was the most able among them. I predicted Andropov would find his greatest challenge to be reviving the flagging Soviet economy and seeking an arms accommodation with the United States. "Andropov will turn out to be a tough defender of Soviet interests around the world," I wrote, "but he will probably also display uncommon sophistication and flexibility in dealing with the U.S. and the West."

The beginning of the Andropov government brought a welcome sense that a firm hand was at last back at the helm, heralding improvements in both the country's internal situation and U.S.-Soviet relations. Andropov was known as a highly intelligent and disciplined leader, someone who might stop the economic stagnation that had developed during the Brezhnev years. His Politburo colleague Viktor Grishin has described him as conservative, ascetic, and rather withdrawn from his colleagues. For more than a decade, Andropov had headed the KGB, which he used to enforce worker discipline, intimidate dissidents, and cut back the flow of would-be emigrants. Declassified Soviet documents show that as KGB chief, Andropov spent years lobbying the Politburo to expel rebellious writer Aleksandr Solzhenitsyn from the country and send into internal exile Andrey Sakharov, the "father" of the Soviet H-bomb but now a courageous voice for human rights and democracy.

Andropov's rise began after Stalin's death when he was named Soviet ambassador to Hungary in 1954. His diplomatic reports to Moscow warned of growing discontent among Hungarians with the Communist regime and contributed significantly to the decision by Nikita Khrushchev and his colleagues to put down the rebellion in 1956 with an invasion force. Andropov returned to Moscow to head the Central Committee department for liaison with Communist countries and was appointed in 1967 to head the KGB. In 1973 he was made a nonvoting candidate member of the Politburo and was raised to full status in 1976 while continuing to direct the political police. He stepped down as secret-police chief in May 1982 to become one of the powerful secretaries of the Communist Party. In short order, he emerged as the second-most-powerful leader after Brezhnev. Like FBI chief J. Edgar Hoover in the United States, Andropov was reputed to have files on all the top political leaders.

Almost immediately, rumors began circulating that the new chief was really not just a disciplinarian; he also wrote poetry, liked jazz, and watched American movies. At the time, I speculated these stories were set in motion by Andropov's close aides, seeking to soften his image for foreign audiences, and possibly for party apparatchiks. However, on reading recollections of some of his aides in later years, I am inclined to think the rumors were simply warmed-over gossip without specific political purpose. Apparently, Andropov did write poetry, had an interest in culture, was well educated, and could switch instantaneously from intellectual to devoted party servant. *U.S. News and World Report* noted the rumors and ran a skeptical box in its November 22, 1982, issue headlined: "A 'Closet Liberal'? Don't Bet on It." On target, I thought.

On November 15, 1982, Andropov presided over Brezhnev's funeral on Red Square. On that blustery day, I stood shivering in the reviewing stands, hoping to catch an exclusive picture with my long lens of Andropov and the other leaders as they carried Brezhnev's open coffin to its resting place behind the Lenin Mausoleum. I didn't succeed; the AP photographer easily outdid me. Following the ceremony, Andropov, sixty-eight, retired to the Kremlin to receive a long line of foreign emissaries, including Vice President George Bush and Secretary of State George Shultz. Shultz wrote afterward, "Andropov made clear that no one should tell the Soviets how to run their internal affairs. He looked more like a cadaver than the just-interred Brezhnev, but his mental powers filled the room. He reminded me of Sherlock Holmes's deadly enemy Professor Moriarty, all brain in a discarded body." I noted in a message to the magazine: "The Americans found Andropov to be tired after the Brezhnev funeral but intelligent and quick-witted. They noted that he spoke in cultivated Russian and gave evidence of understanding English when he answered a question before his interpreter had time to translate into Russian."

The new Soviet administration began as I expected, with a campaign to stop the rot in the national economy. In the January 31, 1983, issue, I reported, "In less than three months after rising to power, Yuri Andropov is cracking down hard on the Soviet Union's three major evils—drunkenness, absenteeism and corruption—in an effort to breathe new life into the nation's sagging economy." I was gratified to see that Andropov soon developed some notable innovations, including slightly more openness than his predecessor. He insisted on announcing Politburo meetings, publicizing the issues that these top rulers had been dealing with, and publishing transcripts of speeches before the full Central Committee of the party. He scored a major propaganda coup in the early fall of 1983 when he invited an eleven-year-old American girl, Samantha Smith, who had written him a protest against war, to come to Moscow with her mother and father to promote peace.

Away from public view, the Andropov team began exploring the possibility of resuming serious arms negotiations with the United States. Ambassador Dobrynin began meeting quietly with Secretary of State George Shultz in Washington in November and December, followed by an unannounced meeting in mid-February with President Reagan at the White House. In March, President Reagan proposed an "interim agreement" limiting U.S. and Soviet intermediate-range missiles in the European theater, and Andropov responded with a counterproposal that the United States, however, found unacceptable.

President Reagan followed up these initiatives with a handwritten note to Andropov on July 11, 1983, urging the creation of a confidential "back channel" to reinvigorate arms negotiations. Andropov replied on August 4 with another proposal that, again, the United States found unacceptable. Both sides continued exploring quietly the views of the other side. In mid-August 1983, Andropov received a group of visiting American senators. They reported that Andropov came over as willing to bargain, if very, very tough. On the surface it seemed that the ice jam in Soviet-American relations was breaking up. Three days later, I filed an upbeat cable to the magazine: "Putting reluctance aside, the Soviet Union is joining the U.S. in a broad dialogue and even some cooperative ventures. This significant shift from the Kremlin's chilly attitude a year ago is bound to cause satisfaction at the White House and prompt U.S. spokesmen to assert that President Reagan is now getting Soviet-American relations 'under control.' But make no mistake about it: the deep ideological rivalry between the two superpowers is not about to fade." I noted, too, in the cable that the United States signed a major agreement with the Soviet Union at the end of August for hundreds of thousands of tons of wheat and corn to Moscow in the coming year, that the two sides would resume talks on a new cultural exchange agreement, the establishment of consulates in New York and Kiev, and that Soviet scientists would be using miniaturized American monitoring equipment to observe monkeys and rats in a new space flight to be launched in October.

Then on August 31, an event occurred in the Soviet far East that threw all expectations into doubt: A Korean Airlines flight from New York to Seoul disappeared off the Soviet coast bordering on the Sea of Japan. At midnight in Washington, Assistant Secretary of State Richard Burt began calling the Soviet Embassy for information, with no result. The next morning, September 1, at six-thirty, Secretary Shultz began receiving intelligence that a Soviet interceptor had shot down Korean Airlines flight KE 007 with 269 passengers on board, including Representative Larry MacDonald (D-GA). He called a press conference for 10:45 A.M. to lambaste the Soviet leadership for committing a barbarous act and revealed incriminating details from monitored radio conversations between Soviet ground controllers and interceptor pilots. He, thus, forced the Kremlin leadership to acknowledge the shoot-down.

Late on that evening of September 1 in Moscow, about twelve hours after the incident, national television reported on its nine o'clock newscast that an unidentified aircraft, flying without lights, had violated Soviet airspace over Sakhalin Island, near the Sea of Japan. The aircraft, according to TASS, refused to reply to any radio communication. Soviet interceptors had been launched and attempted to force the plane to land. TASS concluded: "However, the intruder-plane failed to respond to the Soviet fighters' signals and warnings and continued its flight toward the Sea of Japan."

That first acknowledgment—partly correct but partly false—lay down the line that would become fundamental to all further Soviet explanations. No lights. No response. Attempted escape. The phrase "continued its flight" appeared to us Moscow correspondents as highly suspicious. It was covering up something. But what? The plane had evaded the interceptors? It had been shot down? Or maybe it had crashed flying away from Soviet territory, leaving the Soviet side blameless?

Moscow's response to the convulsions of anger from the West was typical for those Cold War years: the Kremlin's attitude was that the best defense is a strong offense. Blame the other fellow for everything, and shout about it in as loud a voice as possible. I was familiar with this very Russian reaction that continues right up to today. It issues from a deep sense of insecurity, and a belief that Russia is surrounded by unfriendly neighbors. In the ensuing days, the Kremlin dribbled out additional aggressive explanations. On September 2, TASS asserted that the Soviet Union was legally defending its borders, although it regretted the loss of life. From September 3 to September 6, TASS issued statements charging the United States had consciously outfitted a Korean Airlines plane with espionage equipment and directed it to fly over military and naval bases on Kamchatka and Sakhalin. On September 6, the Kremlin issued a formal Soviet government statement denouncing the flight.

Moscow's most dramatic performance came on September 9, three days after a devastating presentation by Ambassador Jeanne Kirkpatrick at the United Nations during which she played eleven minutes of radio conversations between ground control and the Soviet fighter pilots, monitored by the United States. These intercepted conversations included the order to fire, and the pilot's report, "The target is destroyed."

Marshal Nikolai Ogarkov, chief of the Soviet General Staff; Georgii Kornienko, first deputy foreign minister; and Leonid Zamyatin, head of the Communist Party's International Relations Department, presented the Soviet rebuttal at a press conference. I sat in the audience with my tape recorder, captivated by Ogarkov's performance. He stood ramrod straight, pointer in hand, next to a large map depicting the flight of the Korean plane six hundred kilometers into Soviet territory from the established Anchorage-Seoul route. I was struck by his eloquence, his supreme confidence in what he was saying. In reviewing that tape for these recollections, I was impressed again by his absolute lack of doubt. Could it all really be as he said? I was determined to find out, now or later.

Ogarkov declared that a commission of experts had examined all available data and had concluded that this had been an espionage mission. He revealed that a U.S. RC-135 reconnaissance aircraft had been flying parallel to the Korean liner, at about the same altitude, and asserted that it was controlling the Korean plane's movements. He claimed that the radar signatures of these two aircraft at one point totally coincided. The KAL airliner, he claimed, "transmitted short, coded signals, which are usually used for transmitting intelligence information." Ogarkov emphasized that the Soviet side abided by all international rules and that Soviet interceptors were dispatched to identify the intruder and force it to land at a Soviet air base.

In answer to questions, the chief of the General Staff said that one of the interceptors fired 120 tracer bullets along the liner's flight path, and only when the Korean pilots ignored this signal was the order given to shoot down the intruder. We Western journalists were particularly struck by Ogarkov's statement that the shoot-down was ordered by regional commanders without emergency consultations with Andropov or his top aides. This revelation led the front page of the *New York Times* on September 10, 1983.

The press conference, nevertheless, left many questions unanswered. Was the plane really flying without navigation lights? Did the Soviet interceptors realize they were dealing with a passenger plane, and a foreign one at that? And perhaps most important of all, why was this plane so badly off course? Was there really a possibility that U.S. intelligence services had used the KAL flight for the purpose of activating Soviet radars and photographing naval installations at Kamchatka and Sakhalin Island with infrared cameras? Moscow's loud voice ensured that these questions would remain in dispute for years.

A quarter century later, we know much better what actually happened on that night of August 31–September 1, 1983. After the collapse of the Soviet Union, President Boris Yeltsin finally supplied the International Civil Aviation Organization (ICAO) with important materials, including the Russian transcripts of radio conversations between ground controllers and interceptor pilots. The Korean Airlines flight left Anchorage at 4 A.M. local time (1300 GMT) and headed south toward Seoul. It was to follow a well-established international route called R-20 but, for reasons that I will come to later, began to drift eastward almost immediately after leaving U.S. territory. An hour and a half later, it was already hundreds of mile off course when it entered Soviet airspace at the Kamchatka Peninsula and began flying over a major naval and submarine base at Petropavlosk-Kamchatskii, home port to some ninety nuclear-powered submarines. (This, by the way, was not the first time a KAL airliner had strayed over Soviet territory. In 1978, a Paris-Seoul flight over the North Pole mistakenly violated the Soviet Union's northern border and was forced by interceptors to land on a frozen lake near Murmansk.)

As the Korean airliner cruised over two hundred miles of the peninsula, Soviet radarmen were already busy tracking a U.S. reconnaissance plane flying in "lazy eights" off the northern Kamchatka coast. The American plane had been assigned to monitor telemetry of a test flight of a Soviet ballistic SS-25 missile expected that night. Keeping track of such missile tests was a frequent occurrence in 1983: out of some sixty reconnaissance flights that year, several American aircraft reportedly had violated Soviet borders. The Soviet radarmen were keyed up, and one of their officers designated the RC-135 reconnaissance plane "air target 60-64." The Korean airliner was approaching at approximately the same altitude. The radar operators, at first, thought it was a tanker coming to refuel the RC-135. But when it continued on a north-south course, past the circling RC-135, they assumed it was a second RC-135 under the control of the first RC-135. They designated it "air target 60-65."

Informed of the intrusion over Kamchatka, General Ivan M. Tretyak, chief of the Far East Military District, ordered his subordinate commands to force the plane to land or shoot it down according to Soviet rules of engagement. These rules, incidentally, prohibited firing on passenger liners. As the plane flew out over the Sea of Okhotsk, four fighters scrambled to chase it. One interceptor pilot, Major Vassily Kazmin, sighted the plane briefly, but never got close enough to identify it visually. The air defense trackers lost contact with the Boeing 747 over the Sea of Okhotsk because construction of antiaircraft radars covering this body of water had not been completed. However, assuming the KAL liner continued on its heading and did not turn eastward toward Japan, the aircraft would approach Sakhalin Island within two and a half hours. About 5:30 a.m. Sakhalin time on September 1 (11:30 p.m. Moscow time on August 31), the commanding officer of the Sokol-Dolinsk Air Force Base on Sakhalin Island was alerted to the looming crisis. General Alexander I. Kornukov hastily got out of bed, dressed, and prepared for action.

Sakhalin defense radars spotted the Korean airliner as it approached land over the Gulf of Patience shortly before 5:42 A.M. (1742 GMT). This time three Su-15 fighters and a MiG-23 took off to track the plane. One Su-15, piloted by Major Gennadi N. Osipovich, trailed the airliner for some sixty miles over the gulf before sighting it visually as a small flashing dot in the night sky. The moon was half full but mostly obscured by persistent clouds. Ground controllers, having been informed by Kamchatka that air target 60-65 was a spy plane, repeatedly asked Major Osipovich to identify the intruder. He reported back that it was a very large plane, that its strobe and navigation lights were on, and that it might be a Soviet transport. When ground control determined there were no Soviet planes in the vicinity, he was told to interrogate it. He sent off a "friend or foe" radio signal but got no answer because the KAL airliner did not carry a transponder capable of replying to a Soviet signal. He was ordered next to flash his lights and rock his wings, but did so without getting close to the KAL's cockpit. Finally, he was ordered to fire tracer bullets along the plane's path. As it happened, his fighter had not been loaded with tracers, so he shot off 120 ordinary rounds anyway, which were invisible in the night sky.

At this point, Sakhalin ground control ordered Major Osipovich to force the plane to land or shoot it out of the sky. Air controllers were getting nervous that the plane would soon cover the eighty-mile width of lower Sakhalin, and escape over international waters. Major Osipovich was nervous too, he stated later, as he was running low on fuel. He did not try to raise the Korean crew on the international distress frequency of 121.5 MHz because to retune his radio would mean losing contact with ground control. Furthermore, the commanding officer of the Sokol Air Force Base was now repeatedly demanding that he shoot the plane down using cannons or rockets. Commander General Alexander Kornukov was angry and having a hard time controlling himself. At 6:21 a.m. (1821 GMT), Kornukov pressed Lieutenant Colonel Gerasimenko, acting commanding officer of the Forty-first Air Defense Regiment, for immediate action. He blurted out: "Cut the horseplay at the command post, what is that noise there? I repeat the combat task: fire the missiles; fire on target 60-65, destroy target 60-65!" The transcript of their conversation continues:

6:22: LT. COL. GERASIMENKO: Will comply.

6:22: GEN. KORNUKOV: Comply and get Tarasov [pilot of a Su-15 and Osipovich's wingman] here. Take control of the MiG-23 from Smyrnykh, call sign 163, call sign 163, he is behind the target at the moment. Destroy the target!

6:22: LT. COL. GERASIMENKO: Task received. Destroy the target with missile fire, accept control of fighter from Smyrnykh.

6:22: GEN. KORNUKOV: Carry out the task, destroy!

6:22:02: MAJ. OSIPOVICH (call sign 805) to ground control: The target is decreasing speed.

6:22:30: GROUND CONTROL TO MAJ. OSIPOVICH: 805, open fire on target.

General Kornukov knew full well that it would take less than fifteen minutes for "air target 60-65" to overfly southern Sakhalin. Fearing the plane would soon enter international airspace, he began shouting angrily in salty language common among soldiers everywhere, and hardly unusual among Soviet general officers.

6:23: GEN. KORNUKOV: Fuck your mother! How long does it take him to get into attack position? He is already getting out into neutral waters. Engage afterburners immediately. Bring in the MiG-23 as well as a guarantee. While you are wasting time, it will fly right out.

6:23:05: GROUND CONTROL: 805, try to destroy the target with cannons.

6:23:37: MAJ. OSIPOVICH: I am dropping back. Now I will try a rocket.

6:23:51: GROUND CONTROL: 805, approach the target and destroy the target.

6:25:11: MAJ. OSIPOVICH: I am approaching the target; am in lock-on. Distance to target is eight kilometers.

As the drama moved to conclusion, the Korean pilots, blissfully unaware of the catastrophe creeping up on them, asked Tokyo Air Control for permission to climb from thirty-one thousand feet to thirty-five thousand feet, where they would expend less fuel on the home stretch into Seoul. Their voice recorder indicates no sense of imminent danger in the cockpit. When they received permission from Tokyo, they turned the craft westward toward the mainland and pointed its nose upward. Major Osipovich and ground control took that action to be an evasive maneuver, one more "proof" they were dealing with a U.S. spy plane.

At 6:25:30 a.m. Major Osipovich fired two rockets, one a heat-seeking missile to explode on contact and a second radar-guided weapon primed to explode at fifty meters. Thirty seconds later when he observed the hit, Major Osipovich radioed ground control: "The target is destroyed."

But despite what everyone thought, the target was not destroyed. The KAL airliner suffered catastrophic damage—severing of rudder-control cables, failure of hydraulic actuators linked to the steering systems, structural damage on the left inboard elevators, and major holes to the passenger cabin leading to depressurization—but kept flying. On being hit, it pitched upward, reaching an altitude of 38,250, then began to wobble unsteadily, sliding into a right-hand downward spiral at 250 miles an hour.

For the next twelve minutes the crew struggled desperately to regain control as the passengers sat terrified, belted to their seats. The cockpit microphone caught the initial confusion of the crew. Nine seconds after the hit, one pilot noted all engines were performing normally; seconds later he saw that the air brakes suddenly popped up from the wings as the plane gained altitude. The pilot managed to radio Tokyo that they were descending to ten thousand feet. His labored breathing indicated that he had put on an oxygen mask. A minute and forty-four seconds after the hit, power to the cockpit voice recorder failed. The last captured words were of a recorded announcement on the public address system telling the passengers in English and Japanese: "Put out your cigarette. This is an emergency descent. Put out your cigarette. This is an emergency descent. Put your mask over your nose and mouth and adjust the headband. Put the mask over your nose and mouth and adjust . . ."

After Osipovich fired his missiles, there was consternation at ground control. Had the plane really been destroyed or not? Had it fallen over Soviet territory, or had it plunged into international waters? Two interceptors saw the liner's lights go out as it flipped upside down and went into its final death dive. At fifteen thousand feet the liner plunged through the clouds and disappeared out of view of the fighter pilots and of ground-control radar. A Japanese fisherman later reported that he had heard an explosion, seen two flashes of light, and smelled the odor of aviation fuel.

How did the Soviet Union's top leadership really react as the incident played out? At the time, I assumed that the top leaders, assembled as the Politburo, would be dealing with the crisis. Several sources reported a few days later that the Far East Command informed Defense Minister Dmitry Ustinov of the intrusion as it was taking place from Kamchatka to Sakhalin Island in the late evening, Moscow time, August 31. He, in turn, reported to Andropov that a "target 60-65"—an American plane, not a Korean airliner—had illegally entered Soviet airspace. On the basis of Ustinov's report, Andropov reconfirmed the standing orders to shoot down any hostile intruder who refused to land.

As the final moments unfolded, the Far East Command tried to respect the rules of engagement, but totally failed to make visual identification. According to reports circulating in early October in Moscow, a key commander (possibly Kornukov) was summoned to Moscow for questioning. He was alleged to have told a maid at the Central Committee hotel that his mother would never forgive him for what had happened. Immediately after the shootdown, the Soviet military prepared an urgent report for the Politburo, which met in a hastily convened, unannounced meeting in Moscow on the evening of September 1. At this gathering, chaired by the ailing Andropov, the nation's top leaders approved the release of the deceptive TASS statement, which was probably drafted by the staffs of the Defense Ministry and the Committee for State Security under Ustinov's leadership. After the evening Politburo meeting, Andropov flew off on medical leave in the Crimea.

As the story was now rapidly developing, I sent a message to Washington on September 2, alerting the magazine that the Soviet side would probably resort to falsehoods in justifying its actions. My editors probably did not need this advice, as they were skeptical of most Soviet statements. Years later, Major Osipovich acknowledged that he had been forced by superiors to lie. "We shot down the plane legally," he told Izvestia in a 1991 interview. "Later we began to lie about small details: the plane was supposedly flying without running lights or strobe light, that tracer bullets were fired, or that I had radio contact with them on the emergency frequency of 121.5 megahertz. I did not have time for that! To call up that frequency I would have had to tune the radio, that would mean losing contact with ground control." And he added: "From the brass I was given a 'libretto' [script] which was what I was supposed to voice before the cameras." He admitted that he had such a hard time with the "libretto" that he was obliged to down a glass of vodka before going on camera.

On September 3, 1983, the Communist Party newspaper, *Pravda*, reported in an official notice that the Politburo had met on September 2 as the news of the KAL shoot-down ricocheted around the world. The announcement stated only that the agenda concerned worker productivity and population issues. No mention of the Korean airliner at all! This attempt to project an "everything normal" image reminded me of President Nixon's efforts to deflect cascading criticisms during the Watergate crisis. True, the last paragraph of the Politburo announcement referred mysteriously to discussions of unspecified domestic and foreign matters. A decade later—after the collapse of the Soviet Union—the newspapers *Rossiskie Vesti* and *Rossiskaya Gazeta* published a partial transcript that showed that the shoot-down had been the major issue.

Reading the transcript today, you get the feeling that the meeting had been carefully orchestrated by two "elders" of the Politburo, Defense Minister Ustinov, seventy-nine, and Foreign Minister Andrey Gromyko, seventy-four. They would guide the discussion in such a way as to ratify, ex post facto, the shoot-down. Because Andropov was absent, Konstantin Chernenko, formally the number two in the party, chaired the meeting. Gromyko presented first. He emphasized that the United States would undoubtedly take retaliatory action, possibly breaking the grain agreement that had been reached just days before, and thinking up "provocations" against the Soviet airline Aeroflot. He predicted the United States might try to disrupt the planned conference on security in Europe that was due to meet in Madrid a week later. And he urged that all Soviet diplomats be instructed to state that the Soviet Union had acted completely legally in taking action against a challenge to its borders. Gromyko avoided any suggestion, however, that the United States might take some kind of military revenge. He urged a frank acknowledgment of the shoot-down and added, regretfully, that the incident would detract from various initiatives that the Andropov team had taken in arms negotiations.

Following up, Ustinov laid down the hard line that he had prepared with a briefing paper circulated previously to members. He asserted that his colleagues should consider the paper complete and accurate, thereby discouraging any critical questions, if anyone had been so bold as to ask. Ustinov asserted that the fighter pilots had acted within the Law on Borders and that the Soviet Union could not allow intruding planes free access over Soviet territory. He repeated the false information from the September 1 meeting that the plane was flying without lights, that the cabin was not illuminated, that tracer bullets had been fired. The defense minister also reported, according to the transcript, that fighter pilot Osipovich . . . "informed ground control that this was a military plane and it should be destroyed." Interestingly, Osipovich asserted in newspaper interviews in the 1990s that he realized he was following a passenger plane, not a military craft, but was convinced by ground control that it was on an espionage mission. Osipovich's statements contradicted what Ustinov told the political leadership. Furthermore, Osipovich added, he never informed ground control the plane was a Boeing, and "they never asked me."

Mikhail Gorbachev was among the more active Politburo members at this session, interrogating the two ministers a total of four times. I was struck that he asked no probing questions about what had actually happened; to do so in Soviet times would have been risky for his political future. Gorbachev went along compliantly with Ustinov's explanations that a robust defense was what was needed. In that Politburo atmosphere, the subject of an apology or reparations could hardly come up. Keeping in mind that a year and a half later he would be the supreme leader, it is notable that Gorbachev expressed no regrets but was willing to acknowledge what could not be covered up. His concern in 1983 was the bigger picture: what would this incident do to relations with the West?

It is true that Gorbachev was the most junior member of the Politburo at age fifty-two. Fellow Politburo members have commented in their memoirs that Gorbachev was often undemonstrative at meetings, at least until later in 1984, because he did not want needlessly to create enemies. The session ended with Chernenko proposing a working group drawn from the military, Foreign Ministry, and KGB to develop further material. And he stated he would inform the ailing general secretary of the discussion.

Andropov, it turned out, broke off his medical leave and returned suddenly to Moscow. He summoned Ambassador Dobrynin from a holiday on the Black Sea. The ambassador recalled that Andropov looked "haggard and worried." Dobrynin was ordered to return to Washington immediately to try to defuse the situation. Dobrynin recalled the general secretary saying, "Our military made a gross blunder in shooting down the airliner and probably it will take us a long time to get out of this mess." Andropov cursed the generals, calling them "blockheads of generals who care not for grand questions of politics. Just think of all the effort we have expended to improve them [relations with the United States] and there they are making a mess of the whole thing." Andropov arranged for the ambassador to confer with Ustinov, then returned to the Crimea to continue his vacation.

In the immediate aftermath of the shoot-down, much attention was focused on efforts to find the airliner and recover the black boxes. Within
days, a small armada of Soviet, Japanese, and U.S. ships gathered in the Sea
of Japan near the island of Moneron. The hunt was on to spot the remains
of the Boeing 747 and the two black boxes—the flight data recorder and the
cockpit voice recorder. Defense Minister Ustinov reported to the Politburo
the day before Ogarkov's September 9 press conference that some nine hundred items from the airliner had already washed ashore but that no bodies
had been recovered. Later in November, Ustinov reported to Andropov in
a top-secret memorandum that the black boxes were recovered on October
20, 1983 (in the area of 46 degrees 33 minutes north latitude, and 141 degrees
19 minutes east longitude), and transported to Moscow for decoding. He
added that, for purposes of misleading the United States, Soviet vessels
would continue searchlike operations for several more weeks.

Soviet divers, working at a depth of about five hundred feet on sandy bottom, found the remains of the fuselage scattered over a large debris field. Because visibility was limited, they could not get an overall view of the
wreckage. Wheels, engines, and part of the tail fin were spotted, but the fuselage itself had broken into small pieces, the biggest of which was reportedly
about two feet by four feet. Some human remains were spotted. One diver
discovered a headless torso still strapped in a seat. Another diver saw what
looked like a human wrist in a black glove. Others reported ghoulish sights:
a human scalp with long black hair drifting in the water, a jacket strapped in
a seat with human entrails flowing out of it. Divers gathered up many personal objects—documents, passports, paper money, ladies' handbags, pa-
perback books, tapes, teddy bears, slippers—and brought them up for
shipment to Moscow. The Soviets did not collect the small pieces or recon-
struct the fuselage, as the Americans did after the TWA 800 crash in the Atlantic in 1996. Most significantly, they found no espionage equipment in the
debris field. By November 10, 1983, the recovery operation was ended.

Meanwhile, in Moscow a group of experts began decoding the black
boxes. In a secret report to Andropov in December 1983, the defense minister reported disappointing results of the examination but reasserted that
the airliner's intrusion into Soviet territory was deliberate. He noted regretfully that the recorders provided no firsthand confirmation that KE 007
was on a spy mission. Consequently, he came out strongly against sending
the black boxes to the International Civil Aviation Organization and urged
the Soviet government to stand by its statement of September 6, 1983, laying all the blame on the United States. Ustinov also forwarded three reports
that were ambiguous enough to prompt the defense minister to warn
against turning them over to the West. They would only serve the West's

anti-Soviet campaign, he argued. And so this information remained secret until the Soviet Union collapsed.

Why was the plane off course? Was there any truth to the Soviet contention that this was an espionage flight? In the immediate aftermath of the crisis, numerous theories were put forward, including a number of conspiracy theories. Some credited the Soviet version of events that this had been a highly duplicitous action by American intelligence that had installed special reconnaissance equipment on the airliner. The International Civil Aviation Organization final report, issued in 1993, noted that on takeoff from Anchorage, the plane flew on autopilot on a constant magnetic heading of 245 degrees for five and a half hours. This apparently occurred because the Korean crew neglected to couple the autopilot to the inertial navigation system, which would have corrected the course periodically. Amazingly, the crew failed to detect the fact that the aircraft was slipping ever farther west from R-20. The ICAO uncovered no evidence of espionage. In the end, the international organization blamed the deviation on human carelessness.

Another "fact" that the Soviets argued was evidence of espionage was transmission of short bursts of coded material. The final ICAO report noted a short burst of numbers in Morse code but was not able to identify for whom it was intended. What seems clear is that Soviet officials, military and civilian, saw no reason to doubt their own espionage version. As late as August 1988, for example, then Soviet defense minister Dmitry Yazov asked U.S. defense secretary Frank Carlucci why the United States used the Korean airliner for a spy mission when U.S. spy satellites could do the job handily.

In the last months of 1983, Moscow was in no mood to clarify any further details of the incident. In top political circles, to which foreign reporters had no access, there was another preoccupation: Andropov's health. He failed to lead the November 7 revolutionary celebration from atop the Lenin Mausoleum, and his absence began spawning rumors. In December, Leonid Zamyatin, the high Communist Party spokesman, asserted that Andropov was hard at work, neglecting to say he had set up office in Kuntsevo Hospital, where he was being treated. We correspondents guessed that Andropov was very ill, but none of us knew the details. He had suffered from cardiac problems, high blood pressure, and diabetes for years. At the beginning of 1983, unknown to us, his kidneys had totally stopped functioning, and he had to submit to dialysis twice a week. Later, the chief Kremlin doctor, Yevgeny Chazov, revealed that Andropov's condition took a turn for the worse during the KAL crisis and his September break in the Crimea. One evening he went outside for a walk in the fresh air and sat own on a granite bench; he came back inside badly chilled. This led to an infection and the appearance of gangrene, requiring an invasive operation to clean out dead tissue. Chazov noted that Andropov's incision failed to heal, further complicating his health and ability to work. Andropov began intimating to Chazov that he might have to step aside. The health of a Soviet leader in those days was considered a state secret, and TASS masked the situation by claiming that Andropov had simply caught a cold.

As Moscow correspondent, I found *U.S. News and World Report* was far more interested in the future effects of the Korean airliner tragedy on U.S.-Soviet relations than on the details of the catastrophe, however intriguing they might be. In this regard, its view was similar to Gromyko's and Gorbachev's. The magazine was prepared to leave the gruesome morsels to competitors like *Time* and *Newsweek.* So I went out hunting for insights from several of my trusted sources.

Radomir Bogdanov, once KGB chief in New Delhi and subsequently deputy director of the Institute of the USA and Canada, professed to be convinced that the Reagan administration had used the Korean airliner for an espionage operation. "It may be Soviet paranoia," he told me, "but it just shows to what lengths the Reagan administration goes. It bolsters the feeling in some quarters here that the White House wants to destroy socialism as it exists in the Soviet Union today." (How right you were, Radomir!) Alexander Bovin, a former Brezhnev aide and a comparatively liberal *Izvestia* commentator, focused on the evils of superpower confrontation. "If there had been the slightest recognition that this was a passenger plane, it would not have been shot down," he insisted. "In more peaceful times," he said, "the Japanese could have telephoned Khabarovsk [the Soviet Far East air control center]. There is a direct line. They could have said, 'Hey you guys, do you know anything about this plane?' Or Khabarovsk could have called Tokyo to ask what this plane was doing. But nobody could make such a call in the current situation. No one would even think of it."

Following its analytical bent, *U.S. News* wound up the year printing major articles on Andropov and the collapse of his administration with these headlines: "The Kremlin Goes on Automatic Pilot" and "Andropov: A Year of Failure." Reflecting on the misleading, not to say false, versions that Ogarkov and Kornienko set in motion, I am reminded of Henry Shapiro's maxim that a journalist is only as good as his source. And to develop a good source, you must build up confidence with your informant over time. When a source misleads, you contribute to the transmission belt of lies. To some extent, *U.S. News* avoided those pitfalls by requiring its Moscow man to skip the grisly details and simply forecast the future. What emerged so clearly for me was that in war—cold or hot—truth dies quickly; lies and human victims follow.

Chapter 26

Blogging before Blogs

Losing touch with home base has always been a major problem for foreign correspondents. The deterioration begins slowly. You know your host country better than your editors. You see things they do not. You detect the first signs that your host government is about to fall or its economy is on the verge of collapse. The home office does not. Editors send few hints about how your file will fare in the competition for space. They rarely give you an idea what might interest readers. And, finally, they ask questions that reveal their ignorance, and you begin losing respect for them.

The view from the home office is equally dismal. Editors often see the foreign correspondent as lazy, out of touch, rarely responding fast enough to "rockets." They figure that the once trusted reporter has "gone native," enjoying the lack of close supervision. An assignment in Paris means that the correspondent is indulging in long, unproductive lunches. In Hong Kong, he is probably running a nefarious business on the side. In Russia in the 1980s, only God could tell what a correspondent's silence really meant.

To alleviate such misperceptions, I tried to vacation in August and pass through Washington to better orient my story agenda. I tried to encourage top editors to visit Moscow. A transatlantic visitor to Russia was usually received better than the resident correspondent. Using charm and vodka, Soviet officials liked to "snow" the visitor and shun the Moscow resident who probably knew too many embarrassing things. On one such visit home, Joe Fromm suggested I submit a gossip letter regularly, based on daily life in the

Soviet capital and aimed at editors. In today's Internet lingo this would be a blog, before blogs existed. Taking his advice, I titled my protoblog "Info-letter No. 1: The Joys of Returning to Russia." In it, I described the tribulations of landing in Moscow, disabled, and in need of a wheelchair.

The situation developed this way. Ruth, Miranda, Caleb, and I had spent much of August 1983 at Rye Beach, New Hampshire, not far from Pease Air Force Base where FB-111 fighter bombers were ready to launch on short notice to bomb targets in the Soviet Union. Our garage apartment, located directly under their flight path, gave out on the North Atlantic and a spacious lawn where Caleb practiced his gymnastic exercises until the eve of our departure. On that day, he sprained his ankle so badly he was reduced to hobbling on crutches. Ruth, in her usual energetic style, called British Air to request a wheelchair on arrival in Moscow to move Caleb from the plane to the arrival hall.

I was doubtful about the outcome. Despite the fact that there were many paraplegics in the Soviet Union, the industry produced only a tiny number of wheelchairs. "The only wheelchair I've ever seen in Russia," I wrote in "Info-letter No. 1," "was the one Leo Tolstoy used, and that's located at Yasnaya Polyana, 120 miles from Moscow. It's simply useless to expect a wheelchair in Moscow."

Sure enough, on arrival twelve hours after leaving Boston, there was no wheelchair at the Moscow International Airport. Instead, a burly Russian, speaking excellent English, carried Caleb, kicking and screaming, out of the jetliner and into a broken-down ambulance that trundled all of us to the airport medical center. There a grandmotherly doctor examined Caleb's ankle, plied him with solicitude, and wrote a report that apparently cleared the Soviet side of any wrongdoing. The incident reinforced my belief that the centralized Soviet system was incapable of catering adequately to the needs of a multimillion population. The lack of wheelchairs was yet another example of the "rot" that I noticed in my first years in Moscow.

For anyone who lived permanently in the Soviet Union, it was paradoxical that this nation was in such a mess. This was a country extending over one-seventh of the planet, with enormous natural resources, and a population greater than the United States. I often thought that if every nation has a cadre of talented people—say, 1 percent of its population—the Soviet Union could boast no fewer than 2.7 million very talented individuals. They had the potential of driving the nation forward in remarkable ways if only they could be sprung from their box. But they were blocked, their initiative destroyed. The situation was summed up for me by a cartoon in the humor magazine *Krokodil* in 1985. The first panel pictured an inventor full of enthusiasm presenting plans for a new invention. Subsequent panels showed the inventor aging as the invention progressed through an interminable approval process. The final panel showed the inventor with a long, white beard when the product finally came off the production line. Japan, by contrast, officials confided to me, could move from research to production in eighteen months.

We used to joke that to engage in failing welfare programs in health, education, housing, and transportation—as the Kremlin had since the late 1920s—you had to be rich and would become poor. Loyal Soviet intellectuals countered that the Western capitalist system had matured over hundreds of years and that Soviet communism would need no less. Foreign Minister Andrey Gromyko struck a delusional note, I thought, in responding to President Reagan's charge that Russia was an evil empire. He asserted proudly at a press conference, "Never have the stars shone more brightly on the Soviet Union than they do today!" On the whole, I think Prime Minister Margaret Thatcher came closer to the truth when she described the Soviet Union as "Upper Volta with missiles."

The unending missile buildup was one of the hottest issues between the United States and the Soviet Union and a perfect subject for my "Info-letters." The United States began deploying medium-range Pershing II missiles in Western Europe in the late fall of 1983. The Kremlin objected strenuously to this move, conceived to counter the rapid buildup of Soviet SS-20 medium-range missiles targeted on Western Europe. Despite Andropov's proposal to the United States on coming to power, productive talks never got started, in large part because of the Korean Airlines problem and the bad feelings that it engendered. In the absence of negotiations, the Kremlin propaganda machine rolled into action and week after week trumpeted alarms about the present danger.

Warnings about possible conflict with the United States, I speculated at the time, might have been coordinated with Andropov's discipline campaign to make the nation's workers bear down and put in a full day's work for patriotic reasons. Eventually, the population started to become nervous and frightened. To defuse these side effects, Defense Minister Dmitry Ustinov declared in a speech in December 1983 that the Communist Party knew what it was doing and that the times were in no way comparable to the Second World War when the nation stood at the abyss of collapse.

I brought this to the attention of my editors in "Info-letter No. 7" of December 23, 1983, titled "War and Peace in 1984." It was written around a conversation with a construction engineer I met at the Novo-Voronezh nuclear power station. Sasha Konoplyov called me when he came to Moscow on a visit, and Ruth and I invited him for a meal. "What is going to happen?" Sasha asked plaintively. "For the first time, I have the uneasy feeling that war is going to break out." I launched into a long description of the Soviet military buildup that worried the Reagan administration, the nature of Soviet strategic missiles targeted on the United States, as well as the steady deployments of Soviet SS-20 missiles in the western Soviet Union. Sasha was unaware of these facts since Soviet media only gave details of American threats. At the end of my explanation, Sasha seemed relieved. "I feel better," he said. "In any case, I do believe that neither you, nor we, will start a nuclear war. We don't want to commit suicide, do we?" It was easy to agree with Sasha's conclusion.

In the last months of 1983, the Kremlin remained outwardly truculent. In top political circles, to which foreign reporters had no access, there was growing preoccupation with Andropov's health. He had not been seen in public since August, before the KAL shoot-down. On November 29, I had sent Washington "Info-letter No. 6" called "Andropov." What would happen if Andropov died in the near future? I supplied this answer: "Most Soviet and Western observers believe that Defense Minister Dmitry Ustinov would step in to hold the country together. He is the strong man behind the scenes in the Politburo, says one well-informed Soviet source."

During December, we correspondents queried in every way we could the nature of Andropov's illness. I called Bovin on December 28, and he told me he had spoken to Andropov by telephone a few days before. Bovin acknowledged Andropov was being treated in the Kremlin hospital but added that his condition was considered a state secret. A few days later my Danish colleague Samuel Rakhlin, who spoke excellent Russian because he was brought up in Siberia as a child, paid a call on Bovin. This time, without prompting, Bovin showed him a New Year's card from Andropov. "It looks like it was signed by a machine," Rakhlin responded. Bovin countered, "Let's call up Andropov on the *vertushka* [the Kremlin switchboard phone]." The ploy collapsed when a military aide responded, "Comrade Andropov is not available right now." In mid-January 1984, Mike Wallace of CBS had a similar experience when he visited Viktor Afanasyev, chief editor of *Pravda*. The editor offered to call Andropov to satisfy Wallace's curiosity, but then looked at his watch and said, "Oh, no. He won't be available at this time."

Possibly to put an end to these entreaties, Kremlin spin doctor Leonid Zamyatin asserted at a press conference that Andropov was hard at work, fully engaged in the nation's business. Despite the uncertainty of Andropov's situation in December 1983, the days passed at their usual glacial pace, moving slowly over rough terrain, throwing up an occasional rock that we journalists would desperately seize upon. In January 1984, *U.S. News and World Report* reprinted a very astute, humorous cartoon that pictured a pen, unattached to any human arm, mysteriously scrawling out orders all by itself on Andropov's desk. A waiting aide, catching a directive flying toward him, asked, "Will there be anything more, sir?"

My editors began asking me about Andropov's successors. Might Marshal Ogarkov lead a coup to replace the feeble gerontocracy? I suspect their thinking was influenced by General Wojciech Jaruzelski's example of imposing military rule in Poland in December 1981 to prevent a Soviet intervention. I ruled out the possibility. In past decades, the party leadership had dealt harshly with any evidence of military conspiracy. Its system of political control, emanating from the top, reached all levels of the military and the political commissars reported quickly to the Kremlin.

Of possible political contenders, I identified Vitaly Vorotnikov, fifty-eight, recently Soviet ambassador to Cuba; Gaidar Aliyev, sixty, party chief in Azerbaijan; and Mikhail Gorbachev, fifty-two. I gave little thought to Konstantin Chernenko, seventy-two, who held the number-two position in the Communist Party under both Andropov and Brezhnev. My view of Chernenko was frankly negative since former Defense Secretary Harold Brown described him to me following the 1979 summit conference in Vienna as little more than "a cipher."

At the beginning of February, I filed several pieces on the major personnel changes that Andropov had effected during fifteen months in office. I noted that he had named twenty-six ministers and deputy ministers in the government apparatus, appointed thirty new ambassadors, and selected nine new heads of twenty-three departments of the Central Committee bureaucracy. In the 158 jurisdictions of the entire Soviet Union, he succeeded in replacing 20 percent of local Communist leaders with new secretaries of his liking. This was a blow at the lackluster individuals Brezhnev had raised to positions of power. The average age of the Brezhnev Politburo had been fifty-eight when he came to power, but was seventy when he died, compared to an average Politburo age of forty-three under Lenin and fifty-eight under Stalin. "Even if he dies or abandons politics," I concluded, "Communist chief Yuri Andropov will have shaken up Russia's governing apparatus in a way not seen in 20 years."

Still seeking more on Andropov's health, I called on Valentin Falin, a diplomat, historian, and journalist. Fluent in German, Falin served with great distinction in Bonn as Soviet ambassador from 1971 to 1978. However, he developed friction with Foreign Minister Gromyko. Rumor held that Falin might become a rival to Gromyko for the top diplomatic job, and he was transferred back to Moscow to join the International Department of the Central Committee. When Andropov came to power, Falin was offered the job of running Soviet national television but declined because he resisted administrative responsibilities. Instead, he took a sweetheart job with the government newspaper, *Izvestia,* in 1983, where his only obligation was to write one major article a month. During that period, he completed his doctoral dissertation and became available for occasional meetings with foreign correspondents. There was a hidden side to this erudite intellectual, too. His wife's son (by a former marriage) traveled abroad to Austria and refused to return to Moscow. Since such family disloyalty could affect a political career, Falin reportedly divorced his wife and entered a fictitious marriage with his secretary.

This tall, angular man with disheveled hair seemed in a gloomy mood when I called on him on February 8, 1984. On U.S.-Soviet relations, he was downright pessimistic. He asserted one of the things that worried the Kremlin was that U.S. submarine commanders were authorized to launch nuclear-tipped missiles without presidential authorization if communications with the White House broke down in times of conflict. Falin told me he had raised this issue on one occasion with former U.S. defense secretary Robert McNamara, who did not know if this assertion was true but promised to look into the matter. He never reported back to my interlocutor. Falin continued, "It's very difficult to start up the détente process again for a second time. It's like a broken decanter. You can try to put the pieces back together, but it will never be quite right."

Toward the end of our interview, I steered the conversation casually to my main reason for our meeting. Falin was unusually frank, possibly because he felt totally confident in his position, possibly because we were speaking in Russian. Falin admired Andropov very much. He described the leader's hospital quarters and visits that Politburo members were regularly making to him. In a sad tone of voice, he talked about the general secretary's qualities: his broad vision, his desire for productive negotiations with the United States, his interest in the arts, music, theater. The next day, I wrote to Joe Fromm, describing the meeting and suggesting he make a visit to Moscow. "I got the impression," I said of Falin, "that he thought Andropov would be out of it all together in the not too distant future."

Twenty-four hours later, on February 9, Soviet radio interrupted its programs after eight in the evening and began broadcasting Schubert's Unfinished Symphony and other solemn music. That was a heads-up to the nation. I messaged foreign editor Hansen, saying, "Hope your Andropov advancers are close at hand. Stop this may be a false alarm rpt this may be a false alarm, but Moscow radio programs are playing somber music suggesting an important personality has died. Will keep you informed."

The next day, I slipped out of the office for the Byelorussian railroad station to meet one of Miranda's college friends, Miller Tobin, son of a Protestant minister from Massachusetts, who was arriving from Warsaw on his way to China. Greeting Miller, I said, "Welcome to Moscow, you're just in time for a big funeral!" He gasped as I explained and whisked him off to a downtown office to buy a ticket for Beijing. The official death announcement began reverberating from the public radio as we entered the ticket office, but work continued in its usual confusing, smoke-filled way. The only thing that visibly disturbed the routine was my guest's outlandish appearance for those days in Russia—in one ear, he wore a diamond, an incomprehensible adornment for a man.

I learned later that Andropov expired on February 9, the day after I met with Falin. Such deaths were routinely announced with a delay, sometimes as much as twenty-four hours, supposedly because a Russian custom held that a day should pass to make sure the deceased did not come back to life. The twelve-member Politburo began meeting immediately and held sessions again on February 10, 11, and 12. The drawn-out gatherings indicated disagreements. Finally, official media announced that seventy-two-year-old Chernenko had been elected general secretary, and that Gorbachev was named his number two. I was flabbergasted that the Soviet Union, so in need of strong, imaginative leadership, had settled on another sick man to lead the sick nation. Shortly, I ran off to one of my most secret sources for an explanation.

I kept my notes from this source whom I usually called the "Airport Sage." The code name was derived from that section of Moscow where he lived, not far from the airport. I did not want to make it easy for the security police, should they ever secretly search papers in my apartment or office. My friend was a Marxist of liberal bent; in West European parliamentary terms he would probably be called a Social Democrat. He started life as a teacher, but later became a dissident historian who published well-respected books in the West. He employed a number of researchers and had valuable connections in top political circles. My informant believed that the Soviet Union had provided the population with a stable, if inefficient, economy, by no means detested by the people, powerful on the world scene, and not in need of any major structural reforms. What my friend did argue for was greater freedom of expression and inner-party democracy.

The Kremlin came to view my Sage as dangerous and ordered that he be kept under strict surveillance. The KGB, accordingly, established a post with a telephone on the stair landing just below his apartment and manned it twenty-four hours a day for several years to note the comings and goings. The Sage was philosophical about this. He recalled that after Czar Alexander II was assassinated in St. Petersburg in 1881, the police established a guard post in the Summer Gardens to spot suspicious gatherings and maintained the structure right up to the Second World War. Eventually, the Sage felt sorry for his guards and arranged for a light to be installed in the stairwell so they could read and play chess. Since no one was allowed to visit him (not even his researchers), he would take the metro into town to meet individually with me at our apartment. He had relations with several other Western journalists, too, which afforded him some protection against arbitrary arrest. If he disappeared, I and others would be sure to write about him.

What he explained to me on February 20, 1983, was that the Politburo members wanted to reach a unanimous consensus but had trouble achieving it. Their desire for unanimity was dictated by the wish to avoid any conflict in the ensuing Central Committee meeting, which was required to ratify their choice. There were four serious candidates, the Sage said. A major contender was Dmitry Ustinov, the defense minister, a full member of the Politburo. He had an awesome reputation, having headed the Soviet Union's defense industry during World War II while in his midthirties and involved in defense issues for many years. He had canceled a planned trip to New Delhi on February 4, citing "domestic preoccupations" to his Indian hosts. When the crucial voting started, he took himself out of the race, apparently because he professed he was old and tired. He died in December 1984, just a few months before Chernenko did.

Another strong candidate was Grigory Romanov, sixty, the Leningrad Communist Party chief. Romanov had supported Andropov when he was elected general secretary after Brezhnev. He was not well liked by his colleagues, who despised him for the scandals he had been involved in. Reportedly, he had requisitioned a china service belonging to Catherine the Great for his daughter's wedding in the 1970s, and a number of pieces had been carelessly broken during the celebration.

That left Gaidar Aliyev, sixty, a close supporter of Brezhnev, and the fifty-two-year-old Mikhail Gorbachev. Aliyev was formerly party and police chief in Azerbaijan. Later he declared himself a Muslim and made a pilgrimage to Mecca after the Soviet Union collapsed. In the 1920s, such a candidate might have made it to the top, the Sage explained, when internationalism was the byword of the Bolsheviks. Stalin, after all, was a Georgian who spoke Russian with a heavy accent. But in the late twentieth century, Russian nationalism was swelling, as many Russians complained that the country was giving too much aid to African nations and short-changing itself. Gorbachev was the only other viable candidate. Gorbachev had made a hit in the West when he visited Canada in 1983 and was gaining a reputation as an energetic operative. This alarmed the "elders" of the Politburo, who were afraid of losing their cushy jobs if a young reformer took over. The Sage asserted that only three members of that elite policy group of twelve supported Gorbachev.

Why, then, Chernenko? He was a modest man, solicitous of his colleagues, with extensive knowledge of the Communist Party. In internal affairs, he knew all the "go-to" apparatchiks. He had been close to Brezhnev, visited the United States with him in 1973, and participated in the 1979 Vienna summit, but otherwise he had little experience in foreign affairs. His health was poor. In 1983 he was hospitalized for several months with breathing problems brought on by emphysema. The chief Kremlin doctor, Yevgeny Chazov, reported to the Politburo before the succession crisis that Chernenko would probably not be able to maintain his position for long. His personal aide, Viktor Pribytkov, has stated that Chernenko never sought the top post. His physical disabilities became all too obvious on November 7, 1984, when he led the revolutionary day ceremonies from atop the Lenin Mausoleum. On that chilly occasion he could not hold his right hand in salute as the troops marched by, and had so much difficulty breathing he had trouble voicing the traditional holiday speech. In early 1985, I shipped off "Info-letter No. 17," focusing again on the failing health of the latest Kremlin top leader.

The trouble the Kremlin leaders had in selecting a new chief inevitably compounded the complex problems the Soviet Union was facing in 1983. Was the nation stumbling toward collapse? This possibility had been raised as early as 1970 by Soviet dissident Andrey Amalrik, who predicted the disintegration of the USSR by 1984 from internal weaknesses and pressures from Communist China. In December 1980, as I have noted, our magazine suggested the world was seeing the last days of communism, from Cuba to Russia, Eastern Europe, and China.

In Moscow, I gave thought to the Soviet Union's future. But I concluded that the Soviet system, for all its faults, was essentially stable. Living in Russia you got used to the scarcities and learned the ingenious ways the population got around them. The Soviet Union was like a cracked dinosaur egg that, for the moment, was withstanding pressures from the outside world. I thought to myself that the shell might one day crumble under one of two conditions: if a total economic collapse occurred or if a nuclear exchange with the United States reduced its industrial potential to rubble. Then everything would have to be rebuilt.

Oddly, I never put such ruminations in any of my "Info-letters" to Washington. Even though it was 1984—a year that George Orwell had made famous—I never proposed a follow-up to Amalrik's book *Will the Soviet Union Survive until 1984?* Nor did I suggest a second look at our 1980 "Twilight of Communism?" story. And ideas of a Soviet collapse never issued from my editors. It's hard to explain why we were so blinded. American Sovietologists and the CIA were not forecasting catastrophe. In my case, I had no access to the most classified Soviet economic data that might have indicated otherwise. Soviet reality had become my reality, and I was too busy vaulting the hurdles of daily life to imagine the dramatic upheavals of the future. A year later, however, the alarms were clanging in our ears.

Chapter 27

Dangerous Favors

Covering the news in Moscow in the 1980s had evolved considerably since the 1960s. The press department of the Foreign Ministry no longer sought to control contacts between news sources and foreign journalists. The ministry and other government departments put on press conferences that could be described as oral versions of TASS announcements but with the additional element of questions and answers. In 1981, journalists relied far less on newspapers and journals for news than two decades before. Contacts with the U.S. Embassy were no longer as important as before, although journalists were still willing to trade gossip and do a favor—sometimes even a dangerous favor—for an official friend.

In this healthier atmosphere, I met a scientist who would become my *tainyi sovietnik* (secret counselor) as I tried to understand the workings of the Soviet system over the five and a half years of my Moscow assignment. He was Dr. David Moiseyevich Goldfarb, a well-known Moscow geneticist who had fallen out of favor with the authorities because he had made the fateful decision to emigrate. In the minds of many, emigration was treason.

Ruth and I met David Moiseyevich under unusual circumstances. On the afternoon of April 20, 1981—the day I was to fly from Washington to Moscow—I received a telephone call from a Russian biologist who had emigrated to the United States several years before and was working in a laboratory at Columbia University. A mutual friend had tipped him off that I was about to leave for Russia on a journalistic assignment. I tried to put him off since I had only an hour before leaving for Dulles Airport. However, Alex Goldfarb pressed so insistently that I agreed to meet him for only five minutes on our front porch. He quickly explained to me who his father was and urged me to call on his parents. Giving me their telephone number and a box of chocolates, he added, "I think my father would be very useful to you."

Some weeks later in Moscow, I did call on the elder Goldfarb at 44 Vavilov Street, an Academy of Sciences compound. Thus began a long friendship. David Moiseyevich, as I called him, using the polite Russian form of address, was unlike any Soviet citizen I had met during my first Moscow assignment. He was highly educated, well respected in the Moscow scientific community. He had developed a screening test called the Goldfarb Method to identify ten childhood diseases. His fame was such that the Weizman Institute in Israel had offered him a position anytime he could take it up. Furthermore, he was a reflective man, possibly because he was well aware of the frailty of human life: he had lost a leg at the Battle of Stalingrad in 1942. When I first walked into his apartment, he seemed in his early sixties, of medium height with a roundish face, lined around the mouth, black eyebrows, silver hair brushed straight back over his head. He set me at ease immediately as he pushed his crutches aside and plopped down at the kitchen table.

As I got to know David Moiseyevich, he agreed to tape a series of interviews with Ruth and me. He had been born into a liberal Jewish family at Zhitomir, in the Ukraine, in 1921. "My mother," he told me, "finished a special thirteen-year class gymnasium before the revolution. She finished with a gold medal and won the right to teach Russian in Russian schools even though she was not a Christian. My father was one of ten children who came from a nonreligious Jewish family. This was a family of doctors, biologists, and engineers."

David Moiseyevich was brought by his father to Moscow as a small child to escape the Ukraine famine of 1921–1922. "I was sent to a school organized by the company of Isadora Duncan, the American dancer. Between six and seven, I studied ballet, but my ballet career ended when my mother came to Moscow," he recounted. As a schoolboy he showed good abilities in mathematics and physics, but was more attracted to Russia's past. When Moscow State University accepted him in 1936, he decided to study history. Those were troubled years preceding Stalin's Great Terror of 1937. David Moiseyevich recalled verbatim the warning given by one eminent professor who had been educated before the revolution of 1917: "You, who were only children yesterday, have chosen a very dubious road. It is dubious because you must always remember what can be said and what cannot. You must remember that whatever your interpretation is today, it may be the opposite tomorrow."

This introduction to the double life—what can be said publicly and what can be said only around the kitchen table—caused David Moiseyevich to transfer into medicine. "You could say it was something of a crash landing because I was inclined to the humanities, particularly ancient history, Novgorod, Ivan Kalita." Goldfarb finished medical school in July 1941, just weeks after Hitler attacked the Soviet Union. He was assigned as a junior doctor on the western front, then transferred in August 1942 to Stalingrad, scene of the Russian triumph over the German forces commanded by Field Marshal Friedrich von Paulus. On December 16, 1942, as Goldfarb was evacuating the wounded, he was hit in the leg and developed gaseous gangrene. His left leg was amputated.

I would go happily to David Moiseyevich's kitchen table whenever I had a question needing explanation. During good weather, Ruth and I would travel to his country dacha on the electric train to spend the day with him, his wife, Iliya (who had been a nurse at Stalingrad), and their daughter, Olga, a pediatrician. We would talk about the peculiarities of Soviet life, and David Moiseyevich would help me understand context and attitudes. He never passed on any information to me that could be ranked as "news," with one notable exception: he disclosed that one of the Soviet Union's top biologists, Dr. Yuri Ovchinnikov, was engaged in developing biological weapons at a laboratory deep in Siberia in defiance of the 1975 Convention on Biological Weapons.

One of the hazards of working in the more open Moscow was the danger of entrapment. The KGB kept files on correspondents and worked hard at collecting incriminating reports of rowdy behavior, drunkenness, womanizing—anything that could be used later to denounce a reporter in the press or expel him. One trick frequently used was to send an agent, usually a Russian journalist, to ingratiate himself (or herself) with the foreigner. This "friend" would develop a relation of confidence over time and would be in a position to pass on sensitive or secret information to be used later in springing a trap.

The KGB also employed extensive bugging techniques against journalists and diplomats. They bugged apartments and bedrooms. Correspondents and diplomats were relatively easy to trace when they got into their cars; diplomats had red plates, journalists, yellow ones. KGB operatives were capable of placing devices on cars to track their movements around town. If necessary, the KGB could bug theater seats or restaurant tables. Even going out for a walk was not an entirely safe way to talk to special sources. An innocent-looking person across the street carrying a shopping bag could actually be monitoring your conversations. In Moscow the KGB had built up a large network of informers: chauffeurs, maids, secretaries, translators, "sources" who could report on the strengths and weaknesses of a correspondent: his political opinions, drinking habits, relations with colleagues, embassy friends, relations with his wife, sexual dalliances, and so forth. If the correspondent did develop a truly clean relationship with a Soviet citizen, that citizen could be pressured to become an informer on pain of "unpleasant consequences."

Like other correspondents, I had never received any security briefing from my editors before going to Moscow. I doubt that they thought about such things. You learned as you went along, and made an effort to avoid foolish actions like changing money on the black market or keeping suspicious-looking items in your office, like CIA-produced maps that were freely available in the United States. We correspondents should probably have been more attentive, because Article 65 on espionage in the Russian Republic Criminal Code was extremely broad. This crime was described in a single paragraph of forty-eight words stating that collecting state or military secrets, or material detrimental to the USSR, and transmitting it to a foreign government constituted espionage. By that standard, every correspondent in Moscow could be charged with espionage at will. Correspondents and diplomats frequently exchanged information and gossip. Bob Gillette of the *Los Angeles Times,* for example, gave the embassy a Soviet doctoral dissertation with classified information on the economy that fell into his hands. Dusko Doder of the *Washington Post* passed on the classified "Novosibirsk Report" on problems in the Russian economy to a CIA acquaintance in the embassy. And I gave Dr. Goldfarb's tip on biological weapons to a personal friend, Warren Zimmerman, the deputy chief of the U.S. Embassy. Were such favors espionage? Any Soviet prosecutor would have had no trouble accusing us of "impermissible activities" if asked to do so by the political authorities.

The year 1984 turned out to be a bumper year for provocations against me—like the incident at the *banya.* The *banya,* or sauna, is a favorite Russian pastime. It consists of a hot room, the *parrilka* with raised benches, heated to temperatures as high as 230 degrees Fahrenheit. After some ten to fifteen minutes, your arteries and veins expand, your pores open, and you shed the grime of the last week. Next you jump into a pool of cold water for a bracing shock that is supposed to make your blood vessels contract. After an hour or so of these exercises, reputed to be very healthy, you sit down to caviar and salty fish washed down with tea or beer. Such occasions make for uninhibited conversation.

In early 1984, I joined a group of Russian friends who rented a deluxe sauna every Saturday night. Some of these acquaintances were "refuseniks"—

people who sought to emigrate but had been denied permission; the others were friends of refuseniks but still in good standing in Soviet society. This was a useful mix for a correspondent. The refuseniks occasionally disclosed sensitive information; their friends often provided interesting, unofficial views of current events. I was alerted to trouble when one "friend" disclosed he had been summoned to the KGB and told, "Get close to Daniloff." On another occasion, a new member of the group took me aside and revealed that he had worked in an engineering institute beyond the Urals that was developing guidance systems for submarine-launched missiles. This was an obvious "dangle," but I did not bite. I informed my closest friends, and they decided to exclude all nonrefuseniks.

Later that April, I learned that David Moiseyevich had finally won permission to emigrate from the Soviet Union. I was delighted for him, and went over to his apartment on April 8 to say my good-byes. At our meeting, the scientist presented me with a book on the civil war that followed the revolution of 1917. I left with the book in a briefcase he loaned me.

Four days later, I received a mysterious telephone call from an unknown woman, saying, "Your friend Dr. Goldfarb has suffered a heart attack. He is in serious condition, but under no circumstances should you visit him." She hung up before I had a chance to ask any questions.

Two days later, Goldfarb's son-in-law called me with more details. It turns out that shortly after my visit, the KGB had summoned Goldfarb and accused him of trying to smuggle controlled biological strains out of the country with my help. KGB colonel Viktor Gusev confronted him with photographs of my coming to visit, empty-handed, and leaving with the briefcase. The colonel then announced that the KGB had revoked his exit visa. Goldfarb told me later that he replied to the colonel, "I'm an old one-legged Jew, and it's no use threatening me. Whether I go to Israel doesn't make much difference. I don't have long to live anyway."

The KGB colonel warned, "David Moiseyevich, don't underestimate our organization. We have always respected you for your contributions to the nation and have allowed you considerable latitude. But I must tell you now, it is a shame you have been selling your possessions. You will be leaving Moscow soon, all right, but you'll be going east, not west." Then the colonel, accompanied by nine other KGB men, left with Goldfarb to search his apartment. During the search, the colonel demanded that David Moiseyevich call me to the flat, but my friend refused. It was during the search that I received the anonymous warning to stay away.

My editors in Washington, knowing nothing of these events (I did not write about them in my "Info-letters"), asked me in the fall of 1984 to prepare a major story on the role of the KGB in Soviet life. I was not happy about this assignment because I knew it would bring me more KGB attention. Nevertheless, I went along with it. What was I do to, refuse and be accused by Washington of being a timid reporter? So I began interviewing people who had unpleasant contacts with the secret police. One morning when I went down to the inner courtyard to start the office Volvo, I came across a tall, unkempt young man standing near my car. He quickly engaged me in conversation. He said he was the nephew of Stanislav Levchenko, a KGB major who had defected in Tokyo in 1979. I guess that the KGB had gotten wind of my research and put this young man in my path, hoping I would develop a relationship with him. Levchenko's nephew went on to say he wanted to emigrate, but the KGB would not allow it and, instead, confined him on occasion in psychiatric hospitals. From his ramblings, I concluded that the nephew was either crazy or a KGB plant, and possibly both. I had heard of cases where the secret police had taken advantage of mentally unstable individuals to make contact with Westerners for their devious purposes. The nephew soon became a pest, making his way to our apartment on several occasions and demanding help. Finally, I told him in no uncertain terms to go away. He turned to me pathetically and declared that if I would not help him, he would slit his wrists. That was the last I saw of him.

An even more curious event occurred toward the end of the year as Ruth and I were planning a Stateside trip to find a boarding school for Caleb. On December 10, 1984, I got a phone call from someone who said he wanted to talk about the growing interest among young Russians in religion. The rebirth of religion was always an interesting subject in a nation whose government proclaimed itself to be militantly atheistic. However, in this case I tried to put off my caller by suggesting he contact me a week later. Seven days later, sure enough, he called again, and I reluctantly invited him to my office. Such invitations usually discouraged unknowns since they were convinced Western offices were bugged and they would be identified as dissidents. This caller turned out to be an attractive young man, dressed in jeans and a parka. He introduced himself as Father Roman Potemkin of the Association of Russian Orthodox Youth, a group I had never heard of.

As our conversation got rolling, I suggested we go out for a walk in nearby Lenin Hills. "How did you get my telephone number?" I asked. "I was looking for a foreign correspondent to talk to," he replied. "I wanted to talk about church affairs and the interest among young people in the church. I had a friend who referred me to a secretary in the Press Department of the Foreign Ministry. She said that you knew Russian and were a good guy."

His explanation immediately raised an alarm flag for me. Was he trying to flatter me, to soften me up? To say he called a secretary in the Foreign

Ministry I thought doubtful. As we walked on, he launched into the use by the Soviet authorities of psychiatric clinics to confine dissidents. This was another hot topic in the West and the opening to a possible news story. He mentioned a hospital at Belyie Stolby on the outskirts of Moscow, where, he said, patients were being used as guinea pigs.

Roman said that he worked as a deacon and often filled in for sick deacons in churches on the periphery of the capital. He started reeling off examples of how the Soviet government was increasing antireligious propaganda. Much of what he told me about the role of Orthodox priests, the health of Patriarch Pimen, and the future of the Danilovsky Monastery seemed credible.

At one point, I interrupted to ask how he came to religion. He revealed that he had always been interested in icons and kept a few at home. He had been arrested by the KGB and accused of illegal trade. This resulted in a two-year prison sentence in a labor camp cutting timber in the northern province of Komi. Later, he said, he was allowed to work in the camp office because the administration recognized his mental abilities. That revelation really put me on edge. Essentially, he had collaborated with the prison authorities.

In parting, he asked me if I could help put him in touch with other Western newsmen, and I obliged by giving him a copy of *Information Moscow,* a privately printed directory of useful Moscow telephone numbers.

A month later, on January 22, 1985, Roman telephoned again, this time to say he was sending me some information on Russian Orthodox youth. Two days later I retrieved from the large yellow mailbox on my office door an envelope addressed to me that I presumed came from Roman. Ruth and I opened the letter in our kitchen. Inside the envelope was a second one addressed to Ambassador Arthur Hartman, but nothing about Orthodox youth. I immediately suspected something amiss and, dismissing thoughts about privacy of correspondence, opened the second envelope. Inside was a third envelope, addressed in Russian "To Mr. Casey," meaning William Casey, director of the Central Intelligence Agency. Concerned, I opened this third envelope, which contained a letter of some six or seven pages, written by fountain pen in a very small hand. I had difficulty reading it, although I did identify the word *raketa,* meaning "missile" or "rocket." This discovery put both Ruth and me in immediate danger.

The worst thing, I judged, was to keep this unwanted letter in our apartment. Apartments of Moscow correspondents could be searched without notice by spy catchers at any time. For the letter to be found in our apartment, even though I had not solicited its arrival, would be highly incriminating; it would certainly make me look like a spy. The letter had to disappear literally within minutes. But what to do? Should I burn it? Some-

thing within me rejected the burn option. Take the letter to the Foreign Ministry and complain that I was being set up by the KGB? I rejected that option because the letter might contain information valuable to U.S. national
security. By taking it to the ministry, I might cause a dissident scientist to be
arrested and executed. I really disliked that choice. I recalled the conversation many years before with the FBI agent in Washington who wanted my
cooperation in monitoring Soviet diplomats. On that occasion I said I would
be helpful if I spotted some item of national security value. Now it was hard
to suppress a patriotic instinct. If the letter did contain valuable information
or even if it was just the rantings of a crank, the embassy would be in a better position to assess its worth. Within a half hour, we drove to the embassy.
I gave the letter to Ray Benson, the chief cultural affairs officer, and we both
examined it. Benson, who had long experience in Yugoslavia and Russia,
was no better in judging its contents. In leaving it with him, I asked that
Ruth and I be dissociated from any further involvement.

In March 1985, I got a call from Curt Kamman, the number-two man at
the U.S. Embassy, who asked me to drop by. When I arrived, he led me to
the "Bubble," a specially constructed room-within-a-room that could not
be penetrated by Soviet monitoring devices. We sat down at an oblong
table, and Kamman turned on the air conditioner. He asked me to repeat all
I knew about Roman. As I began, the door suddenly opened, and a man in
his early sixties, with a heavily lined face, entered. Kamman introduced me
to this official who, like me, was of Russian heritage. His name was Murat
Natirboff, whose family fled the North Caucasus during the Russian civil
war in the 1920s. I remember seeing Natirboff's name in an embassy directory, where he was listed as a counselor for regional affairs. I guessed his
specialty was the war in Afghanistan.

In an obvious appeal to patriotism, Natirboff said that the letter that I had
brought to the embassy was of great interest to the United States. I was
guessing now that Natirboff was CIA. "An American journalist brought out
a previous communication in his baggage when he left," Natirboff disclosed. "This letter seems to be written by the same person as the letter you
brought to the embassy, and we would like to reestablish contact with the
writer."

I was shocked by Natirboff's assertion that an American colleague had
taken out secrets from a mysterious source. I immediately jumped to the conclusion that the journalist must have been Robert Toth of the *Los Angeles
Times*, although I subsequently learned I was quite wrong about that. Toth
came to mind because he had written numerous well-researched articles on
Russian science. At one point in his Moscow career in the late 1970s, Toth had
received a letter from Colonel Robert Watters, a former U.S. defense attaché

working next for the Defense Intelligence Agency in Washington. In his letter, Watters said the DIA chief praised Toth's reporting and urged DIA analysts to study his articles carefully. He also suggested the DIA was interested in a number of subjects for possible elaboration. Toth had carelessly left this letter in his office, where his Russian staff noticed it and reported it to the KGB. When Jewish dissident Anatolii Shcharansky was arrested for alleged ties to the CIA in June 1977, Toth was summoned for interrogation as a witness. This became a big story in the American press because for a while there was a question whether Toth would be charged with espionage as a coconspirator. In the end, however, he was cleared.

Natirboff questioned me next about Roman, his telephone number, and any identifying marks I could supply. Having covered the Church committee's hearings in Washington on the CIA in the mid-1970s, I was well aware that there was no need for me to cooperate because the agency had been banned from using mainstream journalists. But I did give Natirboff the details about Roman, hoping that this would be my last favor.

Much later, I learned to my astonishment why Natirboff had been so interested in Roman Potemkin. It turns out that in the 1970s and early 1980s, several well-placed Soviet scientists volunteered to spy for the United States. What their motivations were, I never found out for sure, but keeping the United States up to date as a military and political counterweight to the Soviet Union could have been the reason. These scientist-spies made contact with the CIA station in Moscow by dropping material "over the transom"—leaving envelopes containing secret information in unlocked embassy cars near the chancery or getting them into the hands of American correspondents. Adolf G. Tolkachov, an electronics expert at a Moscow aviation institute, dropped packages in four cars in 1978 before the CIA station took steps to contact him. Tolkachov's information turned out to be vastly important, revealing weak spots in Soviet avionics that helped the United States develop its "stealth" technology and save hundreds of millions of dollars at the same time.

In the case of my mysterious letter, the author (or possibly a trusted friend of the author) actually managed to enter the office of a correspondent in the early 1980s. It was unusual for a Soviet citizen to slip by security at foreigners' compounds, but it did occasionally happen. The unknown person, in a highly agitated state, pressed the correspondent to accept a small package. "Get this to the CIA!" he demanded, grabbing the correspondent by the lapels. My colleague pushed the unwanted visitor out of his office, shouting negative comments after him for the benefit of microphones in the walls. The correspondent told me later that he could not make heads or tails out of the information he had been handed and pleaded with me never to identify him. I learned later that the package he received consisted of a spiral notebook, measuring about six by eight inches, crammed with some 250 pages of writing in a minuscule hand. Its pages contained diagrams with arcs that appeared to be trajectories of nuclear warheads.

On return home, the correspondent turned the notebook over to one of his editors, who transmitted it to a high official of the CIA. The Office of Scientific and Weapons Research at the CIA compared the writing in the notebook to that in the seven-page letter that I had delivered to the embassy and concluded it was written by the same hand. The notebook provided detailed information on Soviet nuclear warheads. The experts believed the level of detail was such that the information was genuine, not a KGB provocation. However, there were a few blank spots that begged for additional information. So when the dissident scientist reappeared after years of silence, the CIA asked the Moscow station to make contact with the scientist if ever the opportunity arose.

On April 5, Roman called once again. This time he said that the "March 26 meeting" had gone badly because "your guys" contacted the wrong person. I had no idea what he was talking about, but I suspected the worst. A week later I ran into Curt Kamman at Ambassador Hartman's residence of Spaso House when I went there to cover a press conference by House Speaker Tip O'Neill. In a walk outside, Kamman told me he had been instructed by Washington to warn me to be very careful in whatever I did in the weeks ahead. He did not explain further, nor did he suggest I cut short my Moscow assignment. But he urged, "Be squeaky clean."

In June, Roman called again several times but missed me because Ruth and I were vacationing in Finland. It was during our Finnish vacation that we heard on the BBC that Soviet counterintelligence had arrested a scientist identified as A. Tolkachov, as well as an American diplomat, Paul Stombaugh, whom I did not know. For me, the concern about being caught in some shadowy spy web began to ease when Roman called for a sixth time on June 21. He asked for another copy of *Information Moscow*. Infuriated, I shouted loudly so that the bugs in the office would hear: "I did not get the information about the church that I was expecting from you, and there is no more point in calling me. I wish you well and good-bye." Roman's only comment was "Eto obidno" (That's a shame), and he hung up. Within a year, he would enter our lives again, but this time in rather menacing circumstances.

# Chapter 28

## Gorby for Real?

"The phone's for you," Ruth called out from the kitchen, a hint of concern in her voice. It was a day in May 1985, and we were lunching in the apartment on the floor below the office. I took the phone and breathed a "yes" into the mouthpiece.

"Gospodin Danilov?" a Russian voice responded. "This is the police from the Moscow investigative unit. We are located in the Hotel Moskva. We have a young man here, Dmitrii, who says he has a pair of your son's pants which he wants to return to you. Could you come in right away?"

It was inconvenient, but I responded positively. Then, heart fluttering, I asked if there were any criminal suspicions being raised against Caleb. The policeman answered simply, "No."

Ruth and I got in the office Volvo and drove the twenty minutes to the hotel, then sought out Room 28, a small office on the main floor. Inside were several detectives talking to Dmitrii, or Mitya, as we called him, and one or two girls who looked like young prostitutes. "Do you recognize this young man?" asked the detective who was conducting some kind of inquiry.

I replied, "Yes."

"How often have you seen him? How often does he come around to your house?" the detective continued.

I answered, understating the case, that Mitya came around about once a week. Then yielding to curiosity, I asked what these questions were all about. The detective explained that Mitya had been scooping up clothes from Westerners in Moscow and passing them on to speculators for resale, getting some pocket money in return. "From what he has said himself," the detective went on, "he could be prosecuted as if he were an adult. He is an ordinary swindler." Mitya cowered in a corner, looking pitiful and ashamed as he returned Caleb's pants.

We thanked him and prepared to leave. As we headed for the door, one of the detectives, who had been perfectly polite, said to us, "If I had a word of advice for you, it would be to exercise more control over your son."

And that was that. We drove back to Leninskii Prospekt, upset but relieved.

The police had touched on a nerve. Caleb had been in a Russian school for the first two years of our assignment in Moscow. He had learned Russian well, and developed a host of Russian friends. He had also learned how to smoke, drink, and deceive. As he turned from an obedient eleven year old into a rebellious teenager, he became more and more obstreperous, less and less amenable to anybody's discipline. He had other brushes with the Moscow police, too. During Ted Turner's Goodwill Games in Moscow, the police stopped him in Gorky Park with his friends because he had holes in his T-shirt, which was considered *ne kulturny* (literally, "uncultured" or "inappropriate"). Another time, he had joined his Russian friends at a nearby apartment building. They started drinking and shouting in the stairwell. The neighbors called the authorities, and they were all carted off to a police station. We were summoned to extract him.

By the beginning of 1985, we were convinced the time had come for Caleb to reintegrate into American society. We had planned a two-week trip to Massachusetts and Vermont in February, with approval from the magazine, to seek out a boarding school where Caleb could readjust to the United States. As departure day approached, rumors circulated that General Secretary Konstantin Chernenko was seriously ailing. Were we entering a new succession crisis? He had not been seen publicly since December 28, 1984.

The most hopeful alternative to Chernenko was clearly Gorbachev. We correspondents had followed his fortunes since his elevation to the Politburo in 1979. His 1983 trip to Canada and his December 1984 trip to Britain seemed to augur a more open, more dynamic type of Soviet leader. The fact that he was twenty years younger than most of his Politburo colleagues appeared both a strength and a liability. Gorbachev had been assigned to oversee Soviet agriculture as one of the secretaries of the party. This was usually a dead-end job because of the low productivity and bureaucratic nature of the collective and state farms. But as Chernenko became less and less visible in the second half of 1984, I saw that Gorbachev was beginning to push himself forward. He was taking advantage of Chernenko's illness to encourage his supporters to help him achieve power, at least according to one of his

most severe critics, Viktor Grishin, the Moscow party chief. Gorbachev's maneuvering came to my attention on December 11, 1984, while reading a report he gave to ideological workers. In that speech, Gorbachev made all the
necessary genuflections toward Lenin and party doctrine, but tempered his
remarks with critical comments about falling productivity, lack of innova-
tion, and bureaucratic obstacles. One passage especially struck me:

> Wide-ranging, timely and open information is evidence of trust in people,
> respect for their reason and feelings, and their ability to figure out this or
> that situation. It enhances the productivity of the workers. *Glasnost* [trans-
> parency] in the work of party and government organs is a real means of
> fighting bureaucratic lethargy, obliges a more thought-through approach
> to reaching decisions and achieving control over execution, correcting
> deficits and overlooked considerations. On it depends to a large extent
> the credibility of propaganda, the effectiveness of education, and the se-
> curing of unity of words and deeds.

In the 1980s, *glasnost* was not a commonly used word in Soviet Russia. It
was, on the other hand, part of official vocabulary and appeared in some of
the articles of the Soviet Criminal Code. Russian writer Mikhail Saltykov-
Shchedrin had used the word *glasnost* in describing his efforts to root out
corruption as a nineteenth-century governor. The word was derived from
*golos* (voice) and could be translated as "giving voice" to an idea. Vladimir
Dal's famous nineteenth-century dictionary defined it as "to make public."
Today, it is generally considered the equivalent of "transparency" or "openness." I imagined that Gorbachev's use of this word in 1984 must have worried the Politburo elders who had spent decades enjoying the protection of
a controlled press, and who must have been uncertain what would happen
to them if Gorbachev ever came to power. If he did become top leader, I
thought, Soviet politics would become really interesting.

On February 1, foreign editor Roy Hansen, increasingly edgy about Chernenko's health, fired off one of those nasty messages that editors compose
without much thought, and inevitably make you feel horrible:

> item two february one
> assume you are taking the closest possible reading on the chernenko
> situation and are prepared to delay the stateside jaunt if there appears to
> be an outside chance of some imminent development. stop. we were staff-
> less in moscow for brezhnev and staffless for andropov stop with that
> track record the kremlin should pay you to remain in the capital.
> hansen

I responded by angry note, disputing the Andropov charge, which was clearly untrue, and noting that Ruth, an excellent writer in her own right, had covered us ably when Brezhnev died before I was able to return from Paris. In the end, Ruth, Caleb, and I left Moscow on February 8 and returned without incident on February 20.

In retrospect, Hansen's worries were not unreasonable. Chernenko's life was ebbing, and there was no way to get an accurate fix on the situation. I admit: we risked it, and our timing turned out to be exquisite because elections for the rubber-stamp Russian Federation parliament were being held on February 24 and Chernenko was a candidate. The day before, February 23, Chernenko was to give an election speech to assembled voters, but he never appeared. Rather, his speech was read for him over national radio and TV. Then on voting day, national TV showed him casting his ballot in what looked like a polling place, but actually was a television set, specially constructed at the hospital where he was being treated. Officials at his usual polling station confirmed to some foreign correspondents that his ballot had been sent to the Kremlin hospital at Kuntsevo.

Looking on as Chernenko cast his ballot was Viktor Grishin, taking advantage of the moment to get some national publicity for himself. The subtext was that Grishin might be looked upon as Chernenko's successor. Chernenko seemed gaunt and uncomfortable, clearly a man in distress. On February 27, Chernenko appeared again on TV, to be handed his certificate of election to the Russian Federation parliament. Some of us compared his appearances with a videotape of him voting the year before. In a message I sent to Washington on that day, February 27, I noted that the comparison showed "he has lost considerable weight. The collar of his shirt hangs around his neck. He needs help standing and moving about. His left arm appears to be paralyzed. He looks gaunt, barely speaks. Chernenko is believed to suffer from emphysema."

Later in the message I noted that the Soviet public was either being prepared for Chernenko's resignation—something that no Soviet leader had done to date—or that the Kremlin was again trying to prop up an ailing leader. "Even if Chernenko would like to shuck his political duties and live out his life quietly on pension, as some sources here report, he may not be allowed to do so." On March 7, completely unaware that Chernenko's health was now rapidly deteriorating and top Soviet leaders were urgently consulting each other, I sent another message to Washington for planning purposes:

The double appearance of Politburo member Viktor Grishin by Chernenko's side during his recent appearances raises questions: Is the Kremlin Old Guard maneuvering to hold on to power after the boss goes? Is it conceivable that Chernenko might resign, setting a new precedent in Kremlin politics? Is Grishin a candidate to take over? Is Gromyko? Has Gorbachev beaten back Romanov? Could Shcherbitsky's trip to America aid his political fortunes despite the fact that he is a Ukrainian? What about Aliyev?

Three days later, March 10, Moscow radio began playing somber music again; we noted that heads-up signal, and prepared to pounce on any announcement. The next day, March 11, the somber music continued until late in the evening when the official statement came that Konstantin Ustinovich Chernenko had died at 7:20 P.M. the day before, March 10, of heart and lung failure brought on by worsening emphysema, and that Gorbachev had been selected as the new general secretary of the Communist Party. It seemed so easy, it looked like the wheels had been greased.

Yet within days, rumors began circulating that there had been serious disputes among the Politburo members. These reports were picked up by Western correspondents and broadcast back into the Soviet Union by Western radio. Russian intellectuals, devotees of the BBC and the Voice of America, were soon chattering among themselves; political Moscow was in ferment. I quickly contacted the Sage, who told me, according to the notes I made:

> Chernenko died on March 8 but his heart-lung function was kept going artificially until March 10. Announcement was on March 11 with death said to be on March 10. On March 9, a group of Politburo members gathered, minus Shcherbitsky, who was in the U.S., and Kunayev who was in Kazakhstan.
>
> Romanov proposed Grishin as General Secretary. Vote showed that Grishin and Gorbachev were tied. KGB presented evidence of malfeasance in apartment allocations. Grishin feigned ignorance but withdrew his candidacy. Romanov proposed Gromyko as General Secretary. Gromyko refused categorically. Gorbachev was unanimously elected.

Today we have a much better picture of the bargaining that went on behind the scenes. Ever since Chernenko's selection as general secretary, Politburo members began splitting into two groups. The Politburo knew that in choosing Chernenko, they were merely postponing a succession crisis. By March 1985, his declining strength could no longer be covered up. During Chernenko's long absence from the public scene, the maneuvering between the Old Guard and the Gorbachev "young Turks" intensified. Gromyko recalls that around March 7—when I was alerting my editors about possible leadership changes—the dying leader telephoned him. According to Gromyko, Chernenko said, "Andrei Andreyevich, I feel unwell. . . . And I have been thinking, shouldn't I offer to resign? I want to consult with you."

Gromyko writes in his memoirs, "Wouldn't that be forcing events, not in accord with the objective situation? After all, so far as I know the doctors are not inclined to be so pessimistic."

"So I shouldn't rush things?"

"Right. There is no need to rush. There's no reason."

"Well then, I'll go along with that," Chernenko replied.

Gromyko had acted in a sly manner, not wanting to upset Chernenko personally or, more important, the Old Guard. But that conversation apparently focused Gromyko's attention on the coming crisis as Chernenko slipped into a coma. Gromyko began turning over in his mind who could really take charge of the flailing Soviet Union. The three most obvious candidates were Grishin, Romanov, and Gorbachev. Gromyko is thought to have had reservations about Gorbachev, who was inclined to be more accommodating toward the West than he was—or was it simply jealousy at seeing Gorbachev execute highly successful visits to Canada and Great Britain? On the other hand, Romanov was not popular within the Politburo. He had proved himself to be a loner in his role of overseer of the defense industry and, furthermore, had been involved in a variety of hushed-up scandals, one of which was the use of Catherine the Great's china for his daughter's wedding, during which several pieces were broken. Grishin was too obviously ambitious and likely to put his own interests above that of the nation. So in the final days, Gromyko began taking his own soundings.

He sent his son Anatoly, a graduate of the Moscow Institute of Economics and International Relations, to Dr. Yevgeny Primakov, a Middle East expert closely associated with IMEMO, to ask him to be an honest broker. Primakov, accordingly, paid a call on Alexander Yakovlev, recently named head of IMEMO. This was the same Yakovlev with whom I traveled around the United States in 1970. Together they reviewed the leadership situation and concluded that Gorbachev was, indeed, the only viable candidate. But what did Gorbachev think? Yakovlev went to Gorbachev at Central Committee headquarters and came away encouraged. Gorbachev was concerned that, if named, he needed a strong mandate; he would not be satisfied by simply squeaking into the top position. Yakovlev then telephoned Gromyko's son directly, bypassing Primakov, and the two engaged in a delicate minuet in which they made clear to each other that they did not want to do anything that might precipitate a botched-up situation in which both might be blamed.

The soundings moved a step further when the younger Gromyko confided to Yakovlev that his father was ready to play kingmaker. He said the elder Gromyko was prepared, as a member of the Old Guard, to nominate Gorbachev when the time came. Furthermore, he added, his father was tired of twenty-seven years as Soviet foreign minister and would welcome a change. Yakovlev went back to Gorbachev a second time. This time Gorbachev was more definite and said to Yakovlev, "Tell Andrei Andreyevich [Gromyko] that I always found it pleasant working with him. I'll be happy to continue doing so no matter what positions we occupy. Add to that I am capable of keeping my promises."

Then on the evening of Sunday, March 10, 1985, Chernenko died. Gorbachev, as the number-two man in the party, immediately scheduled an emergency Politburo meeting—as the solemn music played—which got under way within an hour after the leader's death. Twenty minutes before the meeting, Gorbachev and Gromyko met informally and signaled to each that the Anatoly Gromyko–Yakovlev scenario was a "go." Gorbachev writes that he told Gromyko, "Andrei Andreyevich, we have to consolidate our effort, the moment is crucial." The foreign minister replied, "I believe everything is clear." Gorbachev replied, "I will proceed from the assumption that we now have to work together."

The official business of the Politburo meeting was only to make necessary funeral arrangements. But a delicate question soon intruded: who would chair the funeral commission? In recent years, funeral commission chairmen had subsequently been elected general secretary, and if anyone was named to chair the commission that night, the world would greet the news as announcing the new Soviet leader. Neither side wanted to push that issue so far on short notice, and the Politburo meeting broke up about eleven that night with no decision on the chairman. Another Politburo meeting was scheduled for the next day at about two o'clock, when the issue would be decided, to be followed by a Central Committee meeting at five to confirm the choice. Gorbachev and his colleague Yegor Ligachev, a Communist Party secretary in charge of administration and personnel, worked until three o'clock that night, finishing up the paperwork and agreeing to return to Central Committee headquarters early on March 11. Ligachev recalls in his recollections he never slept and was back at work at eight. Shortly before ten, Ligachev was surprised to get a call from Gromyko. The foreign minister was tap-dancing through his own soundings. "Yegor Kuzmich," Gromyko began tentatively, "whom are we going to choose as general secretary?" This was a logical question to put to a party secretary in charge of personnel and administration.

Yegor Ligachev writes that Gromyko knew very well what sort of answer he was likely to get, inasmuch as Ligachev had been encouraging the provincial party leaders to support Gorbachev at the coming meeting of the

Central Committee. "Yes, Andrei Andreyevich, it's a complicated question," Ligachev says. "I think we have to choose Gorbachev. I know you have your own opinion. But since you've asked me, then I'll tell you I have the following considerations. I know that many of the provincial first secretaries and Central Committee members are of the same mind."

Gromyko replied delicately, "I am also thinking of Gorbachev. I think he is the most suitable figure and has some prospects." Then the elder diplomat popped the key question: "Well, what do you think? Who could be the one to make the motion? Who could nominate him as the candidate?"

Craftily, Ligachev replied, "It would be very good Andrei Andreyevich, if you would be the one to do that."

"Do you think so?" Gromyko replied, not wanting to tip his hand too soon.

"Yes, that would be best . . ."

"I suppose I am ready to make the motion about Gorbachev. But Yegor Kuzmich, help me prepare for my speech, and please send me more detailed biographical information on Gorbachev."

Ligachev speculates that Gromyko had probably made up his mind before telephoning and wanted Gorbachev to learn of his decision immediately. In any event, Ligachev would swiftly convey it to Gorbachev.

That afternoon the Politburo meeting got under way at three rather than two, with Gorbachev in the chair as the party's number-two man. Gorbachev carefully sat not in the usual chairman's spot but off to one side so as to discourage any impression that he was lusting after power. Grishin supporters were reported to have prepared their position in advance and were ready to move. However, as soon as the meeting started, Gromyko stood up, his large frame dominating the room. Gorbachev recognized him immediately, thus preventing any other representative of the Old Guard to speak. Gromyko quickly nominated Gorbachev, listing the qualities that would make him an outstanding general secretary.

Politburo practice was to reach decisions by unanimity (or reschedule debate for another time), and in this case Nikolai Tikhonov, the eighty-year-old prime minister, quickly sided with Gromyko. So did Grishin. They could see which way the wind was blowing. At five o'clock Gromyko gave a longer speech in support of Gorbachev, and the Central Committee ratified the proposal. Late in the evening Soviet media announced that Mikhail Sergeyevich Gorbachev had been chosen unanimously to head the Communist Party and lead the nation. In actuality, the selection might have gone the other way but for the understanding between Gromyko and Gorbachev.

The new leader roared into action. At Chernenko's funeral at Red Square on March 13, Gorbachev made a point of meeting individually with top leaders of the Western powers—France, Britain, Germany, and Vice President George Bush of the United States—in a dizzying round of meetings. No sooner had the visitors gone home than Gorbachev began to make a series of public talks and "walk-arounds," meeting with ordinary people in Moscow, Leningrad, and Kiev to hear their everyday complaints and to enunciate hopes for a revitalized nation. "His activism, his instinct for maneuvering and, above all, his speaking abilities came across on television," wrote my colleague Dusko Doder of the *Washington Post.* "He is the first Soviet leader to be a TV personality, bringing with him a casual tone, a dislike of verbosity and sloganeering, a man with a self-deprecating wit and also what many Soviet citizens sense as personal warmth."

I illustrated the problems that Gorbachev was going to confront on the domestic scene with a major four-page article titled "Promises, Dreams: 4 Voices from Moscow's Streets," published on July 29, 1985. I said in the introduction, "The Soviet Union today is a nation in distress, its people trying to cope with a faltering economy, with promises made and broken by their leaders and with what they are told is a military threat from the United States." To back up this gloomy beginning, I interviewed four citizens—a sixty-eight-year-old widow, Klavdia Mikhailovna Petrova, who was born in the year of the Russian Revolution; an unofficial artist, Vlad, a thirty-something painter who had been denied membership in the official Union of Painters; a Communist official, Alexander Yevgenevich Bovin, fifty-five, a member of the Central Auditing Commission (one of the higher party bodies) and a commentator for the government newspaper, *Izvestia;* and a fourth person, Roy Alexandrovich Medvedev, fifty-nine. Although I did not say so in print, Medvedev was the Airport Sage who had told me so much about how the Soviet Union had chosen its most recent leaders. These four interviewees spelled out the many problems of Soviet life—scarcity of food, rising prices, restricted personal freedoms—issues that Gorbachev was now playing on.

Domestic problems were only half of what the new leader had to deal with. The other part, the arms race with the United States, was bankrupting the Soviet Union. By April 1985, Gorbachev was saying publicly he was prepared to meet with President Reagan, and within weeks a summit conference in Geneva was agreed upon by both sides. With the prospect of a Reagan-Gorbachev summit, the magazine finally agreed to send Joe Fromm to Moscow between September 22 and September 28, 1985, to scout out the Russian mood and intentions. I arranged a heavy program that included interviews with Yevgeny Velikhov, vice president of the Academy of Sciences; Vadim Zagladin, the deputy chief of the International Department of the

Communist Party; several Soviet newspaper editors and academic researchers; and Western diplomats. Traditionally, the International Department dealt with relations with other Communist countries, whereas the
Foreign Ministry maintained contacts with the noncommunist world. Gorbachev was determined to bring the International Department more into the
process of foreign policy formation. Until now, Western reporters were
rarely, if ever, admitted to Central Committee headquarters. But under Gorbachev's glasnost, closed power centers were opening up. Telephone numbers of Central Committee departments were becoming available, and even
the office numbers of Politburo members . . . not that you could ever reach
them on the telephone. They would be unavailable at the time of your call.
Shortly after his arrival in late September, Joe Fromm, our translator, Tamara
Devyatkina, and I drove to the Central Committee on Staraya Ploshad.

Once our documents were verified by the entrance guards, we made our
way to Rooms 500 and 501, where Vadim Zagladin, an unusually erudite official who spoke several European languages, was awaiting us. He was
smoking a Marlboro cigarette behind a highly polished desk on which lay
a red folder and sheaves of restricted TASS reports. Behind him hung the
obligatory portrait of Lenin and a map of the world, and on his side table I
counted seven separate telephones. Zagladin greeted us warmly, then
launched into a half-hour discourse emphasizing that the Soviet Union was
entering a new, dynamic era under Gorbachev. "You should not be surprised to see us now offer many new proposals," he told us.

Zagladin also reflected residual wariness about Reagan:

> We have followed the American statements of serious preparations for
> the meeting. But I would say frankly the president takes actions which put
> us on guard. There is the continuing testing of an antisatellite weapon.
> There is the test of a laser against an ICBM [intercontinental ballistic mis-
> sile]. If the president is really serious, why is he doing such things? Why
> is it necessary to do this, to pressure us? Still we are preparing ourselves,
> and we consider that the meeting in Geneva must yield serious results.

Our conversation with Zagladin covered a wide range of topics under-
lining the fact that the world was becoming increasingly interconnected and
that all countries, including the Soviet Union, had to take into account the
legitimate interests of others. "We are for the mutual reduction of strategic
forces," he said, hinting that a 40 percent reduction was not inconceivable.
"We understand that protracted issues will not all be solved through negotiations in Geneva, but agreement at the high level will help the process
along, and we are getting ready very seriously."

Our visit left an upbeat impression. Something might be changing. In those days, there was a tendency in the West to regard Gorbachev's openness as yet another charm offensive. The question everyone asked: is Gorbachev for real? We would have to wait to see. The new openness at the secret heart of the Central Committee was interesting in another way: there was a feeling that a strong master was in charge. Little things, perhaps, but we were impressed by the cleanliness and order of the place—especially the men's room. So often in the Soviet Union public restrooms were disgusting, rarely cleaned and left to fester for days on end. The Central Committee offices we found were not the dilapidated, disorderly Defense Ministry that my grandfather witnessed in 1918. As we were about to leave, Tamara insisted on a visit to the cafeteria. We glanced in, but let her inspect the place by herself. When she returned, she was angry, shaking her head. She had glimpsed a bountiful menu and a wide array of takeout packages including caviar sandwiches at low prices. "It's disgusting the privileges these people get!" she sighed.

Dealing with the United States, Gorbachev and his team could easily declassify information for propaganda and other purposes. What I didn't realize at the time was how daunting the challenge was of spreading this new transparency down the line and getting thousands of officials, millions of citizens, to speak up truthfully. To correct shortcomings in Soviet industry and agriculture, Gorbachev had to persuade workers at all levels to identify problems and propose constructive solutions. To make that happen, he would have to relax censorship and ease off harsh penalties for sensitive disclosures against the natural inertia of the bureaucracy.

Censorship intrigued me; the secrecy that surrounded it made it mysterious. I often wondered what was officially on the forbidden list and what the list actually looked like. It was impossible to know because the content of the list was highly classified, and even its very existence was secret. However, after Gorbachev left power in 1991, I found an editor who was brave enough to slip me a copy, making me one of the few Westerners who has ever held it in his hands. Its real title was "List of Information Forbidden for Publication in the Open Media," and it contained 192 pages divided into 14 chapters and 10 appendixes. All references to the censorship system—its structure, organization, whereabouts, or personnel (with the exception of the top censor, V. Boldyrev)—were prohibited. The system, originally established in 1922, was called Glavlit (for the Main Administration of Literature and Publishing), but by the 1970s it carried the less ideological title of Main Administration for Guarding State Secrets in the Press.

Much of the manual was aimed at the nation's military potential and current strength conceived in the broadest possible terms. This included the structure of Soviet military forces, their organization, deployment, readiness, mobilization plans, logistics, and civil defense. Also restricted were such matters as military industry, military research, cartography, and availability of natural resources, ores, and minerals. By the 1980s, the list showed definite signs of "mission creep" and classified a whole range of activities in agriculture, economics, and criminal happenings censorship of whose reporting an open society would consider intolerable. In farming, the list banned "data (factual, estimated, or probable) of overall harvest, yield or government purchases of grain, peas, cotton, potatoes, beet; production or government purchases of meat, milk, wool, eggs, cattle—in all or by categories—for the previous or current years—throughout the USSR, Union Republics, until their official publication." This prohibition made it difficult for Soviet planners to predict the size of the annual harvest and therefore the shortfalls the nation might experience. That, in turn, made it difficult for central planners to estimate grain purchases from abroad. I remembered from Washington that Soviet agricultural attachés in the 1970s would visit the U.S. Department of Commerce to learn of American projections of Soviet harvests based on satellite images.

Besides agriculture, other sensitive areas were sometimes surprising to a Westerner. Article 8.70, for example, prohibited the disclosure of airports and landing strips for civil aviation. Article 8.76 required facts about airplane crashes to be kept secret, while Article 8.77 required that extraordinary events—hijackings or attacks on a flight crew—be hidden until a decision to release was made by the Ministry of Civil Aviation.

One of the most damaging suppressions was contained in Article 4.21, which called for hiding the consequences of environmental catastrophes that could endanger human life. The motivating factor here, I believe, was the desire to prevent public panic. This hypercautious attitude came into play in 1957 when a discharge of radiation occurred at the secret Kyshtym-40 nuclear plant in the Chelyabinsk region. That article would bedevil Gorbachev and his colleagues in the coming year when a serious explosion occurred at the Chernobyl nuclear power plant, spreading a radiation cloud over northern Europe.

Other prohibitions were no less astounding. No information was to be published about epidemics whose nature had not been established, making it difficult to write about AIDS. Publishing the number of recruits being treated for a variety of illnesses or the incidence of infectious diseases among members of the armed forces was prohibited. Publication of the number of deaths per one thousand from tuberculosis, industrial accidents, or suicides was banned. Forbidden, too, were criminal statistics—the number of persons convicted or their punishments. No mention of particularly serious crimes was permitted, and nothing was to be released about closed trials, without the permission of the judges.

Needless to say, the whole system limited anyone's soaring imagination. Since any infraction could be viewed as anti-Soviet propaganda—Article 70 of the Criminal Code—the whole system conspired to promote self-censorship in the name of personal security. This culture of caution was not something that Russia could overcome in a few months, or even years. The allure of democracy with its requirement for free expression, for free and fair elections, would find it rough going in confronting these restrictions in the long-term. "You unyoke the horse from walking in a circle, raising water from a well, and the horse will continue to walk in a circle," one wit explained to me.

As we got closer to the Geneva summit in early November 1985, one of my oddest undertakings related to a friend of ours, Russian violinist Alexander Brussilovsky, whom we called Sasha. He had been an extremely promising graduate of the Moscow Conservatory and had won several international prizes, including the Jacques Thibaud Prize in Paris in 1975. However, he fell out of favor with the Soviet authorities when he and his wife applied to emigrate. Immediately GosKoncert, the national agency controlling all musical performances, canceled his major appearances within the country, banned him from traveling abroad, and allowed him to perform only in the most desolate parts of the union. To save him from his isolation, Ruth generously insisted we "adopt" him and his wife, Lena. With his help, she arranged a special fiftieth birthday gift for me: Sasha Brussilovsky would give a concert for me and our closest friends in our apartment on December 30, 1984.

Finally, in 1985 after years of waiting, Sasha, his wife, Lena, and his daughter, Alisia, were granted permission to leave for France. But now a new problem hit. The Ministry of Culture would not permit him to take his eighteenth-century Italian violin on the grounds that it was a national treasure. This instrument, made by Niccolo Galliano in 1750, had been given to him by a professor, Yuri Yankelevich, and he depended heavily on it.

He asked me if there was any way I could help, and I decided to seek out Ambassador Arthur Hartman. I had a good relationship with the ambassador, whose forebears had emigrated to the United States in the nineteenth century from Odessa. Once in a while he would ask me for my views, especially about a curious incident in which a fourteen-year-old Soviet boy made his way, past guards, into his residence at Spaso House, and asked to see him. Hartman agreed to meet the boy, and they chatted amiably for more than an hour. "Do you think he really just wandered in, or was he sent?" Hartman asked me. I said I thought the boy must have been part of some probing operation by Soviet counterintelligence, although in Russia not everything can be known with certainty.

Now on this occasion, Hartman and I retired to the "Bubble," and I explained the problem. The ambassador, a strong supporter of the arts, agreed to help. Like all diplomats, Hartman was not subject to any customs inspection on leaving or entering the country. "Bring the violin to Spaso House. Drive into the grounds, park in back of the house, and bring it up to our bedroom. We'll take it when we fly to Geneva." A few days later, after lunch, I put the million-dollar instrument and its case in an old U.S. Army duffel bag. I drove the office Volvo to Spaso House, waved at the Soviet guards at the front entrance, and maneuvered the car down the short driveway and around into the small backyard. I entered the mansion through the rear door, feeling uneasy yet almost exultant. I explained briefly to a member of the ambassador's household staff that I was bringing the Hartmans a package the ambassador had requested, and trudged up to the second floor, no questions asked, to the bedroom. There I laid the duffel bag, with its precious instrument, gently on the still-unmade bed and departed, feeling as guilty as any bamboozler. Within days the violin regained its master in Paris.

The first meeting between President Reagan and Mikhail Gorbachev has gone down in history as the "fireside summit." Reagan wanted to break through the formalities that had usually attended summit leaders and made special efforts to find a less formal meeting place outside the confines of the American mission or the Soviet villa. His aides found a lakeside mansion equipped with a pleasant living room and fireplace where Reagan believed he would be able to talk heart-to-heart with Gorbachev. The Soviet leader was only too willing. From the Soviet side there had been questions about Reagan's age, his mind, and whether he was in control. Prior to the meeting Soviet aides talked a lot about "chemistry." How would the two get on?

To cover these events, *U.S. News and World Report* assembled what looked like a powerful team. This was one of the biggest events the magazine would cover since being bought by real estate developer Mortimer Zuckerman the previous year. I flew to Geneva from Moscow; correspondents Robin Knight and Jeff Trimble arrived from London and Rome. Our coverage, however, soon ran into trouble. Zuckerman, fascinated with international affairs, wanted his news magazine to displace *Newsweek* as America's number-two newsweekly, and he had begun a major reorganization. He had hired Shelby Coffey from the *Washington Post* as managing editor, acquired Reagan's director of communications, David Gergen, as editor, and signed on Hank Trewhitt of the *Baltimore Sun* as chief diplomatic correspondent. The magazine had hardly shaken down under the new ownership, and its journalists were uncertain whether they were to continue the forward-looking projections or revert to colorful coverage of unfolding events. Added to this confusion was the fact that Trewhitt, our chief writer, misplaced his passport early in the summit and was distracted by his urgent pleas to the U.S. consulate to issue him a new one.

The cables we dispatched to Washington were rough and lacked the traditional *U.S. News* forward cast; they needed to be completely rewritten. Our new editor, Shelby Coffey, assigned Joe Fromm, who had remained in Washington, the unenviable task of poring through endless dispatches, trying to make sense out of our chatter. Later, Joe told me, "Coffey came to me and said, 'You're going to have to write this one.' The story you guys sent had no story line, did not project into the future, and didn't tell the reader what the summit meant to the nation or to the individual."

We left Geneva downcast, but perhaps not as unhappy as the Soviet military. Whereas Gorbachev and Reagan initiated a personal relationship, the Russian generals returned to Moscow with no concessions from the United States, no halt to the Strategic Defense Initiative, and no quick fixes for their dwindling finances.

Chapter 29

# Chernobyl

April 26–27, 1986, was a weekend of uneasy quiet. Nothing seemed to be going on despite the fact that Soviet media managers, under Gorbachev, were creating boundless activity (something that had been lacking under previous leaders) with incessant press conferences. For April 28, we had been summoned to a press conference at the Ministry of Foreign Affairs to learn of the "subversive activities" of Radio Liberty, a Washington-financed broadcaster that transmitted uncensored information in Russian, about Russia, into Russia.

When we showed up on Monday, we discovered that the topic was, indeed, out of the ordinary. The chief performer was Oleg A. Tumanov, a Soviet sailor who had defected to the United States in 1965 and now had redefected back to Russia. Abroad, he had joined Radio Liberty and worked on the editorial staff in Munich, West Germany. Now after a twenty-year absence, nostalgia had gotten the better of him, and the Soviet authorities offered him a deal: come home as prodigal son and denounce the malicious ways of the West. He had agreed, and we journalists sat obediently in the ministry's press center to hear his accusations.

The more Tumanov bumbled on, the more irritated I became. I could not stop thinking how the newspaper *Sovietskaya Rossiya* had attacked two of my colleagues, Serge Schmemann of the *New York Times* and Don Kimmelman of the *Philadelphia Inquirer,* for alleged ties to U.S. intelligence and rowdy behavior in public. After Tumanov had spoken for nearly an hour, I raised my hand. Yuri Grimitskikh, the ministry spokesman, recognized me, and I launched into a counterattack. "What bothers me as an American journalist," I said getting straight to the point, "is the rather malicious attack on my colleague Don Kimmelman. I know Don Kimmelman. I know him to be energetic. I know him to be a fair-minded person, a decent person." I plowed on, slowly, deliberately, and calmly. I knew I was totally out of bounds, but I felt something had to be said, and if I was to suffer consequences . . . too bad. "Since the arrival of Mr. Gorbachev to power in this country," I continued, "there has been a great deal of discussion about civility among nations, civility among peoples, and I would hope that it would extend to those who by profession engage in official propaganda, and those who by profession are journalists."

Here Grimitskikh, upset at losing control, interrupted. And I shot back: "I will finish my intervention if I may. I would like to know if the standard of civility is such that Mr. Kimmelman will be given the opportunity to give his version of events. Thank you very much." My Western colleagues burst into applause, and I relinquished the microphone. My mind was grinding over and over what I had done, and what consequences I would suffer. But I felt a satisfying sense of relief. Instead of being the guilty bystander, I had said the right thing.

In the next hours, this little drama faded away as we began receiving reports from Sweden that an unusual cloud of nuclear radiation was sweeping across northern Europe. The Swedes had checked their nuclear stations and found no accidental releases. The Swedish Embassy asked the Foreign Ministry if something had happened in the southwestern Soviet Union, but got no answer.

We now know that the Chernobyl disaster was set in motion at the beginning of the weekend when the plant operators began an experiment as reactor no. 4 was being shut down for routine maintenance. They wanted to discover how much electricity could be produced to run emergency systems by a free-spinning turbine disconnected from its nuclear power source. The shutdown began on Wednesday, April 23, was interrupted, then resumed again on the night of Friday, April 25. On Saturday morning, April 26, a little after one, a series of missteps led to an emergency situation in which the reactor suddenly surged to full power. Water in cooling pipes and associated systems began to boil, pressure tubes burst, and the escaping steam blew the top off the reactor, sending it and its concrete shield through the roof of the reactor building. The Chernobyl plant was not housed in a concrete containment, as Western plants are, and a plume of radiation escaped, rising a half mile (twelve hundred meters) into the air, and drifted northward.

None of this was acknowledged at the time. In fact, inaccurate initial reports of the accident, general confusion, and a desire by the Soviet leadership to avoid panic convinced Mikhail Gorbachev and his colleagues to abide by the censorship code of silence. After hours of deliberation in Gorbachev's office—as we journalists listened to Oleg Tumanov drone on—the leaders finally authorized this boilerplate for the nine o'clock national news: "An accident has occurred at the Chernobyl nuclear power station; one of the four atomic reactors has been damaged. Measures are being taken to eliminate the consequences of the accident. Victims are being helped. A government commission has been created."

Toward midnight, I received a message from Washington saying, "Apparent nuclear mishap with radiation cloud floating westward is lead story this afternoon stop. Obviously we are interested in what you can find out stop. Please keep us advised." This was followed by a message from our daughter, Miranda, in Chicago, asking if Ruth and I were in any physical danger. To her message, we replied no.

The next day, Tuesday, April 29, saw the evil results of silence. Journalists, ham radio operators, people all over the world began digging out rumors and misinformation. The editor of the *Ukrainian Weekly* in New Jersey made contact with a person in Ukraine who claimed fifteen thousand people had died. A Dutch radio amateur monitored a conversation between a Japanese radio operator and a Kiev radio ham who claimed there were "many hundreds of dead and wounded." The *New York Post* picked up a report by my colleague Luther Whittington of UPI and splashed it across its front page: "2,000 Die in Nukemare: Soviets Appeal for Help as N-Plant Burns Out of Control." Luther based his information on a telephone call he made to a woman in Kiev whom he had met accidentally on Red Square several weeks before. I was never convinced that he had correctly understood her, as his Russian was primitive. But this inaccurate report gained sensational worldwide attention, angering the Soviet propagandists who had no clear idea how to counter it.

On Wednesday, April 30, I prepared a lengthy report for my editors in Washington on Chernobyl but found my telex machine would not transmit. As a result, I sent the following message through friends in the UPI bureau:

ex moscow item 1—april 30

yalowitz

a fault has developed on my telex line and i can neither send nor receive. i am communicating to you through upi whose telex number is 64 413424 rpt 64 413424. have your item 1 of april 30 which i confirm. will ask you in a couple of hours to call upi moscow and i will begin transmitting copy to you.

daniloff

A few hours later, I drove the twenty minutes across town to the UPI bureau where I dispatched my account of why such an accident was more
likely to happen in the Soviet Union than the United States, the accident at
Three Mile Island notwithstanding. Looking out my office window before
leaving, I saw several men in our inner courtyard working around an open
manhole. They were doing something to the cables inside, apparently cutting off my communications. I learned that *Newsweek* and *Time* also experienced trouble with their telex communications and American television
bureaus were denied satellite links because Soviet technicians were allegedly too busy with the coming May Day holiday to handle their business.

After the collapse of the Soviet Union, declassified Soviet documents
shed light on these strange events. On that day, April 30, KGB chief Viktor
M. Chebrikov sent a memorandum to the Communist Party's Central Committee, saying, "Measures are being taken by the Committee on State Security to control the behavior of foreign diplomats and correspondents,
limiting their opportunities to collect information about the accident at the
Chernobyl nuclear plant and to break up their efforts to use it for mounting
an anti-Soviet campaign in the West."

May Day was traditionally a workers' holiday in the Soviet Union marked
by an elaborate military and civilian parade through Red Square. The Soviet
leaders would gather atop the Lenin Mausoleum overlooking the square to
review the troops and the latest military hardware, including strategic missiles. This could be an appropriate forum, I thought, for Gorbachev to say a
few words of condolence to victims and relatives and to cast the aftermath in
a positive light, as President Reagan had done when the Challenger spacecraft had blown up in January. Before the parade began, I had a chance to chat
with and photograph Gorbachev's wife, Raisa, in the reviewing stands. She
hoped to visit the United States later in the year with her husband, but
breathed not a word about Chernobyl. Gorbachev, atop the mausoleum, gave
the traditional speech, but remained silent about the explosion. No acknowledgment. No details. No condolences. No reassurances.

Meanwhile, the streets were buzzing. Foreign embassies, worried about
the radiation levels of fruit, vegetables, and meat in the Moscow markets,
called in their experts. U.S. Army specialists with Geiger counters arrived on
May 3. Visiting the Institute of the USA and Canada, I recall one secretary
asking me, "What do your American experts say about radiation levels? I
don't believe a word of what our people say. Is the food in our markets going
to be affected?"

Finally, on the overnight of May 5–6, the news agency TASS released a
lengthy article that would appear in *Pravda* on May 6, reporting the first official details of the tragedy. This story showed some understanding of pub-

lic relations by placing major emphasis on the heroism of the firefighters. The article set the scene for a press conference later in the day led by Deputy Foreign Minister Anatoly Kovalev and Deputy Premier Boris Shcherbina. The Soviet diplomat struck a defensive stance by asserting that the West was using the catastrophe to wage an organized anti-Soviet campaign. He said, in part:

> Claims are being made with regard to the incomplete character of the information we provide. We cannot accept such an argument because at the very moment information was available to us we made it public.
>
> The experience of recent days shows one very unpleasant thing. Another hysterical campaign is being organized from the same center, the United States, and clearly along an already established line.

Deputy Premier Shcherbina, in charge of investigating the catastrophe, adopted a milder tone, acknowledging that plant officials and decision makers in Moscow had been confused at first. They admitted that the radiation dangers had not been fully appreciated and that evacuation of local residents had been senselessly delayed for thirty-six hours. The May 6 press conference was followed by an important statement by Dr. Yevgeny Velikhov, vice president of the Academy of Sciences, on the difficulties of containing the radiation. On May 8, a small group of foreign correspondents was allowed to tour Chernobyl under official supervision, and the Reuters news agency sent back an on-the-spot report. On May 9, Dr. Hans Blix, director of the International Atomic Energy Agency, visited Chernobyl and held a news conference at which he disclosed that the Russians intended to submerge the damaged reactor in a pile of boron, clay, sand, and lead, enclosed by a concrete "sarcophagus."

Finally, on May 14, eighteen days after the explosion, Gorbachev broke his silence and spoke for twenty-five minutes on the nine o'clock news. His speech was a careful balancing act, defending the leadership's cautious reaction, denouncing an allegedly anti-Soviet campaign that ensued, while disclosing in rather general terms details of the explosion. Gorbachev revealed that 2 persons were killed at the time of the explosion, 7 others died subsequently, and 299 were hospitalized with radiation sickness. He finally offered the "profound condolences" of the Communist Party to the victims. And seeking to turn tragedy into opportunity, he suggested a summit meeting with President Reagan in Europe or at Hiroshima (naming Hiroshima seemed a bit opportunistic) "to reach agreement on a ban on nuclear testing."

Chernobyl was more than a technological tragedy. It seemed to me it was also a major challenge to Gorbachev's policy of glasnost. In a crisis you find out how open any organization is. Traditional attitudes in the Politburo resisted Gorbachev's efforts to clarify the situation publicly, but there was no way to prove my speculation, and I tucked the thought away for future exploration.

A decade later, once-secret Soviet documents were declassified, and I found out what had actually happened while we journalists were blindsided. The explosion occurred April 26 at 1:24 A.M., and within fifteen minutes local firefighters were hard at work, risking radiation, to control the blaze. Military firefighters arrived about an hour later to help. This was one case in which the system, which we correspondents tended to view as overly bureaucratic and inefficient, actually worked. At 3:00 the director of the plant, Viktor P. Bryukhanov, woke up Vladimir V. Marin, the Communist official in Moscow in charge of nuclear matters, to report by telephone about the accident and to assure Marin that he had the situation in hand. His report was both inaccurate and self-serving: he denied there had been any radiation release and stated the fire was liquidated by 3:30.

Meanwhile, other political and military leaders had begun receiving reports of the accident. Marshal Sergei F. Akhromeyev, chief of the General Staff, was alerted at home at 2:20 A.M. and arrived at the military command center in Moscow at 3:30 A.M. He immediately took action, ordering special antinuclear mobile units to move in from as far away as Volgograd. The commander of the Kiev military district, Colonel General V. V. Osipov, reported at 6:00 A.M. that the fire appeared to be extinguished but that there really had been a radiation release. At 9:00 A.M., an interdepartmental task force left Moscow without publicity on a special flight to Kiev. An hour later, at 10:00 A.M., Marshal Akhromeyev telephoned Gorbachev that the catastrophe was probably worse than initially reported. At about 2:30 P.M. that afternoon, two members of the interdepartmental team flew by helicopter over the damaged plant and viewed the hole in the roof through which they could see the cracked-open reactor. A dosimeter in the aircraft, flying at an altitude of about four hundred meters, showed that they were in the middle of the radiation plume.

Gorbachev scheduled an "emergency" meeting of the Politburo after Marshal Akhromeyev's telephone call. However, he apparently did not think the situation was so serious that they needed to meet immediately; instead, he set the meeting for Monday. Soviet foreign minister Eduard Shevardnadze, who would come under world pressure in the days ahead, learned details of the accident only on that Monday.

But by Sunday, April 27, word of the Chernobyl accident began reaching a few Soviet journalists. Chief among them was *Pravda*'s science editor, Vladimir S. Gubarev. He began making inquiries, but was told to back off.

Article 4.21 of the "List of Forbidden Subjects" limited coverage of environmental disasters. Leonid N. Dobrokhotov, a high Communist official, later explained that, at the start of the crisis, press handling was traditional. "We had to play down the catastrophe to prevent panic among the people," he said, "and to fight against what was then called bourgeois falsification, bourgeois propaganda."

At the emergency Politburo meeting on Monday, April 28, Vladimir I. Dolgikh, party secretary for nuclear matters, reported what was then known of the explosion. A division of opinion immediately appeared among the top leaders. Gorbachev, Shevardnadze, and other reformers wanted to release as much confirmed information as possible in a timely manner; others, led by Gromyko and Ligachev, urged caution. In releasing information, Gromyko argued for telling the nation's socialist allies such as East Germany and Poland first, and Western countries such as Sweden, Finland, and the United States later. The meeting created an Operations Group headed by Premier Nikolai Ryzhkov and an executive committee headed by Deputy Premier Boris Shcherbina. The meeting approved a brief acknowledgment of the disaster, which, as noted, was read on the evening news.

Still unknown to us foreign correspondents, the Politburo met again secretly on April 29 to hear a fuller report by Dolgikh and to authorize further dumping of absorptive materials on the no. 4 nuclear block. The U.S. Embassy, on President Reagan's orders, quietly offered the Gorbachev government medical and technical help. The offer was shoved aside, I would say, because of excessive national pride. That evening Ryzhkov's Operations Group held its first meeting. The nation was sorely lacking in emergency equipment: radiation counters, protective antiradiation suits, and self-propelled robots to scoop up radioactive debris were either unavailable or in desperately short supply. One member of the Ryzhkov group, Vitaly I. Vorotnikov, recalled: "There is not equipment or materials. You cannot get up to the zone of serious nuclear pollution. There is no means of protection. The situation and method of work of people are not sufficiently well checked."

On Wednesday, April 30, ambassadors from Britain, France, Finland, the Netherlands, and Austria were called to the Foreign Ministry for a briefing. Deputy Foreign Minister Anatoly Kovalev informed them that 2 firefighters had died while attempting to put out the Chernobyl blaze, 18 others were in "critical condition," 197 persons were hospitalized, and 49 had been examined and released. Britain ordered 100 British students, who had arrived two weeks earlier to study in Kiev and Minsk, to leave the country, which they did, protesting all the way. The Finns withdrew a group from Kiev. In this information "brownout," we correspondents scrambled for any information at all, and many erroneous stories were sent out. I had visited a nuclear power plant at Novo-Voronezh a few months earlier and managed to reach my acquaintance Sasha Konoplyov, who said he was trying to find out something himself and to call back. I was never able to reach him again.

By the time of Gorbachev's May 1 silence, it was clear that the Soviet leadership would have to provide considerably more information in the days ahead. Gorbachev could have made an inspection tour, which would have had a positive effect by demonstrating concern at the highest level. But he declined to involve himself publicly, which, I think in retrospect, was a huge mistake attributable to lack of political sensitivity. Ryzhkov and his Operations Group did tour the area, and a small group of trusted Soviet journalists visited on May 4–9. In the journalist group was the *Pravda* science editor, Gubarev, who privately decried the policy of silence. In a confidential memorandum to the Communist Party Central Committee in Moscow, he wrote: "Word about the visit of comrades Ligachev and Ryzhkov to the area of the power station had a positive effect. However, 'the silence' of the Republic leadership in the ensuring days, in my opinion, again precipitated panic, especially when it became known that the children and families of leading officials are being evacuated. More than one thousand people were lined up outside the cashiers' windows of the Central Committee of the Ukrainian Communist party. Naturally in town, everyone knew."

Looking back on the Chernobyl disaster today, it seems to me that a part of the tragedy that has been underestimated was the Soviet Union's long estrangement from the West. Since Stalin's death in 1953, of course, the country had been opening up. I myself could measure the movement from my first assignment in 1961 to my second in 1981. But contacts were still difficult in 1986, and many obstacles were strewn in the way. Had there been normal relations with Western nations, more regular contacts at all levels, the Soviet leadership might have been more attuned to the possible dangers of nuclear energy. As it was, A. P. Alexandrov, the eighty-year-old president of the Soviet Academy of Sciences, had been assuring the leadership that nuclear power was safe. Consequently, insufficient attention was paid to plant construction and safety measures. The KGB, in fact, had noted sloppiness in the construction of the Chernobyl plant as early as 1979. Soviet engineers did have access to the U.S. report on a similar incident at Three Mile Island in Pennsylvania in 1979. However, as so often happens, it took a real catastrophe for critical assessments to have an impact on the nation's leaders.

Had the Soviet Union been less isolated, Gorbachev's team might also have had a cadre of officials, schooled in the West, with public relations skills. Good public relations officers, trusted by the leadership, could have done the government a favor by acknowledging in timely fashion what could not be denied. They could have placed major stress in their an-nouncements on the rapidity and heroism of the first responders that Gor-bachev finally got around to on May 14. This would have projected a picture of the Soviet Union responsibly tackling a tragedy that could have occurred in any Western country, including the United States, France, or Finland. Fear of stoking a panic was a normal-enough reaction that my own Washington colleagues sensed at Three Mile Island. Leaders of a sophisticated industrial society have to find a balance between truth and terror, between public health and panic-making disclosures.

Another problem that Chernobyl pointed up was the compartmentalized nature of communications within the Soviet government. This prevented the free flow of internal communications. By the end of Saturday, April 26, Gorbachev should have known the major contours of the Chernobyl prob-lem and should have urgently convened his top leaders on Sunday at the latest, not Monday. Foreign Minister Shevardnadze should have been im-mediately informed, because it would have been obvious that the radiation problem was going to affect the outside world. Yet he began to learn of the problem only on Monday.

All of this raises fundamental questions about the absurdity of Article 4.21 of the censor's "List of Forbidden Topics." Long-term censorship car-ries with it the seeds of its own erosion. By 1986, much of the reading pub-lic did not believe the Soviet media, or believed that it had to be interpreted "between the lines." This does not mean that every nation should have as few restraints on the media as does the United States. Both Britain and France, for example, place greater restrictions on libel and criticisms of the national leadership than does the United States. Yet good information is crucial to a healthy society. Otherwise, how are faults to be brought to light? How are remedies to be conceived?

The failure of Gorbachev to visit the disaster area also needs to be pointed out. In today's world, where information travels around the globe in sec-onds and is repeated, confirmed, hyped, or distorted, the absence of the ul-timate leader at the scene of a disaster projects a perception of indifference. That was not a good signal for a society like the Soviet Union, which for decades claimed to have the interests of all citizens and humanity at heart.

One of Gorbachev's aides declared optimistically after the Chernobyl tragedy, "You could say that Chernobyl delivered a decisive blow against the mania of secrecy, convincing the country to open up to the world." Did Chernobyl really do that? I will come back to that question.

Chapter 30

Links in a Chain

By the summer of 1986, Ruth and I were looking forward to the end of our Moscow assignment. We had been in Russia five and a half years, a long time for a hardship posting. We had lived through four general secretaries, some of the deepest Cold War chill, the shoot-down of the Korean airliner, and the catastrophe at Chernobyl. We had seen acquaintances die, others get married, and a few children born. Caleb, now fourteen, had gone to a Soviet school, learned Russian, made friends, and lost contact with America.

As we approached the last months of the assignment I increased my efforts to find the surviving traces of my Russian ancestry, something I had totally ignored during my first assignment twenty years before. A number of questions drove me on: Did I have any living Russian relatives I could meet before leaving? What happened during the Russian Revolution to the Frolov and Danilov families? And what was the real story of Alexander Frolov, my grandmother's grandfather, who had been arrested in the mutiny of December 14, 1825?

My father, in his engaging manner, used to make light of Frolov at cocktail parties in America, saying that he was a naive young officer who had wandered into the uprising on Senate Square in St. Petersburg and gotten himself arrested for no reason. Somehow, I doubted my father's version. My uncle Mish, Serge's more academic older brother, once told me that Nicholas I interviewed all the rebels and had a few choice words for our ancestor: "So, puppy dog, you joined that rabble too? We'll teach you!" What a great quote! As a part-time instructor at American University during my Washington tenure, I knew that pithy quotes like that tend to change as they are repeated from person to person. That puppy-dog quote was one of the things that drew me into the hunt for Frolov. Even more important was Frolov's sole surviving ambassador—a steel-gray ring, lined with gold, surmounted by a strange inscription, made by Frolov in Siberia, and worn by my father right up to the mid-1950s when he gave it to me. The ring was a link in the chain of family memory.

My first break had come in November 1981 when I spotted an article titled "From the Chains of the Decembrists" published in the newspaper *Sovietskaya Rossiya*. It described how some of the 121 convicts made rings of their chains once their conditions were eased and they were unshackled. I learned from the article that the author was trying to track down as many rings as possible and had uncovered more than fifteen. I immediately wrote to the newspaper. In those Cold War days, almost every effort at outreach began with a letter, the better to allow the recipient time to consider whether to reply or to inform the secret police. In February 1982, I finally got a reply, inviting me to the newspaper's offices on Pravda (Truth) Street.

On arrival, I was ushered up to room 411 where I met Svetlana Stepunina, a subeditor who was marking up copy. She motioned toward a man of medium build. "This is Comrade Malinovsky, Svyatoslav Alexandrovich," she explained, "the author of the article that interested you." We shook hands and soon were deep in conversation about the Decembrists and their rings. Malinovsky was fascinated that one of these pieces should have traveled as far as America and immediately made clear that he hungered to see it personally to make precise measurements of its size. Couldn't I bring it to Moscow the next time I went abroad? he asked. I demurred. Because of the deep suspicions that both superpowers harbored about each other, I thought it risky to bring the ring to Moscow. At this first meeting, Malinovsky became quite insistent, and, possibly as an incentive for me, promised to research the Frolov family history. We agreed to meet again, and I, in return, promised to dig up whatever else I could find about Frolov from my father, uncle, and Matousievich cousins in France.

Two months later, Stepunina called another meeting. Sure enough, Malinovsky was true to his word. "There were six Frolovs associated with the conspiracy," he informed me, "but your ancestor was the most important." He was given a very severe sentence: life at hard labor, which was eventually reduced to ten years of labor and "eternal exile" in Siberia. Out there he married the daughter of a Cossack. Malinovsky explained there was a wellspring of information on the Decembrists in memoirs, historical studies, and a multivolume collection of legal documents called *The Uprising of the*

*Decembrists* that the Soviet Academy of Sciences began publishing in 1925, the one hundredth anniversary of the uprising.

"Here . . . ," my new friend continued, "here is a diagram of the Frolov family tree." He took a piece of paper from his portfolio and passed it to me. "Why, it's almost exactly the same as the family tree I have put together!" I blurted out. He had determined that Frolov's wife, Yevdokiya, had given birth to a daughter, Nadezhda (Hope), and two sons, Nicholas and Peter. Nicholas was Baboota's father. My grandmother had five siblings, Olga, Yelena, Sophia, Alexander, and Gavriil. Malinovsky had identified three of them but missed two sisters, Yelena and Sophia. As we came to the end of our meeting, Malinovsky announced excitedly, "I have a surprise for you. Do you have time for a little excursion?"

It was a Friday, the day of Ambassador Hartman's late-afternoon briefing for American correspondents, but I was willing to risk missing the meeting to accompany Malinovsky. We jumped into a minibus taxi and alighted at the Byelorussian metro station. In the cavernous interior, Malinovsky drew me aside in the best I've-got-to-be-very-careful Cold War manner. Over the roar of the trains, he confided, "It's not a good idea for me to be seeing you often. My work, my son's career, conditions in general . . . you know. If you need to get in touch with me, use this number and call only from a public phone booth." Feeling somewhat disheartened, I acknowledged his warning.

After changing trains, we emerged at the 1905 Street station and headed for Vagankovsky Cemetery, a place that I had visited before with one of my Russian teachers. This time my guide gave no hint as to what he had in mind, but I guessed it would be a grave of one of his ancestors. We came to a sudden stop not far from the church that stands inside the gates, and Malinovsky pointed to a waist-high monument, a reddish granite cube about a yard square, surmounted by two-thirds of a sphere, highly polished. "*Vot!* Here!" he exclaimed. "Frolov's grave!"

I was stunned to silence. After surveying the grave site, I studied the monument closely. A white marble plaque announced that Frolov died in 1885 at age eighty-one. The fenced plot was also the resting place of Frolov's wife, Yevdokiya, who lived until 1901. I spotted, too, the graves of Baboota's two brothers, Gavriil, who died in 1947, and Alexander, in 1942. Even more surprising—something red caught my eye: three red roses and a sprig of greenery. Did that mean I had living relatives? In a while I would find out.

In July 1982, I took the family back to the United States for a vacation in New Hampshire. During that time, I made the decision to risk taking Frolov's ring to Moscow. When I met Malinovsky again in September, he informed me that the Historical Museum on Red Square planned a yearlong exhibit, Three Stages of the Russian Revolution, and would I be willing to put the ring on display? He suggested we take the ring to the museum and have it evaluated. There, several weeks later, an elderly woman, specializing in antique jewelry, dated it to the late eighteenth or early nineteenth century. She deciphered the inscription on its crown as meaning "December 14"—the date of the mutiny. The experts were much intrigued, and the museum director offered to buy the ring for two thousand rubles. Painfully, I informed him that I could not part with a precious family heirloom. But I did weaken and agreed for it to be displayed. Leaving the museum, Malinovsky confided that he had another surprise for me: he had found a living cousin of mine! Her name was Svetlana Algazina, a former surgeon who now worked in the Central Committee of the National Trade Unions. She was the granddaughter of Baboota's sister Olga. "Unfortunately," he added, "she is not very sociable, and has no interest in Frolov. And she doesn't seem to want to meet you. Probably thinks such a contact could harm her career."

The next break came in December 1982. I knew from Malinovsky there existed a society of Decembrist descendants in Moscow that gathered at the end of every year. He mentioned that there might be a possibility that I could attend, especially since my Russian surname would allow me to pass so long as I did not open my mouth and reveal my accent. The meeting convened on a snowy night, December 21, in a historic building on Gogol Boulevard. It was led by A. K. Narishkin, himself the scion of a family famous in Russian history, and was centered on two rather academic lectures that I found stifling. What interested me more was a slide show of Decembrist graves located in various parts of the Soviet Union. Near the end of the evening, Malinovsky and Stepunina pointed me toward an elderly man with graying hair. "That's Boris Ivanovich Yeropkin," Malinovsky whispered to me. "He is one of the two living grandchildren of Decembrists." He stressed the word *grandchildren,* noting that the uprising took place 157 years before. "Let me introduce you to him," he continued, pushing me in Yeropkin's direction. A few moments later, Yeropkin was explaining how his father had married late in life, making it possible for a grandson to be alive today. It was an awkward conversation, but Boris Ivanovich promised more information in the future.

By 1983, my search was gathering momentum. Russian acquaintances, who became interested in my family background, often helped by informing me of relevant materials in publications and libraries. These bits of intelligence came at unexpected, sometimes totally inconvenient, moments, like the time Yeropkin appeared during the Korean Airlines crisis. He showed up at our apartment without warning, a usual ploy to keep below KGB radar. I had just finished sending a dispatch to the magazine on the troubling TASS announcement that the Korean Boeing had violated Soviet airspace and had flown off toward the Sea of Japan. Ruth and I opened the door after repeated knocks.

This time Boris Ivanovich addressed us in very serviceable English. "I had an English nanny in my youth," he explained, "and it's a pleasure to have an excuse to use English again with a native speaker." We sat Boris Ivanovich down for a cup of tea, and he began to tell us his story. He had been brought up in Leningrad, formerly St. Petersburg, and had received an engineering education. He had lived through the starvation years of the German blockade of Leningrad, and had participated in the creation of a land route over frozen Lake Ladoga by which the city was partially resupplied in winter. He told me that there were still two living grandchildren in 1983: himself and a granddaughter who also lived in Leningrad. He had been born in 1910 from an elderly father, born of Decembrist Dmitrii Zavalishin. "You know," he went on, "your great-great-grandfather and my grandfather got into quite a spat many years ago." I had no idea. I learned later that Zavalishin, a young naval officer in 1825, had accused some of his Decembrist colleagues of homosexuality and various indecent acts. Frolov had protested, defending his comrades' honor in an article published in the May 1882 issue of the journal *Russkaya Starina*.

Boris Ivanovich said he was moved to find me because he had come across documents related to Frolov's presence in the Crimea after his sentence was commuted and he was allowed to return to Russia in 1858. He gave me typed copies of these documents that showed the local police sent secret telegrams to Moscow that former "state criminal" Frolov had left the Crimea without permission in November 1873, apparently to visit his son Nicholas. "I thought you should know about these," Boris Ivanovich told me. I thanked my unexpected guest profusely. As he went out the door, we promised to meet again in Leningrad in the not too distant future.

By now, Frolov's story was beginning to emerge in three dimensions, thanks to the persistence of my secretary, Tamara Devyatkina. The more requests Tamara executed, the more she became intrigued by my search. She confessed that the Decembrists had become her "religion." What she meant was that the Decembrists symbolized hope for her in a despotic world. Their behavior in prison constituted an example for anyone disgusted with the contemporary system that had turned Russia into an abnormal state— a prison state in which people were boxed in, deprived, and prevented from traveling. Tamara recalled that one of the convicted conspirators, facing perpetual exile in a faraway territory, famously declared: "The sun also rises in Siberia." Never give up; there's always tomorrow.

We followed that maxim in our searches, too, and began to learn who Frolov really was. I discovered that in 1825, he was a twenty-two-year-old junior lieutenant with the Penzensky Regiment of the Second Army. His father, Filip Frolov, was the commanding officer of a small fort at Kerch that guarded the straits that connects the Sea of Azov to the Black Sea. Alexander Frolov was home-schooled with two brothers and three sisters and entered the military school at Sevastopol at the age of fourteen. By reading the transcripts of the 1826 investigation into the rebellion, I discovered that Frolov was approached by fellow officers in May 1825 to join a secret society known as the Union of United Slavs. This association, which was in close contact with another secret group known as the Southern Society, was deeply influenced by the antimonarchist sentiments of the French Revolution and the democratic ideas that Russian soldiers encountered when they chased Napoléon out of Russia, back to France, in 1813. Their original goal was to depose Czar Alexander I and develop a democratic constitution for Russia. "The time has come," declared one of the conspirators, Nikolai Bestuzhev-Ryumin, "for the liberation of the people from their exploitation and enslavement. It is unthinkable that the Russians, who have made such a name for themselves by their brilliant achievements in war, liberating Europe from Napoléon, would not throw off their own yoke."

When talk turned to assassinating the imperial family, Frolov told the investigators he felt uncomfortable. "Why should we kill the empress?" Frolov protested. "After all, she does so much good for the poor." Further trying to exculpate himself, Frolov declared he had wanted to quit the secret society and inform the authorities. But he was dissuaded from doing so by another officer who asserted that France, Britain, and Austria would intervene to assist the plotters.

The conspirators had planned to make their move in the spring of 1826, but were thrown into confusion by the unexpected death of Alexander I in December 1825. This accelerated their plans, thinking that they could assassinate Nicholas I when he accepted the oaths of loyalty from his troops on Senate Square, December 14. As the key moment approached, the new czar, frightened by the mutiny, ordered loyal troops to put down the uprising after the governor-general of St. Petersburg was shot dead while addressing the conspirators. This armed rebellion on the first day of his reign pushed Nicholas to have no truck with democratic principles. In a way, December 14, 1825, was for Nicholas I a "9/11" moment, requiring a tough reaction.

Contrary to what my father told me, Frolov was nowhere near Senate Square when the uprising occurred. He was arrested near the Ukrainian city of Zhitomir on February 8, 1826, having been fingered by other rebels. Days later, on February 17, Frolov was delivered to the Winter Palace, where Nicholas insisted on personal interviews with most of the conspirators. Nicholas scowled contemptuously when the guards pushed forward the

disheveled young lieutenant. The surviving evidence shows that the interrogation proceeded pretty much as Uncle Mish described it to me. "You!"
shouted the emperor in rage. "How old are you?" The sovereign used the
second-person singular to emphasize his disdain and kicked the young officer in the shins. "Twenty-two years from birth, your majesty," Frolov stut-
tered. "You *malchishka neschastivyi* [unfortunate kid] were with them, too!
Don't torture yourself. I'll teach you!"

At the end of the meeting, Nicholas turned to his chief investigator and
scribbled on a piece of paper, "Imprison and hold under harsh conditions."
Frolov was carted off to the Peter and Paul Fortress where he was confined
in solitary in cell 15 for the next eleven months. During that period he was
interrogated and made to write supplementary statements that have survived in the official records. They were judged to be of minor value. A special judicial tribunal found him guilty of breaking his oath of loyalty to the
emperor and of having been a member of a secret society that planned to assassinate the imperial family.

One hundred and sixty years later, in March 1985, Ruth and I left for
Leningrad to visit the Peter-Paul Fortress where Frolov had been held. We
informed the authorities in advance of our quest, and were greeted warmly
by the historical personnel. Although they had unearthed no specific notes
about Frolov's time in solitary, they did report that he was held in cell 15. I
had wanted to visit that dungeon to get an idea what solitary might have
been like. Here I was disappointed; the cell no longer existed, and its space
had been converted into an administrative office. "But we can show you
another that would be the equivalent," one of our guides said. When we got
to this second cell, I asked to enter. "Could you close the door, so I can feel
what it was like for Frolov?" As the heavy door swung shut, I sensed the
world closing in with frightening finality. It was like being buried alive in a
damp mausoleum, alone and without recourse.

What I lacked now were the details of Frolov's life at hard labor and in exile.
The official documents, though revealing, were laconic reports—departure
by sledge, arrival at the penal colony, years in the mines of Petrovsky Zavod.
How did he survive hard labor? Who were his comrades? How was he exiled
to the tiny Siberian town of Shusha, where seven decades later another conspirator, the founder of the Soviet state, Vladimir Lenin, was exiled in 1897?
By persistent requests to Moscow repositories, we learned in July 1985 that
the Archive of Art and Literature had turned up an unpublished manuscript
about Frolov written for the one hundredth anniversary of the uprising in
1925. I immediately recognized the author's name: it was Sasha Manganari,
Baboota's cousin! I remembered that peculiar name from my walks with her
forty years before. Manganari was the lad who jumped off a clothes closet in

a vain effort to fly. Now I was going to get acquainted with him despite space and time. Tamara and I laid out his 116 outsized pages on the archive reading table and began perusing the handwritten text.

From the very first page, Sasha seemed to be talking directly to me, emphasizing the need for human details. "I've given myself the task to paint a colorful portrait of my grandfather Alexander Filipovich Frolov," he wrote. "For such a portrait you need background. You need it to understand his transition from Decembrist-revolutionary to colonist and transmitter of culture. You need it simply to paint, without abstract judgments, the beautiful, honest, hardworking life of a good man."

Right on, I thought. Tell me more.

The worst time for Frolov, Manganari reported, was the eleven months in solitary in the Peter-Paul Fortress. With no distractions, no Bible, nothing to read, Frolov was tortured by a restless mind constantly worrying what would happen next. Intermittently, he would be called for interrogation, followed by periods of clammy oblivion. To occupy himself, he slipped the whalebone stays that puffed up his uniform jacket and made crude knitting needles. Then he would unravel his woolen socks, winding the yarn into balls. "Now I had yarn and needles," Manganari recalled him saying, "so I could continually be knitting my socks. I would knit, undo, knit, and undo, and so my thoughts gradually became happier."

Frolov had been found guilty by the military tribunal and ranked in the second category of state criminals. He was sentenced to twenty years at hard labor (later commuted to ten) and "eternal exile" in Siberia. On the night of January 20, 1827, Frolov was shackled at the ankles and dispatched unceremoniously with several others by sledge to Siberia, more than three thousand miles from St. Petersburg. After more than two months of travel from St. Petersburg, Frolov arrived at Chita, across Lake Baikal from Irkutsk. They were assigned to a road gang and ordered to move sand for long hours every day. They worked in a pit called "the devil's grave." As they shoveled, the sand cascaded down on them, seeping into their clothes, lodging under their fingernails, making them constantly dirty and itchy. "We labored in chains, tied to our wheelbarrows," Frolov had told his grandson. "Sometimes we would get orders to move faster, and the guards would make us shovel ten hours a day. We were punished for any unguarded grimace or a rude remark." Frolov's group was quartered in a small house inside the stockade. "At first, in the Chita prison our conditions were truly terrible. Sixteen men lived in a small room with plank beds. When we lay down to sleep, we had less than an *arshin* [twenty-eight inches] for each. You couldn't turn over at night without waking up your neighbor."

In time, Nicholas I, under pressure from highly placed relatives, agreed to ease the condition of the prisoners. Their chains were removed, and they were allowed to form two cooperatives: the Greater Artel, in which they pooled their financial resources, and the Lesser Artel, to help departing prisoners settle in exile. These educated men also created a Free University in which they taught a wide variety of courses from Latin and Greek to history, chemistry, agriculture, and medicine.

Dr. F. B. Volf, a staff doctor and Decembrist, became close to Frolov in incarceration. He often gave lectures on anatomy and medicine. "Volf instantly understood that my restless, volatile nature was no good for the high sciences," Frolov told his grandson. "For that reason, I did not try to learn languages, philosophy, or gracious speech—something my more talented comrades did. Instead, I studied the natural sciences. It seems as though one of the great purposes of his life was to make something worthwhile of me. It's not for me to judge whether I justified the time he spent, but I am in his debt in that he gave me a chance to live life to the fullest and not fear any kind of work."

Frolov's hard labor came to an end in 1836, and he was shipped off with a fellow Decembrist, former lieutenant colonel P. I. Falenberg, to exile in the hamlet of Shusha in southeastern Siberia. Although the winters were long, the summers were hot and the ground fertile. Those who lived there often referred to this part of Siberia as "Little Italy." After getting through the first winter of 1836–1837, Frolov began to emerge from subsistence living. He sold the first cabin he built, and constructed a larger house in his second year. Receiving seeds from Russia, he began to farm in a serious way, acquired chickens and livestock. Still, he yearned to return home. He applied, as did some of the other Decembrists, to fight in the Caucasian wars that Nicholas I was waging against insurgent Islamic rebels headed by Imam Shamil. But he was turned down.

More important, however, was that the war in the Caucasus opened his way to marriage. Two fellow Decembrists, the Belyayev brothers, in the neighboring town of Minusinsk had devoted their exile to educating the local population. One of their outstanding pupils was twenty-two-year-old Yevdokiya Makarova, daughter of a Cossack border guard. Alexander Belyayev, who was accepted as a soldier for the Caucasus, decided to abandon Yevdokiya and pass her on to Frolov. She was not consulted on this switch, Sasha Manganari informed me. He recalled that he would ask her how she met Frolov, a subject the paterfamilias was not inclined to discuss. Manganari quoted Yevdokiya explaining the change in marriage plans this way: "I do remember that to prevent the Belyayevs' work on me from being wasted—they spent two years pounding wisdom into me, teaching me every kind of science, how to comport myself so I would be equal to them—they came to a decision to give me away to Alexander Filipovich. The question of protesting never arose, and anyway there was nothing to protest. I knew that if I went with him, I would always be safe."

Together, Alexander and Yevdokiya produced five children in Siberia: Nicholas born in 1846, Nadezhda in 1849, Peter in 1852, and twins, Alexander and Vladimir, in 1855 who survived only a few months. The year 1855 proved to be a turning point in Frolov's life for another reason. Nicholas I died suddenly that year, and his son Alexander, whom he had taken in 1825 to witness the uprising on Senate Square, became emperor. Czar Alexander II quickly turned his attention to the thirty-five surviving Decembrists and decided to pardon them. By his decree of 1856, the "state criminals" were given permission to return to Russia and settle anywhere except Moscow and St. Petersburg. Frolov, who had built up an enviable farm, could easily have stayed on in this fertile part of Siberia. But he quickly made up his mind, without consulting his wife, to return. He sold off his holdings at bargain prices, outfitted a wagon with five horses, and set out for home.

Their parting from Siberia was touching. They headed north toward Minusinsk, where they would cross the powerful Yenisei River and head for Kazan, some three thousand miles away. They lumbered along slowly, accompanied by Yevdokiya's father, Makarov, on horseback and their dog, Kakvaska. When they reached the river crossing, Manganari wrote, they looked back and saw the old man standing on the eastern bank with the dog, slowly waving his hat in a final good-bye, knowing they would never meet again. Frolov headed for Yelizavetgrad for an emotional reunion with his mother and settled initially in the Crimea to raise sheep. Finally, at age seventy, he decided to disregard the ban on returning to Moscow and secretly left the Crimea to rejoin his elder son, now an army captain. Frolov suffered a stroke in 1882 that left him partially paralyzed and nearly blind. He died on May 6, 1885, gasping painfully for breath. "He had a rebellious soul, my great, beautiful falcon," Yevdokiya later told her grandchildren. "As a rebel he lived, and as a rebel he died."

Naturally, I was curious about what Frolov looked like. By 1985, all I knew of Frolov's looks was the 1827 police description on his arrival at Chita for hard labor: "Face, somewhat dark, round, clear; eyes dark brown, large nose with a hump and bent slightly to the right; hair and eyebrows, reddish brown." A Russian historian advised me to visit a famous art expert, Ilya Zilbershtein. Tamara and I finally arranged a meeting with him on July 21, 1985. We found this eighty-one-year-old connoisseur dressed in a gray suit, a shirt without tie, and thin suspenders, his hands trembling from Parkinson's disease. He led us slowly into his large apartment, down a long corridor to his two workrooms, once elegantly painted sky blue but now suffering from years of wear and tear. Some of the plaster had cracked off the ceiling, revealing the slates above. A long table was pushed against the window through which the sun was streaming as we sat down a little before noon. The room was stuffed to overflowing with books, some piled waist-high on the floor, others lying in a fine antique cabinet with glass-paneled doors, beveled at the edges.

I explained my search to Zilbershtein, who seemed suitably impressed by this American guest. It became apparent that I knew more about the Frolov family than he. But he had what I wanted. Frolov's picture was among the watercolors of the Decembrists included in his 675-page book, *Khudozhnik-Dekabrist Nikolai Bestuzhev* (The Artist-Decembrist Nikolai Bestuzhev). "If you had raised this with me six months ago," he acknowledged, "I could have published a picture in color of Frolov in the next edition. The original watercolor is in the Pushkin Museum, you know."

"Where did you find these watercolors?" I asked Zilbershtein. My expert seemed reluctant to answer, but on pressing, he began to recount his own search for these pictures, which had vanished from view for nearly a century. Nikolai Bestuzhev, like many of the other Decembrists, was well educated and a fine artist. He had painted most of his comrades who were sent to hard labor in Chita, particularly after the prison commandant, General Leparsky, had eased their conditions of confinement. On Bestuzhev's death in 1855, the watercolors passed to his sister, who brought them to a famous Moscow art dealer, Koz'ma T. Soldatenko. However, Soldatenko held on to the watercolors for forty years, never offering them for sale. Shortly before his death in 1901, he gave them to two associates who were supposed to, belatedly, fulfill the sister's wish that they be sold or at least made known. However, the associates, in turn, failed to carry out the assignment. They stashed the watercolors and forgot about them until Zilbershtein began poking around in the 1940s.

As a young man, Zilbershtein had started a literary review called *Literaturnoye Nasledstvo* (Literary Heritage) in the 1930s and became intrigued by references in historical sources to the Bestuzhev watercolors. He began hunting in every conceivable corner. Finally, during the Second World War, the director of manuscripts at the Lenin Library in Moscow gave Zilbershtein the names of two old men living in the suburb of Kuntsevo who, he said, might know something. In the winter of 1944, Zilbershtein trekked out to Kuntsevo and called at the first address, only to discover that its elderly resident had died several years before. He then tracked down the second address. At his knock, the door was opened by a very old man, with a flowing, well-trimmed beard. Zilbershtein engaged him in conversation, and gave him a copy of his literary journal. The old man was struck by its rich material—text and pictures—of the poet Pushkin and began inquiring about the stranger's bona fides. In the end, the old man asked him to return in a few days. At the second meeting, the old man presented him with a box. "I opened the box and was flabbergasted," Zilbershtein told me. "There inside were the watercolors. They had not been opened for forty-five years and were as bright as the day they were painted. Watercolors fade, you know, if they are exposed to light. The man told me to take them and to bring the money another time. 'You're doing me a favor,' he said. 'I promised Soldatenko to take care of them years ago. And I failed in my duty to him. You've put the situation right.'" Zilbershtein added that the old man refused to identify himself, apparently to avoid attracting any shame to his name.

Within weeks, I made my way to the Pushkin Museum, where curators were happy to produce the original for me. I held the 150-year-old watercolor uncertainly in my hands. It was a moment of communion: twentieth-century America touching nineteenth-century Russia, or maybe it was the other way around. The picture showed Frolov as a thirty-two-year-old in a white shirt and dark-gray waistcoat, right arm hooked over the back of a chair. He had a full head of chestnut hair, curving sideburns, thinner than English pork chops, extending down his cheeks, and a reddish brown mustache. He had piercing eyes, a Greek nose with a clearly defined hump. Beneath the picture, in flowing Russian script, were the words *Alexander Frolov.*

At the end of December 1985, Tamara learned that an exhibition of Decembrist artifacts would be held at the Pushkin Museum. When we arrived, we were astounded to find that some of Frolov's possessions were on display with the belongings of other Decembrists. His contributions were an icon and a small, richly decorated *shkatulka* (casket). Most surprising to us was the current owner, a person I had never heard of—Boris Glebovich Shtein. After our visit, Tamara spent hours tracking down Boris Shtein. The surname might be Jewish, but from family recollections I knew of no Jewish connection to the Danilovs or the Frolovs. Finally, Tamara was able to persuade the museum to give us Shtein's telephone number, and three months later, on March 21, 1986, Tamara and I paid a visit to him and his wife, Anna Dmitrievna.

Boris Glebovich turned out to be a Moscow literary figure who lived in a large apartment building near the panorama monument to the Battle of Borodino on Kutuzovsky Prospekt. Entering the apartment through a long hall, we found him and his wife ensconced among floor-to-ceiling bookcases filled with books, manuscripts, and files. He greeted us warmly and motioned for us to sit down on the four chairs they had drawn together in the living room. Speaking in a calm voice, occasionally punctuated by an emotional high, he began to explain how he was related to Baboota's younger brother, Alexander Frolov. "Alexander," Shtein explained, "was born in 1877 and at the turn of the century began to follow the family's tradition by serving in the army in Poltava. There he fell in love with a married woman—Alexandra Iosiofna Vinitskaya. She had a daughter, Yelena, who was born in 1894." The romance broke up Vinitskaya's marriage, but her husband refused to agree to a divorce, which forced Alexander and Alexandra to live in sin. Finally, Mr. Vinitskii relented, and the couple was married. Boris Glebovich continued:

> Alexander, who had an artistic temperament, left the army and in the years before the First World War—somewhere around 1910–1913—went to Paris to study art and theater. He was supported by his wife, who apparently had money.
>
> Returning to Moscow, they settled in a large apartment near the Bolshoi Theater. Alexandra ran a fashion shop with several seamstresses below the apartment. After the war, in 1918, the daughter, Yelena, married a man whose name was originally Gleb Vonshtein. He was a Russian of German heritage. You know there were quite a few of those in old Russia.

Because of the anti-German feelings spawned by the First World War, the Vonshtein family dropped the German particle *von* and went simply by the name Shtein. Thus, my host turned out to be Yelena's son, a nephew-twice-removed of Baboota. "Alexander Frolov, my grandfather, used to live in the Kremlin," Boris Glebovich said, "because the Decembrist's son Nikolai was an artillery officer assigned to the Kremlin arsenal. We sometimes used to walk together in the gardens below the Kremlin, and my grandfather would point up to the walls and say, 'That's where we used to live!'" That little fact confirmed for me Baboota's boast of having been born in the Kremlin.

The Frolov family was very sociable, frequently having dinner parties. Alexander Frolov favored stylish dress, and was always well turned out, even in the hardest of times. When the revolution struck in 1917, the family was plunged into poverty. They were not political by nature, and accepted the new government without protest. But an *ukaz* (order) by the new regime forced the wealthy to accept poor people into their homes on a permanent basis and created the phenomenon of communal apartments that lived on until the collapse of the Soviet Union. The Frolov family was forced to live in what had been Madame Vinitskaya's office of thirty-eight square meters. They divided that space into five individual cubicles.

A friend of the family, the former Prince Shakovskoi, used to joke about the changes brought about by the revolution. "Once, I went with Prince Shakovskoi to a magic shop where we bought a trick tube," Boris Glebovich continued. "You could put things in both ends of the tube. Then you covered the tube with a shawl, opened the ends of the tube, and the articles disappeared. Shakovskoi would say, 'It's like the revolution. They throw a red shawl over us, and we disappear!'"

Boris Glebovich knew quite a lot about Baboota's cousin Sasha Manganari. It turned out that Sasha, like Alexander, also had an artistic bent and became a painter and engraver. He produced for me some of Manganari's engravings of nudes, and told me that many of his paintings were in the Art Museum in Leningrad, now again called St. Petersburg. "He was a strange man," Boris Glebovich recalled, "with long hair and a beard. He limped and walked with a cane. In a way, he looked like Karl Marx." That description tallied with what Baboota had told me in New Hampshire about Sasha injuring a leg when he tried to fly by jumping off a closet with homemade wings. "He disappeared around 1932," Boris Glebovich went on. "He was returning to his mother, Nadezhda, at Frolov's dacha in the Crimea when he was hit with typhoid. He died, was taken off the train, and apparently buried in an unmarked grave."

The Second World War had a devastating effect on the Frolov family, especially on Alexander and Alexandra. Boris Glebovich continued:

> These people had lived through the revolution and civil war. When the second war came, Alexander was sixty-seven, the same age that I am now. I literally saw the life ebb out of him before my eyes. The family was used to eating and drinking well. Now there was *golod i kholod* [famine and cold]. There was little vodka to be had, but when they got a bottle they would share one or two shot glasses among themselves. My grandfather seemed to wither away. I sometimes could get him something special to eat and drink, and he would cheer up. He died in 1942, and I buried him at Decembrist Frolov's grave site. His wife, Alexandra, seemed to start losing her mind after my grandfather's death. She began selling things from the apartment until she was committed to the Ganushkin Hospital. There she would bewilder the other patients with her stories, and she would often mix up her words, going suddenly from Russian to French and back again. Often she would begin, "Now when I was living in Paris . . ." She died in 1947.

My newfound relative didn't seem to know anything about my grandmother other than her marriage to General Danilov. That was not so surprising since the Second World War broke off communications among family members in Moscow and those who fled abroad. I learned from the Art and Literature Archives that the wife of Baboota's brother Gavriil was still alive in 1967, and, theoretically, I might have met her during my first Moscow assignment. But I had no hint of that at the time. The last letter we received from Moscow, according to my father, came in 1942. And anyway, as a youth in my late twenties, I was still years away from wanting to know what came before me.

My last effort to resurrect Frolov occurred in June 1986, when Ruth and I boarded the trans-Siberian train to Novosibirsk on our way to Shusha in Siberia. Reports surfaced occasionally in some Moscow newspapers that Frolov had built the house where Lenin lived when he was exiled to the same Siberian hamlet under Nicholas II. On arrival, we visited the museum and historical park devoted to Lenin's life in exile. We were amused by a notation in one of the records of 1895 that the police kept a regular, if careless, watch on this latest revolutionary who, like the Decembrists, was plotting the overthrow of the Romanov dynasty. One police notation reported on Lenin's activities this way: "He is reading something, and writing something." In fact, Lenin was carrying on an active correspondence with socialist and communist revolutionaries all over Europe and drafting his famous tome, *The Rise of Capitalism in Russia*.

The director of the museum, Yuri A. Ivanov, whom we contacted ahead of time, had arranged for us also to meet with a number of Siberian historians. Archivist Ludmilla Sisoyeva, who flew in from Krasnoyarsk, generously brought with her more documents about Frolov's life. We learned, for example, that their twins, Vladimir and Alexander, born in April 1855, died in infancy. We also discovered that Frolov got into a quarrel with one of the neighbors and was brought to court. Possibly the most significant detail we learned was that Frolov did not build the house where Lenin lived, but there was a connection. Frolov had built a guesthouse that was later bought by one of the residents and moved to another location. This became a village clubhouse where Lenin would come to play chess with the locals. A massive fire in the 1880s destroyed Frolov's main house, which he had abandoned when he left for Russia. Today the land that he owned has been covered over by blacktop, and a bank stands in its place.

Standing on this unrecognizable spot where Frolov built his house so long ago, I took out my blue notepad and scribbled these thoughts:

> There was a mysterious feeling. Why am I here at all? What is pushing me to uncover my roots? It is probably not comprehensible intellectually. Yet it carries an increasing urgency. To some extent it may be mixed up with a desire to try to further a dialogue between the United States and the USSR. In that sense it is more than just a selfish desire. And judging by the warm way I was received and the conversations that I had, something

came of it. There was communication, and even though nothing was resolved, there was a sense of hope.

My travels in Russia convinced me of this: We are all links in a chain. To
know yourself, to know your family, or—on a grander scale—to know the
world, or Russia, or America, you have to understand that chain. You have
to know the rings, the links. The past is indeed prologue to the present and
threshold to the future.

Chapter 31

The Gulag's Vestibule

On Saturday, August 30, 1986, Ruth and I were finally preparing for a roundabout trip through Russia back to the United States. We planned to travel on the trans-Siberian railroad and leave from the Pacific coast for Japan. A bit before eleven in the morning, I slipped out of the apartment to meet Misha Luzin, my Russian friend from Kirghizia. Misha had been very helpful during the past few years in providing insights into the toll that the Soviet intervention in Afghanistan was taking. For this last meeting, I planned to give him a half-dozen novels by Stephen King that he longed for. I thought he might bring me some newspaper articles that would show how Gorbachev's policies of glasnost and perestroika were developing in central Asia. As I walked out the door I had not the slightest idea of the trap I was stepping into. Perhaps I should have. A week earlier the FBI in New York had arrested a Soviet physicist working for the United Nations Secretariat and charged him with espionage.

As agreed, we met at the Leninskii Prospekt subway station, and we walked down to the Moscow River embankment not far away. This was a park surrounding the river where we often met before. Moscow correspondents preferred to talk to their most precious sources outside their offices, away from the microphones hidden in the walls of their offices. We settled comfortably into a little A-frame shelter by the river. I explained I was winding up my Moscow assignment but hoped to return in March of the next year when I would be sure to look him up. He pulled out an envelope from his jacket that he said contained the clippings on perestroika in central Asia and some photographs from Afghanistan; I handed him the Stephen King novels.

I tried to persuade Misha to come back to the apartment to meet my replacement, Jeff Trimble, and his wife, Gretchen, but Misha seemed unenthusiastic. That was not unusual; in the Soviet Union sources of information usually developed on a personal basis and were nontransferable to the next correspondent. Excusing himself, Misha got up to leave. The abrupt way he ended our meeting was a disappointment, but it raised no alarm bells. I offered to walk with Misha to the Sportivnaya subway station for which he was heading, but he declined. The first inkling that something was amiss came when I spotted a white unmarked van coming my way down a road rarely used by automobiles. Then, suddenly, the van's door slid open, and six men jumped out and sailed toward me. My attackers threw me against the van and forced me into handcuffs. The thought whipped through my mind, as I was being pushed into the van, that I would be hurt if I resisted.

It all happened so quickly, I did not drop the white plastic bag I was carrying with Misha's envelope. To be detained in this manner, with no warning, unhinged me momentarily. I knew I was in trouble; I guessed it was the KGB. But why? As we took off at high speed, I sat lodged between two husky men. One fished in my pocket and pulled out my wallet and Soviet press card. "A foreigner!" he declared as if he had no idea whom he had been sent to arrest. I was getting more and more frightened, but had the self-control to remain silent.

On arrival at Lefortovo Prison, I was lined up outside the prison wall and photographed still holding the white plastic bag. It dawned on me this was to be a propaganda picture that would probably be published with a title along the lines: "Spy Caught Red-Handed." Next, I was pushed into the prison entrance and marched up to interrogation room 215 where I found two men waiting for me. One was a young man with a sallow complexion, the other a tall man in a well-cut business suit, probably a senior official in his sixties, with black hair combed straight back over his head. "You have been arrested on suspicion of espionage," said this imposing figure. "I am the person who ordered your arrest."

I remained silent. But inside, I cringed. All thoughts of leaving the Soviet Union with Ruth on that extensive homeward journey evaporated. I wondered how she was going to react. The way this senior officer said that last sentence was threatening. It made me suspect that I was in for a lengthy struggle whose outcome was uncertain.

The official ordered the arrest team to remove my handcuffs and dismissed them. Then he asked for witnesses to be ushered in. I had no idea who they were, or why they were summoned. One was a middle-aged woman who looked as if she had been out doing her Saturday shopping, or maybe she was just a prison secretary. The other was an athletic-looking man, about thirty-five, possibly a passerby, but more likely one of the prison guards in civilian clothes. The investigator motioned for them to sit down at a long table that extended from his desk. Behind them, a still photographer took up a position to record the scene. The investigator indicated I should sit facing the camera and opposite the witnesses. He then pulled Misha's envelope out of the white plastic bag. "What have we here?" he said extracting the contents. "Negatives, black and white photographs, newspaper clippings, maps!" I immediately sensed a false excitement in his voice, as if he knew very well what was in the envelope.

We squinted at the pictures, but they were hard to make out because some were overexposed. Finally, he laid out the maps on the table. "The first one shows part of Afghanistan and has handwritten markings on it, symbols noting the deployment of troop formations," he announced. "And the second is a hand-drawn diagram of a region indicating where military equipment is located. The map contains a variety of code names—Abakan, Shushenskoye . . ." I was taken aback by those names; they were places that I had visited in June during our trip to Siberia. What did that mean? Was this some kind of intricate plot whose details were to be revealed later? I never did find out the answer to that one.

It was clear that the authorities intended to print these pictures for all the world to see. By now I had settled down a bit, and an idea came to my head. I remembered the sailors of the ill-fated USS *Pueblo,* captured by North Korea in 1968, had been photographed as spies and, in defiance, had given "the finger" to signal their mood of resistance. I decided to do the same. I extended both middle fingers of my hands and placed them ostentatiously on the maps. I counted on this gesture conveying abroad that this was a setup. The two KGB officers made no comment, but other authorities must have understood. The pictures were never published.

The photo op over, the senior official introduced himself in perfectly civil tones, "I am Colonel Sergadeyev, Valery Dmitriyevich, of the Committee of State Security, investigative section." He paused.

"Valery Dmitriyevich," I interrupted in Russian. "I don't know why I have been brought here. My arrest very much resembles that of my colleague Robert Toth a few years ago."

The colonel frowned threateningly and said, "I would say your case is quite different."

I continued, "I have a request. I was expected home at one o'clock. I would be grateful if you would call my wife and tell her that I will not be there on time. Tell her I am in reliable hands. Also, if I remember correctly,

I have the right under the U.S.-Soviet consular convention to telephone my embassy immediately and inform them I have been detained."

"All agreements will be observed," the colonel replied coolly.

I could feel a growing panic within me. What should I do? What were my rights, if any? I tried to remember what a Soviet dissident, Vladimir Albrekht, had said in an underground pamphlet on coping with searches and interrogations. As far as I could recall, Albrekht recommended not trying to deny the undeniable, to avoid comment on third parties, and to answer questions relating only to the case at hand. Since his advice strengthened the hand of a defendant, the authorities considered his pamphlet to be anti-Soviet and tried to suppress it.

Just then, Sergadeyev broke into my thoughts. "I would like to inform you of your rights. You have the right to legal counsel *after* the preliminary examination. You may take notes; you may use a tape recorder. You may present your own affidavits and explanations." He handed me a copy of the procedural code and urged me to study it. I looked at it blankly for some minutes, not knowing what to do. I flipped over some of the pages, finding it impossible to concentrate. Needless to say, I completely missed Article 46, the right to remain silent, and Article 142, the right to explain why I might refuse to sign any papers. The colonel had carefully avoided alluding to them.

"Now, then," Sergadeyev resumed the interrogation, his interpreter translating awkwardly into English. "Tell me about your relationship with Misha. I should tell you that he has been arrested on suspicion of treason under Article 64 of the criminal code and is being interrogated at the same time as you. I would urge you to be honest and sincere. I think you will find that cooperation will be to your ultimate benefit."

I found Sergadeyev's statement difficult to digest. Since first meeting Misha in the central Asian town of Frunze (now renamed Bishkek) in 1982 with my colleague Jim Gallagher of the *Chicago Tribune,* we had both judged that Misha might have connections with the KGB. However, during the next three years, Misha visited us several times in Moscow. He turned into a good source on the mood in central Asia about the Soviet war in Afghanistan. He occasionally showed me scrapbooks, songs, and photographs that the young Soviet recruits in Afghanistan kept. For our part, we introduced Misha to pizza, which he came to like a lot. He left us with the impression that he was a Russian lad who had grown up in central Asia who was seeking ties to the outside world. He seemed to me to be suitably intimidated by the KGB and urged me to do nothing that would bring him to the attention of the secret police. Looking back on this friendship later, it was clear that Misha had a relationship with the KGB and his actions were intended from the start to build a sense of trust between us. A close relationship would have advantages for the KGB, like using this channel to insert incriminating information into my hands. It was hard to assess whether Sergadeyev was telling the truth about Misha's arrest. I turned the possibilities over in my mind, but decided the only thing I could do was to wait and see.

At five o'clock, after four hours of interrogation, Sergadeyev brought the proceedings to a halt. "You may make your call now," he told me. "Here, use this phone," he said pointing to one of three on a small table beside his desk. For a moment, I thought of dialing 252–2451, the embassy number. But it was Saturday afternoon, and I knew I would get only a marine guard who wouldn't know what to answer. So, instead, I dialed 137–5024, the number of the *U.S. News and World Report* bureau. My replacement, Jeff Trimble, answered. I explained what had happened and where I thought I was. Jeff replied cheerily, "It's in retaliation for the arrest of Gennadii Zakharov in New York. He was refused bail . . ." So that was it: tit for tat. "Where's Ruth?" "She's coming just now."

When Ruth came on the line, I repeated the essential facts. As I gazed at the telephone, I saw its number was taped to its base. "Have you got a pencil?" I asked. "Write down this number: 361–6556. That's where I am." Sergadeyev looked at me blankly.

"Got it," she replied. Her voice was calm and businesslike. That was the best news of the day. She and Jeff would know to share the number with my journalistic colleagues. They would be on the story like a shot, and my case would not disappear into a dark dungeon. "How long do you think you will be held?" Ruth asked.

"I would guess weeks at this rate," I replied, glancing at the colonel and his translator, who remained expressionless. In the next minutes, Ruth and I completed our conversation. Her warmth and support stayed with me until the colonel distracted me with his next order. "The guards will take you to the place you will spend the night," he said as if he was referring to a pleasant country inn. Two guards marched me, hands behind my back according to prison protocol, down to the basement of Lefortovo Prison and opened the door to Cell 26. The cells all had solid metal doors with a peephole and a small window through which food could be passed. When the door slammed shut, a wave of claustrophobia swept over me. I was in a chilly, eight-by-ten-foot cell and wanted to shout, "Let me out!" But the words failed me. I felt desperately alone, as if buried alive. Suddenly, a stranger moved toward me out of a corner, and introduced himself as Stas Zenin. "Welcome to the Gulag's vestibule," he said cheerily, stressing the word *Gulag*. On this occasion and in the days to come, Stas did his best to restore my sense of calm.

On the following day, I was taken to be officially entered into the prison's records. Two guards took my fingerprints. "It's still the same old technology," one of them said, as he rolled my fingers over an ink pad almost apologetically. After the usual mug shots, they took out a form to set down in words a description of my face. They noted that I was middle-aged, with brown hair, brown eyes, and "a nose with a slight hump." The words were almost the same as in the police description of Frolov in 1827. This coincidence was unsettling . . . It became clear to me much later that in our family, many of us have "a nose with a hump." But at the moment I didn't know what to make of this physical similarity, passed down genetically from generation to generation. I was definitely a link in the Frolov chain!

During the next thirteen days, Colonel Sergadeyev called me nearly every day for lengthy interrogation. Early in our sessions, he asked if I was satisfied with his interpreter. Having noted that my Russian was considerably better than his English, I told the colonel we could dispense with the interpreter. I thought that speaking directly to the interrogator would make it easier for me to explain any actions that might look suspicious. That decision, I came to realize, was my first big mistake. To work through an incompetent interpreter has advantages. For one thing, it is bound to draw out the proceedings, thereby preventing the interrogator from getting quickly to the most useful information from his point of view. Second, using an interpreter is like having a buffer between yourself and your tormentor. One of the problems any reflective person has in an interrogation is to guess what is coming next and how to prepare for it. My spontaneous decision deprived me unwittingly of those two aces.

Day after day, we worked in the following way. Sergadeyev would question me closely about my sources of information. Frequently, he would suggest that I was acting on direct orders from the CIA station in the U.S. Embassy. Sometimes, when he was playing "good cop," he would compliment me on my Russian and on my self-control. "You are really a very accomplished spy," he would say. To this I would reply over and over again, "I am not a spy. I have never been a spy." Then, during the same session, he could turn himself into "bad cop" and drill me with leading questions to which any answer looked incriminating. When I objected to his choice of words, he asserted that if I did not like his manner I could request a different investigator. I passed up that suggestion, believing for the moment it was better to cooperate with the known devil. That was probably my second mistake. Today I think that what I really should have done was refuse all cooperation. However, at the time I was frightened and spooked myself by dreaming up horrible consequences for silence.

Following interrogation, Sergadeyev would write out in longhand, in my presence, his questions and my answers. I could edit and amend my responses. These transcripts would be sent overnight to a secretary who would type them up. The next day, we would go over the typed-up version, and he would ask me to sign them. I was unhappy about signing. I did not realize I could refuse. Ignorant of the provisions of the procedural code, I made it a rule to read over my answers in Russian at least three times. I flirted with the idea of signing "Nicholas B. S. Daniloff"—again a ploy to signal to the outside world if these documents were ever published that I was signaling a setup. In the end, I simply signed my name.

These daily sessions were interrupted by a number of visits from Ruth, Caleb, and the American consul, Roger Daley. In the first visit, the American official asked me to sign a waiver of the Privacy Act so that the embassy could comment freely on my case. Try as I might, I could not get Colonel Sergadeyev to understand what the issue was about. In the end, I just told him it was an American *formalnost'*, a formality, and he agreed to let it go at that.

These visits were important to me for other reasons. Ruth reassured me that a worldwide reaction had set in and that the story was the top news topic in the United States. She whispered to me that she rejected the advice of the embassy to stay silent while the diplomats tried to unscramble the mess and intended to shout as loudly as possible about the frame-up. After twenty-five years of marriage, her passion did not surprise me, and it gave me strength.

Whenever she came to the prison, she brought along a bevy of newsmen. On one occasion a TV crew placed a ladder against the outside prison wall in an attempt to shoot down inside. If there ever was proof of love and devotion, this was it. In the interrogation room, Colonel Sergadeyev was mightily displeased. "Is your wife aggressive?" he asked me. "What do you expect?" I replied. "She is defending her husband." Sergadeyev shot back, "I must protest to you that the reporters she brought to the prison were very disorderly. One of them even put a ladder against the wall. Against the wall! Against government property. Hooligans!" His scowling frightened me.

But he was not always "bad cop." When he was playing "good cop," he would try to make me relax by engaging in informal conversation. "If we were doing this interrogation in America, how would it go?" he asked at one point. It did seem to me that the interrogation was proceeding in a nineteenth-century sort of way. "I don't know," I answered. "I've never been under arrest before. But I am sure of one thing: if we were in American you'd be using a computer."

"Ah," the colonel sighed, "we in Russia are not there yet."

On another occasion, I asked him about his family and where he lived in Moscow. He replied he had two daughters and lived in the Izmailovskii district near a large, pleasant park. He questioned me about how the media in the United States work. It was clear that he thought the media took their direction from the government. I tried to disabuse him of that notion. Whenever I appeared intimidated by his questioning, he shot at me, "Nikolai Sergeyevich, why do you always look at me as if I were pointing a gun at you?" "Because you are! Anything I say, you try to make me look guilty." "You know how I know you are a spy?" he said during one session. "Because of that article you wrote in your magazine about the KGB." He was referring to my article the magazine published in its March 25, 1985, issue about the vast extent of the secret police organization. "It was dictated to you by a CIA source." "Nonsense," I replied. "I based it on readings published in the West about your organization and on interviews with Soviet citizens who have had contacts with you." That evening I left the interrogation room somewhat heartened. If this was the best he could produce, I thought, he was not going to get very far. I felt I had achieved a small victory.

On Sunday, September 7, 1986—oddly enough, this was my father's birthday—he proved that he still had the upper hand. On that day, I was called for interrogation in the afternoon. That was unusual because Sundays and Saturdays, too, were considered sacred rest days in the Soviet Union. When I walked into the room, accompanied by two guards, I was confronted by a rotund man wearing a fine leather jacket over a sweater. Sergadeyev introduced this newcomer as a general from the military court system. I did not catch his name. The general then disclosed that they had decided to issue an indictment against me. "Espionage," he said, "is a particularly severe crime. It is punishable by heavy sentences up to the death penalty." The reference to execution took my breath away. My head became clouded; I felt my blood pressure going through the roof, but I remained silent. "Aren't you concerned about the death penalty?" the general asked in an irritated tone, drumming his fingers on the table. "Of course," I replied.

He then pushed in front of me a paper that accused me of three counts of espionage: (1) collecting, on the instructions of the CIA, and transmitting to the CIA information of an economic, political, and military character detrimental to the Soviet Union; (2) assisting the CIA in making a conspiratorial contact with a Soviet citizen; and (3) other espionage activities.

We had come to a turning point. I could sign the paper the general was pushing forward at me and thereby, I hoped, bring further interrogations to an end. Or I could refuse any acknowledgment and categorically deny any wrongdoing. I weighed these possibilities over in my mind. I felt almost too weak to fight back. If I was going to be true to myself, however, I really had no choice, so I refused to sign or acknowledge the sections laying out the substantive indictment. I did sign the third section that stated I had read and understood the accusations. That was a fact, which according to Albrekht's advice, I could not deny.

Immediately after signing, the general got up and left me alone with Sergadeyev. I was dying to go back to my cell to collect my thoughts about what had just happened. But the colonel had other ideas. On this Sunday he had turned into "bad cop." Staring at me, he said, "We have something more to discuss: Father Roman. Tell me about Father Roman. We know you received a letter from Father Roman. What did you do with it?"

This was one subject I had hoped would not come up, but now there was no way to avoid it. For a while, I remained silent, turning over in my mind what to say next until, under the colonel's prodding, I finally replied. "The envelope contained a second envelope," I said, "and it was addressed to Ambassador Hartman, so I took it to the embassy." "But whom exactly did you give it to at the embassy?" he snapped.

I hesitated. Giving the KGB the names of third parties did not sit well with me or with Albrekht. I was reluctant to implicate anyone. "I'd rather not say," I replied, knowing that the answer immediately made me look guilty. Sergadeyev was not swayed. He could see that he was at a crucial point. By forcing me to answer that question, he would break a hole in my dike. If he could do that, it would be easier for him to breach my resistance a second, and a third, time.

"It's useless," the colonel said. "Nikolai Sergeyevich, you must tell us. We can show you photographs that will make you tell us everything." I was distinctly not happy to see any photographs. I had no idea what photographs he could produce that would make me talk. Photographs of me with CIA agents under diplomatic cover? Photographs doctored to be incriminating? I was afraid that by looking at any photographs, my body language, my facial expression, my general reaction, might betray something. "You must tell us, Nikolai Sergeyevich," the colonel said in a tone that suggested he had many unpleasant means to open my mouth. He could see my resolve was weakening. I finally gave him his answer: "I gave it to our chief press counselor, Ray Benson."

A look of satisfaction passed over Sergadeyev's face. He had obtained what he was looking for and won a psychological victory. He knew that I knew that too. Taking advantage of his victory, Sergadeyev plowed on. His tack was to tie me directly to the CIA. "Now," he said, pulling on his cigarette, "I want to know about your relationship with Paul Stombaugh," a logical question from his point of view. Paul Stombaugh, a CIA officer working at the embassy under diplomatic cover, had been expelled from the Soviet Union in June 1985 for making contact with a dissident scientist who supplied much valuable information on Soviet avionics. I acknowledged I was aware of that incident but never met Stombaugh or had any relation with him.

The colonel did not believe me. "We have reason to believe you did," he insisted. "In fact, we know that Stombaugh telephoned Roman and introduced himself saying, 'I am a friend of Nikolai's.' How do we know? We recorded the conversation. We have it on tape. It clearly suggests that you were a friend of Stombaugh's and that you worked together. What other explanation is there?"

I was stunned. "Not only that," he continued. "We intercepted a letter from Stombaugh to Father Roman in which you figure prominently. Let me read you a passage." He pulled out a photocopy of a letter typed on a single sheet of paper and read with evident delight: "Dear and esteemed friend . . . We would like to assure you that the letter you sent to us through the journalist on January 24 reached the destination you indicated. We value your work highly . . ."

Sergadeyev tried to convince me of the authenticity of the letter and flashed it in front of me. It was written in Russian and contained some spelling mistakes. The colonel made light of the errors, saying that Americans usually had trouble writing ordinary Russian. The letter was signed "Michael" in Russian and spelled incorrectly.

"But," I protested, "Stombaugh's first name is Paul, not Michael." "So what makes you think he would sign his real name?" I had no answer.

"And another thing . . ." Sergadeyev's smug expression showed that he felt he was on sure ground. "This letter was typed on your office typewriter!" Here he was pushing beyond his knowledge, hoping I would cave.

I took the letter from him, terrified at what I might find. The copy was clear and perfectly in focus. I could make out the typeface easily. "It was not," I protested. "These letters are smaller, and the type is bolder. I had absolutely nothing to do with this!" I threw the paper back at him. "Anyway, I've told you over and over again: I had no contact with these CIA people." I was relieved. I thought at the time this was a phony document, proof that the KGB was stooping to false evidence to make their case.

Sergadeyev was implacable. "Are you trying to tell me that Murat [Natirboff] involved you 'in the dark'?" That was a Russian expression that I did not know, but could guess from the context. "You mean unwittingly?" I replied. "Yes, if I understand the Russian language correctly. If Natirboff and Stombaugh used my name, they did so without my knowledge, and without my permission. It was done 'v temnuyou,' as you say, 'in the dark.'" Here I thought I had won a victory. Judging by his expression, Sergadeyev seemed to accept that there might be another explanation besides direct, explicit cooperation with the CIA.

Years after these interrogations, people have asked me whether I was physically tortured in prison. I was not tortured physically. There were no beatings, no sleep deprivation, no stress positions, no naked grillings, no growling dogs, no deprivation of food. However, that is only part of the answer. To be held in prison, to be denied legal counsel, to be called constantly for hostile questioning, to be denied access to the outside world except at the pleasure of the investigator is duress . . . and duress is mental torture. I felt it keenly. I was constantly trying to figure out what was going to hit me next, and that scared me to the point that I could hardly reason with myself. It slowly dawned on me why prisoners ask for a Bible or a Koran. You have to while away anxious hours before the next blow, and the scriptures can both occupy and calm you. As an agnostic, I recognized how belief in the Deity could be of enormous help. In confinement, faith still escaped me; I envied the believers.

To cope, I turned my thoughts to history. I recalled Alexander Frolov, who had joined the conspiracy to overthrow Nicholas I, his arrest in St. Petersburg, and his exile in Siberia. Strange as it seems, I also thought about the American founding fathers and the constitution they put together in 1787. Several aspects of the U.S. Constitution made an impression on me as I reflected on them: An independent judiciary that can prevent "star chamber" trials—executive power imposing its will on a court. The prohibition against cruel and unusual punishment. And, of course, the First Amendment and its interpretations by the U.S. Supreme Court. Sitting in Lefortovo Prison, I realized how little I really knew about American constitutional history, in fact about American history. Harvard had required little of American history from me. I told myself that one day I would delve more deeply into those subjects.

Of course, I wondered constantly what was happening in the outside world. The Reagan administration had been caught off guard during the August vacation season. White House spokesman Larry Speakes had said publicly that the plans for a Reagan-Gorbachev summit would go ahead despite my arrest. As time went on, officials split into two camps. On one side, hardliners in the National Security Council, the Department of Justice, and Congress demanded a trial for Zakharov and my unconditional release. Jack Matlock, of the National Security Council and later ambassador to Moscow, has described the tough position he forwarded to Secretary of State George Shultz but was brushed aside.

On the other side, President Reagan and top State Department officials realized full well that I was arrested for a purpose—the freeing of Zakharov through negotiations. If I were tried and sentenced, a summit meeting would become politically impossible. Secretary of State Shultz has described the complexity of reaching any decision in this split atmosphere in his memoir *Turmoil and Triumph*. In the end, a dominant feeling emerged that I was owed a helping hand for two reasons: I had done the United States a favor by delivering the letter from Father Roman, and CIA operatives had compromised me through professional carelessness. As time went on, the prison authorities eased my conditions, and when events moved toward resolution, I began receiving visits from the prison commandant, Alexander Petrenko, who supplied me with extra blankets and an improved diet.

Later, I learned that the Central Intelligence Agency had invoked the "Gavrilov Channel," a rarely used link to the Soviet spy agency. It had been established on KGB initiative some years before, somewhat in the spirit of the White House–Kremlin hotline. Its purpose was to inform the other side of items of urgent concerns, such as terrorism or other serious problems. The Gavrilov Channel was yet another example of Cold War rules of behavior, not unlike the electronic signaling by the Strategic Air Command when Soviet submarines approached too close to American shores. Needless to say, those Cold War conventions were more reliable than the haphazard communications during the current war on terrorism.

During my imprisonment, CIA officials traveled to Vienna to inform their KGB counterparts that I had no connection with the CIA and that I was being pulled into this episode unfairly. One of the Soviet representatives was KGB Major General Rem Krassilnikov, who I am confident did nothing to inform Colonel Sergadeyev of the CIA message. To do so would have undermined his investigation. Rather, Krassilnikov argued that Zakharov should be let off lightly because he was a naive graduate student. Actually, he was a major in the KGB masquerading as an academic.

*U.S. News* owner Mort Zuckerman, much to his credit, came out strongly in support of me. Foreign correspondents cannot always count on strong backing from the home office when things go wrong for reasons I have suggested earlier. Zuckerman and his top editors were in constant contact with the State Department and other officials. Mort made a special trip to Moscow and visited me in Lefortovo Prison, telling Colonel Sergadeyev he wished to take me back to the United States with him on his return journey. The colonel replied dryly, "I think Mr. Daniloff will be taking another flight."

Meantime, President Reagan received assurances from the U.S. intelligence community that I had no connection with the U.S. government. On the advice of his national security team, he sent Gorbachev a letter modeled on the letter that President Kennedy sent to Khrushchev asserting that Professor Barghoorn was not a spy and requesting immediate release. For the president of the United States to involve himself personally in the calamity of a single individual was extraordinary. I attribute this to Reagan's ability to empathize with individuals in distress. On September 5, 1986, Reagan wrote Gorbachev:

I am sure that you have been monitoring, as I have, developments relating to the detention by Soviet authorities of the U.S. News and World Report Moscow correspondent, Nicholas Daniloff. I would like you to have in mind two points as you consider how to handle this case.

First, I can give you my personal assurance that Mr. Daniloff has no connection whatever with the U.S. government. If you have been informed otherwise, you have been misinformed.

Second, there are no grounds for Mr. Daniloff's detention, nor any attempt to link him to any other case. If he is not freed promptly, it can only have the most serious and far-reaching consequences for the relationship between our two countries. That would be an extremely unfortunate outcome, and I therefore thought it important to emphasize personally the gravity with which this situation is viewed in the United States.

Gorbachev, the tough guy, replied the next day, brushing aside Reagan's assurances and angering the president, who considered the response to be needlessly arrogant. Gorbachev said in his missive:

Your letter of September 5 prompted me to ask for information regarding the question you raised. As was reported to me by the competent authorities, Daniloff, the Moscow correspondent of the U.S. News and World Report magazine, had for a long time been engaged in impermissible activities damaging to the state interests of the USSR. Now an investigation is being conducted by the results of which we shall be able to make a conclusive judgment about this entire case.

I think that we both should not permit the use of questions of such kind to the detriment of the Soviet-American relations whose improvement and development are extremely important.

On receipt of Gorbachev's letter, President Reagan immediately fired off a reply by the Washington-Moscow hotline, barely disguising his growing anger:

I am disappointed that your letter of September 6 contains no indication that Mr. Daniloff will be freed promptly. This is difficult for me to understand inasmuch as I have given my assurances that he has not conducted any activities on behalf of the U.S. government. If he continues to be held, we can only consider his detention an attempt by the Soviet authorities to create a hostage, and we will have to act accordingly.

Needless to say, this situation, in and of itself, does great harm to our relations. The longer it persists, the greater the damage will be. In fact, there is no way very serious and far-reaching consequences can be avoided if Mr. Daniloff continues to be retained by your authorities.

Given the gravity of this issue and the urgent requirement to solve it, I have asked that this message be delivered by the most rapid and direct means available.

Gorbachev did not immediately reply but spent time contemplating how best to bring developments back to the major political question of arms reduction. In mid-September he dispatched Foreign Minister Eduard Shevardnadze to the United States to attend the fall meeting of the U.N. General Assembly and to call on the president. The minister carried a Gorbachev letter dated September 15 complaining of the unpredictable crisis in U.S.-Soviet relations. He hinted that certain forces in the United States seemed to create obstacles whenever the chances for improvements or a summit meeting appeared on the horizon. He noted:

Among such incidents—of the kind that have happened before and that, presumably, no one can be guaranteed against in the future—is the case of Zakharov and Daniloff. It requires a calm examination, investigation, and a search for mutually acceptable solutions. However, the US side has unduly dramatized the incident. A massive hostile campaign has been launched against our country, which has been taken up at the higher levels of the United States administration and Congress. It is as if a pretext was deliberately sought to aggravate Soviet-American relations and to increase tensions.

Between Reagan's last letter and Gorbachev's September 15 reply, officials on both sides began plumbing the archives for precedents and reached an interim arrangement. On September 11, they agreed that Zakharov and I would be released into the custody of our respective ambassadors. I got the news in Sergadeyev's interrogation room that evening from a stocky, white-haired official dressed in a dark suit who announced, "At three o'clock this afternoon a political agreement was reached under which you will be released into the custody of your embassy." He seemed to be relaxed and in a good humor. I asked him for his name, but he declined to give it. My guess today is that this was Major General Krassilnikov, of KGB counterintelligence, who participated in the Vienna meeting with the CIA officials from Washington.

We two prisoners were duly freed to wait for diplomats to fashion a satisfactory final settlement. Unknown to me, Deputy Foreign Minister Yuli Vorontsov, the same diplomat I had known in Geneva and Washington, informed the U.S. Embassy of the case the Soviets were building against me.

The implication was that the Soviet side would produce plenty of information at a trial that would embarrass the United States. That prompted the editors of *U.S. News and World Report* to ask me to write a list of all actions that the Soviets might cough up. I wrote a list of some dozen points, the most important of which were:

—An allegation by Soviet spokesman Gennadii Gerasimov September 13, 1986 that I sought secret information when I visited the Novo-Voronezh nuclear power plant. I did ask detailed questions about reprocessing and disposal of nuclear wastes for a story published in the October 10, 1983 issue. Throughout the whole trip I was accompanied by an official minder from the Ministry of Energy who watched every step I took.

—A charge by Gorbachev when he met with local residents during a walk-about at Krasnodar on September 18, 1986 that I had been spying "in many places, some not far from here." However, I never visited Krasnodar or its environs, although Ruth did go there on one occasion to visit a stud farm for Arabian horses.

—An accusation by investigator Sergadeyev during my prison interrogations that I delivered a book of 200 pages (contents unspecified) to the U.S. Embassy in May–June 1981. I categorically denied this during the questioning and have no idea to what the investigator was referring.

Following my provisional release, the dominant feeling in Washington was that a one-on-one exchange was unacceptable and that the Soviet side would have to pay a premium for any final solution. Eventually, U.S. officials persuaded the Soviet side to change Zakharov's plea from not guilty to nolo contendere, not a formal guilty plea but an agreement not to contest the charges. I am happy to say that Dr. Armand Hammer, chief of the Occidental Petroleum Corporation, whom I once interviewed in Washington for UPI, flew especially to Moscow in his corporate jet to urge his high-level political contacts to endorse this development. In the end, Zakharov would get a nonjury trial before the federal court for the Southern District of New York, be declared guilty (the evidence was clearly in hand), and banished from the United States for a period of five years. I would be free to leave simultaneously with Zakharov's departure from the United States.

Additionally, as the premium, Moscow agreed to free one leading dissident and allow about a dozen other Soviet citizens to travel to the West for medical treatment. President Reagan's list was headed by academician Andrey Sakharov, or his wife, Yelena Bonner, or dissidents Ida Nudel and Yuri Orlov. And now President Reagan undertook one surprising, secret initiative. He asked the U.S. Embassy to summon Ruth to look over his personal list, comment on it, and add any person she felt strongly about. Ruth arrived at the embassy about one in the morning, dumbfounded by this presidential request. "I didn't know quite what to say. The president of the United States asking me to assess his list?" she recalled. "In the end, I decided to add the name of Dr. David Goldfarb."

The final details were agreed on September 29, and Ruth and I flew to Frankfurt, West Germany, that evening. The next day we flew, accompanied by a host of newsmen, to Dulles Airport, outside Washington, D.C., where we learned that the Reagan-Gorbachev summit would be held in Iceland, October 11–12. Our homecoming, minus our Jack Russell terrier, Zeus, left behind temporarily, began with a private family meeting at Dulles Airport. My son, Caleb, had left Northfield Mount Hermon School in western Massachusetts, by Hartford, Connecticut's, Channel Five helicopter to Bradley Field to catch a flight to Dulles. Miranda arrived from Chicago. Shortly afterward, I faced the journalists, almost all of them close colleagues from previous years. It was a dramatic and pleasant moment.

Heavily on my mind in those days was the need to thank members of Congress, Secretary Shultz, and President Reagan for the enormous efforts they put into my case. In doing the rounds, I was introduced to Judge Abraham Sofaer, legal counselor of the State Department. He explained to me how he broke down resistance in the Justice Department to a political solution by stressing the favor I had done for the U.S. government and the peril I had been put in. "You were innocent," he told me during our meeting in the State Department, "but you were convictable."

The high point came on October 1, 1986, when Ruth, Miranda, Caleb, Mort Zuckerman, David Gergen, and I visited the Reagans in the Oval Office. Also attending were Chief of Staff Donald Regan, White House spokesman Larry Speakes, Vice President George H. W. Bush, and Assistant Secretary of State Rozanne Ridgway. The setting was impressive. The president and I sat next to the fireplace as if I were a visiting head of state. The president sought to put us all at ease by reeling off a series of jokes. Then he turned serious. "Did you know, Mr. Daniloff," he continued, "that the KGB wanted to arrest you several times before?" "Really," I replied, "tell me what you know."

Reagan's account focused heavily on the KGB's interest in Dr. Goldfarb and their efforts to entangle me. These were things that I knew about only too well. After that, Nancy Reagan took over. She was clearly interested in conditions of life in the Soviet Union, and she alone lobbed question after question at me. The president, whose Alzheimer's disease was beginning to show, remained silent for the most part. Apparently, the other officials felt courtesy required them to defer to Mrs. Reagan. I was pleased to answer her questions; it made me feel that after our five years in Moscow, I had something worthwhile to say at the highest levels of government and society.

After nearly an hour, the meeting came to an end, and the president and I walked through the french doors to the Rose Garden, where my journalistic friends had gathered for a press conference with their "celebrity" colleague. I noted, to my surprise, that the president wore tiny flesh-colored hearing aides in both ears and sometimes had trouble hearing. ABC's Sam Donaldson, known for a loud voice and blunt questions, was determined to challenge the president for allegedly giving in to a one-on-one swap. "Mr. President," he boomed, "why did you cave?" Seeing the president hesitate, I jumped into the fray: "Come on, Sam," I scolded, "if the president had not found a mutual solution, I would be spending the next ten years in Siberia!"

The rest of 1986 turned out to be a depressing time. True, I was assigned by the magazine to cover the Iceland summit with the rest of the *U.S. News and World Report* team, but my role was cosmetic and insignificant. The Russians made clear they did not want to see me at any Gorbachev press conferences, and my contributions to the files were minimal. My life as a Cold War correspondent had come to an end, and I was unlikely, I thought, ever to return to the Soviet Union. So Ruth and I settled in Vermont, where I wrote *Two Lives: One Russia,* comparing my detention in 1986 to the arrest of my great-great-grandfather in 1826.

For a while, I was in constant demand as a speaker, a profitable and occasionally pleasant offshoot of momentary fame. But my private concern was to bring the "Daniloff affair" to an end by getting the Soviet authorities to close the case against me. I wrote letters to Prosecutor General Rekunkov and other high Soviet officials and lobbied Secretary of State George Shultz for help. Finally on March 24, 1988, Soviet Ambassador Yuri Dubinin wrote me that the case had been dropped by an act of clemency approved by the Supreme Soviet, the country's rubber-stamp legislature. Although I did not like this method of ending the case, I realized that Moscow had to find a face-saving way to end the affair. The text stated:

> The Ministry of Foreign Affairs of the Union of Soviet Socialist Republics, responding to the note of the Embassy of the United States of America No. 505 dated November 17, 1987, reports that the case against American citizen Nicholas Daniloff has been terminated on the basis of a Decree of the Presidium of the Supreme Soviet of the USSR, which states: Nicholas Daniloff, citizen of the United States of America, born 1934, is to be freed of criminal responsibility for actions under article 65 of the criminal code of the RSFSR as an act of clemency.

The note was curious in some respects. It did not cite the date or number of the decree of the Supreme Soviet. Was there really such a decree? Or was this just a way for an authoritarian government to rid itself of an annoyance? After President George H. W. Bush took office in January 1989, I asked the new secretary of state, James Baker, to see if he could get my name erased from any blacklist, and within a year he succeeded. Once that occurred, I found that Russian diplomats, especially after the collapse of the Soviet Union, were extraordinarily friendly toward me and Ruth, and we began, again, visiting Russia.

On May 15, 1992, Mikhail Gorbachev publicly acknowledged that my arrest had been a prime example of Cold War retaliation. On a visit to the United States, he appeared at the Kennedy School of Government at Harvard University. Three hours before his performance, Ruth and I took up seats in the balcony of the Arco Forum. After Gorbachev had made his preliminary remarks and answered a first question, I was recognized as the first speaker from the floor. To the former Soviet leader, I said, "I want to welcome you here and hope that in the future our countries will be great friends. Friends need to discuss the future and the past and to speak in a critical and open manner. In 1986, you were preparing to meet with President Reagan when a Soviet physicist was arrested in New York. In retaliation for that action, the KGB arrested an American correspondent in Moscow. I am that correspondent. I would like to know who in your apparatus thought up that bright idea!"

Murmurs of amusement rippled around the hall. Gorbachev, looking tense and defensive, interjected before the translation was complete: "That was perfectly normal for the Cold War." He went on to explain how action and reaction, retaliation and counterretaliation, worked during the decades of superpower rivalry, citing an example in which Prime Minister Margaret Thatcher expelled a number of Soviet diplomats from London. Gorbachev noted that he retaliated with equal expulsions of British diplomats from Moscow. Prime Minister Thatcher responded with a second round of expulsions, and Gorbachev threatened to continue the tit for tat until both sides finally agreed that enough was enough. "Thank God all of that is over," he concluded at the Harvard meeting, which was recorded on videotape. "And you are a living example of how relations operated." Then turning to my original question he remarked, "Specifically, I cannot tell you anything. I don't know the answer to your question other than it was a retaliatory move."

The episode was finally over, but there were still a few questions. What happened to Zakharov? I learned later that he was feted in Moscow on return from the United States and honored for taking risks—intelligence agencies like to reward risk takers. He was reportedly raised in rank from major to colonel and given new responsibilities for collecting and coordinating intelligence data on the United States.

And Roman? He surfaced again toward the end of 1986 when he telephoned the bureaus of both the *Washington Post* and the *New York Times* to learn if and how his name had been reported in the Western media. Both bureaus declined to deal with him. CIA officials confirmed that Father Roman had cooperated actively with the Soviet authorities but had given them a hard time; the KGB concluded he was almost impossible to control.

As to Misha, I assumed that he had been rewarded in some way for his help to the KGB. Fifteen years later, in March 2001, I got an unexpected message from Misha on my office telephone. He followed up with an e-mail message on April 10, recalling the pleasant times we had enjoyed in Moscow, eating pepperoni pizza. His real name, apparently, was not Misha Luzin but Alex Iatskovski, and he revealed that he had left Russia and settled in the United States in 1991. (A former KGB officer told me he thought Misha probably had been sent to infiltrate the growing Russian community in the United States.) Misha said he would be happy to "spend a couple of hours at a dinner table in a small quiet place with a nice glass of good old wine, and reminisce." Intrigued, I messaged back that I would be happy to hear his side of the story but that, first, I believed he owed me and my family an apology for the way he had betrayed me in August 1986. To this he responded, "I personally do not see a reason for me to be apologetic . . . Remind me again, what you see as the reason for my apology. After all, each of us was doing his job—each in his own way."

I found his response inappropriate, even ugly. And there was a curious element: He claimed in his message that he had never been to the town of Frunze (today Bishkek), yet that is precisely where I met him with Jim Gallagher of the *Chicago Tribune* and even included a picture of him, taken in the center of that city, in my book *Two Lives; One Russia*. As of this writing, we have yet to meet again.

# Chapter 32

## A Story to Tell

In my post–Cold War career, I turned from journalist to writer to professor at Northeastern University in Boston. Inevitably, my experience in the Soviet Union played a big role in my teaching. Living in Moscow during the Cold War tended to clarify your identity as an American and make you respect America's positive achievements. I soon found myself promoting democratic values, especially freedom of expression, persuading my jaded students they were wrong to believe the U.S. government, even after 9/11, had really destroyed freedom of expression in favor of censorship. They had no real idea how pervasive Soviet censorship and control had been. In the ensuing years, I lectured, too, to foreign audiences, especially in the Caucasian and central Asian parts of the former USSR about the benefits of free expression, of confronting reality head-on, and even of airing dirty linen in public. They believed me about as much as my American students.

My interest in the North Caucasian provinces of Dagestan and Chechnya grew as I learned more about this unique region that straddles Europe and the Middle East, Christianity and Islam, and harbors thirty different languages and cultures. In the ensuing years, Ruth and I came to admire the Caucasian traditions of hospitality and respect for foreigners and for elders. We traveled through Dagestan and Ingushetia, although we never set foot in Chechnya. Still, we came to know a fair number of Chechens and respected their boundless hospitality. Back in the United States, we assisted Ilyas Akhmadov, foreign minister of the democratically elected government of

President Aslan Maskhadov—a government the Russians eventually denounced as terrorist and a minister they declared should be tried and executed. How I migrated from journalistic voyeur to silent partner in Chechnya's struggle for home rule and independence needs explaining.

I can trace the beginning of that process to October 3, 1986, shortly after our meeting with the Reagans. On that date Ruth, Miranda, Caleb, and I boarded a Disney Corporation jet sent to attend a bicentennial celebration of the U.S. Constitution in Orlando, Florida. I was pleased to be invited, especially after my ruminations in prison about the founding fathers. Supporting and promoting democracy seemed to me then—and seem to me today—very worthwhile endeavors. I was billed only as "the mystery guest." The agreement with Disney was that I would have words of praise for democracy, but I would not be photographed with any of the Disney characters. The Constitution and the Bill of Rights should be admired for their own sake and not trivialized, no matter how useful these figures might be in engaging the youngest generation. For that reason, on arrival, we secreted ourselves in our overnight quarters, out of reach of Mickey and Minnie.

My thinking was disgustingly elitist, of course, and almost from the beginning pressure began building to weaken our reserve. When the ceremony got under way the next day, Mickey Mouse appeared on stage, before an audience of fifteen thousand, seeking to shake hands with each participant. When Ruth spotted this from the wings, she exploded, yelling, "Get that fucking mouse off the stage!" Then she turned on Michael Eisner, chief of the Disney Corporation, and declared, "For the last month I've been dealing with the insolence and bad faith of the KGB in Moscow. I did not expect to find those same qualities here!" Taken aback, Eisner apologized and tried to smooth over the situation. Meanwhile, unaware of what was going on backstage, I burst onto the platform, brushing past the fluttering hand that Mickey was thrusting in my direction. Our rejection did not go down well. Ruth later received letters from members of the audience who had gotten wind of the confrontation with Eisner. One letter began, "You insulted our Mickey! You should have your mouth washed out with soap and water."

It was a momentary thunderclap that passed in the hours that followed. At the end of the performance, we were charmed by the avuncular personage who had led the ceremony, an elderly man in a rumpled blue suit with ill-matching brown shoes—the chief justice of the United States. We chatted with Justice Burger at length, and, I must say, he got me very excited about the Constitutional Convention of 1787. When we parted, he gave both of us copies of the Constitution. On mine, he inscribed these touching words: "You have seen and felt the difference. Warren Burger."

Since college days, I have been attracted to the academic life but had avoided it, believing I lacked the "right stuff." Now, in the fall of 1986, I began receiving tempting proposals. Universities and foreign affairs councils from Massachusetts to California, Minnesota to Oklahoma, invited me to lecture on the future of the Soviet Union. Yale asked if I would spend a year in residence. The Carnegie Endowment for International Peace in Washington sounded me out for a position as an analyst of Soviet affairs. The Russian Research Center and the Shorenstein Center for the Press, Politics, and Public Policy at Harvard University both offered me the status of associate fellow, which I accepted concurrently through 1988. Finally, the School of Journalism at Northeastern University in Boston invited me to become a visiting professor with the possibility of moving up the academic ladder. In the fall of 1989, I took up Northeastern's offer and moved slowly through the ranks from assistant professor on tenure track to associate, then to full professor and director of the School of Journalism.

I found that the College of Arts and Sciences was very receptive to hearing my views about Russia. To this end, I helped organize two conferences at Northeastern in 1993 and 1994 on Russian politics and free speech after the breakup of the USSR. On organizing trips to Moscow, I would often query people on the streets about democracy and their interest in accepting it as a system of government. When I left Moscow in September 1986, I had predicted that it would take two generations—forty to fifty years—for a semblance of democracy to develop in Russia. The answers I got in 1991 confirmed that opinion. "Democracy? It's everything in the stores," said one citizen. "It's rock-and-roll and chewing gum," quipped another. A third proclaimed, "It's the road to the stars." A fourth confessed, "It means I can do anything I want, anytime." A fifth gave me what I thought was the closest approximation: "It's live and let live." No one said that democracy was a system of government and not a cash cow. No one said anything remotely approaching Lincoln's words in the Gettysburg Address—"government of the people, by the people, for the people."

Hosting Russians in Boston occasionally illustrated how pent-up demand for goods, services, travel, wealth—in short, the "good life"—has led to aggressive self-seeking. Three specific examples struck me. Take the case of Sergei K., a journalism student. He wanted desperately to come to the United States. I think what attracted him were consumer goods and MTV. When he accidentally met a Northeastern professor of engineering and his daughter in Moscow one summer, he saw his chance. The professor and his wife were so impressed by Sergei that they facilitated his entering our university as a graduate student in journalism. In Boston, he courted their daughter and charmed the family. The professor's wife helped Sergei with his English, edited the essays he wrote for me, and arranged for extensive dental treatment. In December, Sergei came to me with a delicate problem. He said he wanted to move out of the professor's house. Knowing nothing of his personal life, I turned to my engineering colleague with the news that Sergei needed to move because his wife was about to arrive! The professor's family was deeply shocked. They had no idea that Sergei was married and were devastated by his betrayal of their daughter. "It totally ruined our Christmas," the professor meekly confessed to me later. I thought the professor's attitude should have been a thousand times harsher.

Then there was Max A., who came to Northeastern under the student exchange program that my colleagues and I put together with Moscow State University in 1990. Between 1991 and 1992, we exchanged students. The Russians would arrive for six months, usually with little pocket money. Max, however, was energetic and imaginative. Soon tiring of redeeming beer bottles, he turned to one of the fertility clinics in Boston, where he contributed sperm three times a week for something like twenty-five dollars a shot. How he qualified for this unique job, I never learned. Later, he came up with an even better scheme. He applied for a position as a guard with a private security firm at Logan International Airport. With the help of a letter he forged on Northeastern stationery falsely stating that he was a permanent resident, he landed the job. During the last months of his stay, he worked secretly forty hours a week at the airport. When it came time to return home, he packed his uniform and badge and flew off to Moscow. In Russia, he had a residual military obligation, and that summer of 1992 he spent some weeks in the provincial town of Vladimir in training. On weekends, he would dress up in his Logan uniform and parade around the town. The local girls called him "the American" (*Amerikanets*), and apparently he enjoyed great success. His downfall came when I, visiting Moscow, received an urgent message from Northeastern informing me of the scam and demanding the return of the uniform. Logan officials were concerned that Max might eventually sell the uniform to terrorists on the black market. With help from journalism faculty at Moscow University, I managed to contact Max and repatriate the uniform. Max got a severe reprimand from the journalism dean but otherwise suffered no damage. When last heard from, he was doing business in Switzerland.

A third incident occurred during a conference, "The Struggle for a Free Press in Russia," that we put on at Northeastern on March 21–22, 1994. We invited a Russian delegation consisting of Vitaly Tretyakov, editor of *Nezavismaya Gazeta*; Mikhail Lubimov, host of a popular TV interview show; Alexander Meltsaev, a political journalist from Nizhny Novgorod; Dr. Magodmedkhan Magomedkhanov, a specialist on the North Caucasus; and Leonid Nikitinsky, legal affairs writer of the government newspaper, *Izvestia*.

The first hint of trouble hit when Nikitinsky got off the plane at Logan, drunk and incoherent. In the course of a week, he never sobered up, never attended a single conference session. He sat in his hotel room drinking whiskey in his underpants and throwing his cigarette butts on the wall-to-wall carpeting. The hotel finally announced that they would expel him from the hotel. When he refused to budge, they called the police. When the police tried to arrest him, he refused to let them into his room, proclaiming his human rights.

Lubimov, a former assault paratrooper, volunteered to take matters into his own hands. He declared he would move Nikitinsky by force and take him to a hospital to dry out. Nikitinsky resisted successfully and kept on smoking.

Then the wily Magomedkhanov whispered to me he would try another ploy. "Khan," as we called him, began to plead with Nikitinsky to get dressed, pointing out that he had been drunk the whole time, had embarrassed his American hosts, and was a disgrace to both Russia and *Izvestia*. Then, bargaining as if he was at a Caucasian bazaar, Khan unleashed the winning phrase. "Look, Lonya," he said, "the conference is coming to an end, and you have not appeared at a single session. We are getting ready to leave. Our wives and children"—here Khan put heavy stress on *wives and children*—"are awaiting our arrival back in Moscow. You've got to come now, or you will be left behind."

Slowly, Nikitinsky stumbled to his feet, throwing another butt on the floor. He struggled into his trousers, grasped his bag, while Lubimov and Magomedkhanov propelled him forward into an ambulance that took him to a local hospital. There he was supposed to quit smoking and dry out. But when we took him to the airport the next afternoon with the rest of the delegation, we found him puffing away and still inebriated. He had found a former Soviet doctor, now licensed to practice in the United States, who had apparently slipped him some spirits to keep him quiet. Ruth scolded Nikitinsky severely before he boarded the plane, saying, "Promise me you will take care of your drinking problem when you get back to Moscow." He replied with a straight face, "What drinking problem? I have no drinking problem." It turned out that Nikitinsky had been treated for alcoholism in Moscow before coming to Boston with an antialcohol patch called a "Torpedo." Drinking while using this patch was strictly forbidden because of the possible consequences we had just lived through. The day after their departure, Lubimov called on his cell phone from Moscow to say they had all arrived safely and gone their separate ways.

To me these were sad encounters. Such urgent, thoroughgoing hedonism, multiplied across millions of Russians, it seemed to me, would erode any democratic values that might be burgeoning in Russia. Could traditional corruption be reduced or eliminated when the wealth of the nation was not equitably distributed, when a vast majority were living near subsistence level, while the fabulously successful were flaunting their wealth? Could free and fair elections really be held with such public patterns of dishonesty? Or an independent judiciary? Or independent media? Partly because of this, my academic focus began drifting away from Russia to the newly independent republics of Georgia, Armenia, and Azerbaijan, and other areas of the Russian Federation such as Sakha in Siberia, Chechnya in the North Caucasus, and Uzbekistan in central Asia, all of which wanted to loosen ties with Moscow. This shift was spurred on by Ruth who had visited Dagestan, bordering on Chechnya, and had become fascinated with the cottage industry of rug weaving that Dr. Magomedkhanov was successfully reviving. Since 1991, we maintained regular contact with "Khan." In 1994, he won a fellowship to the Kennedy School of Government at Harvard, and in 1995 we visited him in Makhachkala by flying from London to Baku, the capital of Azerbaijan, then traveling by taxi to Russia's southern border, walking over the bridge spanning the river, and entering Dagestan. It was a troubled time, because after the collapse of the Soviet Union, Chechen president Dzhokhar Dudayev had declared independence from Russia and gone to war to assert it.

Until that time, we had followed President Dudayev's activities only slightly. Now Khan introduced us to a group of Chechen intellectuals who traveled through their war-torn territory to meet us at dusk in a field inside the Dagestan border. By candlelight we feasted on lamb, slaughtered before our eyes, washed down with wine and vodka. Until late that night, they danced and we talked while sporadic gunfire echoed in the distance. We discussed at length the grievances of the small Muslim population, brutally deported by cattle car to Kazakhstan in 1944. We learned that the Chechens were (and are) quite distinct from Russians. Though numbering only a million in a province the size of Connecticut, they have their own traditions, culture, language, and customary law, the *Adat*. Since Frolov's time and before, they had been repressed by the Russians, sometimes in genocidal ways. Yet they have maintained their devotion to their own interpretation of Islam. A rational solution to the Chechen independence problem—if reason could ever prevail over war—would involve cooperative agreements on trade, defense, and foreign affairs with Moscow and a large amount of self-rule.

In the months ahead, our interest in the Chechen problem grew as the Chechen freedom fighters, denounced by Moscow as *band-formirovaniya* (bandit formations), got the better of the ill-trained troops President Boris

Yeltsin had dispatched in December 1994 to put down the insurgency. We began to make contact with American experts familiar with the region, among them a woman who had become a confidante of Dudayev. Dr. Diane Roazen, originally a Latin American expert, had traveled to Chechnya in the early 1990s with an American group interested in exploring oil resources. She had struck up an amicable relation with Dudayev, who sometimes used his rudimentary knowledge of Spanish in conversation. In those days it was prestigious for Soviet ethnic groups to cultivate relations with Americans, who, they hoped, might use their influence to further their local causes. Over the years, Dudayev would include Diane in some of his meetings and maintain contact with her by satellite phone. She counseled against exporting war and terror into Russia and moderated Dudayev's more extreme views.

The Russians preferred force over talks to keep the Chechens in line. At a time when they were hunting down Dudayev, Diane arranged on February 14, 1995, a conversation by satellite phone for the Russian Research Center at Harvard with the Chechen president, who once again called for peace talks from his mountain lair. The hour-long session ended on a humorous note when Dr. Marshall Goldman, deputy director of the center, thanked Dudayev for his views and quipped, "Send the telephone bill to Yeltsin." With Diane's help, I interviewed the general on three occasions toward the end of the year (between November 30, 1995, and January 26, 1996) by telephone from the comfort of her Massachusetts living room. The interview was published by *Demokratizatsiya: Journal of Post-Soviet Democratization* in 1996. Some pertinent passages:

Q: What would be necessary for peace to return to Chechnya?

A: For peace to return, Russia must withdraw its troops and return to the bargaining table under international supervision and guarantees of international law. The only country in the world that can give us guarantees is the United States of America . . .

Q: And what are your main points?

A: The most important point, important for Russia, is to make Chechnya a demilitarized zone, and also the Caucasus, a demilitarized zone. The second issue is the economic cooperation in extraction of oil and gas, refining, delivery, energy resources as a whole. On the long term, on agreed upon conditions, a reliable partnership. These are the two key questions. The remaining ones flow from these two. We can resolve the other issues on mutually agreed terms: education, culture, history, mutual relations, and so forth. These are not difficult issues . . .

Q: What's your attitude toward terroristic acts that are aimed at encouraging movement towards peace in Chechnya?

A: I declare that I am against any terroristic acts and I am prepared to do everything in my power to make sure that terrorism does not grow. But it is growing, and through no fault of ours. It has been provoked by Russia, on our territory, and it has spread further afield. And if the world community does not cooperate, this danger will increase.

Dudayev's argument in 1996 hit on that enduring paradox: terrorism has become the planet's new world war, but in responding with violent means, nations encourage an upsurge of revenge killings and suicide bombings. Use of force by the strong encourages terrorism by the weak. Dudayev was killed in April 1996. The nature of his death has still not been satisfactorily explained. The Russians claimed they struck him with an air-launched missile, but some Chechens assert Dudayev's death was an inside job. By now, the violence in Chechnya was escalating, and as in all modern wars the chief victims were innocent civilians, particularly women and children. Appalled by these human tragedies, Ruth and several friends established a charity to send medical aid to children in Chechnya. They called their group the International Committee for the Children of Chechnya, and it succeeded in sending modest supplies of medicines.

For a moment in 1996 it seemed that political compromise might prevail over further force. President Yeltsin sent General Alexander Lebed to sign a peace agreement with Colonel Aslan Maskhadov, Dudayev's chief of staff. The Khasavyurt Agreement provided for a cease-fire and withdrawal of Russian troops and checkpoints within two months, and prohibited the use of force forever in the future. The agreement put off a final settlement of Chechnya's political status for five years, until the end of 2001. In January 1997, Maskhadov was chosen to replace Dudayev as Chechen president by elections that were judged to be free and fair by the Organization for Security and Cooperation in Europe.

Yet almost immediately, the hardliners in the Soviet military and security services began to undermine the Khasavyurt Agreement. Their argument was that a great state such as Russia could never yield to a ragtag group of guerrillas. To allow Chechnya to receive full independence, they argued, would encourage other ethnic groups within the Russian Federation such as Tatarstan or Sakha (Yakutia) to try to secede, although no other group, I believed, was likely to present the armed resistance that Chechnya did. Furthermore, Chechnya was (and is) a major oil-refining center; an oil pipeline from Baku on the Caspian Sea passes through Chechnya on its way to the Black Sea port of Novorossiysk. Chechnya's geographic position is highly strategic, as it borders on the newly independent republic of Georgia and the province of Dagestan, in close proximity to Azerbaijan in the south, where Western nations are establishing a presence aimed at securing imports of Caspian Sea oil. Moscow felt it was losing control of its own backyard, just as the United States has been troubled for a half century by the presence of a Communist government in Cuba.

By 1999, the disorderly internal situation in Chechnya deeply concerned Russia. The Chechen government was increasingly hostile to its Russian residents. It revealed the names of Russians and Chechens who had cooperated with the NKVD secret police (forerunner of the KGB) in the mass deportation of 1944, precipitating a wave of emigration by Russians. Maskhadov proved to be a weak political leader and was unable to put down increasing civil disorder. Gangsters roamed the country, attacking trains, kidnapping for ransom, and assassinating their enemies. Islamic fundamentalists began arriving in Chechnya, whose borders were ill-defended, in an effort to spread the Wahhabi version of Islam throughout the region and promote the creation of a North Caucasus caliphate. In early August 1999, field commander Shamil Basayev with a band of 2,000 men attacked several towns in Dagestan, which he hoped would join with Chechnya in seeking independence from Russia. The incursion proved to be the straw that broke the camel's back.

Russia now resolved to end the crisis in the South by overwhelming force. Premier Vladimir Putin declared in September, "We will kill terrorists where we find them and drown them in the toilets!" Moscow began a campaign of carpet bombing and deployed some 150,000 troops into the republic. It dropped a half-million antipersonnel mines, some disguised as toys designed to maim the unwary, mostly children. It released criminals from prison to earn their way back into society by serving in Chechnya, conducting brutal clean-up operations and engaging in gratuitous killings. Chechen fighters, numbering perhaps 3,000, continued to resist, and the conflict with Russia dragged on well into the twenty-first century. The main casualties turned out to be Russian soldiers and Chechen civilians, largely women, children, the elderly, and the infirm. Human-rights groups in the West criticized Russia for conducting a war that looked like genocide.

On the night of January 31–February 1, 2000, a particularly dramatic episode took place. The Russians announced they would allow an evacuation of civilians and Chechen fighters from the capital city of Grozny. Some 4,000 evacuees trooped over a snowy field, seeded with mines, toward the Grozny suburb of Alkhan Kala. At least 170 people were killed in the process, but 300 arrived at a small clinic in search of medical aid. There a courageous Chechen surgeon, assisted by a small nursing staff, operated for two days and nights without sleep on Chechen fighters, Russian soldiers, and hapless civilians. Among those he saved was Basayev, the warlord who would go down in history as the mastermind of the Moscow theater takeover over in 2002 and the Beslan school tragedy of 2005.

We watched this drama at a distance, appalled by the unwillingness of Russia to accept any outside brokering for a peaceful settlement. We became more and more convinced that Chechnya was a distinct society that deserved respect for its cultural heritage and a high measure of autonomy, either within or without the Russian Federation. In May 2000, the *New York Times* published an article about Dr. Khassan Baiev, the Chechen "protector" of Alkhan Kala who had treated the wounded of February 1 and 2. Dr. Baiev fled the conflict shortly after this incident, carrying with him evidence of the abuse of human rights perpetrated by Russian soldiers. When we learned that the organization Physicians for Human Rights was bringing him to Boston in May 2000, we requested an interview.

We met with Dr. Baiev in Physicians' offices in Boston. He spoke in a flat, calm voice, but his trembling hands suggested he was deeply affected by trauma. He revealed that during those awful days of February, he had operated nonstop for more than forty-eight hours during which he did sixty-seven amputations and seven brain surgeries. Toward the end he was near collapse, and his nurses had to rub his face with snow to keep him conscious. He described, too, how earlier some Chechen extremists had held him in a pit for nine days and nearly executed him for collaborating with the Russians, and how the Russian military sought to arrest him and put him out of business.

After hearing his tale, we invited him to spend the rest of the day with us, visiting the town of Concord, where the Revolutionary War against Britain began in April 1775. We walked to the bridge where three British casualties of the fighting of April 19, 1775, are buried. Later we took Dr. Baiev for tea at the Concord Inn. Dr. Baiev looked downcast and exhausted. "I also have a story to tell," he said quietly. We sensed at that moment that we would likely put aside our own projects to record his tale.

In the course of the next six months, we met occasionally with Dr. Baiev, who was staying with acquaintances in Washington, D.C. Little by little, we began to tease out his story. He had been born in Alkhan Kala, along with his twin brother, Hussein. He and his brother were indifferent students but enthusiastic wrestlers. The family was always interested in medicine; his father was particularly versed in traditional means of healing. Khassan convinced himself he wanted to become a doctor, and was eventually admitted to the Institute of Medicine in the Siberian city of Krasnoyarsk. There he was struck by the Hippocratic Oath cut into the wall of the entrance hall. In the following years he studied earnestly and made the Soviet national judo team. In the early 1990s, he went to Moscow for advanced training as a cosmetic surgeon but returned to Alkhan Kala when war broke out in 1994.

During the conflict, he organized a small hospital of his own and turned himself into a war surgeon. He treated all in need. The Russian military wanted to arrest and try him; the Chechen extremists held him in a pit for nine days, bringing him up for punishment that turned out to be a mock execution. By December we were convinced that he was willing to speak truthfully and at length. Together we conceived a book that would explain much about Chechnya and its war for independence. During the next three years, we interviewed, wrote, translated our work back to him, listened to his comments, amended the words, and retranslated everything to him, until we had a final text, published in October 2003 as *The Oath: A Surgeon under Fire*. The book was a literary success and was published in more than a dozen countries, including Israel, Japan, Turkey, Canada, France, Britain, Finland, Poland, and the United States. What we did not fully realize at the time was that Khassan was welcoming us into his family and into the Chechen diaspora in the United States.

In the course of those years, we became acquainted with Ilyas Akhmadov. He was named to his post of foreign minister on August 29, 1999, and confirmed by the Chechen parliament in September. One of his first acts was to denounce Basayev's invasion of Dagestan and to fly to Moscow to confer with the head of the Organization for Security and Cooperation in Europe in an effort to negotiate a cease-fire that might deter a Soviet invasion and preserve the Maskhadov government. When the Russians refused to be drawn into negotiations and invaded, Akhmadov believed his mission was to explain the Chechen situation to the world. He took up residence in Baku until he was invited to the United States in May 2002 by the American Committee for Peace in Chechnya. This bipartisan group was headed by Dr. Zbigniew Brzezinski, President Carter's national security adviser; General Alexander Haig, President Reagan's first secretary of state; and Ambassador Max Kampelman. Its purpose was to create a "back channel" of communication on Chechnya with Moscow and encourage negotiations.

In the meantime, Akhmadov began lecturing around the United States. When his Russian passport expired, he applied for political asylum. One of his notable contributions was a detailed plan for the peaceful resolution of the Chechen crisis. His proposal would put Chechnya under U.N. trusteeship for a period of twenty years while civil institutions would be created. The spirit of this initiative was similar to the resolution of the East Timor independence problem and the Carter administration's willingness to transfer the Panama Canal and the Canal Zone to Panama.

Moscow would hear none of it. As the Putin government intensified the second Russo-Chechen war, the Russian army and security services began targeting the Chechen separatist leaders, eventually assassinating President Maskhadov in 2005. They claimed, too, to have killed Shamil Basayev in 2006, although he may have perished as the result of an accident while transporting explosives. Simultaneously, the Kremlin authorities denounced Akhmadov and demanded his extradition. At one point, a Russian diplomatic note reportedly charged that Akhmadov was Osama Bin Laden's personal representative in the United States, although Akhmadov had never been to Afghanistan, never met Bin Laden, and repeatedly denounced the jihadists.

The more Ruth and I studied the situation, the more we felt that Russian officials were deeply mistaken about Akhmadov. A lanky, soft-spoken man, Akhmadov had served as a top sergeant in the Soviet army at a missile testing site in Kazakhstan. He was particularly skilled as a diplomat, well versed in history, and spoke beautiful Russian. He worked tirelessly for a peaceful resolution of the crisis. Although he had fought in the first Russo-Chechen war, he had not been involved in terrorist activities. He had the respect of many influential Americans who backed his efforts for a peaceful resolution.

Akhmadov was essentially living on a shoestring. The Chechen government had sent him abroad with five hundred dollars, and that money had run out long ago. For a while, some Chechen businessmen supported him. We came to his rescue by giving him a place to live in 2003 and 2004. When his request for asylum was rejected in February 2003, he appealed the decision. Both Russian and American friends submitted affidavits of support to the federal immigration court in Boston. On March 18, 2004, Dr. Brzezinski testified in Akhmadov's favor before Judge Leonard Shapiro. No representative from the Russian Embassy attended.

The government's attorney argued tenaciously against asylum, pointing to documents that Moscow had submitted to the United States demanding extradition and asserting Akhmadov was a terrorist. Akhmadov's pro bono lawyer rebutted the allegations, stating that the Russian documents were more political than legal. In some of these documents Akhmadov was incorrectly identified as Ahmed Ilyasov; in other places, he was confused with members of a criminal gang in Chechnya run by a group of Akhmadov brothers unrelated to Ilyas. A number of the documents were blatantly backdated, and some of the Russian testimony against Akhmadov had been given under duress and was of doubtful credibility. These documents contained no statement from any authoritative Russian official describing Akhmadov's alleged activities, the lawyer said.

Undeterred, the government's attorney aggressively questioned Brzezinski, systematically trying to cast doubt on his credibility. He suggested the former national security adviser was hardly objective, was actually an advocate for Chechen separatists, and hated the Russians. At one point, he intimated that the U.S. decision to supply arms to Afghan resisters following the Soviet invasion of 1979 was evidence of Brzezinski's anti-Russian bias. Visibly piqued, Brzezinski retorted sharply, "It was the policy of the U.S. government under Democratic and Republican administrations and your question is a fascinating indication, for some reason, that you are inclined to go very far in supporting Russian policy, and in this particular case, Soviet aggression directly threatening to the United States. I find your question—and I want to say this on the record—amazing!" To this Neville shot back, "My response is that I ask the questions and you are to answer them."

But Brzezinski's outburst broke the momentum, and the hearing came to an end a few minutes later. Within weeks, Judge Shapiro found in favor of asylum for Akhmadov, acknowledging that he would face probable execution if returned to Russia. Homeland Security subsequently confirmed the judge's decision in favor of asylum, although for a while we had our doubts. General Haig pressed Tom Ridge, head of Homeland Security, and Ridge ordered an FBI investigation after which he, too, concluded the judge's decision was correct.

The year 2005 smiled on Ilyas. The National Endowment for Democracy, a U.S.-supported think tank in Washington, D.C., awarded Ilyas a fellowship and the opportunity to undertake further work on elucidating the Chechen problem.

The Russians were furious at the grant of asylum. The Kremlin denounced the decision publicly as more evidence of America's double standards in the war on terrorism. Russian leaders never seemed to understand, or did not want to understand, that the decision was arrived at through a judicial process independent of the White House. Independence of the judiciary, division of powers, and checks and balances are democratic concepts that go back to such eighteenth-century thinkers as Baron de Montesquieu and John Locke but, in the twenty-first century, have yet to infect the Russian political class.

# Afterword

I close on the fiftieth anniversary of my entry into journalism in the fall of 1956 at the *Washington Post*. In those five decades, much has changed in journalism and in international relations. In 1956, the major dynamic in international affairs was the superpower competition and its adjuncts. Germany was divided into two countries by World War II, which ended with unconditional surrender of the Axis but without a peace treaty. Eastern Europe was turned into a buffer zone around the Soviet Union and was heavily influenced by Moscow. The United States and Soviet Union competed to put men on the moon. The developing countries of Africa played each superpower off the other in an effort to secure the best terms for economic assistance.

In American journalism in those years, the *New York Times* was supreme and set the daily news agenda for all other media. The *Washington Post* was only just entering the battle with the "Good Gray." The rivalry between the Associated Press and United Press International was intense and tended to keep both of them honest. Three national television networks were in operation: ABC, NBC, and CBS, the latter, advanced by the legendary journalist Edward R. Murrow, at the apogee of its prowess, earning the name the "Tiffany Network."

Following the death of Stalin in 1953, American news media took an increasing interest in the closed society of the USSR. In those days and in the years following, some remarkable assets developed. Henry Shapiro served UPI a total of forty years from Moscow until he retired in 1974; Edmund Stevens, who went to Moscow in 1934, covered the country for a span of fifty years, with a few breaks in between, for the *Christian Science Monitor* and *Look* and *Time* magazines. Several Moscow bureaus developed enviable archives and Russian personnel, such as *Time*, the *New York Times*, and the *Baltimore Sun*. By the early 1960s, the American television networks began opening Moscow bureaus; American correspondents began to study the Russian language seriously.

Today, in the year 2008, the landscape has totally changed. The Cold War has ended, and U.S.-Russian relations have entered a new friendlier stage but certainly not one without frictions. A tacit agreement seems to have been reached between President George Bush and President Vladimir Putin to keep criticisms within certain bounds. Bush does not criticize Russia for the brutal way it repressed the Chechens; Putin does not criticize Bush for the American intervention in Iraq or Afghanistan. Both wish to cooperate in the war on terrorism, which gained new momentum with the terror attacks of September 11, 2001. The Israeli-Palestinian crisis has taken on new urgency with the Israeli-Hezbollah war, waged largely on Lebanese territory in 2006, and the growing political power of Hamas.

In journalism, we see dramatic transformations and fragmentation of the media. The *New York Times*'s influence has declined, as has that of ABC, NBC, and CBS. Cable TV channels and the Internet have eroded the position of the news leaders of fifty years ago. Their constant demand for content encourages commentary, speculation, and sensation, especially when there is no new news to report. And a new wild card had appeared—the citizen journalist, writing and photographing for the Web, unchecked by any gatekeepers.

The paradigm shift is reflected in the declining status of the Moscow correspondent. ABC has been expelled, and the other networks have reduced their Moscow staffs. Similarly, newspapers have often withdrawn their Moscow correspondents and replaced them with local Russian hires. As the costs of covering the war in Iraq and Afghanistan have soared, sending crisis journalists into hot spots—"parachute journalism"—has replaced the long-term commitments of the likes of Shapiro and Stevens.

There is a paradox in these developments. Today, thanks to the Internet, there is more international news available than ever before for the ordinary American citizen. Yet it is not packaged in such a handy way as it was in the past; it is fragmented over hundreds of outlets, and one can no longer rely on the *Times* for all the essentials of the day. You have to go scratching for it. The result is, I think, that many Americans are actually less well informed on international affairs than in the past. And the American public, never all that concerned with what happens outside U.S. borders, is vulnerable to heavy influence from an articulate and insistent administration in Washington.

Yet despite these changes, some things have remained the same—*plus ça change, plus c'est la même chose*. People still want to know what is going on in the nation and the world; they still demand news, whether "just-the-facts-ma'am" news or advocacy news. The public still devours gossip, sensation, and hype. Journalism remains a fascinating craft that requires confidential sources and reporting in an independent fashion. And a Moscow assignment can still be an enormously enriching experience.

Are journalists born or trained? I think I know the answer to that question now: they are sometimes born but not always, and they can be trained. But the indispensable element to success is curiosity, wanting to know more, and digging for it. Ethical behavior continues to be the big journalistic challenge. When is it right to use deception to get a story? When does the public good require writing or voicing details that will surely embarrass some individuals? When should a journalist cooperate with an intelligence agency? Is it right to tell the truth and let the chips fall where they may? These are subjects I often raise in my course on ethics and journalism at Northeastern University. The short answer is that the public good tends to override all other considerations.

The common weal is greatly assisted by an open society and a culture that has accepted the necessity of washing dirty linen in public. In this regard, few societies are willing to go as far as the United States. The Clinton–Monica Lewinsky affair is a good example. The scandal embarrassed me as I taught journalism at Western University in Baku, Azerbaijan, in 1997. "You should not be embarrassed," one of my Azeri acquaintances said. "It shows that in your country, your president will be held accountable. America is a great example. If such a scandal happened here, it would be totally covered up."

The cover-up is still alive and well in many societies, including Russia. Despite the fact that I came to admire Russian literature, Russian language, and the Russian people, I have to admit there are still dark corners in the land of my ancestors. When I left twenty years ago, I recited a verse that a dear Russian friend brought to my attention from nineteenth-century poet Mikhail Lermontov:

> Farewell unwashed Russia
> Land of slaves; land of lords.
> And you, the blue police uniforms
> And you, the people bound to them.
> Perhaps behind the ridge of the Caucasus
> I will be able to hide from your pashas
> From their all-seeing eyes
> From their all-hearing ears.

What I see happening in Russia today is the failure of strong, independent media to develop—what Benjamin Franklin called the "bulwark against tyranny." The Kremlin has caged national TV broadcasting that reaches the masses, while allowing a small amount of critical reporting by newspapers that reach a comparatively small number of people. Meanwhile, enrichment of a very small section of society to the detriment of the overwhelming majority continues. Such a disparity in the distribution of wealth of the nation can only prolong the endemic corruption that existed under the czars and was perpetuated under the Soviets. The mentality of getting around official rules is highly corrosive and will inevitably cast doubt on the fairness of future Russian elections. The notion that the executive should in some manner be able to direct an "independent" judiciary is another broken leg of Russian democracy. At best, what we see is a managed democracy—an authoritarian government with populist pretensions.

As I conclude this backward glance, word comes from Moscow that Anna Politkovskaya, one of the most courageous Russian commentators on Chechnya, was murdered by contract as she returned to her apartment from shopping. For some time, she had realized that her truthful reporting could lead to disastrous consequences. She had received death threats before, and she acknowledged in one of her last pieces that she would likely be killed for speaking out about the abuses of power in Chechnya. Her death was followed by the strange murder in London of Alexander Litvinienko, a dissident Russian intelligence officer, with the controlled radioactive substance polonium 210.

President Putin announced official investigations, but their outcome remains uncertain. Many Russian journalists have been murdered in the post-Soviet years. In the five years of Putin's tenure, twelve Russian journalists were killed in contract-style murders. Yuri Shekhochikhin, an investigative journalist reporting on corruption and an acquaintance of mine, died of poisoning. Dmitrii Kholodov, investigating corruption in the Russian military for *Moskovskii Komsomolets*, died when a bomb blew off his legs. Vladimir Listev, a television personality, was gunned down like Politkovskaya. Paul Klebnikov, the crusading American editor of *Forbes Russia*, was assassinated on a Moscow street in 2004.

This is the darkest side of the new Russia. And even though I am far away, it touches me deeply. I learned, for example, that in 1997 Vadim Biryukov, my *nyanka* (nursemaid), was tortured and murdered, probably because he was engaged in monetary machinations that angered some influential persons. And my good friend Yuri Korolyov, the UPI photographer, was detained by persons unknown on November 8, 1994, when he stopped to fill up his car with gas on the Minsk Highway. When he resisted, he was overcome by force, tortured, and murdered. The motive here may also have been revenge. His body was dragged across the road, drenched with gasoline, and set alight. His car was discovered some distance down the road, where police found an expensive watch and other valuables—signals that this was not a robbery gone wrong but a warning to others. A few buckets of gasoline are not sufficient to incinerate a body, and his wife, Tonya, easily identified Yuri's corpse by the socks he was wearing.

I'll pass over Tonya's grief and desperation that lasted without relief until she died several years later. On November 28, 1994, I wrote in the *Boston Globe*, "My friend Yuri Korolyov, who served Russia as an outstanding photojournalist and a decent human being, never lived to see his country become a democracy. Will Russia live to see that day?"

That question remains open.

# Notes

Russian family names can sometimes be confusing for Westerners. In Russian, all nouns are either masculine, feminine, or neuter. Feminine proper names usually end in an *a*. Thus, the family name of Mr. Ivanov's wife will be Ivanova, not Ivanov.

All Russians have a middle name known as the patronymic that is derived from their father's first name. Thus, if Vassilii Ivanov has a father called Dmitry, his middle name will be Dmitryevich.

Furthermore, the polite form of address in Russian is the first name and patronymic, rather than an honorific such as Dr., Mr., Mrs., or Miss and the last name. Thus, it will be polite to address Vassilii Ivanov as Vassilii Dmitryevich, rather than Gospodin ("Mr." in Russian) Ivanov.

In transliterating Russian names into English, we have been guided by *Webster's Biographical Dictionary*. In transliterating Chinese names, we have followed the official Chinese romanization system pinyin.

## Chapter 1. A Peck of Trouble

For numerous details of my arrest, incarceration, and release, see Nicholas Daniloff, *Two Lives, One Russia* (Boston: Houghton Mifflin, 1988). Not available for that book were the texts of President Reagan's and Soviet leader Gorbachev's correspondence, or subsequent developments including correspondence with Soviet ambassador Yuri Dubinin and my nemesis, "Misha from Frunze."

The text of the espionage contract that Gennadii Zakharov asked Leakh Bhoge to sign was given to me by an official of the Justice Department.

Details of the arrest of Zakharov were related during a meeting of the New England Chapter of the Association of Former Intelligence Officers, September 17, 1988, at Marlboro, Massachusetts. Although a videotape was shot of the meeting, none could be found when I asked the association to review the conversations. Consequently, I relied on my own two-page memo of the discussion.

## Chapter 2. Serge

I based my account of Serge's arrival in the United States in 1918 on a 221-page manuscript he wrote in 1924 and published in a shortened version in the youth magazine *Open Road* in 1925.

## Chapter 3. Russia in My Life

This chapter draws on my recollections and family memorabilia. I commented on my mother's death in April 1950 in my journal of that time. However, that volume of the journal was lost in returning from France to the United States in 1952.

I translated my grandfather's account of Czar Nicholas II's abdication from the French as published in *La Rue des Deux Mondes,* January 1, 1929, 59.

## Chapter 4. Cards I Was Dealt

During college, my life was so hectic I stopped keeping a journal, so here, again, I rely on memory.

I wrote to Albert Camus on February 5, 1956, in connection with my senior honors thesis examining the relationship of man to the state. I received a reply dated February 23, 1956, from Camus with some minor clarifications. A copy of our correspondence is contained in the Camus Archives, I believe.

## Chapter 5. The Magic Dateline

I kept the better pieces that I wrote for the *Washington Post* during the period 1956–1957 along with letters of recommendation from managing editor Alfred Friendly. Among the curiosities I preserved were photographs of our double-decker London bus that we drove to Moscow and snapshots of some of the participants.

By 1959, I was carefully collecting the pieces that I wrote for the UPI wire, knowing that they might be important in seeking a better job sometime in the future.

## Chapter 6. London, Paris, Geneva

Historical details about United Press operations come from the standard histories of American journalism such as those of Frank Luther Mott, *American Journalism* (New York: Macmillan, 1962); and Edwin Emery and Michael Emery, *The Press and America* (Boston: Allyn and Bacon, 1996).

Other details come from memory, occasionally supplemented by conversations and correspondence with Norman Runnion, a top UPI rewrite man in London and Washington, and Greg Jensen, a top UPI rewrite man in London. Runnion was later editor of the *Brattleboro Reformer* in Vermont but quit to become a Protestant minister.

## Chapter 7. Genri

When he retired from UPI in 1973, Henry Shapiro received an offer from a New York publisher to write a book about his forty years in Moscow. To the chagrin of many, he never managed to do so. But he did write a series of sixteen thousand words for UPI summing up the high points of his career.

Much of what I have written is drawn from casual conversations with Henry when I was working for him in Moscow.

When Henry took up a position at the University of Wisconsin at Madison, he was interviewed for the William E. Wiener Oral History Library of the American Jewish Committee. The resulting two typewritten volumes are contained in the Henry Shapiro Papers in the Manuscript Division of the Library of Congress, Washington, D.C. I drew on these volumes to check my memory of the many stories Henry related to us in Moscow and for additional information and quotes.

I also conferred with Henry's wife, Ludmilla Shapiro; his daughter, Irina Corten; and his granddaughter, Alexandra Corten. I am very grateful to them for their insights, suggestions, and correction of errors, although I cannot say that they approved of everything I wrote.

The assassination of Czar Nicholas II has also been described by Mark D. Steinberg in *The Fall of the Romanovs* (New Haven: Yale University Press, 1995).

## Chapter 8. Henry's Bureau

As time has elapsed, memories of the alliance system have dimmed. I thought it important to give my description, as an insider, of how the system evolved, generally, to everyone's benefit in the 1960s. By the 1970s, some correspondents, particularly Jerrold Schecter of *Time* and Murray Seeger of the *Los Angeles Times*, became very critical of Henry. Between them they believed that Henry was using the alliance system to boost his own feeling of power and to impose his views, or even the Soviet government's views, on others. When Schecter published his book *An American Family in Moscow,* Henry protested the author's description of himself in a seven-page, single-spaced letter, dated March 18, 1976. At the start of the letter he said, "Some of your allegations are not only grossly inaccurate, as are your innuendos and value pronouncements, but malicious and defamatory. Totally unworthy of the man I once thought Jerry Schecter was." This opening quote set the tone for the rest of the letter, which I considered "over the top." In a note to me, Henry added, "The enclosed is self-explanatory. It is the second draft of a much harsher piece I wrote which I softened somewhat at Ludmilla's insistence."

I have tried to give a balanced picture of Henry, noting his qualities but also his weaknesses as I perceived them. Three books describing the alliance system and Henry are relevant: R. Whitman Bassow, *The Moscow Correspondents: Reporting on Russia from the Revolution to Glasnost* (New York: William Morrow, 1988), 201–2 (Bassow, who held a doctoral degree from the University of Paris, worked as Henry's assistant when he returned to Moscow in 1956); Murray Seeger, *Discovering Russia: 200 Years of American Journalism* (Bloomington, Ind.: AuthorHouse, 2005), 375, 389, 423; and Leona Schecter and Jerrold Schecter, *An American Family in Moscow* (Boston: Little, Brown, 1975), 184, 186–87.

## Chapter 9. The Cuban Crisis of 1962

Besides quoting from my own dispatches, I have reviewed press coverage of the time and conducted interviews with a number of personalities, including Marvin Kalb, then of CBS, and Norman Runnion, chief rewrite man of UPI in Washington, D.C., during the Cuban crisis. Murrey Marder, former diplomatic correspondent of the *Washington Post,* was very helpful in recounting how the Soviet Embassy tried to influence his reporting.

See also Michael Beschloss, *The Crisis Years* (New York: Edward Burlingame Books, 1991), especially chaps. 17–18; Fedor Burlatsky, *Vozhdi i Sovietniki* [Leaders and Advisors] (Moscow: Izdatel'stvo Politicheskoi Literatury, 1990); Aleksandr Feklisov, *Za Okeanom na Ostrove* [Abroad on an Island] (Moscow: DEM, 1994), 222ff (this book gives Feklisov's description of his lunch with ABC correspondent John Scali, which differs sharply from Scali's account); A. A. Fursenko and Timothy Naftali, *Khrushchev's Cold War* (New York: W. W. Norton), chap. 19, "Cuban Missile Crisis," 485ff, especially for details of the Soviet feeler for resolving the crisis transmitted by Feklisov; Max Frankel, *High Noon in the Cold War* (New York: Ballantine Books, 2004), especially 133–34 on Soviet signals for a resolution); Raymond L. Garthoff, *Reflections on the Cuban Missile Crisis* (Washington, D.C.: Brookings Institution, 1989), 64, where Garthoff reports Penkovsky's signal of an imminent Soviet attack); and Ronald R. Pope, *Soviet Views on the Cuban Missile Crisis* (Lanham, Md.: University Press of America, 1982), which contains the transcripts of the Khrushchev-Kennedy correspondence during the Cuban missile crisis.

## Chapter 10. The Paradox of Censorship

For an account of how the censors worked under Stalin, see Masha Gessen, *Ester and Ruzya: How My Grandmothers Survived Hitler's War and Stalin's Peace* (New York: Dial Press, 2004), 274.

On the KGB plot to poison Harrison Salisbury of the *New York Times,* I refer to an e-mail message to me from Dr. Fred Starr, 2004. Masha Gessen also refers to this plot in her book.

On the rescinding of external censorship and on the dirty trick played on UPI correspondent Aline Mosby, see Bassow, *Moscow Correspondents.*

For Vadim Biryukov's connection to the KGB, see Jerrold Schecter, *Sacred Secret: How Soviet Intelligence Operations Changed American History* (Washington, D.C.: Brassey's, 2002), 227.

## Chapter 11. Life and Death in 1963

For more on the 1962 journey of ASNE editors to Moscow, see Robert H. Estabrook, *Never Dull: From Washington Editor and Foreign Correspondent to Country Publisher* (New York: Hamilton Books, 2005).

Documents concerning Professor Barghoorn are kept at the John F. Kennedy Library in Boston. My request for access to all papers was denied since one or two folders remain classified. I suspect they would show that Barghoorn undertook a mission for the CIA.

UPI files from the day President Kennedy was assassinated can be found in the Henry Shapiro Papers, Manuscript Division, Library of Congress, Washington, D.C.

## Chapter 12. The Mystery of Mr. Khrushchev

In writing about our coverage of Soviet leader Nikita Khrushchev, I engaged in an extensive e-mail correspondence with Robert J. (Bud) Korengold, one of Henry Shapiro's top assistants from 1958 to 1962.

Ludmilla Shapiro gives an excellent account of her acquaintance and marriage to Henry Shapiro, life in Moscow, and many other vignettes, in Ludmilla Nikitina-Shapiro, *V Gostyakh u Proshlogo: Stranitsy Zhizni Odnoi Moskvichki* [Guest of the Past: Pages from the Life of a Muscovite] (St. Petersburg: Sudarynya Publishers, 2002).

On Khrushchev's overthrow, see the excellent biography by William Taubman, *Khrushchev: The Man and His Era* (New York: W. W. Norton, 2003). See also Martin Page, *The Day Khrushchev Fell* (New York: Hawthorn Books, 1965).

I found the information about Sam Jaffe's KGB sources in the Jaffe Family Papers. They contain numerous U.S. government documents that the family obtained through the Freedom of Information Act. They were made available to me by his daughter Deborah Jaffe of Hollywood, California.

## Chapter 13. Something Rotten

Any correspondent who spent decades in Moscow during the hostile period of the Cold War (like Henry Shapiro; Edmund Stevens of the *Christian Science Monitor* and *Time;* Ralph Parker, formerly of the *New York Times;* Robert Dagleish of the *Anglo-Soviet Journal;* and Jennifer Louis of the *Times Educational Supplement*) was bound to prompt questions about his or her motivations and loyalties.

Henry Shapiro spoke little of his sources when I worked for him in Moscow. To speak openly would have been considered poor etiquette. I have tried to discover whether Henry had any really special sources in the Kremlin. I found none. He always maintained that his scoops came from long experience and shoe-leather reporting. I am deeply grateful to his wife, Ludmilla; his daughter, Irina; and his granddaughter, Alexandra, for their willingness to share recollections with me.

On the space flight of March 18, 1965, see UPI dispatches in mid-March 1965 contained in the Henry Shapiro Papers. On Korolyov's death, see the Russian-language newspaper *Novoye Russkoye Slovo,* October 21, 1979. The post-Soviet journal *Soversheno Sekretno* [Top Secret] expanded on this report in 1992. Also extremely interesting, especially on the extreme security measures surrounding the Soviet space program, see James Harford, *Korolev* (New York: Wiley, 1997).

On the assault against Horst Schwirkmann, see John Barron, *KGB: The Secret Work of Secret Agents* (New York: Reader's Digest Press, 1974), 10–11.

## Chapter 14. Whose Side Are You On?

On President Warren Harding's gaffe on the Naval Limitation Treaty, see the *New York Times,* December 21, 1921.

On Professor Richard Pipes's gaffe, see his memoir, *Vixi: Memoirs of a Non-Belonger* (New Haven: Yale University Press, 2003), 159–60. In a note from my journal, March 20, 1981, I reported that I had called Reuters correspondent Jeff Antevil, who was convinced that Pipes was pushing his own personal line and was perfectly well informed on the "background" rules. In my note to myself, I wrote, too, that at a reception in the Soviet Union, Russian diplomats asked me whether President Reagan would now fire Pipes. I replied that I doubted it.

On the confrontation with Secretary of State Dean Rusk, John Scali reported in the *Washington Journalism Review* (1981) about his version of the exchange. See also Dean Rusk, *As I Saw It* (New York: W. W. Norton, 1990).

On editor Ben Bradlee's effort to alter the background rules, I obtained his views when interviewing him on December 9, 2003. The transcript is in my personal archive.

## Chapter 15. Dancing with Spooks

I drew details of Sam Jaffe's troubles with the intelligence community from government papers his daughter Deborah Jaffe obtained from the FBI and the CIA through Freedom of Information Act requests. See also Michael Beschloss, *Mayday* (New York: Harper and Row, 1986), 329–31, 336–37.

Jaffe's apparent relationship to intelligence agencies was always mysterious for his colleagues. I think that Sam himself was not entirely clear how deeply he had become involved. One of the best descriptions of his relationship with the KGB, I think, came from my interview with Jamie Jameson, a former analyst with the CIA, June 26, 1976.

The eulogy of ABC commentator Ted Koppel is contained in the Jaffe Family Papers.

## Chapter 16. America, 1970

Articles, notes, schedules, and other ephemera of the Soviet editors' trip are contained in my personal archives.

For a description of Alexander Yakovlev, a key adviser to Mikhail Gorbachev during perestroika and glasnost, see Loren Graham, "A Man of Fervor," in *Moscow Stories* (Bloomington: Indiana University Press, 2006). Dr. Graham was a graduate student at Columbia University when Yakovlev was there in 1958 as one of the first Soviet exchange students after Stalin's death.

See also Lev Tolkunov, *Mify i Realnost'* [Myths and Reality] (Moscow: Izvestiya, 1971).

## Chapter 17. Good Snoop, Good Gossip

Bureau manager Grant Dillman (1918–2001) was an excellent editor. But he could make snap judgments about people that were hasty and sometimes unfair. A man about whom Dillman made a snap judgment was Marlin Fitzwater. See, for example, Marlin Fitzwater, *Call the Briefing* (New York: Times Books, 1995).

On Armand Hammer: the author's collection of recorded interviews.

John Downey was reluctant to talk about his ill-fated mission to China in 1950. My account is drawn from the evening with Downey at the home of Professor Jerome A. Cohen in Cambridge, Massachusetts, in March 1974. See also John Downey, "To China and Back, Once Again," *Yale Alumni Magazine* (1984).

## Chapter 18. Au Revoir

I covered the White House during the end game of the Nixon crisis along with Helen Thomas, a longtime UPI correspondent there. Working with her was an education. She surpassed most journalists in dedication and determination to report every detail, large or small. In later years, as a professor of journalism at Northeastern University, I did a television interview with Helen when she came to Boston to receive an honorary doctorate at Northeastern University.

In writing this chapter I found two books especially helpful: Jonathan Aitken, *Nixon: A Life* (London: Weidenfeld and Nicolson, 1993); and Bob Woodward and Carl Bernstein, *Final Days* (New York: Simon and Schuster, 1976).

See also Nicholas Daniloff, "Falling," *Nieman Reports* (1974): 3–8.

## Chapter 19. Adventures with Kissinger

Traveling with Henry Kissinger was a challenging experience. Whatever you think of the former secretary of state, he was a highly intelligent man. He enjoyed the company of journalists and liked to bounce ideas off them. We were his peers, unafraid to challenge his points of view. On homeward flights, he would regularly devote an hour and a half "off the record" to journalists. Sometimes transcripts were made of these conversations. Reporters made tape recordings. I made a few recordings, but like many of my colleagues failed to preserve them. See Nicholas Daniloff, "Kissinger and the Press: A Mutual Malaise," *Foreign Service Journal* (July 1976): 6–8, 17; and Richard Valeriani, *Travels with Kissinger* (Boston: Houghton Mifflin, 1979), especially 176, 332.

On Donald Maclean, see Ruth's article in the *Washington Post*, December 16, 1966.

On meeting with Brezhnev, see Henry Kissinger, *Years of Renewal* (New York: Simon and Schuster, 1999), 3:854.

On Woodford McClellan, see journal entry for September 26, 1971; interview with Professor McClellan, April 1975; and *Richmond Times Dispatch*, July 13, 1976.

## Chapter 20. The Devil's Details

The Congress of the United States is a reasonably open place, employing no fewer than ten thousand people. I found that a great advantage of this assignment was to speak to opponents of the administration in the White House. Often, they were only too eager to leak classified information to create obstacles to the president's policies. Covering Congress also gave me the possibility of conferring with any representative or senator as I wished.

Additionally, I consulted the following: LeRoy Ashby, *Fighting the Odds: The Life of Frank Church* (Pullman: Washington State University Press, 1994).

On Senator J. William Fulbright, see my interview with the senator in *Harvard Magazine* (March 1975): 22–26.

On Richard Perle, see notes from my journal, 1974–1979. See also Kissinger, *Years of Renewal*, vol. 3, chap. 27; and *Vanity Fair*, December 2006.

## Chapter 21. The Rogue Elephant

I can't say that I "covered" the Central Intelligence Agency or ever wanted to. But the secrecy surrounding espionage operations always made the CIA a tempting target for national security journalists. I was invited once with a small group of colleagues to lunch with CIA director Stansfield Turner when he was trying to demystify the agency.

For this chapter, I consulted primarily the following: Carl Bernstein, "The CIA and the Press," *Rolling Stone*, October 20, 1977; Central Intelligence Agency videotape, *Burial at Sea*, 1992; William Colby, *Honorable Men: My Life in the CIA* (New York: Simon and Schuster, 1978), and the French edition, *30 ans de CIA* (Montreal: Presse Select LTEE), which contains more details on what was found in the Soviet submarine; hearings before the Committee on Armed Services,

U.S. Senate, 1973; John Ranlagh, *The Agency: The Rise and Decline of the CIA* (New York: Simon and Schuster, 1986); Harrison Salisbury, *Without Fear or Favor: The "New York Times" and Its Times* (New York: Times Books, 1980); Sherry Sontag and Christopher Drew, *Blind Man's Bluff: The Untold Story of American Submarine Espionage* (New York: Public Affairs, 1998), 79, 194; Angus Thuermer, telephone conversation, March 20, 2005; and *Washington Post,* October 23, 1977, A1.

## Chapter 22. The Infamous Zone

The fate of the Panama Canal and the Canal Zone consumed enormous political energy at the end of the 1970s. The canal, built by Americans, was undoubtedly vulnerable, and to protect it might have required a deployment of one million American troops. The danger was that the Panamanian nationalists might sabotage the canal as an act of protest against the Canal Zone, a veritable American colony that divided Panama in two.

David McCollough, *The Path between the Seas: Creation of the Panama Canal* (New York: Simon and Schuster, 1977), is an excellent description of the engineering feat involved in the creation of the canal.

Useful background material and photographs appeared in the *Panama Canal Review* (Winter 1977).

The UPI series on Panamanian drug running that caused the White House such anguish was published in the *Washington Star,* February 19–21, 1978. It was also featured in the *Arkansas Gazette, Hartford Courant, Indianapolis Star, Longview Morning Journal, Main Sunday Telegram, New Hampshire Sunday News, Palm Beach Post-Times, Providence Journal, Rutland (VT) Herald,* and *San Francisco Examiner.*

I reconstructed the UPI confrontation with White House spokesman Jody Powell using the White House transcript of February 17, 1978, and my own notes and tape recordings.

My sketch of Senator Robert Byrd appeared in the *Peekskill (N.Y.) Sunday Star,* May 14, 1978.

## Chapter 23. War Machines

History unveils mysteries that confounded observers at the time they were happening. My grandfather's unpublished writings revealed to a great extent why he participated in the last Soviet delegation to the Brest peace treaty in 1918. Equally interesting were details of the military side of the Cold War confrontation that I learned in my trip to the headquarters of the Strategic Air Command in Omaha, Nebraska, and to a Minuteman missile site at Great Falls, Montana.

Also useful were *Armed Forces Journal* (August 1979); General Y. N. Danilov, unpublished manuscript titled "Chapter from My Recollections" (a copy is in Houghton Library, Harvard University) and *Na Puti k Krusheniiu* [On the Road to Collapse] (Moscow: Voennoe Izadel'stvo, 1992), 247 (copies of the original manuscript are in Houghton Library and the Military Historical Archive in Moscow, Russia); Nicholas Daniloff, "How Russia's Military Tried to Undermine Lenin's Separate Peace," *Foreign Service Journal* (June 1980): 18–22; Alexandr Lyakhovsky, *Tragediya i Doblest Afgana* [The Tragedy and Valor of the Afghanistan Veteran] (Moscow: Iskona, 1995), 109–12; and from my personal archive a taped interview with General Richard Ellis, commander in chief of the Strategic Air Command, February 8, 1980.

## Chapter 24. Russia in 1981

This chapter is built around my dispatches to *U.S. News and World Report* from April to July 1981. I preserved all my correspondence and stories with the magazine, month by month, for the five and a half years we lived in Moscow during the 1980s.

I included my complete self-interview, published in the July 13, 1981, edition, to give the reader a firsthand sense of how life had changed in Moscow during the past twenty years. *U. S. News and World Report* graciously gave permission.

Ruth's article that got editor Marvin Stone so upset was published in the *Washington Post* on April 26, 1981. His letter to me was dated May 27, 1981.

## Chapter 25. The KAL Shoot-down

How could the Soviet government be so certain that the Korean airliner was actually on a furtive espionage mission? How could Marshal Ogarkov speak with such confidence at the Moscow press conference? Answers to those questions emerged a decade later, after the fall of the Soviet Union. The following were extremely useful in discovering the answers: Yevgenii Chazov, *Zdorovye i Vlast'* [Health and Power] (Moscow: Novosti, 1992); Anatolii F. Dobrynin, *In Confidence* (New York: Times Books, 1997), 537; Viktor V. Grishin, *Ot Khrushcheva do Gorbacheva* [From Khrushchev to Gorbachev] (Moscow: ASPOL, 1996), 69; International Civil Aviation Organization, *Destruction of Korean Airlines Boeing 747 on 31 August, 1983* (Montreal, Canada: International Civil Aviation Organization, 1993); *Izvestia,* January 28, April 24, May 27, 1991; Roy A. Medvedev, *Neizvestnyi Andropov: Politicheskaya Biografia Yuriya Andropova* [The Unknown Andropov: Political Biography of Yuri Andropov] (Moscow: Prava Cheloveka, 1999), 356ff; Don Oberdorfer, *The Turn: From the Cold War to a New Era* (New York: Poseidon Press, 1991), 55; from my personal archive, "Info-letter No. 6" of November 29, 1983, and memos on my conversations with Radomir Bogdanov on September 9, 1983, and Alexander Bovin on September 13, 1983; Politburo transcript, September 3, 1983, published in *Rossiskie Vesti,* August 25, 1992, 1–4; Politburo transcript, September 8, 1983, published in the Moscow press; Joshua Rubenstein and Alexander Gribanov, *The Secret KGB File on Andrei Sakharov* (New Haven: Yale University Press, 2005); Murray Sayle, "KE007:

A Conspiracy of Circumstance," *New York Review of Books,* April 25, 1985, 44–54; George P. Shultz, *Turmoil and Triumph* (New York: Scribners, 1993), 126; and the report of Dmitry Ustinov, minister of defense, to General Secretary Yuri Andropov, November 1983, published in *Izvestia,* October 15, 1992.

## Chapter 26. Blogging before Blogs

Why didn't Moscow journalists predict the collapse of the Soviet Union? Why didn't Sovietologists? Why didn't the CIA? I thought about the possibility of a Soviet collapse, but never had enough hard evidence to cast it as a story. Had blogging and the Internet existed, I might have shared my ruminations more fully with my editors. I should have mentioned the possibility in my "Info-letters."

In writing this chapter, I consulted my dispatches to *U.S. News and World Report,* 1983–1984; my letter to Joe Fromm, associate editor of *U.S. News and World Report,* about Falin, February 9, 1984; Chazov, *Zdorovye i Vlast';* personal collection of seventeen "Info-letters," 1983–1985; and Viktor Pribytkov, *Aparat* [The Apparatus] (Moscow: Molodaya Gvardiya, 2002).

## Chapter 27. Dangerous Favors

Being tracked by the KGB was par for the course in Cold War Moscow. What really surprised me was how innocent, or careless, many of us were. The most astounding event that I learned of was the willingness of one correspondent to deliver critical material on Soviet nuclear warheads to the CIA. This correspondent agreed to talk to me on condition that I never identify him. And I have not.

I consulted the following: Milton Bearden and James Risen, *The Main Enemy* (New York: Random House, 2003), 50ff, on the dissident scientist's description of nuclear warheads; my interview with Ben Bradlee, former editor of the *Washington Post,* December 9, 2003; my *Two Lives, One Russia,* on Bob Gillette's favor to the U.S. Embassy; Dusko Doder, *Shadows and Whispers* (New York: Random House, 1986), 186ff, on his transmittal of the "Novosibirsk Report" to the U.S. Embassy; from my personal archive taped interviews with Dr. David Goldfarb, Moscow, 1984, and "Careless Correspondents" (memo to files), December 29, 1992; and Robert Toth, "Toth's Story: From the Chilling to the Ludicrous," *Los Angeles Times,* June 19, 1977, supplemented by e-mail correspondence with Toth in June 2000.

## Chapter 28. Gorby for Real?

One of the great mysteries of the Cold War concerned the choosing of the top Soviet leader. Neither intelligence services nor Western correspondents had any direct access to Kremlin decision making. After the collapse of the Soviet Union, when censorship was abolished, many of the decision makers began publishing their accounts of events. I consulted the following: A. M. Alexandrov-Agentov,

*Ot Kollontai do Gorbacheva* [From Kollontai to Gorbachev] (Moscow: Mezh-dunarodnye Otnosheniya, 1994), 126ff; Chazov, *Zdorovye i Vlast'*, 176ff; Dusko Doder, "Gorbachev: Soviet Leader in a Hurry," *International Herald Tribune* (Paris), August 1, 1985, 1; Grishin, *Ot Khrushcheva do Gorbacheva*, 69ff; A. A. Gromyko, *Pamyatnoye* [Memoirs] (Moscow: Izadel'stvo Politicheskoi Literatury, 1988), 1:392–93; Yegor Ligachev, *Inside Gorbachev's Kremlin* (Boulder: Westview Press, 1996) and *Zagadka Gorbacheva* [The Puzzle of Gorbachev] (Novosibirsk: Interbook, 1992); *Perechen' Svedenii, Zapreshchennykh k Otkrytomu Opublikovan-niiu* [List of Information Forbidden for Open Publication] (Moscow: Glavlit, 1987); from my personal archive, dispatches from bureau files, March 1985; Pribytkov, *Aparat*, 12ff; V. I. Vorotnikov, *A Bylo Eto Tak . . .* [It Was This Way . . . ] (Moscow: Soviet Veteranov Knigoizdaniya, 1955), 56–59; and Alexander Yakovlev, *Omut Pamyati* [Whirlpool of Memory] (Moscow: Vagrius, 2001), 5ff.

## Chapter 29. Chernobyl

The explosion at the Chernobyl nuclear power plant posed a major challenge to Mikhail Gorbachev's policy of glasnost, or transparency. Now we know that the leaders in the policy-making Politburo divided roughly into two groups: those who wanted to release as much information as possible and those who were worried about saying too much.

In reconstructing what happened at Chernobyl, I found the following par-ticularly useful. A selection of Politburo documents relating to the Chernobyl catastrophe was declassified in 1994. These documents are from Arkhivy Kremlya i Staroi Ploshadi (Archives of the Kremlin and Old Square) and repre-sent a partial collection of discussions among top leaders. They are in Fond 89, Opis 28–32 and 50–54. Microfilm copies are located in Harvard University's film archive in Lamont Library. I also used S. F. Akhromeyev and G. M. Kor-nienko, *Glazami Marshala i Diplomata* [Through the Eyes of a Marshal and a Diplomat] (Moscow: Mezhdunarodnye Otnosheniya, 1992); Nicholas Daniloff, "Chernobyl and Its Political Fallout: A Reassessment," in *Demokratizatsiya: Jour-nal of Post-Soviet Democratization* (Winter 2004): 117–32; Mikhail S. Gorbachev, *Memoirs* (New York: Doubleday, 1996), 189; David Marples, *The Soviet Impact of the Chernobyl Disaster* (New York: St. Martin's Press, 1988); Grigory Medvedev, *The Truth about Chernobyl* (New York: Basic Books, 1989); from my personal archive, a tape recording of the press conference with Oleg A. Tumanov; Eduard Shevardnadze, *The Future Belongs to Freedom* (New York: Free Press, 1991); Georgii Kh. Shaknazarov, *Tsena Svobdy* [The Price of Freedom] (Moscow: Zevs, 1993); Vorotnikov, *A Bylo Eto Tak . . .*; and Yakovlev, *Omut Pamyati.*

## Chapter 30. Links in a Chain

I found that in middle age, I became increasingly interested in my roots. The Russian side of the family was particularly intriguing because of Decembrist

Alexander Frolov. To find his traces in Moscow and elsewhere in Russia, the following were useful: Academy of Sciences of the USSR, *Vostaniye Dekabristov* [Uprising of the Decembrists] (Moscow: Nauka, 1975, 1986), vols. 13 and 16; Daniloff, *Two Lives, One Russia;* Alexander V. Manganari, *Istoriya Dekabristkoi Zhizni: Dekabrist Aleksandr Filipovich Frolov* [The Story of a Decembrist Life: Decembrist Alexander Filipovich Frolov] (manuscript submitted to the journal *Zemlya i Fabrika,* December 15, 1925, and preserved in the Archives of History and Literature, Moscow); from my personal archive, notebooks from the trip to Siberia, May 1986; and Ilya Zilbershtein, *Khudozhnik-Dekabrist Nikolai Bestuzhev* [The Artist-Decembrist Nikolai Bestuzhev] (Moscow: Izobraziltel'noye Isskustvo, 1977), 20–22.

## Chapter 31. The Gulag's Vestibule

Being nabbed off a Moscow street and thrown into Lefortovo Prison without warning was a shocking experience. Although the Soviet authorities treated me correctly, I had only very limited access to news from the outside world. I am, of course, very grateful to the attention that President Reagan and other high-level American officials paid to my case. The following sources reveal how the crisis was defused: Daniloff, *Two Lives, One Russia;* Robert M. Gates, *From the Shadows* (New York: Simon and Schuster, 1996), 365–68; Jack Matlock, *Reagan and Gorbachev: How the Cold War Ended* (New York: Random House, 2004), 198–216; from my personal archive, e-mail from Misha, April 10, 2001, and letter from Ambassador Yuri Dubinin, March 24, 1988; Ronald Reagan, *An American Life* (New York: Simon and Schuster, 1990), 666–74; Shultz, *Turmoil and Triumph,* 728–50; and a videotape of meeting with Mikhail S. Gorbachev at the Kennedy School of Government, Harvard University, May 15, 1992.

## Chapter 32. A Story to Tell

In later years, Ruth and I became interested in the development of democracy and a federal system in Russia following the collapse of the Soviet Union. The status of Chechnya in the new Russian Federation posed an enormous challenge to Russian federalism as well as to freedom of the press. The two Russo-Chechen wars showed that Moscow felt more comfortable relying on force rather than persuasion and compromise to settle this internal dispute. For more information, see Kh. Z. Baiev, with Ruth Daniloff and Nicholas Daniloff, *The Oath: A Surgeon under Fire* (New York: Walker Books, 2003); Zbigniew Brzezinski, testimony to the Boston federal immigration court, March 18, 2004, CD in the possession of Ilyas Akhmadov of Maryland; and my interview with Chechen president Dzhokhar Dudayev in *Demokratizatsiya: Journal of Post-Soviet Democratization* (Spring 1996): 233–41.

# Index

Page numbers for illustrations appear in *italics*

Defense Intelligence Agency (DIA), 324
Demichev, Petr N., 210
Democratic values, ND's promotion of, 385, 386
Deutsche Presse Agentur (DPA), 39, 111
Devyatkina, Tamara, 335, 336, 354, 357, 359, 361
Diem, Ngo Dinh, 245
Dien Bien Phu, French defeat at, 138
Dillman, Grant: and ND's Torrijos files story, 252, 253, 254, 255, 258; and ND's trip with Soviet journalists, 155, 156; praise for ND from, 209, 215; as UPI Washington bureau manager, 132, 133, 190–91, 194, 201, 225, 226, 266, 268, 278
Dimitrov, Georgii, 90
Disney World, Constitution bicentennial at, 386
Dmitrii ("Mitya"), 326–27
Dobrokhotov, Leonid N., 347
Dobrynin, Anatoly F., 75–76, 77, 78, 84, 162–63, 234, 235, 293, 302
Doder, Dusko, 319, 334
Dolgikh, Vladimir I., 347
Donaldson, Sam, 382
"Doomsday plane," *183*, 274, 275
Douglas, Cathy, 281
Downey, John, 194–98
*Dr. Strangelove* (film), 141
Dubinin, Yuri, 382
Dudayev, Dzhokhar, 390, 391–92
Duncan, Isadora, 65, 317
Duranty, Walter, 57–58
Dykema, Annette, 25
Dykema, Jere, 25

Eisenhower, David, 199
Eisenhower, Dwight D., 45; Khrushchev's U.S. visit and, 74, 107, 117; Santiago motorcade of, 133; U-2 incident and, 45, 149
Eisenhower, Julie Nixon, 199
Eisenhower administration: Bay of Pigs invasion and, 72; mainland China and, 197; Rogers as attorney general in, 140; Russian ambassador during, 75; Washington, D.C., during, 27
Eisner, Michael, 386
Elections, U.S.: of 1960, 47, 118, 202; of 1972, 143
Ellis, Richard, 274
Ellsberg, Daniel, 242, 243
Emigration: Russian Revolution and, 7, 12, 48, 49, 259, 290; of Russians from Chechnya, 393; from Soviet Union, 97, 285, 292, 316, 319–20, 321, 338, 363. *See also* "Refuseniks"
England: as daughter Miranda's birthplace, 95, 96, 100; ND's first visit to, 30–33; post-WWII austerity in, 38. *See also* London; Oxford University
Ensz, Gus, 85
Espionage: ND's disavowal of, 281, 320, 322, 323, 371; Russian Republic criminal code on, 319; in U.S. cities by Soviets, 1. *See also* Central Intelligence Agency (CIA); Defense Intelligence Agency (DIA); KGB; Zakharov, Gennadii
Estabrook, Robert, 99–100
Evans, John, 2–3

Falenberg, P. I., 358
Falin, Valentin, 310–11, 312
"Family Jewels" (CIA internal report), 243–44
"Father Roman." *See* Potemkin, Roman
Fecteau, Richard, 195–98
Federal Bureau of Investigation (FBI): ND and, 247, 3233; Sam Jaffe and, 148, 151, 152, 153–54; and Zakharov case, 1–4, 5
Fedorov, Yuri V., 147
Feklisov, Alexander (Alexander Fomin), 82
Feldkamp, Robert, 251
Felt, Mark, 143
Ferguson, Harry ("Fergie"), 47
*Final Days, The* (Woodward), 203, 206
First World War: Armistice announcement by UP, 40;

TASS (*cont.*)
confidential sources within, 110, 111, 121; KAL shootdown and, 294, 295, 300; Khrushchev overthrow and, 204, 205, 207; office in Moscow, 63, 79; as official news source, 55, 92, 104, 115, 118, 122, 124, 137, 316, 335, 344–45, 353–54
Tatarian, Roger, 32–33, 37, 38, 43, 45, 132, 133, 134, 189
Tehran, U.S. diplomats' hostage crisis in, 269, 270–73
Television networks: in Russia, 401; U.S., 52, 53, 398, 399
Telex machines: demands imposed by, 67–68; in Moscow news bureaus, 91, 101
Tereshkova, Valentina, 93, 120, 121
Terrill, Ross, 194
Terrorism: Chechnya and, 391–92, 393–94, 396; international incidents of, 289; war on, 86, 143, 276, 377, 392, 397, 399
Tet offensive, 138–39
Thaler, Karol C., 42, 51, 110
Thatcher, Margaret, 308, 383
Thomas, Helen, 190, 193, 201–2, 209, 266
Thomas, William F., 241
Thompson, Fred, 7
Thompson, Llewellyn, 77, 78–79
Thomson, James C., Jr. ("Jim"), 194, 200–201
Thornberry, Paddy, 40–41
Three Mile Island accident, 344, 348, 349
Thuermer, Angus, 238, 242, 247
Tikhonov, Nikolai, 333
*Time* magazine, 91, 210, 215, 241, 305, 344, 398
Titov, Gherman, 109, 117, 119
Tolchakov, Adolf G., 324, 325
Tolkunov, Lev N., 156, 157, 158, 159, 164, 165
Tolstoy, Leo, 307
Tonkin Gulf Resolution, 227
Toon, Malcolm, 105
Torrijos, Moises, 250, 252
Torrijos, Omar, 250

Toth, Robert, 323–24, 368
Tretyak, Ivan M., 297
Tretyakov, Vitaly, 388
Trewhitt, Hank, 339, 340
Trimble, Gretchen, 1, 367
Trimble, Jeff, 1, 5, 339, 367, 370
Trotsky, Leon, 35, 49, 261
Trujillo, Rafael, 245
Tsarapkin, Semyon K., 47, 48–49, *167*
Tsiolkovsky, Konstantin, 119, 126
Tukhachevsky, Mikhail N., 58–59
Tumanov, Oleg A., 341, 343
Tyreman, Donald, 38

Udall, Morris, 77
Uganda, hijacked airplane rescue in, 270
Ulrich, Vasilii, 59
Umstead, William ("Uncle Bill"), 132
United Nations: Cuban missile crisis and, 80; Geneva headquarters of, 45, 47; Jaffe's coverage of, 144, 148; KAL shootdown and, 295; Khrushchev shoe incident at, 109, 111; in New York, 52; post-Six-Day-War session of, 137; Scali appointment to, 140; Soviet Mission to, 157
United Press (UP): advice on getting ahead in, 37, 95; Berlin bureau of, 89; Eisenhower's Santiago motorcade and, 133–34; exclusives and, 40–41; London bureau of, 32–33, 36, 37, 55, 58, 120; Moscow bureau of, 32, 33–34, 36, 58, 89, 94; in rivalry with AP, 40, 41, 42
United Press International (UPI): in Columbus, Ohio, 190; correspondents' letter of protest and, 210; in Des Moines, 250; diplomatic coverage and, 42; exclusives and, 40; in Geneva, 45, 46, 47–51, *169*; "hotline" experiment and, 86; as international service, 39, 43; Khrushchev scoops and, 108–9; ND's resignations from, 131, 278–79; New York headquarters of, 68,

# About the Author

Nicholas Daniloff is Professor of Journalism at Northeastern University. His previous books include *The Kremlin and the Cosmos* and *Two Lives, One Russia*. He lives in Andover, Vermont, and Cambridge, Massachusetts.